THE NUREMBERG RAID

30−31 MARCH 1944

MARTIN MIDDLEBROOK

CASSELL&CO

Cassell Military Paperbacks

Cassell & Co
Wellington House, 125 Strand
London WC2R 0BB

British Library Cataloguing-in-Publication Data
A catalogue record for this book is available from the British Library

ISBN 0-304-35342-6

Printed and bound in Great Britain by
Cox & Wyman, Reading, Berks

*This book is dedicated to all who
lost their lives flying with R.A.F.
Bomber Command over Germany and
Occupied Europe 1939–45, and
particularly to Flying Officer
Theodore Archard, a navigator in
50 Squadron, who returned safely from
Nuremberg but died at Mailly-le-Camp
on the night of 3–4 May 1944.*

Contents

List of Maps

*Maps and diagrams by Leo Vernon from preliminary drawings by
Edward Sylvester*

List of Plates

Introduction

The first R.A.F. bombing action of the Second World War took place on 4 September 1939, just twenty-four hours after Britain's declaration of war. In mid-afternoon, fifteen Blenheims and fourteen Wellingtons took off from their airfields in East Anglia to attack German capital ships reported by reconnaissance aircraft to be in Wilhelmshaven harbour and off Brunsbüttel.

Flying in rain and cloud ten of the bombers failed to find their target and returned. Three more nearly bombed British warships but turned away when the ships showed the colours of the day – these three aircraft also returned without bombing. One aircraft bombed the Danish town of Esbjerg, a navigational error of 110 miles. The British Government apologized to the neutral Danes and paid compensation for the resulting deaths and damage.

Forced by the low cloud to fly at less than 500 feet, most of the remaining fifteen aircraft attacked Wilhelmshaven but were heavily engaged by anti-aircraft guns which found the bombers an easy target at that low height. The battleship *Scheer* was struck by at least three bombs but these failed to explode, while other hits on the cruiser *Emden* caused only slight damage. Five Blenheims and two Wellingtons were shot down.

The Operational Record Book of Bomber Command Headquarters recorded: 'An eye-witness account obtained from secret sources shows that the action by the Blenheims was a most gallant affair and according with the best traditions of the Royal Air Force.'* This was certainly true, but almost half of the bomber force had failed to find a daylight target 270 miles from the English coast and of those which did find the target almost half again had been lost. It was a disappointing start.

The last R.A.F. raid of the war against Germany took place on the night of 2–3 May 1945 when 125 Mosquitoes attacked the port of Kiel. They bombed in two waves, making use of a

* Public Record Office AIR 24/200.

sophisticated navigational aid called 'Oboe'. The bombing was accurate, many fires were seen in the target area and the official comment on the opposition was 'Defences Nil'. All the Mosquitoes returned safely, some of them to the same air-field at Wyton near Huntingdon that had despatched the unfortunate Blenheims to Wilhelmshaven over five years earlier. Four days later the war in Europe was over.

These two raids, both by twin-engined bombers and both against maritime targets, mark the temporal limits of Bomber Command's war, yet neither in the type of aircraft nor in the targets raided are they typical of what happened in the intervening years. Between the gallant but ineffective start at Wilhelmshaven and the complete dominance and technical efficiency of Kiel there stretched a five-and-a-half-year campaign by Bomber Command of a kind unique at the time and which will almost certainly never be repeated. The main feature of this was the sustained offensive against German industrial cities and towns carried out by heavy bombers operating mostly at night. This later became known as the Strategic Bomber Offensive.

This book is intended to describe one twenty-four-hour period in this campaign in the greatest possible detail. On the night of 30–31 March 1944 R.A.F. Bomber Command raided the city of Nuremberg in northern Bavaria. In its aim this raid was typical of hundreds carried out during the war but in its execution it met almost all the difficulties and dangers which enemy defences and the weather could between them produce. These and a measure of bad luck combined to turn a routine operation into a tragedy. The Nuremberg Raid gained an evil reputation among Bomber Command men and, for several reasons, became one of the turning-points of the bombing war. Because the raid portrayed so dramatically the hazards faced by bomber crews during the war and because of its significance in the Strategic Bomber Offensive I will attempt to tell its story and that of all other Allied air operations carried out on that night, in great detail.

I freely admit the huge advantage of hindsight and the benefits gained by the recent release of contemporary documents, from the recollections of several hundred participants and, above all, from the opportunity to study at leisure which enables one to comment now on the actions of those who bore the terrible responsibility of directing Bomber Command under the intense pressure and urgency of war-time conditions. I hope to use these advantages without abuse.

Firstly, however, it will be necessary to describe the course of the bombing war from 1939 to the eve of the Nuremberg Raid, the characters and the hopes of the British bomber leaders, and the composition of both Bomber Command and the German night-fighter force at that period in the war. This will help the reader to follow more easily the actual description of the raid and its importance as a turning-point in the bombing war.

1973

The main purpose of issuing this revised edition of *The Nuremberg Raid* is to enable me to comment on a suggestion made in a book published in 1975 that details of the Nuremberg operation had been deliberately passed to the Germans before the raid by an Allied organization in order to help gain a major intelligence advantage. For this reason, Chapter 17 in this edition is almost entirely composed of new material.

The basic Nuremberg story has stood the test of time well and there are no other major changes, although I have taken the opportunity to correct a number of minor errors in the text and to present Appendix 4 in a new form.

1980

The Early Years of the Bombing War

In spite of many attempts between 1918 and 1939 to achieve an international agreement to regulate the use of aerial bombing in time of war, nothing was ever settled. Although there were elaborate rules under the Geneva Convention for the conduct of land and sea warfare the Second World War opened with no limitations whatsoever on the use of bomber aircraft.

The policy of the R.A.F.'s bomber leaders was that the proper use of the aeroplane in war was to strike at the enemy's means of production and deprive his armies of supplies of war materials. If this could be done on a large enough scale, the defeat of the enemy in land battle would automatically follow. The bomber was to be the R.A.F.'s primary weapon.

This is a simplification of a philosophy that had been evolving slowly since 1917. It was held by R.A.F. officers with varying degrees of conviction. Some genuinely felt that a large enough bomber force, properly handled, would be the decisive weapon in the coming war, that land warfare would cease to be the primary means of defeating an enemy, and that the R.A.F. should be the senior service with the major say in the conduct of the war. Other officers did not go this far but all saw that strategic bombing, by destroying the source of the opposing side's war material, would at least be an essential prerequisite to victory in land battle.

When war broke out Roosevelt, President of the United States, appealed to those countries at war not to engage in unrestricted bombing. France asked Britain not to bomb any German land targets because France was more likely to suffer the retaliation. Britain agreed to both requests, pleased to have more time to build up her forces. Bomber Command continued its daylight raids on German naval targets until December, but then it lost, to German fighters, twenty

Wellingtons out of thirty-six dispatched on two raids. The assumption that self-defending bomber formations could attack their targets and survive was obviously mistaken and the raids ceased.

The only night activity was leaflet flights. These had started on the first night of the war when ten Whitleys from Linton-on-Ouse had dropped over 5,000,000 propaganda leaflets on several German cities. These leaflet flights continued for several months. It is unlikely that German morale was affected but the bomber crews gained invaluable operational experience. Bad weather was the main hazard and navigation was, as always, a problem.

By May 1940, when the 'Phoney War' abruptly finished, Bomber Command had flown 990 night sorties for the loss of twenty-eight aircraft and 393 daylight sorties from which forty-five aircraft had been lost. It had been estimated that Bomber Command could not sustain a loss-rate of more than 5 per cent in continuous operations. The daylight rate had averaged 11·5 per cent while that for the night flights had been an acceptable 2·8 per cent. In this way Bomber Command was forced to become primarily a night-bombing force.

Throughout the history of the bombing war there are a number of dates which, in retrospect, can be seen to have been distinct turning-points; 10 May 1940 was such a date. At dawn of that day the Germans opened their *Blitzkrieg* or 'lightning war' against France, Belgium and Holland, and Luftwaffe units bombed any town that stood in the way of their armies. It was obvious that Western Europe was to be treated no differently than Poland had been, where many civilians had been killed in so-called 'tactical' bombing of cities and towns.

One significant incident occurred on that day. A formation of twin-engined aircraft appeared over the beautiful German town of Freiburg and unloaded their bomb loads. Fifty-seven people were killed including thirteen children who had been playing in a school playground. The Germans were, initially, furious and accused France or Britain of bombing a peaceful town of no military importance. It was soon found, however, that the bombers were German who had thought they were over the French town of Mulhouse. This error of thirty miles on a short daylight flight shows that navigational difficulties were not confined to one side.

On the same day Winston Churchill became Prime Minister. There was immediate pressure that R.A.F. bombers should be let loose. That night thirty-six aircraft were allowed to attack München-Gladbach, a town on the west bank of the Rhine and a key point behind the German invasion of the Low Countries. Among the four people killed in this raid was an English woman living in that town.

For four more days permission for an all-out attack on Germany was refused. But on 14 May, the last restraints gave way when Rotterdam was bombed by the Germans. Huge fires broke out and many civilians were killed. The raid was widely reported and throughout the world the news was received with revulsion. To be fair to the Germans this raid should be explained further.

The German army units attacking Rotterdam were held back by strong Dutch resistance at a certain point in the city. The Germans issued an ultimatum: if the Dutch did not surrender, bombers would be called in to attack the Dutch positions. As the ultimatum ran out 100 Heinkel 111s took off en route for Rotterdam. During their flight the Dutch finally surrendered and a recall order was sent out to the bombers. Forty-three turned back but fifty-seven had already dropped their bombs. Only 250-kilogram high-explosive bombs were used and these were dropped accurately but they started fires with which the Dutch fire brigade were unable to cope. It was the resulting blaze that caused most of the damage and casualties. This was not a 'terror raid' but a tactical raid that went wrong. It must also be said, however, that the raid was in support of a completely unprovoked invasion of a country that had been neutral even during the First World War.

Because of this raid and the rapid advance of the German ground forces Churchill and his new War Cabinet finally gave permission for the R.A.F. to attack industrial targets east of the Rhine and, on the night of 15 May, ninety-nine aircraft bombed oil refineries and railways in the Ruhr.

The events of 1939 and early 1940 have been described here in some detail to show that, whatever happened later in the war, the British Government held back the R.A.F.

bombers for over eight months after the war had started and
for four days after the German invasion of France, Belgium
and Holland. Britain had tried to avert the bombing of
built-up areas in which German civilians might have become
casualties, in the hope that the Germans too would restrain
their bombers. But now, the theory that strategic bombing of
industrial centres rather than the tactical bombing of ships
and military targets could decisively influence the course of
the war was to be put to the test. The Strategic Bomber
Offensive which started on 15 May 1940 would last for
almost exactly five years. For Bomber Command it was to be
a long, hard road of agony and disappointment, of wonderful
courage and many triumphs. It would end in doubt and controversy.

We can pass quickly over the next year and a half. From
May 1940 to the end of 1941 Bomber Command operated to
its full capacity, flying 43,774 sorties. Losses of aircraft
amounted to 1,019 in this period but the loss-rate of 2·3 per
cent was still an acceptable one. No records exist for the
cause of these losses but it is probable that German anti-
aircraft guns – 'Flak'* to all R.A.F. aircrew – was the main
cause, followed by mechanical failure and bad weather, with
losses to German night fighters only beginning to be serious
late in 1941. It would be useful to describe briefly a typical
Bomber Command operation of this period so that the
developments of the following years may be more easily
followed.

There was an air of amateurism and individuality about
these raids that a bomber-crew member of 1944 or 1945
would find hard to imagine. Between 100 and 150 aircraft
might be detailed to attack a particular town. Times for
take-off were not rigid and often left to the discretion of the
aircraft captain. Nor were routes laid down and each crew
would choose its own way to and from the target. After the
German capture of France and the Low Countries the R.A.F.
bombers operated under a permanent disadvantage. To reach
any part of Germany they had to fly over the sea or over
German-defended territory for at least 200 miles, while a
German bomber based in France had merely to fly across the
English Channel. To reach Berlin the British bomber had to

* 'Flak' is from the German word *Fliegerabwehrkanone* (anti-aircraft gun).

fly 500 miles, the German had only to cover eighty miles to London.

In spite of many directives given to Bomber Command the choice of targets was limited at all times to what was tactically possible, and a pattern quickly evolved that was to continue for most of the war. Quite simply, far-distant targets could not be reached in summer because of the short nights. Only the Ruhr, Cologne and the German North Sea ports could be raided at these times; Berlin and other targets in central and southern Germany and in northern Italy could be reached only in the long winter nights. The Germans took advantage of this pattern and deployed their fighters and anti-aircraft defences accordingly. Little attempt was made to bomb targets in the occupied countries by night for fear of causing casualties to friendly civilians.

Over the target each crew chose its own bombing time and height; this last could be anything between 20,000 to 8,000 feet depending on the visibility, the German defences and the determination of the pilot. There was no target-marking and, in the early days, no Zero Hour. When bombing times did become regulated, an attack could last for up to four hours. With almost unbelievable optimism crews were allocated to bomb individual buildings within the target town.

Some effort was made to start fires early in the raid by incendiary-bomb loads so that later crews had something to aim at; this was fine if the fires were in the correct place or if the Germans did not light decoy fires. When a few bombing cameras became available these were given to the best crews who, by means of a photo-flash, took a photograph of their bombing position. Most of the high-explosive bombs were 250- or 500-pounders although a few 1,000- and 4,000-pounders were becoming available in 1941. The average aircraft bomb load was one ton. Moonlight nights were obviously best and precision targets could only be attacked during these periods – journalists called it the 'bomber's moon'. When cloud obscured the target, or on moonless nights, crews navigated by dead-reckoning, released their bombs and hoped for the best. Navigational errors of up to 100 miles were not uncommon.

The autumn of 1941 produced three events which marked this period as another turning-point in the bombing war, although not a sharply defined one.

By August of that year Bomber Command had been operating for fifteen months in its strategic role of bombing German industrial targets. Although none had expected the small force available to be decisive in this time, questions were being asked as to whether the bombing had even been effective. The Government ordered a survey to be carried out on the results of the increasing number of bombing photographs being brought back by crews. The results of 100 raids were carefully considered. Out of 4,065 aircraft claiming to have hit their targets the survey suggested that only one third had bombed within five miles of the Aiming Point, that is, in an area of seventy-five square miles around the allocated target. Put in the simplest terms, the majority of the effort had been wasted by inaccurate navigation and faulty bomb-aiming. It was a bitter disappointment.

At about the same period the War Cabinet decided not to proceed with a previous though tentative plan to produce a force of 4,000 heavy bombers. With the Battle of the Atlantic raging, with Russia, the new ally, demanding a Second Front invasion of Europe, with the Suez Canal threatened and war with Japan looming, Britain had not the resources to meet all demands and the Cabinet would not gamble on the unproven theory that the war could be won by bombers alone. Bomber Command would continue to be a major attacking force but it could not claim priority in industrial capacity over all other service needs.

As 1941 slipped away Bomber Command faced a fresh danger – the increasing effectiveness of the German defences and the wintry conditions were causing unacceptable losses. The climax came on 7–8 November when 400 aircraft were dispatched to three different targets in Germany and over 9 per cent were lost. Five days later Bomber Command received a directive stressing the necessity to preserve its forces and urging the avoidance of heavy losses. Long-distance raids ceased.

This was undoubtedly the lowest point in Bomber Command's war. The leaders had reluctantly to accept that many of their ambitions and claims had been too optimistic. The aircrews had little to show for their endurance and the loss of so many of their comrades.

It would have been easy at this time for both the bomber force and the strategic-bombing theory to be abandoned in favour of waging war by more conventional means, but this did not happen. Churchill still believed in the bomber as a weapon. The operational experience gained had been invaluable, new tactics were being developed and better aircraft were becoming available in greater numbers. But what above all changed the course and fortunes of the bombing war was the appointment on 22 February 1942 of Air Chief Marshal Sir Arthur Harris as Air Officer Commanding-in-Chief of Bomber Command. It was Harris's leadership which enabled Bomber Command to turn its back on those bad days at the end of 1941 and to emerge as a new and powerful fighting force which would play a major role in the eventual victory.

2

The Middle Years

There are a lot of people who say that bombing cannot win the war. My reply to that is that it has never been tried yet. We shall see.

Sir Arthur Harris, 1942

There are at least two reasons why some space should be devoted to introducing the new leader of Bomber Command. Firstly, he was to retain his position for the remainder of the war and his influence during this time on the Strategic Bomber Offensive was immense. Secondly, two questions will later be put and answered: how did Bomber Command come to be raiding Nuremberg at all, and why did the raid take place on the particular night of 30–31 March 1944? The answers to both questions will be found in the character and philosophy of Sir Arthur Harris.

Harris was born in England but had gone to live in Rhodesia as a youth. He had fought with a Rhodesian army unit in German West Africa in 1914 before coming to England and joining the Royal Flying Corps. He served as a fighter-pilot for the remainder of the war but was one of those who were much impressed by the bombing of London by German Gothas in 1917. At the end of the war he was a major with a permanent commission in the new Royal Air Force. Between the wars he commanded squadrons of bombers and of flying boats. As a bomber-squadron commander in the Middle East in the 1920s his two flight commanders were Flight Lieutenants Robert Saundby and the Hon. Ralph Cochrane. These three were to meet again twenty years later as senior officers in Bomber Command. It was in this squadron that the practice was first introduced of placing an aircrew member on his stomach in the nose of a bomber to aim and release the bombs.

When war broke out Harris commanded a group of Hampden squadrons but he became Deputy Chief of the Air Staff late in 1940 under Portal. Harris stayed at the Air Ministry for only six months before being sent to the United States as head of the R.A.F. delegation in Washington. When a new leader was being sought for Bomber Command following the survey of bombing results late in 1941 it was Harris who was chosen as the new Commander-in-Chief.

No man reaches high command in time of war and retains that command unless he has certain unique qualities. Looked at in retrospect these may seem to be less than admirable and few war-time commanders retain the permanent affection of the country they serve. This is one of the hazards of their profession.

There are many adjectives applicable to Sir Arthur Harris. He was ruthless, dedicated and single-minded. He was supremely confident of his own judgement and without patience for those outside Bomber Command who failed to agree. But he was neither cunning nor devious; he was blunt but also honest. After the war he wrote a book – *Bomber Offensive* – which is a model of what a war-time leader's memoirs should be. In this he explained clearly what had been his aims and hopes for Bomber Command. He made no attempt to alter the views he had held during the war but which did not appear so attractive now that the war was safely over. His explanations of complicated tactics are concise and lucid.

It was Harris's opinion that the decisive weapon of the First World War had been the submarine, but that this was now obsolete and the strategic heavy bomber had taken its place. He felt that the R.A.F. should be the senior of the services; it cannot be said that he co-operated easily with other service chiefs. Harris recognized in 1942 that an invasion of the Continent would be necessary. Like most of the senior officers in the R.A.F. he had flown over the battle-fields of the Somme, Arras and Passchendaele in the First World War. He wanted to ensure that such a prolonged agony did not take place again. He was convinced that if he could be given both the necessary resources and freedom of action Germany could be brought to her knees by bombing alone. It was his intention systematically to smash their principal industrial cities and so demoralize their inhabitants that Germany would collapse. The Army could land as a mopping-up and occupation force after this had happened. Any departure from this simple method was, to Harris, a waste of time and a dissipation of precious effort. It was a powerful and attractive argument that fitted well the theory of the strategic bomber long held by the R.A.F.

It was to be over two years before Europe was invaded, although that was not known in early 1942. Harris was lucky. He was typical of the commander who comes to power after others have muddled through the dangerous early years with weak forces and obsolete equipment. He arrived at Bomber Command just when the improved aircraft and navigational aids were coming into operational use. He was the first to have both the opportunity and the means to prove the theory that the strategic bomber could win a war.

For more than three years Harris ruled Bomber Command from his headquarters at High Wycombe. Very few of his bomber crews ever saw their chief for he did not often visit the airfields, but they all knew him and all were somehow infected with his dynamism. He galvanized a dispirited force and, although there were plenty of bad times ahead, there was never a return to the despondency of late 1941. I asked one staff officer at High Wycombe about the mood there following the heavy loss of the Nuremberg Raid, quoting a report I had read that there had been 'deep gloom'. The reply of this officer was, 'I do not remember a single day after the arrival of Sir Arthur Harris which could be described as one of deep gloom.'

In many ways Harris, at High Wycombe, can be compared with Field Marshal Haig at the Headquarters of the British Expeditionary Force in the First World War, although Harris would not like the comparison. Haig never went into the trenches; Harris never flew in a bomber over Germany. Haig thought his front was the decisive one of his war; Harris thought the same of his bombers, and both hated forces being allocated to other commanders. Once they had got into their stride both men became optimists who felt that one more effort would open the way to final victory. Both played a large part in winning their respective wars, yet when peace came both were held to have been responsible for too great a loss of life and public opinion turned from them.

At High Wycombe Harris found his old flight commander, Robert Saundby, was the Senior Air Staff Officer. These two continued together until the end, in later years Saundby in the newly created position of Deputy Commander-in-Chief. It was not a partnership – Harris was too strong a character for that – but they were very close. Saundby always supported his chief whatever his own private views, protected

Harris from unnecessary visitors and placed his fine brain at the disposal of his bluff leader for, as another senior officer noted, 'Saundby was an intellectual, one of the few in the top leadership.'

Harris created two records of the destruction caused by his bombers. One was the *Blue Book*, an album of photographs showing smashed cities, which was sent to Downing Street, Buckingham Palace and even as far as Russia to show what Bomber Command was achieving. The other was a room at High Wycombe, called by Harris the Conversion Room, which contained similar evidence in order to impress important visitors. His memoirs express disappointment when the Chiefs of Staff of the Army and Navy declined to visit him and be 'converted'.

To the press and the public Harris was 'Bomber' Harris and to his close associates, Bert. To his crews, however, he was always known as 'Butch', short for the Butcher. This term must be explained carefully. His men recognized Harris as a hard-driving commander who would not hesitate to send men to their deaths for as long as the war lasted. But they recognized also that all this was necessary for final victory. If anything went wrong it was always 'Butch' who was cursed but rarely with real malice. One man has described it as a 'love–hate relationship'. Others have expressed it in similar ways:

In your book *please* don't refer to Air Chief Marshal Harris as 'Bomber' Harris. This was not his true nickname in the R.A.F., he was always referred to as 'Butch'. He was very highly regarded by all aircrew who believed that the highest safety measures for the benefit of his crews were a prime factor in his mind when considering targets and deployment of forces. The nickname was typical cruel service humour but was not intended to reflect our opinion of him – we would have had no hesitation in doing anything he wanted. (Sergeant E. Wilkins, 626 Squadron) *

Harris was the Big Chief and he could do no wrong. We were going to get stuck into the Germans and his were the brains that were going to lead us. I still think he was the best man for the job and I don't blame anyone for what happened. Someone has got to

* Ranks and units in these quotations will be those of 30 March 1944. All quotations both by Allied and German contributors are from men who flew on the night of the Nuremberg Raid or men and women who were closely associated with the planning and preparation of the raid or the effects of it.

do the job and mistakes will be made sometimes. (Sergeant N. Wilmott, 10 Squadron)

This man's Halifax was shot down on the way to Nuremberg and four of his fellow crew-members were killed. Only a very small percentage of ex-Bomber Command men would fail to be proud that they had served under 'Butch' Harris.

In his post-war Dispatch on War Operations Sir Arthur Harris divided his campaign into three parts. The period from February 1942 to February 1943 was the first of these – the Preliminary Phase. Harris had inherited a mere 400 front-line night bombers, nearly 100 fewer than were available three months earlier when the order had been issued to conserve the bomber force over the winter months. There were two reasons for this decline in strength. The pre-war Hampdens, Whitleys and Blenheims were being rapidly phased out while production of new types was only slowly developing. Secondly, Bomber Command was forced to give up trained squadrons for other work – mainly to the Middle East and Coastal Command. Harris bitterly resented this weakening of his force, but it was something he was unable to stop and the loss of his precious crews and squadrons continued for some time.

If the numerical growth of Bomber Command in 1942 was disappointing there was, however, sound progress in the quality of the aircraft and equipment and in the development of operational techniques. The new heavy bombers – the Stirlings, Halifaxes and Lancasters which were coming into service – were far superior to their twin-engined predecessors in range, performance and, above all, in bomb-carrying capacity. In addition, the navigational and bomb-aiming difficulties which had plagued the Command in the early years had stimulated intense research and the first of the new aids – code-named 'Gee' – was now ready for use.

Gee was a device that enabled a bomber's navigator to fix his position by consulting an instrument – the Gee Box – which received pulse signals from three widely separated stations in England. The Gee Box computed the difference between receipt of these signals and gave the navigator an instant 'fix'. As it was a line-of-sight device its range depended on the aircraft's height and range. A bomber flying at 20,000 feet 400 miles from England could just receive the signals; beyond that, they were blocked by the curvature of the earth. But as with all devices depending on signals from a land-based station there was a danger that the enemy would jam or distort the signals.

The Air Ministry had, by now, produced its answer to the 1941 bombing survey. It was decided that precision bombing was beyond Bomber Command's capabilities and when Harris arrived at High Wycombe he found there an eight-day-old directive which laid down a new policy: 'The primary object of your operations should now be focussed on the morale of the enemy civilian population and in particular of the industrial workers.' * In the absence of the ability to hit individual factories the whole town was to be attacked and its life brought to a halt. The official administrative buildings, the public utilities, the workers' homes and, with luck, the factories would all be hit. The new policy became known as Area Bombing. The directive rescinded the order holding back the bombers during the winter months and Harris was urged to embark on intensive operations making use of Gee before the device was jammed by the Germans. The German industrial worker and his family were now in the front line and the long agony of the German civilian population was about to begin.

Unfortunately the initial use of Gee was disappointing. Starting on 8 March 1942 Bomber Command raided Essen eight times in two months. But the Flak and searchlights of the Ruhr, the ever-present industrial haze, the clever use by the Germans of decoy fires and the inexperience of the bomber crews in using Gee all combined to make the raids a failure. Bombing photographs indicated that only about 10 per cent of the crews had hit Essen.

More successful was the trial of another bombing theory – that old towns could be destroyed by fire. In the list of targets in the February directive was the Baltic port of Lübeck, the centre of which was known to be of medieval construction. Lübeck was beyond Gee range but the device did help on the approach flight and the town's position at the mouth of a

---

* *The Strategic Air Offensive Against Germany 1939–1945*, vol. IV, page 144. Hereafter this work will be referred to as the Official History. I would like to acknowledge that this has been relied upon heavily during the first two chapters of the book.

river made its final identification easy. On 28 March it was
attacked by 191 bombers. Three quarters of these carried all-
incendiary loads; the remainder mostly carried the new
4,000-pound High Capacity bomb. In an attack lasting 140
minutes against this lightly defended town the bombers were
able to fly as low as 2,000 feet. In the new terminology of
Bomber Command 200 acres of Lübeck were 'devastated'.
Four factories, of which one made aircraft, the main railway
station and the electricity works were all severely hit but so
too was the cathedral, many old buildings and 2,000 dwelling
houses. The town records of Lübeck show that 302 people
were killed. It was Bomber Command's first real success in
Area Bombing.

Two months after Lübeck came a further success – the
Thousand-Bomber Raid on Cologne. To assemble this huge
force Harris had to bring in his training units and was also
loaned, not always willingly, bombers from other commands.
The heartening effect of the raid on the British public and the
advantage it gave Harris in demanding more bombers are
well known, so we might look at the less obvious tactical
aspects of the raid.

The German defensive system had now become well
established. It was based on a chain of radar stations and a
sophisticated fighter-control system which enabled the night
fighters to take an increasing toll of single bombers flying
anywhere over German-occupied territory. All approaches to
Germany were split up into 'boxes', called by the Germans
'rooms', each patrolled by its own fighter which could be
swiftly vectored onto any bomber flying through that box.
To counteract this the Thousand-Bomber Raid made use for
the first time of a bomber-stream. All attacking aircraft
would now fly by the same route to and from the target and
each was allocated its own place and height in the stream.
Although all were ordered to fly at exactly the same speed
the obvious risk of collision, especially at turning-points on
the route, was accepted but it was hoped that the stream
would smash through German fighter-boxes in such numbers
that the controllers would be unable to single out any bomber
for attack. In addition only those fighters whose boxes were
being flown through could be brought into action; all others
would be patrolling empty boxes.

Another experiment was also attempted. It was thought

that the shorter the duration of the attack, the more successful it was likely to be. The German fire-fighting services
would be overwhelmed with fires starting at many points;
those which could not be reached would take good hold and
eventually join together, and the one great blaze would cause
greater destruction than would the many smaller ones. The
anti-aircraft guns, too, would have shorter time in action and
the concentration of aircraft overhead would prevent them
from engaging individual aircraft. Again, the risk of collision
over the target was accepted. The attack was timed to last
only ninety minutes compared with the four-hour raids of
1940 and just over two hours at Lübeck.

The attack was another great success. Six hundred acres of
Cologne were destroyed and, despite ideal conditions for
German night fighters and the inexperience of many of the
bomber crews which were provided by training units, only
forty bombers from the 1,046 dispatched were missing – a loss-
rate of 3·8 per cent. Lübeck was a success against a minor,
ill-defended target but Cologne was Bomber Command's
first success against a heavily defended major industrial city.
In a tactical sense, too, it was a distinct turning-point. The
use of the bomber-stream and the increased concentration in
the target area had been found successful and these became
the basis of future raids.

There is only one other significant event of 1942 – the
creation of the Pathfinder Force. The idea of a separate force
containing experienced crews to find and mark the target for
the remainder of the bombers had been suggested several
times since 1941. There were two schools of thought on this
within the R.A.F. The first felt that the creation of such a
force would dilute the other squadrons in Bomber Command
and lower morale there. It was thought too that Bomber
Command could now hit large towns effectively and that
provided the weight of bombs was consistently dropped the
desired effect would eventually be achieved. Harris and most
of the group commanders thought on these lines. The
proponents of the Pathfinders were to be found among the
more senior of the operational aircrew who felt that much
more could be done in the way of bombing accuracy. It was
the argument of the 'area-bombers' against those who felt
that precision bombing was both possible and desirable. The
Pathfinder group found their champion in a certain Group

Captain Bufton, a staff officer at Air Ministry with much operational experience behind him. Bufton, Deputy Director of Bomber Operations, pressed the Air Staff to establish a specialist target-finding force within Bomber Command. Harris protested that the move was unnecessary and objected to a staff officer of junior rank interfering in his work. Bufton and the Pathfinder lobby won the day however, and on 11 August 1942 Harris was ordered by the Air Ministry to create the Pathfinder Force.

Having stated his case and lost Harris accepted with good grace and for the next eighteen months at least the Pathfinders were to have his full backing. Four days later the new force was formed as a separate unit directly under the control of High Wycombe. The bomber groups, with varying degrees of enthusiasm, filled up squadrons with experienced but volunteer crews and sent them off to the new force. An Australian officer, Group Captain Donald Bennett, an acknowledged expert on navigation and an operational pilot, was promoted to Air Commodore and appointed to its command.

It is a measure of Harris's hard-driving methods that he ordered the Pathfinder squadrons to be ready for operations on the evening of the day that they assembled at their new bases. In the event there were no operations that night but they did operate three nights later. They had some of the most experienced crews in Bomber Command but no special aircraft or equipment, and Gee, their only useful navigational aid, had been discovered by the Germans and jamming had started six nights earlier. However, under the leadership of Donald Bennett, the Pathfinders were destined to play a vital role.

The R.A.F., which had persevered with its strategic bombing for over two and a half years, was now joined by an ally. The Americans too had their bomber enthusiasts and were prepared to base a force of heavy bombers in England to join in the attack on Germany. The methods they chose were different from those of the R.A.F. but it was intended that the two air forces should have a common aim. In January 1943 the Prime Minister, the President and their Combined Chiefs of Staff met at Casablanca to co-ordinate their policy. The result was the famous Casablanca Directive sent to both bomber forces and stating that the 'general concept' of the overall aim was 'the progressive destruction and dislocation of the German military, industrial and economic system, and the undermining of the morale of the German people to a point where their capacity for armed resistance is fatally weakened'.* The directive suited Harris and his philosophy well.

Bomber Command was about to embark upon what Harris, in his post-war Dispatch, called the Main Offensive. This started in March 1943 and ended just over one year later with the raid on Nuremberg. Bomber Command made the most during this year of several distinct advantages. Harris was allowed a freer hand in that period in the direction of his operations than at any other period in the war. An increasing number of bombers and better equipment gave him, for the first time, the means to strike a really decisive blow at German industry and that elusive target, the will of the German people to resist.

During that year Harris mounted three separate offensives against three distinct targets. In each offensive the bombers were sent again and again to the same target in the hope of destroying it completely. Alternative targets had to be raided sometimes both to keep the Germans defences guessing and because of weather factors, but the Germans realized what was happening and concentrated their defences at the main target. This resulted in such fierce opposition for the bombers that the conflicts were later classed as 'Battles' and history has named them as such – the Battle of the Ruhr, the Battle of Hamburg and the Battle of Berlin.

These three battles were not only struggles between man and man and of aircraft against aircraft, but a contest also between the British introduction of electronic devices and the ability of Germans to produce counter-devices which would render the British equipment useless or, even worse, make use of the impulses given off by the devices to hunt down and destroy the British bombers. The scientists had perfected two further aids to replace Gee and these were to play a major part in the coming battles.

The first of these, code-named Oboe, was more a blind-bombing device than a navigational aid. Like Gee, it depended upon signals transmitted from ground stations in

* ibid., page 153

England. Two beams could be laid with great accuracy over targets as small as a factory building, and a receiver in the bomber guided it exactly to this point. But there were also disadvantages. Unlike Gee, which could be made use of by an unlimited number of aircraft, only one bomber could use a pair of Oboe stations at any one time. Even when three pairs of stations were established only eighteen aircraft could use Oboe in an hour. Further, the aircraft making an Oboe-controlled bombing run had to fly absolutely straight and level for several minutes, the worst possible conditions for evading German fighters and Flak. The range of Oboe was also limited by the curvature of the earth.

Bomber Command overcame all of these limitations. The new Mosquito bombers could reach 30,000 feet and, with their superior speed, flying straight and level was not the danger it would have been for the heavy bombers. The Mosquito's height advantages also increased the range at which it could make use of Oboe. To make the best use of the limited number of aircraft that could use the device, the Oboe Mosquitoes were used primarily as marker aircraft.

It was in a way a most interesting experience. One had to navigate to an exact point in space and be there within about thirty seconds of a stated time. Then, on receiving your call sign, the Oboe set was switched on and the pilot flew straight and level for about fifteen minutes and was directed by means of dots and dashes to the dropping point. The bombs were dropped on receipt of a signal and when one returned home one was told how much off the target the bomb had been. We averaged about 100 yards error on Ruhr targets. (Flying Officer H. C. Boyd, 109 Squadron)

Used in this manner, the Mosquito was the perfect Path-finder aircraft. Their target indicator bombs, though limited in numbers, were highly accurate. When the Oboe Mosquitoes were not required for marking they were employed as individual precision bombers and, providing they could land and take off, could bomb in any weather conditions.

The Germans soon found that the single Mosquitoes which they plotted on their radar and which bombed so accurately were difficult to shoot down. Because of this the Germans probably never captured an Oboe set in good condition for they certainly never produced an effective jamming method. This was undoubtedly the biggest single piece of good fortune enjoyed by Bomber Command during the war.

The other new device is more easily explained, for it was simply an airborne radar set which could be carried in any aircraft and which displayed on a small screen in the navigator's position a rough radar picture of the ground over which the aircraft was flying. For readers now grown used to radar the use of such sets may sound simple and obvious, but these first airborne radars were a complete novelty for bomber crews. Mechanical failure was frequent, reception of the reflected impulses was often uncertain and confused, and above all, the interpretation of what the navigator saw was difficult, for one built-up area could look much like another unless it had distinct radar properties such as a well-defined river or coast-line. The code name 'Stinker' was suggested first for the new aid but this was soon changed to its permanent name – H2S.

H2S could be used both as a navigational aid supplementing the navigator's dead-reckoning and visual sightings and also as a blind-bombing device, but its use in this last role was always erratic. The radar displays were not in such detail that markers or bombs could be aimed accurately. The great advantage of H2S was that, being carried in the aircraft, there was no limit to its operational range.

The first H2S sets were issued to the Pathfinders' heavy bombers and proved useful in getting these to the general area of their target; it was also employed in some of their target-marking techniques when operating beyond Oboe range. As further sets became available the bombers of the Main Force were equipped but it was to be over a year before every bomber had its own H2S.

By a cruel stroke of luck the Germans captured an intact H2S set from a Stirling shot down on only the second raid in which H2S was employed. The Germans gave it the code-name *Rotterdam* after the location of the crashed Stirling. As it was not dependent on land-based signals they could not jam it but they quickly produced two H2S-tracking devices. From ground receivers they were able to track accurately the course of any force of bombers using H2S and, with another type of receiver fitted to some of their night fighters, they could home onto individual bombers. When bomber crews realized that the Germans were making such use of their H2S impulses prolonged use of the device was discouraged, morale suffered and it became doubtful whether an H2S set was more help than hindrance to a bomber crew. But this was all in the future.

The Battle of the Ruhr opened at 20.58 on 5 March 1943, when an Oboe Mosquito of the Pathfinder Force dropped its target-indicator bombs where two Oboe beams crossed in the atmosphere nearly six miles above the Krupps factory in the centre of Essen. During the next forty minutes more Oboe-guided Mosquitoes re-marked the target while, from a lower height, Pathfinder heavy bombers backed up these accurately placed markers with further target indicators.

This particular raid marked another of those turning-points in the bombing war. Essen, one of the most important industrial towns in Germany, with its industrial haze and fierce defences had been the most difficult to hit of Bomber Command's targets. But now, for the first time, clear sight of the ground was not needed. The bomb-aimers in the Main Force had merely to find the red or green target indicators glowing clearly through the haze 20,000 feet below to place their loads accurately. The results of this raid were most impressive. More than 600 acres of Essen were destroyed or badly damaged, the Krupps works being particularly hard hit, and only fourteen bombers were lost from over 400 taking part.

Using the Oboe marking technique Bomber Command dealt the same fate to nine other towns in the Ruhr, but targets outside that area had sometimes to be visited to keep the German defences from concentrating exclusively on the Ruhr. In this way eleven widely spread, more distant targets were raided during the course of the battle, but it was immediately obvious that bombing results beyond the range of Oboe could not achieve the same accuracy as the Ruhr attacks and accurate marking of these distant targets remained a basic problem for the remainder of the war.

Within the period of time covered by the Battle of the Ruhr took place the famous Dams Raid. The story of this gallant effort is well known and will not be repeated here. The long-term significance was that an attempt had been made to hit a vital target from low level using heavy bombers – a clear and desirable alternative to the acknowledged weaknesses of Area Bombing. To achieve this, however, an élite squadron had spent eight weeks out of the front line undergoing special training and had suffered a 42 per cent loss-rate which kept it off operations for a further long period.

The Battle of the Ruhr lasted until 14 July and included forty-three separate raids, of which two thirds were against the Ruhr itself. Photographic evidence showed that enormous damage had been done to Germany's principal industrial area. It was an undoubted success for Bomber Command and, with some justification, Sir Arthur Harris wrote to Portal, 'If we can keep this up it cannot fail to be lethal within a period of time which in my view will be surprisingly short.' The operative words were 'If we can keep it up'. The Battle of the Ruhr had cost Bomber Command 872 aircraft and their crews a loss-rate of 4·7 per cent!

Before that month of July 1943 was over, Harris had already opened the next battle – the short, sharp and highly successful Battle of Hamburg. The heavy losses of the past three months, although approaching the critical 5 per cent rate, had affected the command surprisingly little, for the aircrew-training programme and the bomber factories had more than replaced those losses. At the beginning of 1943 Bomber Command had only 483 bombers available for night operations but by the end of the Battle of the Ruhr its strength had risen to over 800.

In addition to its ever-growing force of aircraft, Bomber Command was about to produce a further tactical novelty which was to prove a major breakthrough against the German defences. In the technically complicated electronic war then being waged this next move was based on an article of the utmost simplicity – a piece of paper roughly one foot long and half an inch wide, one side aluminium foil, the other black paper. If these strips could be dropped from bombers in sufficient quantity the slowly descending clouds of paper produced a barrier through which the German radar could not 'see'; it was hoped that the German fighter-controllers would not be able to estimate the strength or exact course of the bomber-stream, the radar-predicted Flak batteries would be unable to distinguish and engage individual aircraft and night-fighter crews would find it difficult to pick out the British bombers on their airborne radar sets. Two thousand such strips, costing just four old pennies, produced a radar echo similar to that of a heavy bomber. Once introduced, the R.A.F. would drop 250 million strips of this paper, code-named 'Window', weighing 100 tons, in an average week's operations.

The British had known the value of Window for over a year but it was feared that the Germans would copy it and use it to mount a new bombing campaign against England. For this reason its use over Germany was banned until a British night-fighter radar could be produced that was immune to Window jamming. This was ready in July 1943 and Window was released for the Battle of Hamburg. Ironically the Germans had already made their own Window and they too had banned its use by their own bombers in case the British copied it! They had not, however, taken the precaution of producing Window-proof radar sets.

Hamburg was beyond the range of Oboe but, situated on a wide river and being close to the sea, it had good H2S characteristics. The plan was a simple one – to bomb this one city until it was completely destroyed. In the absence of Oboe, the Pathfinders planned to carry out their target-marking by the light of masses of flares dropped by H2S-equipped aircraft. Window was to be the surprise that would nullify the German defences and the Americans were prepared to take part with Fortress raids by day. The stage was set for the destruction of Hamburg.

It was soon over. Within the space of ten nights and nine days from 24 July to 3 August Hamburg suffered four massive R.A.F. night raids and two daylight ones by the Eighth Army Air Force. Although the accuracy of the marking by H2S – and therefore of the bombing – was not as good as that achieved by Oboe, enormous destruction was caused. Approximately 50,000 people were killed and 40,000 injured. Most of this human loss had been caused by a firestorm which had developed when a multitude of small fires had joined to create one huge blaze. More people were killed in Hamburg than were killed in Britain by air raids during the whole war.

The use of Window had thrown the Germans into complete disarray and only twelve British bombers were lost on the first night. The Germans soon discovered the strips of Window, naming it *Düppel* after the location where their own experiments with a similar device had taken place – and immediately changed their tactics. British losses increased in the remaining three raids: seventeen in the second raid and thirty each in the last two raids. But from the 3,095 sorties sent against Hamburg only 2·8 per cent had been lost. The use of Window had probably saved between thirty and forty bombers and their crews.

With Hamburg reduced to smoking ruins the Germans were given cause for serious thought. Before the Battle of the Ruhr the R.A.F. bombing had certainly angered them but had not seriously affected their war effort. Their pride had been hurt more than their factories. Each tactical move by the bombers had been followed by a counter-move by the German defence and the scattered damage caused by the bombing had always been repaired in the lull following each raid. But the sustained attacks on the Ruhr and Hamburg had altered this pattern. Albert Speer, the intelligent and highly efficient Reichsminister for Armaments, has recorded in his memoirs that if the R.A.F. had systematically followed up the attack on Hamburg with similar campaigns against other key cities then Germany might not have been able to withstand the resulting damage. The *Gauleiter* of Hamburg begged Hitler to make a personal visit to his stricken city. Hitler declined and even refused to see a delegation of the rescue workers.

Both Hitler and Speer were soon to find that Harris had already chosen his next target – Berlin.

We are now, in August 1943, only eight months away from the Nuremberg Raid and have reached another turning-point. It is desirable that this should be examined carefully, for the decisions taken after the Battle of Hamburg were to lead directly to Nuremberg.

Until early 1943 all directives, that is all orders, received by Bomber Command had originated with the British War Cabinet or in the Air Ministry. Bombing policy was, there-fore, entirely British in origin and largely based on the operational capabilities of the British bomber force. But, from the Casablanca Directive of January 1943 onwards, the directives originated with the British and American Com-bined Chiefs of Staff and were issued as orders jointly to the Eighth Army Air Force and to Bomber Command. Each major directive laid down both the common aim of the Strategic Bomber Offensive and targets for each bomber force which were intended to be within the capabilities of that force.

In June 1943 a new directive was issued. The German fighters had been taking an increasing toll both by day and by night of the Allied bombers. It was feared that, unless checked, this growing German fighter force could prevent the complete air supremacy that was deemed essential as a prerequisite to a successful invasion of Europe then being planned for the spring of 1944.

The new directive stated that while the main aim remained the general destruction of German industry and morale it had become essential that the German fighter force in particular and the Luftwaffe generally should first be destroyed. Both Bomber Command and the Americans were ordered to attack the ball-bearing and aircraft industries; ball-bearings were believed to be essential to the German aircraft industry. It was realized that Bomber Command could not hit the individual factory buildings but the directive urged the command to attack the towns in which the factories were situated. This directive became known as the Pointblank Directive and the R.A.F. reaction to it was to have important consequences.

The targets referred to in Pointblank were mostly situated in small or medium-sized towns in central and southern Germany and because of the short summer nights could not then be reached by Bomber Command. But with the approach of winter the situation changed. Bomber Command with two victories behind it and steadily increasing its strength was now available to play its part in the Pointblank plan.

Harris, however, hated being ordered to bomb such targets. He was firmly convinced that Germany could be beaten before the invasion by the general destruction of her industrial cities and not by attacking selected industrial systems. He called such targets 'panaceas' and did all he could to prevent the effort of his bombers from being diverted to them. In addition he believed that it was beyond Bomber Command's capability to find and destroy the smaller towns beyond Oboe range where the Pointblank factories were to be found. Harris successfully presented these views to his R.A.F. superiors and the Air Ministry secured an amendment to Pointblank whereby Bomber Command would pursue the main aim, the attack on German industry and morale, leaving the American daylight bombers to attack the ball-bearing and aircraft factories.

The Americans, too, were having difficulties. Their

heavy-bomber formations had started in August 1943 to attack the Pointblank targets but had swiftly discovered, as had the R.A.F. in 1939, that the self-defending bomber formation could not survive against German fighter attack. For two months they persisted, suffering terrible losses in the process: on 17 August sixty bombers were lost from 376 attacking Schweinfurt and Regensburg; on 10 October thirty from 274 sent to Münster and, finally, on 14 October, sixty from 291 to Schweinfurt. Schweinfurt was the main centre of the German ball-bearing industry and was destined to become a focal point in the bombing war. By chance, it will also enter into our Nuremberg story.

No one could accuse the Americans of not having tried to follow Pointblank, but after their second raid on Schweinfurt raids beyond the range of the existing Allied daylight fighters had to stop until a long-range fighter could be developed.

Bomber Command had won the first two battles of 1943; now, with the approach of the longer nights, Harris wanted to go for what Bomber Command called the 'Big City' – Berlin, the capital of all Germany. The third great battle of 1943 was about to begin.

During the next few weeks Harris made a number of statements which give a precise indication of his hopes and intentions. First he announced in the press that he planned a great winter campaign with the intention of forcing a German surrender by the following spring. Then, on 3 November after his offensive on Berlin had begun, he wrote to Churchill, 'We can wreck Berlin from end to end if the U.S.A.A.F. will come in on it. It will cost between us 400 and 500 aircraft. It will cost Germany the war.'* Finally, on 7 December, he sent a letter to the Air Ministry pleading for priority for the production of the Lancaster, his best bomber. This time he omitted any reference to the U.S.A.A.F. but stated, 'The Lancaster force alone should be sufficient but only just sufficient to produce in Germany by 1 April 1944 a state of devastation in which surrender is inevitable.'†

Harris went on to state his requirements for this grand aim; most of these were granted but there was no German surrender in April 1944 or indeed for a further year.

Many military commanders and politicians make ill-fated

* ibid., vol. II, page 9.   † ibid., page 56.

forecasts which return to haunt them for the rest of their lives. One can call to mind Lloyd George's 'land fit for heroes', Chamberlain's 'peace in our time' and Goering's boast early in the war, 'My name is not Goering if an enemy aircraft is ever seen over Germany.' These claims that he would 'wreck Berlin from end to end' and produce 'a state of devastation in which surrender is inevitable' were to dog Harris in the following years.

The destruction of Berlin in Hamburg style was certainly an ambitious plan. The city lay deep in Germany and was certain to be defended to the utmost by the Germans. It was beyond Oboe range and its H2S characteristics were very poor. It was a sprawling modern city; its industry was not concentrated as was Essen's; it would not burn well as had Hamburg or the unfortunate medieval town of Lübeck.

The campaign against Berlin started at the end of August 1943. Three raids were sent to the capital in a week but the bombing results were very poor and, due to a partial recovery by the Germans from the Window setback, 7·2 per cent of the bombers dispatched were lost. These losses could not be borne for such poor results and the raids were stopped to await the re-equipment of the Pathfinder bombers with an improved H2S set.

It would be useful to describe here a typical raid of this period. The British tactical advances of the preceding months and the response of the Germans had been such that raids at this time bore little resemblance to those of earlier years; moreover the Nuremberg Raid was of the late-1943 pattern and this will save wearisome technical explanations later.

Bomber Command mounted a major raid on a German target on an average twice each week during this period of the war. It had the potential to carry out far more frequent operations but was prevented from doing so because the position that had prevailed earlier in the war when bombers had gone out on moonlit nights had changed. Such conditions were now ideal for German night fighters and the bombers were forced to operate on dark nights only, relying on their new electronic devices for accurate target-marking and for bombing – the 'bomber's moon' had become the 'fighter's moon'. Because of this there was a lull during the moon period of each month and intensive operations during the dark nights. A typical raid would involve about 600 aircraft, capable of delivering over 2,000 tons of bombs.

The bomber-stream first tried on the Cologne Thousand-Bomber Raid was still the mainstay of the tactics used. It had been found that the number of aircraft lost in collisions had not been serious and the stream had been steadily condensed. The bombers took off from their bases and the stream assembled as each aircraft, at its allotted time and height, flew over a pre-determined point. By the time the enemy coast was crossed the stream was complete – a seventy-mile-long swarm of aircraft 4,000 feet deep, the width depending on the accuracy of the navigation. It was always forcibly impressed on crews that safety lay in keeping well tucked into the bomber-stream.

The greatest problem for bomber crews, other than the avoidance of Germans, continued to be that of navigation. It was desirable that not only should all crews find the target but that all should be on time. To reach the target area too early could lead to its premature disclosure to the Germans. If a bomber arrived late it could find that the Pathfinders had gone home and that it had lost the protection of the stream. The strength and direction of the wind was the all-important factor in navigation. Forecasts given before take-off could be no more than a rough guide and, to discover 'actual' winds while in flight, navigators had to obtain regular and accurate 'fixes' of their position – not easy to achieve by night with Gee jammed and only about a quarter of the Main Force aircraft equipped with H2S.

Two expedients were used in an attempt to keep the stream compact. Pathfinder aircraft dropped target indicators as 'route-markers' at the turning-points to rally a scattered stream for the next leg of the flight, but a more complicated aid to navigation was the 'Broadcast Wind' or 'Zephyr' system. Experienced crews with H2S were chosen to fly at the head of the bomber-stream as 'Windfinders'. Their navigators would obtain fixes and calculate the wind strength and direction. The Windfinder wireless-operators transmitted these back to England in code every half-hour. The results were averaged at Bomber Command H.Q. and fifteen minutes later this average was broadcast again, in code, to the remaining bombers whose relatively inexperienced navigators would use this until the next Broadcast Wind was received half an hour later. The system was fine in theory but often failed to work. The Battle of Berlin contains many reports of scattered bomber-streams and late or early arrivals at the target.

The actual attack on the target was, of course, the climax of any raid. The German tactics during the earlier part of the Battle of Berlin concentrated on the defence of the target and they made their main effort against the attacking bombers at that point. These tactics will be described in detail later. The British answer was to concentrate the bombing still further and the four-hour attack of 1940 and that of ninety minutes on Cologne in 1942 was now down to a mere thirty minutes.

The Battle of Berlin is partly the story of the Pathfinder Force, for the ground was rarely visible to Main Force bomb-aimers from 20,000 feet on those moonless winter nights and the success of every raid depended on the accuracy of the marking. Target-marking will play an important part in the Nuremberg story so a brief description here of the marking methods used by the Pathfinders beyond the range of Oboe will be useful.

The Pathfinders naturally achieved their best results when vertical visibility was good. Flying ahead of the Main Force were two groups of Pathfinders: the Illuminators who dropped masses of flares, and the Visual Markers who would attempt to place their target indicators on the Aiming Point by the light of these flares. If visibility was good enough for this then the desirable 'Newhaven' marking-method had been achieved; when the first of the Main Force arrived at Zero Hour the bomb-aimers, four miles up, would find a mass of up to sixty target-indicator bombs cascading around the Aiming Point. These would be backed up by further Pathfinder aircraft for as long as the raid lasted.

Seldom, however, were conditions as good as this. Haze, fog or thin cloud would necessitate the use of the marking method known as 'Parramatta', much the same as a Newhaven but with the Aiming Point being marked by the uncertain H2S. When thick cloud was present target indicators were invisible and the whole of the marking had then to be done with coloured flares attached to parachutes, these 'release-point flares' being more commonly called sky-markers. The Pathfinders had to place these at a point in the sky in such a way that Main Force bombs would pass through that point and hit the target below – a most difficult task in calm conditions and almost impossible in strong winds which blew the skymarkers off this aerial Aiming Point as soon as their parachutes opened. This skymarking was code-named 'Wanganui'. It often resulted in inaccurate bombing but it was better than allowing the Main Force to bomb blindly and indiscriminately through cloud.

There is an interesting story about how the three marking-code names were chosen one day at Pathfinder Headquarters. The Australian Pathfinder commander, Bennett, chose 'Parramatta' after his own birthplace. A New Zealand officer contributed 'Wanganui', his home town, and a W.A.A.F. clerk, known as 'Sunshine', was invited to provide the third. Her home was at Newhaven in Sussex.

Often there was a Master Bomber (sometimes called the Master of Ceremonies), a senior Pathfinder pilot who would orbit the target throughout the raid assessing the accuracy of the marking and broadcasting advice to the crews of the Main Force. The less experienced crews received a tremendous uplift in morale when they heard in their headphones the calm voice of the Master Bomber calling them into the target and telling them which were the best-placed markers. Again, however, the system did not always work smoothly. The compiler of a Canadian squadron's records may or may not have had his tongue in his cheek when he wrote after a Berlin raid six days before Nuremberg, 'Several crews reported their resentment at the language used by the Master of Ceremonies.'*

The intention, in Area Bombing, was always to set the target city alight and destroy it by fire. For this reason the Aiming Point was usually close to the centre of the city, the older buildings there being the most promising place in which to start a good blaze. The first crews over the target carried only high-explosive General Purpose bombs to block the streets and force the German firemen to keep under cover, but the Main Force loads were mainly composed of 4,000-pound High Capacity bombs and incendiaries.

The 4,000-pounders – called 'Blockbusters' or 'Cookies' – were simply thin-skinned cylinders packed with explosive. They had no penetrating power and were not very accurate but they produced a tremendous blast-effect. One Blockbuster

* Operational Record Book, 420 (Snowy Owl) Squadron.

jettisoned over a Cologne suburb on the Nuremberg Raid destroyed only two houses but caused damage to 793 others! The Germans called them *Luftminen* – 'air mines' – possibly because the earliest ones had been dropped by parachute. There were several types of incendiary bomb of which the most commonly used was the four-pound magnesium incendiary – *Stabbrandbomben* or 'stick incendiary bombs' to the Germans. Over half a million of these small incendiaries would be scattered over a German city on one raid. The Blockbusters were intended to blow in the roofs and windows of the old buildings in the centre of the German cities, the incendiary bombs to set them afire.

Unfortunately Bomber Command's insatiable demand for bombs meant that less dependable types had to be used and there are many reports of the high number of these that did not explode; one says that 60 per cent of all General Purpose and Medium Capacity bombs were useless and another that 25 per cent of all high-explosive bombs failed. Neither report is backed by reliable research but a German survey of 30,434 bombs dropped on their oil refineries later in 1944 shows that 18·9 per cent of the R.A.F. bombs and 12·2 per cent of U.S.A.A.F. bombs did not explode. It is a tragedy that, on this evidence, so much of Bomber Command's effort was wasted. *

Another cause of waste was that certain bomber crews did not press home their attacks properly. There are many reports during this period of bombs being jettisoned over the sea and pilots lightening their loads to gain height when fighters attacked the bomber-stream. Again, at the target, some crews failed to fly right up to the Aiming Point but bombed early and turned away. The result of this was known as a 'creep-back' in the bombing which despite all efforts could never be eliminated. Photographic evidence showed that the creep-back on one Berlin raid measured thirty miles, but this is an extreme example. In a report on morale during the Battle of Berlin Air Vice-Marshal Bennett derisively refers to these crews as 'fringe merchants'. Despite these human failures bombing accuracy had increased greatly, thanks mainly to Bennett and his Pathfinders. All aircraft were now fitted with cameras and, in 1943, these showed

* Details of the German survey are taken from the Official History, vol. IV, page 519.

that nearly two thirds of the bombs fell within three miles of the Aiming Point.

While bombing techniques and accuracy improved the dangers to bomber crews had increased. The Germans were applying an increasing determination and ingenuity to the defence of their cities. Flak continued to take its toll but the bombers' main enemy was now the night fighter. These were responsible for roughly two thirds of the losses in the Battle of Berlin. The bombers were armed only with small-calibre machine-guns which were outranged by the night fighter's cannons. Air gunners were ordered not to open fire until attacked; concealment in the dark and evasion were considered safer than fighting it out with an attacker. Once attacked, the corkscrew manoeuvre was considered the best escape from a fighter. One German night-fighter ace followed a corkscrewing Lancaster for forty-five minutes without once getting into a firing position.

In an effort to deliver a decisive tonnage of bombs during the Battle of Berlin the Lancasters' bomb loads were increased. But these increased loads also robbed the bombers of their manoeuvrability. German night-fighter pilots state that they could tell exactly when the loads were increased and victories became easier for them from that moment. In general, once a good night-fighter pilot had found a bomber, the odds against the bomber escaping destruction were very high and it is not surprising that Bennett's 'fringe merchants' lightened their loads to even the odds a little.

Just as the operations of 1939 had shown that the self-defending bomber could not survive in daylight so the increasing efficiency of the German defences in the winter of 1943 was robbing the bombers of the protection of darkness. The bomber losses were becoming so heavy that an increasing effort was being devoted to ensure their survival in sufficient numbers to keep Bomber Command a viable force.

For some time the bombers had been fitted with a variety of devices and the records of this period contain a mass of code names. 'Mandrel' was a device for jamming German ground radar, and 'Tinsel', a small transmitter fitted near one of the bomber's engines, was switched on when orders to night fighters were being broadcast. 'Monica' and 'Fishpond' both gave warning of the approach of German fighters but, as many bombers were also nearby, there were frequent false alarms. Even worse, the Germans had discovered Monica as soon as it was introduced early in 1943. They had produced an airborne counter-device to home upon the Monica impulses. In July 1944 a German night fighter equipped with this device landed by mistake on a British airfield. When tested by the R.A.F. it was discovered, with horror, that the German equipment could pick up Monica transmissions from a bomber flying 130 miles away! That was the end of Monica.

Another, more successful, device was 'Airborne Cigar', this code name being shortened to 'A.B.C.' The aircraft of one Lancaster squadron were each fitted with three transmitters manned by an extra German-speaking crew member to jam the German fighter-controllers' instructions. These A.B.C. Lancasters carried a normal bomb load and were mixed into the bomber-stream of all major raids. The Germans knew all about A.B.C. soon after its introduction but there does not appear to have been any serious attempt to home onto its transmissions. In its turn A.B.C. certainly caused the German controllers difficulty and they had to employ a variety of expedients to overcome these and other jamming efforts. *

In addition to the effort provided by the bombers themselves, support from long-range Mosquito night fighters had also to be sought although the close escort of night bombers was impossible. Low-level fighters had been flying deep into Europe for several years attempting to shoot down enemy aircraft, particularly those taking off and landing. These aptly named 'Intruders' were now harnessed directly to the R.A.F. bomber raids by patrolling known German night-fighter airfields within range of the route of the bomber-stream. A later development was the 'Serrate' Mosquito – the Serrate being a special radar which could home onto the German airborne radar sets being used in 1943. Both the Intruders and the Serrate Mosquitoes were scoring a steady trickle of victories, but the problem of providing an effective fighter defence for night bombers remained immense.

The reader need not remember all these weapons and the

---

* The reader may like to refer to an excellent and comprehensive book on the subject of the radio counter-measures war – *Instruments of Darkness* by Alfred Price, published by William Kimber.

jumble of code names. Only the Serrate and Intruder Mosquitoes and the A.B.C. Lancasters with their German-speaking crew-member and his jamming equipment will play an important part in the story of the Nuremberg Raid.

Further aid was being given to the bombers by the use of 'spoof' raids. The Battle of Berlin period saw the introduction and the development of such tactics on a large scale. Training aircraft or obsolete bombers would assemble and fly towards the enemy coast before, or at the same time as, the main bomber-stream and then turn away at the last moment. Other diversions would be provided by small groups of Mosquito bombers who would fly deep into Germany and then attack a spoof target with flares and target indicators. The 'raid' would then fizzle out while the Mosquitoes made their escape at high speed. All these diversions dropped plenty of Window so that the German radar could not easily distinguish the small diversionary force from the main attack. The object of all these ploys was to confuse the German fighter-controllers and force them, if possible, to commit their night fighters at the wrong time or place.

These then, briefly, were the tactics of a raid of the Battle of Berlin era. The simple bomber raids of 1940 and 1941 had given way to an intricately planned, highly complicated operation with the night sky full of aircraft, heavily laden or speedy, with electronic transmission being emitted, reflected, echoed, received and homed upon, often bringing death to whoever tried to use them to escape death. The bombing war had become almost a contest of technology but each bout resulted in the loss of a large number of human lives. Let us look next at how the opposing forces had organized themselves in this deadly game.

3

Bomber Command

Just as the policy and tactics of the bombing war gradually evolved, so too did Bomber Command itself. The mighty force available at the end of the war grew from the brave but fragile squadrons that had raided Wilhelmshaven in September 1939. This chapter will examine Bomber Command at a precise moment during these years – 30 March 1944, the day of the Nuremberg Raid.

Bomber Command's front line was the great chain of fifty-four operational airfields stretching through eastern England from Darlington to Cambridge. About one third of these had been the R.A.F.'s pre-war stations with extensive facilities and comfortable accommodation. Postings to these 'gin palaces' were much sought after by aircrews. The less fortunate had to make do with the more spartan Nissen huts of the temporary airfields built since the beginning of the war. Sir Arthur Harris at his headquarters near High Wycombe was fifty miles from his nearest bomber station, Gransden Lodge, and over 200 miles from the Canadian station at Middleton St George in County Durham. Between Bomber Command H.Q. and the operational squadrons were three intermediate levels of command – group, base and station – although all major decisions were made by Harris. Rarely has a military commander had such a powerful and flexible force under his own personal control.

The group was a long-established organization containing an average of a dozen squadrons ideally all equipped with the same type of aircraft. In March 1944 Bomber Command contained seven operational groups, three training groups and a signals group. The base was of recent innovation. As the groups had grown in size and bomber operations had become more complex, this small extra link had been inserted in the chain of command. The base was commanded by an air commodore and was housed on an operational airfield; it controlled that airfield and usually two more. These became unofficially a 'clutch'. The setting-up of the base system was

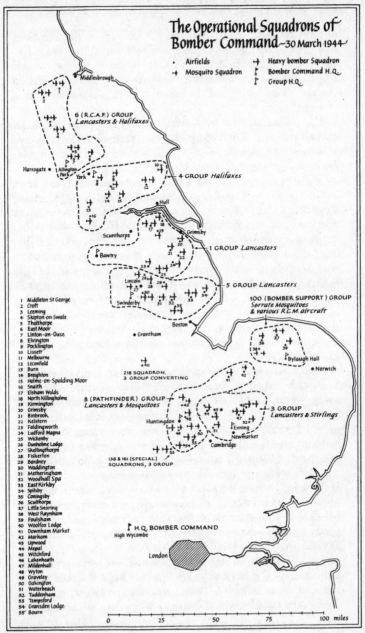

The Operational Squadrons of Bomber Command ~ 30 March 1944

Legend:
- Airfields
- Mosquito Squadron
- Heavy bomber Squadron
- Bomber Command H.Q.
- Group H.Q.

6 (R.C.A.F.) GROUP
Lancasters & Halifaxes

4 GROUP *Halifaxes*

1 GROUP *Lancasters*

5 GROUP *Lancasters*

100 (BOMBER SUPPORT) GROUP
*Serrate Mosquitoes
& various R.C.M. aircraft*

218 SQUADRON,
3 GROUP CONVERTING

8 (PATHFINDER) GROUP
Lancasters & Mosquitoes

3 GROUP
Lancasters & Stirlings

138 & 161 (SPECIAL)
SQUADRONS, 3 GROUP

H.Q. BOMBER COMMAND

Middlesbrough
Harrogate
Allington Park
York
Hull
Scunthorpe
Grimsby
Bawtry
Lincoln
Swinderby
Boston
Grantham
Bylaugh Hall
Norwich
Huntingdon
Exning
Newmarket
Cambridge
High Wycombe
London

1 Middleton St George
2 Croft
3 Leeming
4 Skipton-on-Swale
5 Tholthorpe
6 East Moor
7 Linton-on-Ouse
8 Elvington
9 Pocklington
10 Lissett
11 Melbourne
12 Leconfield
13 Burn
14 Breighton
15 Holme-on-Spalding Moor
16 Snaith
17 Elsham Wolds
18 North Killingholme
19 Kirmington
20 Grimsby
21 Binbrook
22 Kelstern
23 Faldingworth
24 Ludford Magna
25 Wickenby
26 Dunholme Lodge
27 Skellingthorpe
28 Fiskerton
29 Bardney
30 Waddington
31 Metheringham
32 Woodhall Spa
33 East Kirkby
34 Spilsby
35 Coningsby
36 Scuthorpe
37 Little Snoring
38 West Raynham
39 Foulsham
40 Woolfox Lodge
41 Downham Market
42 Marham
43 Upwood
44 Mepal
45 Witchford
46 Lakenheath
47 Mildenhall
48 Wyton
49 Graveley
50 Oakington
51 Waterbeach
52 Tuddenham
53 Tempsford
54 Gransden Lodge
55 Bourn

0   25   50   75   100 miles

Map 1

not yet complete and it will play little part in the events of this book. The final link in the chain joining the commander-in-chief to his squadrons was the station – the permanent organization on a bomber airfield, commanded by a group captain, that provided facilities for the squadrons that operated from it.

The squadron, led by a wing commander, was the basic operational unit. The average bomber station contained either a three-flight squadron of thirty bombers or two double-flight squadrons with forty bombers in all.

The seven operational groups were situated in three distinct areas – Yorkshire, Lincolnshire and East Anglia.* Together in Yorkshire were two groups which between them operated all of Bomber Command's Halifax squadrons. 6 Group, with six airfields in the Vale of York and one just over the border in Durham, was a unique group in that it was Canadian – its thirteen squadrons were all of the R.C.A.F., its commander was a Canadian officer and most of the running costs of the group were met by Canada. In spite of this, 6 Group was fully integrated operationally into Bomber Command, a fine act of faith by the Canadian Government and typical of that country's total commitment to Britain's war.

Each Canadian squadron incorporated an individual name in its title. Most of these were of Canadian cities or of the country's wild animals or birds but other names had less obvious origins. 428 (Ghost) Squadron was supposedly so named because for many months after its formation no crew had survived a full tour of operations while 425 (Alouette) was predominantly French-Canadian. 427 (Lion) Squadron was adopted by the Metro-Goldwyn-Mayer studios of Hollywood, whose emblem was also a lion. Their aircraft, decorated with suitably painted motifs, were all named after M.-G.-M. film-stars, and members of the squadron were given a special pass which entitled them to two free seats at any cinema showing an M.-G.-M. film.

Two of the 6 Group squadrons had been equipped with Lancasters and others were gradually being converted to this superior type. Some of these Lancasters were the comparatively rare radial-engined Mark II which had a mid-under or

* Appendix 2 contains Bomber Command's full Order of Battle on 30 March 1944.

ventral gun position; the Canadians were also fitting similar gun positions into the bellies of its other aircraft as fast as they could get the necessary conversion sets from the United States. This extra gun position necessitated an eight-man crew but it will be seen to have important consequences.

6 Group was formed in January 1943 but had a bad time in that year. Its rapid expansion had left it short of experienced squadron and flight commanders and a run of very heavy losses had badly affected morale, but by the end of the year the group had settled down and solved many of its problems. A new commander had taken over in February 1944; this was Air Vice-Marshal C. M. McEwen, a First World War fighter ace nicknamed 'Black Mike' for his dark complexion. Drastic measures by McEwen had increased still further the efficiency of the Canadian squadrons.

An example of the difficulties met in building up the Canadian group can be seen in the formation of 433 (Porcupine) Squadron at Skipton-on-Swale. Five crews, most of whom had been in trouble at previous squadrons, were posted in to form the nucleus of the squadron together with new crews who had just finished training. Three of the five experienced crews promptly went missing. The two surviving experienced pilots were an English flight sergeant who was once 'officer' in charge of night flying, normally a squadron leader's job, and an American who had been turned out of the Pathfinders and found himself the most experienced pilot on this squadron with the lowly rank of pilot officer.

This pilot, Christian Neilson, was one of 6 Group's 'characters' and was nicknamed 'the Mad Dane'. On one occasion he was taking off fully loaded when the hydraulics of his Halifax failed so that wheels, flaps and bomb-doors all dropped down. Neilson barely maintained height as his flight engineer, Flight Sergeant Chris Panton, a Lincolnshire gamekeeper's son, whose ambition it was to be a pilot himself one day, pumped furiously at the manual controls and pressure was regained just in time to clear an approaching hill. At this moment Neilson broke the sacred radio silence and was heard to say in a bored voice, 'O.K. Jesus. I've got it!'

It was the presence of such people as Neilson, an American citizen of Danish extraction flying in a Canadian squadron from England, that the Germans found so hard to understand.

A close neighbour of the Canadians was 4 Group, based in south and east Yorkshire with nine R.A.F. squadrons, and the Australian 466 Squadron at Leconfield. This was a pre-war group, the original night-bombing group whose Whitleys had flown to Germany dropping leaflets on the very first night of the war. Now it was equipped throughout with Halifaxes. 4 Group was never one of the glamorous groups with a specialist role or élite squadrons. It had been tucked away in the north of England since 1939, plodding away at the bombing war, usually operating inferior aircraft and taking higher-than-average losses. It was the workhorse of Bomber Command.

The group commander was Air Vice-Marshal Roderick Carr, a New Zealander with a sound reputation, but parts of his group were undoubtedly in a poor state of morale at the time of the Nuremberg Raid. When the Stirlings were taken off major raids in November 1943 the Halifax crews, with a lower ceiling than the Lancasters, had become the 'ground bait' for the German night fighters and 4 Group's losses in the hard-fought Battle of Berlin had been severe. Unlike 6 Group there had not been a recovery. Carr and many others may protest that morale in 4 Group was not low but it is certain that heavy losses in continuous operations with inferior aircraft had left their mark. Some squadrons were in better shape than others but it is significant that, in March 1944, a 4 Group staff officer was touring the airfields lecturing crews on 'early returns' and Carr himself is recorded as having talked to all station and squadron commanders on this subject.

Coming south, the next bomber area was Lincolnshire with two large all-Lancaster groups. In the north of the county was 1 Group under Air Vice-Marshal E. A. B. Rice, a South African badly crippled from a First World War leg wound. Rice was a friend and admirer of Sir Arthur Harris. His philosophy and that of his group was to dispatch the heaviest possible bomb load as often as possible to Germany.

1 Group contained eleven squadrons of which three merit special mention. 101 Squadron at Ludford Magna was the squadron whose aircraft were fitted with the Airborne Cigar

(or A.B.C.) jamming equipment and its eight-man Lancasters were sent on every long raid. For this reason 101 Squadron often operated when their own group was resting and it claimed to have taken part in more bombing raids than any other Bomber Command squadron. 460 Squadron at Binbrook was the senior of the four Australian squadrons in Bomber Command, and 300 (Masovian) was the only Polish squadron in the command. The Poles had flown until early in March 1944 with the last operational Wellingtons; at the time of the Nuremberg Raid they were converting to Lancasters so they had the good fortune to miss that raid.

Next came 5 Group, whose airfields were on the low hills of mid Lincolnshire. If any part of Bomber Command can be said to have had 'glamour' then 5 Group, possibly with the Pathfinders, had this quality. 5 Group was the first to be equipped with that popular bomber, the Lancaster; it had raised and now maintained 617 Squadron of 'dam-busting' fame and, during the course of the war, its airmen were awarded more than half of Bomber Command's V.C.s. In March 1944 it was the largest of the groups and among its thirteen squadrons were 44 (Rhodesia) Squadron at Dunholme Lodge and two Australian squadrons, 463 and 467, at Waddington. It was 463 Squadron that provided a special Lancaster for the R.A.F. Film Unit which produced the thrilling films of bomber raids shown on cinema newsreels during the war.

5 Group had been commanded by Harris earlier in the war and other commanders felt that he still favoured his old group. This is possibly so but the reason may be as much that the present commander, Air Vice-Marshal The Hon. Ralph Cochrane, had more to offer than many of his contemporaries. Cochrane was an English officer with a naval background: he had flown airships with the Royal Naval Air Service in the First World War. He was a reserved, austere man who was always trying to improve bomber tactics in general and bombing accuracy in particular at a time when many others felt that in Area Bombing a pattern had been established that would suffice to the end of the war.

On a lower level, aircrew in other groups were envious of 5 Group's position and its members were sometimes called 'the Snobs of Bomber Command'. Critics of 5 Group also felt that too many men from the group were recommended for V.C.s and that it managed to obtain more than its share of press publicity. Whatever the means used, it is certain that both Cochrane and 5 Group made an immense contribution to the bombing war and morale in its squadrons was high.

The top brass in 5 Group certainly managed to inspire a fine brand of enthusiasm in aircrews. I remember that before we left H.C.U. [Heavy Conversion Unit] at Swinderby on our way to the squadron, we came away from a talk by a wing commander, absolutely sure that we were in the best group in Bomber Command and feeling rather sorry for those crews who had the bad luck to be in other groups. (Flying Officer J. Chatterton, 44 Squadron)

The two Lincolnshire-based groups, being both strong in squadrons and equipped with the Lancaster, were to carry a greater tonnage of bombs to Nuremberg than the other five groups in Bomber Command combined.

Situated south of the Fens were the remaining groups, all completely different – 3 Group, 8 (Pathfinder) Group and 100 (Bomber Support) Group.

3 Group, with its airfields around Ely, had started the war with the sound Wellington and would finish it fully equipped with the equally sound Lancaster, but March 1944 found it in a sorry state. It had converted from the Wellington to the Stirling but this aircraft had become obsolete in 1943. The group then started to change again, this time to Lancasters, but the heavy losses of the Battle of Berlin had meant that most of the Lancaster production had been diverted to replacing losses in squadrons of other groups and 3 Group's conversion had languished. After four months only four squadrons had Lancasters, two were converting and three were still stuck with their old Stirlings. These aircraft did not take part in major raids and were being used on a variety of odd jobs – mining, short raids to France and supply-dropping to Resistance units in France. This last was considered by the crews a useful and popular task but, generally, the Stirling squadrons were fed up and anxious to obtain their Lancasters.

Two of the Lancaster squadrons, 115 and 514, were operating the Mark II Lancaster. While 6 Group were fitting as many downward-firing guns as they could, 3 Group were taking similar gun positions out of their Mark IIs to save just 122 pounds of weight and the need for an extra crew-member.

3 Group contained three squadrons of interest. At Mepal was 75 (New Zealand) Squadron, an R.A.F. squadron but containing many New Zealanders. Like the Polish squadron, it was in the process of converting to Lancasters and missed the Nuremberg Raid. Stationed at Tempsford were 138 and 161 (Special Duty) Squadrons, those responsible for taking Resistance agents and supplies to all corners of German-occupied Europe. They were equipped with a wide variety of aircraft for this task – Halifaxes, Hudsons, Liberators and Lysanders. Their crews flew as far afield as Norway, Poland and Yugoslavia, sometimes landing in Russia or North Africa after a long flight. They spent so much time over enemy territory that their tour ended at 250 operational hours if this came before the normal thirty completed flights.

3 Group's commander was Yorkshireman Air Vice-Marshal R. Harrison. He was older than the other group commanders and was typical of the senior R.A.F. officer who had been promoted steadily since the First World War. He was a quiet man, a bachelor and a keen fisherman. He was a respected commander but his influence on the bombing war was confined to the running of his own group.

In complete contrast to the quiet Harrison was his close neighbour Air Vice-Marshal D. C. T. Bennett of 8 (Pathfinder) Group, one of the most interesting of the bomber commanders.

Donald Bennett, from New South Wales, had served in the R.A.A.F. and the R.A.F. from 1930 to 1935. He had then joined Imperial Airways where, among other things, he piloted the small flying boat *Mercury* in the Mayo Composite where a large seaplane took off with a smaller one carried pick-a-back on its upper wing surface. The smaller plane, *Mercury*, could in this manner carry a far greater fuel load than if it had taken off under its own power. Once released from *Maia*, its 'mother', *Mercury* had a tremendous range. In 1938 Bennett broke the existing distance-record of 4,000 miles by flying this small machine for forty-two hours to cover 6,000 miles with only a wireless-operator as a companion. In 1940 he had helped to establish the Atlantic Ferry by which American-built aircraft were flown to England until, in September 1941, he returned to the R.A.F.

where he was given the rank of Wing Commander and command of a Halifax squadron in 4 Group. In 1942 he was shot down while attempting to bomb the *Tirpitz* in Norway but he escaped to England via Sweden.

When the Pathfinder Force was formed late in 1942 Harris personally selected Bennett as its commander, resisting pressure to accept a more senior Regular officer. When Pathfinder Force became 8 Group, Bennett was promoted to Air Vice-Marshal at the age of only thirty-two, having risen from Wing Commander in just over a year.

Bennett's rapid promotion was not surprising. He was a brilliant navigator and his ability as a pilot, engineer and wireless-operator was probably equal to that of any man in his group. He was completely dedicated to bombing Germany and he set the highest standards for his crews. He had a disconcerting habit of seeing crews off on a raid, taking off himself an hour later in a Beaufighter or a Mosquito and orbiting the target throughout the raid. When the Pathfinder crews returned, they would find Bennett calmly waiting for them at debriefing knowing more about the raid than they did. After one such raid a tired Pathfinder crew admitted to dropping their Wanganui skymarkers down-wind instead of up-wind. Without further ado Bennett ordered the whole crew to be off the station and out of 8 Group by ten o'clock that morning.

Bennett's relations with some of his contemporaries were not good. He believed that not only Pathfinder methods but all navigation and routeing recommendations also should be accepted by the others without question. He called those group commanders who opposed his views 'the unruly barons of Bomber Command'. In turn they found it difficult to work with this brash young officer who had been appointed by Harris to the most interesting job in Bomber Command. Such clashes of personality are not unusual in time of war and there is no evidence that the relationships ever became petty or spiteful. Bennett and Cochrane were often in conflict on tactics and, as we shall see later, this brought about a radical change. On the other hand Carr, Bennett's old commander in 4 Group, thought Bennett 'a brilliant man whom I always backed'.

Few were neutral where Bennett was concerned but of one thing there was no doubt – he had the complete and absolute confidence of the Pathfinder aircrews. They may have found him intolerant and hard to please but, because of his ability as an aviator and his powers of leadership, they followed him without question. 'If you were not religious you thought Bennett was Jesus Christ. If you were religious, he was the next best thing.' (Flight Lieutenant C. S. Chatten, 97 Squadron)

In March 1944 Bennett's 8 Group had seven Lancaster squadrons, five Mosquito squadrons and the Meteorological Flight also with Mosquitoes. Each of the Lancaster squadrons was 'supported' by the bomber group which had originally contributed it on the formation of the Pathfinder Force and it continued to draw replacements from that group in the shape of volunteer crews who were at least half-way through their first tour. There were, however, flaws in the system and there were many grumbles that the groups failed to encourage their best crews to go to the Pathfinders. Bomber Command had decreed that the Pathfinders should only get two thirds of their crew requirements in this way; the remainder came from training units, Coastal Command, the Middle East, from any place where suitable men could be found. These were usually good men but the Official History refers to the Pathfinders as sometimes having to 'struggle with a dead weight of ex-O.T.U. crews'. One would not question the courage of men who had all volunteered for a longer tour than that of crews serving with ordinary squadrons, but there is evidence that the Pathfinders' general level of experience and competence at the end of the Battle of Berlin was much lower than Bennett would have liked.

Two of the Mosquito squadrons are worthy of particular mention. 139 (Jamaica) holds the distinction of being the only squadron to take part in both the first and last bombing raids of the European War – Wilhelmshaven and Kiel. The 'Jamaica' in the title was to acknowledge an earlier gift of money from that island for the purchase of aircraft for the R.A.F. but the 1944 members of the squadron were probably more interested in the continuing gift of Jamaican rum. Another gift of money for aircraft, this time from the British community in Buenos Aires and other Allied sympathizers there, had been rewarded by the incorporation of the organization's name in a squadron title. In this way 692

(Fellowship of the Bellows) Squadron had received its strange but quite official title.

There was great competition by pilots and navigators to be posted to Mosquito squadrons and this privilege was usually reserved for those who had completed a previous tour on heavy bombers or had spent much time as instructors in training units. Pilots were usually required to have at least 1,000 hours flying experience as first pilots for the Mosquito required careful handling. These qualifications led to Mosquito crews often being the 'old men' of Bomber Command.

To compensate for a longer tour and rigorous standards, the Pathfinder crews had two rewards. Once accepted as a qualified Pathfinder, that is after passing tests set personally by Bennett, each man was promoted by one rank and also awarded, temporarily only, the Pathfinder Badge – a small R.A.F. eagle which he wore beneath his aircrew brevet. Only if he completed his tour satisfactorily or went missing did the award of this highly prized badge become permanent and a certificate to that effect issued. On the other hand, Bennett let it be known that there would be no Victoria Cross awards to living in the Pathfinders and there never were.

The last Bomber Command group to be formed was 100 (Bomber Support) Group stationed in north Norfolk. The successes of the German night fighters in 1943 had led directly to the creation of a number of units whose task it was to support the bombers in various ways. In November of that year these units had been collected into a new group whose sole object was to help the night-bomber force. Its commander was Air Commodore (later Air Vice-Marshal) E. B. Addison, an expert in signals and radio counter-measures.

100 Group was to do great things in the last year of the war but at the time of the Nuremberg Raid was not fully effective. It had three Serrate Mosquito squadrons equipped with ancient aircraft and out-of-date radar sets (an ordinary radar was needed as well as the Serrate equipment). These were achieving a trickle of successes but, for example, to the end of March 1944 239 Squadron had shot down only three German night fighters but had lost six Mosquitoes on operations or in training. A fourth Mosquito squadron, for low-level Intruder work, had been posted to the group but was not yet operational, nor was a squadron of American-built Fortresses that no one else in the R.A.F. seemed to

want and which were being converted to a jamming role. 192 Squadron, with Halifaxes and Mosquitoes, was the only operational radio counter-measures squadron in the group and this could muster no more than a handful of aircraft which flew with the bomber-stream and spied on German radar signals. 100 Group had not yet the capability to do any jamming.

This then is Bomber Command on the eve of the Nuremberg Raid – seven groups, seventy-six squadrons, about 1,000 aircraft. Morale, with some exceptions, was high and there was no shortage of crews but recent heavy losses had dangerously reduced the average level of experience. Let us look more closely at the men who had to fly to Nuremberg.

After a period of trial and error the standard heavy-bomber crew was now composed of seven specialist members – pilot, navigator, air bomber (usually called the bomb-aimer), wireless-operator, two air gunners and a flight engineer.

These men had been trained only in their own personal duties before coming to Bomber Command. The pilot, navigator and bomb-aimer were always classified separately by the R.A.F., being called the P.N.B. group. For their specialist training these men had all been abroad to either Canada, South Africa or Southern Rhodesia under the Empire Air Training Scheme, or to the United States under an agreement concluded before that country had become involved in the war. It was possible for such men to have spent several years training. The remaining crew-members had been trained in England.

The crew would start to form at a Bomber Command Operational Training Unit when all but the flight engineer and one of the gunners commenced crew-training on Wellingtons or Whitleys. Sufficient men for the sixteen crews on a course would be assembled in a hangar or large hall and left to sort themselves into crews. In this casual manner men would band themselves together to face what was to become for most the supreme test of their lives. At the end of the course a flight engineer and mid-upper gunner would be added to complete each crew.

Everyone wanted to be a pilot and those young men who survived the rigorous selection and training can be considered 'the cream of the cream'. There were frequent complaints from other aircrew that it was 'a pilot's air force' and to some extent this was true. Promotion and decorations certainly came plentifully to the bomber pilots but it should be remembered that at all times in the air the pilot was responsible for six lives other than his own and it was often by his decision that the others lived or died. In the event of a crash it was always the pilot who had to remain at the controls until the other crew-members had safely escaped. Every pilot knew that when the moment of danger came he stood the least chance of survival.

My research included interviews or correspondence with over 350 men who flew on the Nuremberg Raid. I know that this is not a large enough sample for a scientific survey but I was impressed with the high proportion of ex-pilots, particularly those who had flown more than one tour, who had since suffered medical, nervous, alcoholic or marital trouble. I am certain that the burden of command in prolonged bomber operations had affected these men.

A bomber crew worked as a mutually dependent team and each man made a contribution to the survival of the crew and its success on operations. It fell to the navigator to keep the aircraft on track at all times, to reach the target, avoid defended areas and, at the end of each flight, to find the home airfield. In Canadian squadrons the navigator was even the aircraft captain if he out-ranked the pilot. The navigator could never relax for more than a few minutes on a flight and had to carry out complicated calculations. Many suffered from airsickness.

Navigators were considered to be an introspective, reserved breed, probably the least war-like of all aircrew. Many were sensitive and well educated men and there was a high proportion of former or future schoolmasters. They had a reputation for being clannish and navigational troubles were often quietly dealt with by the 'navigators' trade union'.

The bomb–aimer had been introduced into the bomber-crew in 1942; until then the navigator had aimed and released the bombs. Now, when the aircraft was on its bombing run over the target the bomb-aimer, lying in the prone position pioneered by Squadron Leader Arthur Harris in Iraq twenty years earlier, took over control of the aircraft and the pilot obeyed his directions until the bombs were released and the bombing photograph taken. In French squadrons the bomb-aimer was the aircraft captain. In the Pathfinders and in other squadrons where aircraft had H2S the bomb-aimer was often trained to operate the H2S set sitting alongside the navigator. Otherwise he would attempt to map-read from his position in the nose. Other bomb-aimer duties were the dropping of Window and the manning of the front gun turret when necessary. The bomb-aimer also received a little pilot training and he became the reserve pilot in an emergency. Often they were men who had failed to complete a pilot's course.

If the pilot, navigator and bomb-aimer were the 'brains' in a crew then the remainder – the wireless-operator, flight engineer and the two gunners – were the 'tradesmen' but there was hardly any real snobbery and much genuine comradeship between the two groups, more than existed in any other service. Most crews hardly realized that the two groups officially existed.

The wireless-operator sat near the navigator and was responsible for all messages to and from base. As bomber operations were invariably conducted in wireless silence as far as the bombers were concerned, the wireless-operator had little to do except listen in to the half-hourly broadcasts from base. These contained the coded Broadcast Winds, the occasional recall signal but rarely anything else. For this reason the wireless-operator was usually the odd-job man. He was trained as a reserve gunner, he operated the 'Fishpond', an extension of the H2S that gave warning of approaching fighters, and he could be sent by the pilot to cope with minor emergencies in any part of the aircraft. If the aircraft got into difficulties, however, the wireless-operator became a vital crew member. His radio fixes could establish instantly the aircraft's position and if a ditching in the sea became inevitable he had to remain in his position to the last moment sending out the distress signal.

The flight engineer had also been introduced into the crew in 1942 when the old crew position of second pilot was dropped. He acted in many ways as co-pilot, monitoring the instruments and helping with take-offs and landings. In an emergency he too became essential, for his fuel calculations had to be accurate. In action he became a useful extra lookout man and he was also the reserve bomb-aimer.

Flight engineers came from two distinct groups. The first

and largest group was mainly composed of city men with a mechanical background and there were a high proportion of men from the engineering areas of the West Midlands. A smaller group were the younger men who could not find a place in the pilot-training programme and who flew as flight engineers in the hope of becoming pilots later. Almost all of Bomber Command's flight engineers at this time were from the United Kingdom.

All the above five crew-members worked together in the front part of the bomber. This was heated and each man had a certain freedom of movement. The two gunners, however, were completely isolated in their respective turrets. Dressed in cumbersome electrically heated suits, forced to remain in their cramped turrets for many hours, they had the most uncomfortable and boring job in the crew, yet on their vigilance depended the safety of the whole crew. Although trained to a high standard of marksmanship, their main duty was to advise the pilot on evasive action by anticipating the movements of an attacker. In a combat it was the 'patter' of the gunners that effectively controlled the aircraft. Those gunners who actually completed their tour of operations often did so without once firing their guns in anger. The best gunner was often the man who knew when to hold his fire and not draw attention to his aircraft's presence. The average flight for a gunner consisted of sitting for six hours or more in extreme cold, staring into the darkness in the hope of seeing a German fighter before it opened fire.

Collectively, the aircrews of Bomber Command in 1944 represented the cream of the young manhood of the British Empire with a sprinkling of men from other Allied countries. Every one was a volunteer who had passed rigid physical and intellectual tests. In spite of the grim losses there was never at any time in the war a shortage of applicants, and even when selected for aircrew training there was often a long wait before that training could begin. In a service where it was not family or education but ability that was the only criterion, the best of all found themselves in the front line of Bomber Command.

These men joined for many reasons; there was some genuine patriotism, a desire to crush Nazism and avenge the bombing of Warsaw, Rotterdam, London and Coventry, but it was more often a desire to fly and to embark on an adventure that would test their courage to the limit. It was Ernest Raymond, writing about the men who went to Gallipoli in 1915, who wrote, 'Youth is ever proud to visit the margins of death.' The bomber crews can be compared in many ways with the men who flocked to join Kitchener's Army in 1914. The casualty rate was roughly equal for both. In this new war no body of fighting men suffered a casualty rate comparable with that of the bomber men.

By 1944 there were hardly any pre-war Regulars still flying with the bomber squadrons; promotion or attrition had removed all but a handful. Bomber Command, like the rest of the R.A.F., had become a command structure of professionals directing a mass of civilian volunteers. The youngest were the nineteen-year-old air gunners and flight engineers whose shorter training periods brought them onto operations more quickly than other crew members. The vast majority were in their early twenties with only a handful of men in their thirties. Unlike the R.A.F. of today, only a quarter of the aircrew were officers.

The R.A.F. of 1944 was more truly an Empire and an Allied force than any of the other services. In Bomber Command only two thirds of the squadrons and individuals were provided by the R.A.F., the majority of the remainder being provided by the Empire countries. It is to the credit of these countries that early in the war when they were not remotely threatened by Germany they should place their men in the hands of the R.A.F. and stand four-square with their mother country. It is to the particular credit of Australia and New Zealand that this support should continue through that period of the war when they were in danger of invasion from Japan.

There was no such thing as a completely national squadron in Bomber Command, all squadrons being made up with men from other countries. The crews too were mixed and there were few that did not contain men from at least two countries. This mixture of nationalities went right through to the highest level of command. The Commander-in-Chief was a Rhodesian and, of the seven group commanders, there were three Englishmen, a Canadian, an Australian, a New Zealander and a South African.

There were many opinions held on the relative abilities

of the men from the different countries. Some thought the phlegmatic and conscientious character of the United Kingdom men better suited to bomber operations and that the proximity of their homes to Europe and the war itself gave them an extra dedication. Harris, in his book, says that such men were as brave as any and more effective than most due to their being better educated than overseas crews. These may be valid points but it is a fact that, due to a shortage of manpower, the United Kingdom content of Bomber Command gradually diminished as the war progressed and Harris had to rely on men from other countries in increasing quantities.

The Canadians were easily the largest overseas contingent in Bomber Command. They were usually happy-go-lucky men, great gamblers and very fond of and successful with the girls. Their transatlantic national character set them somewhat apart from other Empire men. They were not always noted for their flying discipline and some consider their dashing attitude more suitable to fighter operations. However, the Canadians contributed about one fifth of all Bomber Command aircrew, and hence losses, during the war.

The Australians, about one man in ten in 1944, came next in numbers. It was thought by many that Australia selected her finest airmen for service in the R.A.F. and that the Australian crews were the best in Bomber Command. The pilots particularly were felt to have had a natural flair for bomber operations and aircrew with Australian captains felt they were in good hands with a better-than-average chance of survival.

New Zealand supported one squadron in Bomber Command throughout the war and also sent many individual airmen. They were quiet, reliable men with a high reputation. One bomber squadron included 'Rhodesia' in its title and men from both Northern and Southern Rhodesia were posted to it but there were barely enough to maintain one flight of Rhodesians. There were a few men from many of the other Empire countries and also a surprising number of Southern Irishmen. There were also Americans, men who had joined up in Canada or England before Pearl Harbor. After America's own entry into the war some transferred to their own Air Corps but many stayed on with the R.A.F.

The presence of men from countries occupied by the Germans is easier to explain. The Poles had their own squadron, the Norwegians had a flight in a Halifax squadron and two French Halifax squadrons came to 4 Group later in 1944. These units all fought with fierce determination but all dwindled due to lack of reinforcements and had to be made up with other crews.

These, then, are the men who flew with Bomber Command in 1944. It is easy to describe them in statistics – so many Canadians, so many air gunners, so many N.C.O.s – but they were real men. A pilot describes his crew.

We were certainly a mixture in origin, size and personality. The flight engineer and the gunners were English; the nav and the bomb-aimer were Kiwis; the wireless op and myself Aussies. Earlier in the war the mid-upper shot down an enemy aircraft while serving with an ack-ack unit. He re-mustered to aircrew to avenge the death of his twin brother who was killed on ops. Our bomb-aimer was 'scrubbed' as a pilot, having wiped off two aircraft in training. Later he was failed and jailed as a trainee navigator for tossing his instruments out of an Aggie-Anson over Canada during a fit of frustration. He was seldom seen wearing a cap or buttoned-up tunic and gave the impression of being somewhat lonely without a swag and a dog. Nevertheless he was a terrific bloke with a perpetual grin and no sense of fear. The tail gunner had come top of his training course. The nav was barely 5 feet tall. He was very quiet, mainly because his mouth was invariably stuffed full of pencils. Our engineer, the only married member, had a most earnest desire to live. We were all surprised when he volunteered for a second tour but he survived. My Aussie wireless op and self were typical non-professionals. I in particular bucked the system; not only did I survive the war but also a Court of Inquiry charged me with flying a Lancaster below Blackpool Tower and down a street in Clevelys. On the ground we were not much to look at but in the air on ops I truly believe we reasonably met the ability and standards aimed at by the Empire Air Training Scheme. (Pilot Officer R. Curling, 622 Squadron)

It was after a man had volunteered for flying duties, carried out his initial training and been assessed as suitable for a heavy-bomber crew that he started what may be regarded as his 'contract' with Bomber Command. Approximately 4,500 such men arrived at the Operational Training Units each month and formed themselves into crews. The three-month course here on the Wellington or Whitley was followed by a shorter period converting to four-engined flying on the Halifax or Stirling at a Heavy Conversion Unit. For those crews destined for Lancaster squadrons there was then a further course at one of the newly formed Lancaster Finishing Schools. The crew was now available for posting to an operational squadron but not all had reached this stage. To those who had failed to satisfy the instructors had to be added those who were killed or injured in flying accidents. Over 8,000 aircrew died in these training units; one in seven of all Bomber Command's casualties occurred there.

On a squadron the newly arrived crews were known as Freshmen and had to undergo a final period of training during which the pilot had to go on one or two raids as a passenger with an experienced crew. The veterans hated taking these 'second dickeys' who cluttered up an already cramped cockpit and whose presence was often regarded as unlucky. Many a new pilot was lost serving this last apprenticeship and his crew, now known as a 'headless' crew, had to return to a training unit to pick up a new pilot – a depressing sequence of events. Those who survived this hazard were now ready for the major event of their contract with Bomber Command – the operational tour. The length of this for all types of R.A.F. operations was decided by the Air Ministry. These notes are accurate for the March 1944 period but bomber operations at other times do not vary greatly from them.

The normal heavy-bomber tour was the equivalent of thirty operational flights. All raids to Germany counted as one operation but bombing raids on Belgium and Holland and on France as far as the 6° east line of longitude, and laying mines in the sea off those countries, counted as one third of an operation only. Mining in German waters and inside certain heavily defended French harbours, however, still counted as a full operation. Leaflet raids did not count towards the tour but the records show that a leaflet crew was entitled to an 'operational egg' – the jealously preserved symbol of the operational aircrew. An aborted operation, known officially as an early return and unofficially as a 'boomerang', did not count unless bombs had been dropped on Germany. Crews in Mosquito bomber squadrons had to do fifty operations and those on Serrate and Intruder squadrons thirty-five.

The Pathfinder tour was forty-five operations but this

included any flown with another squadron before joining 8 Group. If they wished, Pathfinder crews could go straight on to do sixty, in which case, the extra fifteen counted as a second tour and they could not be called for further tours. These tours compare with a Fighter Command tour of 200 operational hours' flying, a Coastal Command one of 800 hours and one of twenty-five daylight operations for the American heavy-bomber crews.

If possible, new crews were introduced to operations gradually by being sent first on mining operations or to easy short-distance targets. However, during the fiercely pressed Battle of Berlin there were few such targets available and one new crew in 57 Squadron at East Kirkby started its operational tour in January 1944 with three Berlin raids in four nights.*

The crucial question for the men involved was simply 'Shall I live to see the end of my tour?' For the individual the answer to this was a matter of luck and could not be known until the end, one way or another. There are however plenty of statistics. During the war Bomber Command dispatched 364,514 bombing sorties by day and by night. From these operations 8,325 aircraft were missing, giving an overall loss-rate of 2·28 per cent. Based on these figures 50·06 per cent of crews would survive a first tour – almost the exact even chance.

Within these overall figures there were wide variations. The men who flew in the Battle of Berlin may feel that theirs was the worst period of the bombing war but this is not so. The most dangerous year for bomber casualties (not counting 1939 with its small number of sorties) was 1942 – the first year of Harris's command, the first year of Area Bombing; the year which saw the Thousand-Bomber Raids, the development of the bomber-stream and the introduction of the Pathfinders. In that year the average loss-rate was exactly 4 per cent and only three crews in ten could expect to survive their first tour.†

A tour could last for anything from four months to a year and during this time the aircrew lived a peculiar double life.

---

* Pilot Officer J. Castagnola and his crew shot down a Junkers 88 on the Nuremberg Raid. They survived the war.

† These and other comments on survival-rates are based on various tables in volume IV of the Official History and on calculations kindly made by the Actuarial Department of the Phoenix Assurance Company Ltd. For this last help I wish to thank M. H. Field, F.I.A., and Geoff Marriott, both of that company.

For perhaps forty hours each month they were flying on raids with all the danger that this entailed. For the remainder of the time their life-style, compared with other servicemen, was one of great comfort and privilege. Their involvement in the war was almost part-time and they pitied the soldiers and sailors who lived in discomfort or continual close contact with the enemy. Not for them, either, the long grinding hours of the airmen and airwomen of the ground staffs who served the aircrews so devotedly.

There were many 'perks' for aircrew – little discipline and much leisure time on non-flying days, flying pay. Every station had a contingent of W.A.A.F.s; the aircrew had easily the best chance both with these and the girls at the local dance-halls. Every station, however, had its 'chop girl', a W.A.A.F. who had been friendly with a succession of men who had subsequently gone missing or 'got the chop'. These poor girls could do nothing about their unwanted reputations and their position on an airfield could become quite miserable as they were eventually shunned by the aircrews.

All aircrew were entitled to one week's leave every six weeks and promotion during a tour, for those who survived, was rapid. One of my contributors rose from flight sergeant to squadron leader in the course of an eight-month tour, and another managed to come from Australia and make squadron leader at the age of twenty. Promotion to officer rank was a simple process. One day a man was a member of the Sergeants' Mess, the next he moved in with the officers without any formality, special training or graduation. Pilots who completed a tour without blemish were usually awarded the Distinguished Flying Cross – these being known somewhat cynically as 'survival gongs' – but an 'immediate' decoration awarded during a tour, especially the Distinguished Flying Medal to an N.C.O., was highly prized.

In spite of all the privileges and rewards, aircrew lived under conditions of great stress. A new crew, keen to get on-to operations, usually started with high morale despite being aware of the odds against their survival. There was a great feeling of 'It won't happen to me' and they were anxious to comply with the unofficial R.A.F. motto of 'Press on regardless'. Such crews were certainly the most conscientious of all. Their greatest period of danger was during the first five trips, when some 40 per cent of all losses occurred. Those who survived this initiation and having seen what they were up against became fatalistic and a little 'couldn't care less'. The early high morale would start to decline. Crews passing the twenty-operation mark began to think that they might, after all, have a chance of survival and they began to fly very carefully. It was probably among these crews that Bennett would find his 'fringe merchants'. The last few flights of a tour was a time of terrible tension when the loss-rate again rose.

A man's best defence against strain was undoubtedly to work hard for the solidarity and strength of his crew and it was the best of good fortune if he found himself in a good, well-balanced one. The squadron and even the flight meant almost nothing; one kept close company with one's own crew and perhaps with one or two others who had arrived at the same time. It was tragic to watch an incompatible crew gradually fall apart and almost surely go missing.

Inevitably some men cracked up and could not or would not continue flying. Genuine medical cases were dealt with in the normal way but for those who refused to carry on there was a harsh fate. They were publicly shamed by being declared L.M.F. – Lack of Moral Fibre. They were then reduced in rank and deliberately put to menial duties. There were remarkably few such cases on bomber squadrons. All aircrew were volunteers and the faint hearts had mostly gone during training. Many men must have thought of refusing to fly but did not do so partly due to loyalty to their crew, partly for fear of being branded L.M.F.

Many thought that the treatment of men who refused to fly was harsh and *Hansard* reveals, in April 1944, that certain Members of Parliament were trying to get the Air Ministry to soften the treatment. But the R.A.F.'s outlook was a simple one. The man had volunteered for aircrew duties knowing full well the implications. He had taken up a great amount of the war effort in being trained and he was expected to fulfil his part of the bargain. On the other hand, the airman had usually seen more danger in half an operational tour than the men who made the rules would see in a lifetime. Bitter comparisons were also made with civilian workers on strike.

And so the bomber crews had to continue through to the end. Serious ill-discipline by an individual or a crew was punished with a spell at the quaintly named Aircrew Refresher

School at Sheffield. Many took refuge in hectic romances, and particularly bad times were drowned in a heavy 'thrash' in the Mess or at the local.

The war found me racked by conflicting emotions – on the one hand an intense patriotism coupled with a desire to match my father's bravery and fortitude in the First World War and on the other a haunting fear of having my life squandered in some action on the lines of the disasters of 1914–18. In my young, immature mind I rationalized these thoughts by deciding that I would serve but that I would join an arm of the forces where individual courage skill and verve were at a premium (or so I thought). It now seems ironical that I should have finished up by flying with Bomber Command in the winter of 1943–4, the arm that had to take the war to the enemy, that had to display the 'Press on' spirit that had characterized the offensives of the first war and that suffered a higher proportion of casualties than any other branch of the forces.

That winter was a tough time to be operating and the losses were appalling. It didn't require an actuarial mind to see that the chances of surviving a tour were slender in the extreme. I find it difficult to recall just what it was that sustained us – fear of showing the white feather I suppose. By the time of the Nuremberg Raid the morale of our crew was undoubtedly getting rather worn and even our phlegmatic Australian pilot was showing signs of strain. (Flying Officer H. G. Darby, 514 Squadron)

Darby's crew was shot down seventy miles north of Nuremberg and only he and the navigator survived.

For the 50 per cent who were more fortunate than Flying Officer Darby's crew the safe return from the last operation of their tour was the sign for great celebrations, particularly in a squadron that had not seen a crew survive its tour for several months. As the training units were now turning out plenty of replacement crews, squadrons that had suffered particularly severe casualties were permitted to release crews before their full tour had been completed to ensure a 'feed-back' to the training units and also as a morale booster for more junior crews.

The tour-expired crew then split up and were posted as instructors to various training-units within Bomber Command for a minimum rest-period of six months. After this they could volunteer for or be called back for a second tour at any time. This second tour was twenty operations for heavy bombers, thirty for Mosquito bombers and twenty-five for

Serrate Mosquitoes. Many men who had once hoped for nothing more than to see the end of their first tour became quite anxious to embark on a second. They often hated training others; they missed the excitement of an operational station and the pride of being in the front line.

The feeling of security based on previous experience shown by many men starting a second tour was dangerous. The tactics of night bombing developed so rapidly that second-tour crews were often badly out of touch and those optimistic ones who arrived at a squadron thinking that they 'knew it all' or that 'God had got us through the first tour and was sure to see us through the second' often went missing immediately.

Those who survived this second tour, however, could not be forced to fly on bomber operations again. It was possible to volunteer for a third tour, 617 Squadron being the only non-Pathfinder squadron allowed to take third-tour crews in 1944, and some men managed to take part in more than a hundred operations having defied all the mathematical odds in the process. The Empire Governments tried to insist that their men should be returned home after sixty flights, so the highest performers were mostly English.

Most men, however, were prepared to call it a day after their second tour and were released from Bomber Command for duty elsewhere in the R.A.F. They had fulfilled their 'contract'.

How many had survived? Based on the overall 1939–45 casualty figures for both aircraft and aircrews, the table below is an estimate of what happened to any 100 aircrew who first joined up into heavy-bomber crews at an Operational Training Unit and for whom the war lasted long enough for them to serve the full cycle of service with Bomber Command.

Killed on operations	51
Killed in crashes in England	9
Seriously injured in crashes	3
Prisoners-of-war (some injured)	12
Shot down but evaded capture	1
Survived unharmed	24

4

The Germans

The night raids started by the R.A.F. in May 1940 found the Luftwaffe without a night-fighter force, for the Germans had not foreseen that they would be menaced in this way. Just two months later, at exactly 02.50 on 9 July, a Messerschmitt 110 twin-engined fighter converted for night work shot down a Whitley near Heligoland – the first of at least 5,000 British bombers that were to fall to the guns of German night fighters in the years to come.

The German response developed steadily as the British raids persisted. Specialist night-fighter units were formed and stationed at every approach to Germany. The night sky was divided into a series of boxes each of which had a patrolling night fighter, two ground radar sets and a small control room. Any bomber approaching Germany had to run the gauntlet of one or more of these boxes. The system served the Germans well for many months but it was rendered obsolete, firstly by the bomber-stream tactics of 1941 and finally by the use of Window in July 1943.

The Germans reacted incredibly swiftly to the Window setback and introduced two new defensive tactics, code-named *'Wilde Sau'* and *'Zahme Sau'* – Wild Boar and Tame Boar. When Bomber Command launched the Battle of Berlin that autumn, it was hoped that Window would still give a clear advantage but, instead, it met the two Boar tactics and it was these that were mainly responsible for the loss of 1,047 bombers in the next seven months. The story of Wild Boar and Tame Boar is also the story of Nuremberg.

The Germans were prepared to adopt desperate expedients to prevent their cities suffering as Hamburg had suffered when Window was first used. A comparatively junior bomber-pilot, Oberst Hans-Joachim (Hajo) Herrmann, presented an idea to the Luftwaffe. Window was causing trouble both to the ground radars that detected the bombers initially and to the radar sets fitted in the orthodox night fighters. The Germans had plenty of single-engined day fighters which normally would have been considered un-suitable for night work as they carried no radar set or radar operator. There was also a surplus of bomber pilots with experience of the instrument flying that was essential for night flying. It had been noticed that when a city was being raided, a high-flying German pilot could see bombers below silhouetted against the glare of burning buildings or of search-lights on cloud. Herrmann's idea was that single-engined fighters could use these conditions over a target to carry out visual attacks on the bombers.

The idea was accepted and the tactic was named Wild Boar, for once the pilot had taken off and been directed to the target city he was free of ground control and any success was the result of his own roving efforts. New single-engined fighter units, manned largely by the ex-bomber-pilots, were formed and stationed close to the big cities.

Wild Boar had one major disadvantage. When the short endurance of the small fighter was nearly exhausted it had to land quickly. There were frequently crashes as the Wild Boar fighters all tried to land on a limited number of local airfields after having been in action over the target city.

Post-war German opinion is that Wild Boar was a mis-take and the heavy loss of experienced pilots and of aircraft crippled the Luftwaffe. However, the expedient certainly achieved initial success and helped fill the gap in the German defences caused by Window.

Before we can move on to Tame Boar it is necessary to describe two adjuncts to it: the operations rooms of the fighter divisions and the running commentary. The defence of Germany against air attack was in the hands of five fighter divisions which between them covered all approaches from England against both day and night attack. Each division had an underground operations room. The fighter division was roughly the equivalent of an R.A.F. Fighter Command group and the operations rooms were similar in some ways to those from which the Battle of Britain had been fought.

By the end of 1943, however, the Germans had been refining their control techniques for three years in the face of continuous bombing attacks. Their operations rooms were far more sophisticated than had been Fighter Command's in 1940. Information from a multitude of sources was col-lected here and displayed on a huge screen. As the same information had also been sent to the other divisional operations rooms, what was happening in Holland, for example, would be known just as quickly at Metz, Berlin or Munich. I cannot do better than quote a description of one of those operations rooms by General Adolf Galland who was at that time Inspector General of Fighters.

The magic centre of attraction was a huge frosted-glass panel on which were projected, by light spots and illuminated writing, the position, altitude, strength and course of the enemy as well as our own formations. The whole was reminiscent of a huge lighted aquarium, with a multitude of water-beetles scuttling madly behind the glass walls. Each single dot and each change to be seen here was the result of reports and observations from radar sets, aircraft spotters, listening posts, reconnaissance and contact planes, or from units in action. They all merged together by telephone or by wireless in this centre, to be received, sorted and, within a few minutes, transposed into transmittable messages. What was represented here on a giant map was a picture of the air situation in the sector of a fighter division, *with about one minute's delay* [my italics] . . . Here was the fundamental instrument to lead the entire defence of the Reich. *

These 'Battle Opera Houses', as they were called by the Germans, had been the nerve-centres for the fighter divisions and, until the coming of Window, each division had fought its own battle from its own operations room with many controllers directing small groups of fighters or even individual aircraft. With Window, such close control had become impossible. The response of the Germans was to introduce the 'running commentary'.

Each division retained the responsibility to order its fighters to take off but, once in the air, only one man in the best-placed operations room now broadcast to all the fighters. The object of this was not so much to give detailed orders as to provide a continuous broadcast of the bomber-stream's progress and particularly of any changes in its course. Attempts were also made to forecast the probable target as early as possible. The night-fighter crews made use of this flow of information to find the bomber-stream but, then, they had to find their own targets in the stream using their radar or even visually if the visibility was clear enough. If the fighter lost the stream he switched on his running com-

* From *The First and the Last*, pages 192–3.

mentary again and attempted to get back among the bombers once more. This was Tame Boar fighting.

It was the running commentary that was the target of the jamming carried out by the German-speaking crew members in the A.B.C. Lancasters of 101 Squadron and of the other radio counter-measures. On one notable occasion late in 1943 the order 'All butterflies go home', broadcast from England on the German night-fighter frequency, caused many German pilots to land. The Germans reacted by switching frequencies constantly, increasing the power of their transmitters and the employment of many other devices. This radio contest continued for the remainder of the war but Galland, in his book, claims that although the British efforts caused great difficulties they never succeeded in stopping all methods of ground-to-air communication at any one time.

In the early days of Tame Boar the Germans had been satisfied to get their twin-engined fighters to the target at the same time as the bombers or to catch them on the return flight. As the tactic was refined, however, the fighters started to intercept the bombers en route to the target and the running battle which resulted could last for a considerable time.

Although fighters were responsible for the majority of bombers destroyed at this period of the war, the anti-aircraft and searchlight defences that had been so successful earlier were not a spent force and their disposition and efforts were complementary to the night-fighter defence.

Anti-aircraft guns (Flak) and searchlights worked together. Earlier in the war they had stretched in a great belt covering the approaches to Germany and had backed up the fighter-box system. The bomber-stream had rendered this form of defence obsolete and the Flak had been pulled back to Germany and was now to be found around the main centres of population. In some places the proximity of several cities caused the defended zones to overlap. In this way, the Ruhr in particular and to a lesser extent the Frankfurt–Mainz–Mannheim area became huge Flak and searchlight zones sixty miles across.

Light Flak, which produced masses of colourful tracer, did not much trouble the high-flying bombers at this time but the heavy-calibre Flak, especially when radar-predicted and engaging single aircraft, could be deadly accurate. In a heavy raid it soon lost the advantage of radar and became barrage Flak. When the Wild Boar fighters were in action Flak was restricted to a certain height leaving the fighters free to hunt above that height. With civil authorities anxious for maximum protection there was often conflict over this and many a German fighter was hit by its own Flak.

Not all the Flak was near the German cities. The entire Channel and North Sea coast was Flak-defended and there were even Flak ships off shore to extend the area of danger. Perhaps the most effective Flak were the special mobile batteries of heavy guns mounted on railway trucks which could appear unexpectedly at places not marked on the bomber crews' Flak maps.

A Bomber Command report early in 1944 shows that there were an estimated 20,625 anti-aircraft guns and 6,880 searchlights deployed in Germany and the West, and another report says that nearly 900,000 people were needed to man these.* Many of these were women, old men, part-time schoolboys and Russian prisoners. The German historian Hans Rumpf tells how one Flak commander jokingly addressed his unit in the following terms, 'Ladies and gentlemen, fellow workers, schoolboys and *tovarishtchi*.'

Rumpf also shows how it took an average of 3,343 88-millimetre shells to shoot down one heavy bomber. As each shell cost 80 Reichsmarks this puts the cost of each Flak victory at £27,000 or $107,000. This was still a bargain, for the bomber had cost £40,000. Rumpf questions the value of Flak but does say, 'The tremendous cannonades sent up by the Flak batteries, vigorously slinging whole munition dumps into the sky, did give the people down below the feeling that they had not been abandoned altogether and this was probably the main value of the operation.'†

The value of Flak should not, however, be judged only by the number of aircraft destroyed. It forced the bombers both to fly high at all times, with a consequent loss of bombing accuracy, and to avoid the major Flak areas unless they were actually attacking a target within that area. This led to considerable limitations in the routes available to the Bomber

* The Official History, vol. II, page 296nn.
† The two Rumpf quotations are from *The Bombing of Germany*, page 197.

Command planners and gave a corresponding advantage to the German fighter-controllers.

These then are the tactics and tools with which the German defended his cities in early 1944 – Wild Boar and Tame Boar fighters, Flak and searchlights. There remain two more items which should be explained – the radio-monitoring service and the fighter beacons – but these can be incorporated into a short description of a typical night's operations as seen from the German side.

The Germans started preparing for each raid long before the bombers actually took off. They already knew of Bomber Command's limitations – that distant targets could not be attacked in summer and major raids were not usually undertaken during the full-moon period. Next, they studied the weather conditions of that day and also the pattern of recent raids. All this gave them a certain amount of help in deciding whether and where the R.A.F. could attack that night.

The Germans had a highly efficient radio-monitoring service with dozens of listening-posts covering all possible frequencies. Every single transmission was noted. Being in code, the content was usually unintelligible but the origins and numbers of signals disclosed much. The equipment was so sensitive that it could detect both radio and H2S sets being switched on and tested in a bomber standing at dispersal on an English airfield. The volume of such traffic during the day told them whether aircraft were being prepared for a major raid that night. The results of this monitoring service were, of course, immediately passed on to the fighter operations rooms. Senior German officers alive today cannot stress too much the value of this information.

So, in the early evening, the night-fighter units were warned to expect another raid. As soon as the British wireless-operators and navigators switched on their wireless and H2S sets to warm up, the German monitoring service could tell that the take-off was imminent. The bombers' H2S impulses were tracked as they flew on the first stage of their flight so that the Germans already knew the approximate path of the raiders even before these had come within range of their coastal radar stations. And so it continued, with radar reports and then visual sightings all being fed into the five fighter-division operations rooms.

The division usually made its own vital decision as to when to order its aircraft into the air. They had to assess the future course of the stream, the probable penetration of the raid and the possibility of further attacks developing that night. They had to distinguish spoofs from the real raid. One by one the divisions ordered their fighters up; those divisions not directly threatened sent their fighters into the area of those through which the bomber-stream was passing. A night-fighter crew could have tea in France and breakfast in Denmark.

The fighters navigated by means of a series of beacons – *Funkfeuers* or radio beacons for the twin-engined fighters and *Leuchtfeuers* with a flashing-light signal for the Wild Boars. There was one of each in close proximity and sharing a single code name. The beacons were a useful navigational aid to the night-fighter crews but their main use was by the fighter controllers as assembly positions. The locations of these beacons were all known to Bomber Command and presented a major headache when planning routes over Germany, for no part of any approach from England was more than forty miles from a beacon.

Success for the Germans depended on two things – the timing of the orders to take off and the skill of the officer broadcasting the running commentary. A badly judged take-off or the incorrect assessment of a feint or spoof raid or the selection of the wrong beacon could lead to the fighters missing the bomber-stream. If all went well, however, almost the whole of the German night-fighter force could be brought into action.

The young men who flew the German night fighters were very much like the airmen of any other air force. A desire to fly and an admiration for Hitler after a childhood spent in the depressing conditions of post-First World War Germany led them into the Luftwaffe. Now they had easier consciences and purer motives than any others who served Hitler. They were fighting simply to prevent their cities and homes from being smashed and burned.

The original night-fighter crews had mostly come from the Messerschmitt 110 day fighters that had flown in the early campaigns of the war. These experienced men formed the nucleus of the night-fighter force and those who survived long enough became the unit commanders and high-scoring aces of this new Luftwaffe arm. As the force expanded these originals were joined by many others – newly trained men or men from other Luftwaffe units.

Basically I was not a night-fighter pilot at all. I had flown in Poland, France, the Balkans and Russia as a Panzer-reconnaissance pilot and had been chased around so much by fighters that after one Russian winter, I decided I would prefer to be a fighter-pilot myself and I was sent to the night fighters. It was a deadly business that night fighting and one really had to be a good pilot to survive. I was shot down three times. It was a tremendous contrast, one moment you were fighting in a combat like a fighter-pilot, the next you were flying quietly home like a bomber-pilot. I was an old man by the time the war finished. (Oberleutnant Helmut Schulte, II/NJG 5)*

During the early years of the war life for the night-fighter crews was not unpleasant compared with that of their comrades flying on other fronts. Their successes were well publicized in the German newspapers; there was regular leave with their homes not far away and decorations were plentiful. As in all German military units promotion was slow; many of the junior pilots were only Gefreiter (lance corporals) and the officer commanding a Gruppe of up to forty fighters might only be a Hauptmann (equivalent to a flight lieutenant). Promotions were usually announced once a year on 20 April – Hitler's birthday.

In one respect at least the German airman differed from his R.A.F. or U.S.A.A.F. counterpart: there was no such thing as an operational tour in the Luftwaffe nor was there any regular rotation of units in the front line. A night-fighter crew member would be posted to an operational unit and there he would usually remain until removed by death or serious injury.

There were at least two results of this system. Night-fighter units which were stationed in areas over which the bombers often flew, such as the approaches to the Ruhr, had plenty of opportunity both for action and for studying the tactics of their enemy. Such units and individual crews in

* II/NJG 5 means the Second Gruppe of the Fifth Night-Fighter Geschwader. This will be further clarified later. In these quotations the German's Christian name rather than initials will be quoted as this is normal German usage.

those units were thus able to build up impressive scores. Although propaganda usually exaggerated the total number of victories gained by the night-fighter units, the fact that nearly all the bombers destroyed fell on German-occupied soil meant that individual claims could be and were carefully checked, and a certificate was issued by the Luftwaffe for each confirmed victory.

The record for a night-fighter pilot was 121 credited victories, nearly all of them over British bombers, held by Major Heinz-Wolfgang Schnaufer. He was stationed at Saint-Trond in Belgium for a long period and scored many of his successes against bombers attacking Cologne and the Ruhr. There were many night-fighter pilots with confirmed scores of over fifty bombers and it was possible to have a log-book showing more than 300 operational flights if one survived long enough. The 'aces' were decorated with pro-gressively higher grades of the Knight's Cross, often by Hitler himself. These decorations were, and still are to those still living, a source of immense pride.

However, the second result of the system whereby crews did not get regular rest was not so good. The key man in a night-fighter crew was undoubtedly the pilot. To fly an aircraft by night took a great deal of skill and to become a proficient night-fighter pilot required the most careful train-ing. The practice of keeping crews in the front line all the time simply meant that there was little feed-back of opera-tional pilots as instructors to the training units. As the original band of experienced pilots gradually dwindled, they were replaced by less-well-trained men. These, in turn, suffered an even more rapid wastage and were replaced again by even greener pilots – and so the progressive deterioration continued.

By the time of the Nuremberg Raid the German night-fighter units were strong both in aircraft and crews, but it cannot be stressed too strongly that the pilots were composed of a small number of first-class men leading a mass of strug-gling beginners. These latter scored the occasional victory but frequently became casualties themselves. The unit com-manders could see what was happening but under the relent-less pressure of Bomber Command's operations there was little time for advanced training in the front-line units. In every air battle a large proportion of the German pilots took off and were simply so engrossed with the basic needs of night flying and survival that they were largely ineffective against the British bombers. At the same time the experienced men were scoring on nearly every raid.

German aircrew say that casualties in the night-fighter units were caused in four ways – by accidents due to technical failures, by crashes in bad weather or on strange airfields at the end of a long night operation, by Mosquitoes and by the air gunners of the British bombers. Opinion is unanimous that losses from accidents and crashes were far higher than those caused by R.A.F. action. The Mosquitoes were certainly a great nuisance and any German pilot shooting down a Mosquito was credited with a double victory. As for being shot down by British bombers, some surviving Germans say that they only attacked unwary victims. Once they had been spotted they broke off their attack and went hunting elsewhere. It is probable that those Germans shot down by the bombers or involved in long, inconclusive shooting matches were clumsy, inexperienced pilots trying to secure their first victory. It is significant that none of the well-known aces met their deaths in combats with bombers and a man from IV/NJG 1, the ace group at Saint-Trond, says they suffered no losses from bomber action over a seventeen-month period.

For a short time in 1943 the night-fighter units had been exposed to a particular hazard which caused them heavy losses. In an attempt to stop the U.S.A.A.F. daylight raids Messerschmitt 110 night fighters had been ordered into action but, untrained in daylight tactics and outclassed by American fighters, their losses had been heavy. Direct attacks on the bomber formations had then been stopped but night fighters were detailed to deal with straggling bombers and also to screen the approaches to Sweden and Switzerland where many American bombers tried to get down. Even so, the Messerschmitt 110s were easy victims for roving Mustangs when these long-range American fighters began operating. One commander took his own steps to stop his crews being lost in this manner.

We received a great number of silly orders. Once I was told to have four aircraft standing by to go for American bombers that were straggling. On the first day I lost all four planes and they sent me two replacements. Then I lost four more and got two more replacements. The 110 was no match for a Mustang. The next day I declared that all my aircraft were unserviceable and I heard nothing further about it. (Major Wilhelm Herget, I/NJG 4)

On the other hand the Germans threw away one great opportunity to cause heavy loss to Bomber Command. Late in 1940 and through most of 1941 they had a very efficient force of Intruders, equipped mostly with the Junkers 88, which achieved much success over Bomber Command airfields. Then, suddenly, in October 1941 the German Intruders stopped operating. Hitler had decreed that, to improve civilian morale, the night fighters were to fly only in direct defence of Germany where their victories could be seen by the civilians. This purely propaganda decision was a great mistake. German Intruders could have caused havoc when the much expanded Bomber Command was taking off and landing in the later war years.

In many ways it can be seen that the Germans had never anticipated a long war while Britain, even before the war had started, realized that a prolonged effort would be required before she could win. This position can be seen at its best in the development of aircraft. The Luftwaffe in 1939 was the most modern air force in the world but had few new aircraft being developed. Britain and the other Allies achieved parity in both numbers and design after about two years of war and thereafter steadily pulled ahead in both.

Night bombing had caught both sides without a purpose-built night fighter. The Luftwaffe reacted by converting for night use a heavy fighter, the Messerschmitt 110, and two medium bombers, the Junkers 88 and the Dornier 17. Of these, the Messerschmitt 110 had been preferred partly because it was, at that time, faster and more suited to night fighting than the other types but more, one thinks, because with the disappearance of day bomber attacks on Germany the Messerschmitt 110 was now redundant in its original role whereas the two bomber types were much in demand. The expanding force was therefore fitted mainly with the Messerschmitt.

This aircraft soon lost its superior position in the German night-fighter force however. The crew of two – pilot and radar/radio man – was increased when a rear gunner, whose real role was that of an extra look-out man, was added. The

Germans called this third crew-member '*das Holzauge*' – the 'wooden eye' – that is the eye in the back of one's head. Also four large covers to conceal the flaming engine exhausts were found to be necessary for night fighting and the number of radar aerials fixed to the nose steadily increased. All these extra burdens robbed the comparatively light 110 of vital speed. Then, when the Tame Boar tactic came with its longer flights, the fuel capacity often forced the crews to land too soon. In this way, the 110 declined.

At the same time the Dornier 17 and later the 217 were found wanting as they were too slow. The Junkers 88, however, was fast and powerful enough to carry the extra loads. It was never as manoeuvrable as the 110 but, eventually, it had an advantage over it of about eighty kilometres per hour in speed and two hours' flying endurance. The Luftwaffe recognized all this and started re-equipping the Messerschmitt 110 units with Junkers 88s, but the latter type was much in demand elsewhere and the conversion went slowly.

In March 1944 the first of the newly designed types of night fighter, the Heinkel 219 and the newer Messerschmitts, were just being introduced but it was a question of too little and too late. The comparable position with the R.A.F. night fighters was that while the Luftwaffe was relying on the prewar Messerschmitt 110 and Junkers 88, the R.A.F. had used and discarded the Blenheim, then designed and introduced the Beaufighter which had, in turn, been superseded by the Mosquito. The resulting situation whereby German night-fighter crews were chased around by Mosquitoes over their own country in 1944 was a direct consequence of Hitler's hope for a short, sharp war while Britain had prepared for the long slogging-match.

However, the balance of power in night fighting did not depend on aircraft alone but also on radar. The earlier radar set fitted to German fighters had been the Lichtenstein. This was an efficient set but had been badly jammed by Window and was also being homed upon by the Serrate sets in 100 Group's Mosquitoes. The German scientists quickly produced a new radar – the SN-2. This was an improvement as it was hardly affected by Window, and it could also pick up a bomber at four miles' range as against the Lichtenstein's two miles. In the early months of 1944 the Germans fitted the SN-2 to their night fighters. The British had yet to identify the new radar so the Mosquitoes' Serrate sets had not been adjusted to the frequency of its impulses. The pendulum had swung again and the German night fighter had a clear advantage.

The Germans had also introduced a weapon of which the R.A.F. seemed to know little or nothing. This is another integral part of the Nuremberg story so must be explained in detail. The orthodox night-fighter attack had been the stern chase on radar leading to a visual sighting and an attack from behind, as far below as the German pilot could manage so as to avoid the fire of the bomber's rear turret. The German name for this attack was '*von unten hinten*' – simply 'from under and behind'.

The new weapon had its origins in the accidental shooting-down of some of their own aircraft by the Germans. Their pilots were ordered to fly directly underneath their quarries and obtain a positive identification before dropping back and opening fire. The Germans found to their surprise that it was possible to fly in safety underneath a Lancaster or Halifax indefinitely, for no member of the bomber crew could see directly beneath it. The Germans experimented with two 20-millimetre cannons mounted in the roof of a Messer-schmitt 110 cockpit to fire almost vertically upwards and slightly forwards. The pilot flew underneath his target, obtained his identification, calmly aimed through a sight in the roof of his cockpit and opened fire. The result, according to one German, 'was almost 100 per cent booty'. The new weapon was given the code name of '*schräge Musik*' – the literal translation is 'slanting music' but the term really means 'jazz music'.

The *schräge Musik* was recognized as a great success but due to a weakness in the methods by which new weapons were developed by the Luftwaffe it was not installed in newly built aircraft for many months. In the interval, front-line units made the necessary modifications themselves but so few kits were available that only the best crews had their aircraft so modified. This, of course, widened the gap between the experienced men and the struggling beginners still further.

A *schräge Musik* attack started in the same way as the *von unten hinten*, that is with a radar approach from the rear. As soon as the bomber was sighted, and this nearly always hap-pened without the bomber's tail gunner seeing the fighter due

Night Fighter Attack Methods

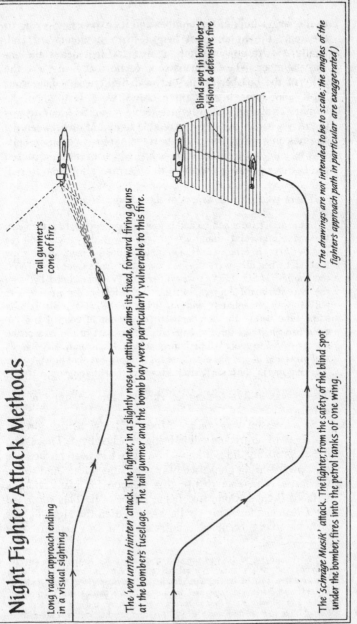

Long radar approach ending in a visual sighting

Tail gunner's cone of fire

The 'von unten hinten' attack. The fighter, in a slightly nose up attitude, aims its fixed, forward firing guns at the bomber's fuselage. The tail gunner and the bomb bay were particularly vulnerable to this fire.

Blind spot in bomber's vision & defensive fire

The 'schräge Musik' attack. The fighter, from the safety of the blind spot under the bomber, fires into the petrol tanks of one wing.

(The drawings are not intended to be to scale: the angles of the fighter's approach path in particular are exaggerated)

Diagram 1

to the larger bulk of the bomber and its exhausts glowing to the rear, the fighter lost height, then flew forward and, finally, slowly upwards until it was 100 feet below the unwary bomber. The Germans soon found that firing into the belly of the bomber on its outward flight was a dangerous habit and some night-fighter crews were lost when the bomber exploded violently just above them. So accurate was the new weapon that they were able to aim at or between the engines on a wing. One short burst of explosive cannon shells was usually sufficient to start a fire which eventually caused the bomber to crash but gave the German pilot time to pull safely away.

There was another aspect of the *schräge Musik*:

In the attack from behind and below using the forward armament, the most important thing was to cut down the defence of the bomber first. In other words one aimed at the fuselage, at the crew first, and when they were finished the petrol tanks came next. With the *schräge Musik* attack it was different. We just aimed between the two starboard engines, setting the petrol tanks on fire, and pulled away immediately without firing at the crew at all. It took some time before the bomber went down out of control and the crew had plenty of time to bale out. It was part of the idea of the *schräge Musik* to avoid killing human beings. Many an R.A.F. flyer is still alive and in one piece because his aircraft was shot down by the 'slanting music'. (Major Rudolf Schoenert, Nachtjagdgruppe 10)*

There was still a feeling of chivalry among some of the aviators.

So successful was *schräge Musik* that few British aircraft managed to return and tell of being attacked by it. Those who did so probably did not know how they had been hit because the upward-firing guns used only very faint tracer. And so the Germans were able to use this weapon for many months without Bomber Command being aware of it. This surprised the Germans, for many civilians worked on the night-fighter airfields in the occupied countries and it was assumed that

* Nachtjagdgruppe 10 was the unit responsible for testing new aircraft, weapons and radars under operational conditions. Its home base was at Werneuchen, east of Berlin, but its aircraft often operated from Hangelar airfield near Bonn and took part in the night air battles. Rudi Schoenert, credited in all with sixty-four victories, was the commander of this test unit. I would like to thank him and also Willi Herget for their critical examinations of this chapter.

details of the installation would be passed by the Resistance to England.

It can be seen now how tragic it was that 3 Group was removing the ventral turrets from its Mark II Lancasters, for the *schräge Musik* was only made possible by the existence of the blind spot under the bomber. It cannot be said for certain but it seems that 6 Group must have had at least an inkling of the new weapon and this is why they were fitting their mid-under gun positions as fast as they could. Some English squadrons also knew of it but 4 Group papers, as late as May 1944, contained constant complaints that gunners were keeping a poor look-out and were being surprised by 'unseen fire'. It is interesting that, for some time, both the Germans' *schräge Musik* and the Canadians' mid-under guns were essentially local 'lash ups'.

It might be that in *schräge Musik* lies the origin of a legend – that of the Scarecrow. In the winter of 1943–4 bomber crews began to report that they had seen a new type of Flak shell. It exploded at operational height and was supposed to simulate a fully laden bomber exploding. A huge flash was followed by flaming debris falling to earth just as though an aircraft had blown up but there had been no preliminary combat. Even experienced crews reported the occurrence claiming that it was undoubtedly a German shell and that they had seen so many real aircraft crash that they could definitely distinguish the fake from the real thing. It was assumed that the Germans fired such shells – christened Scarecrows by Bomber Command but Scare*crews* by the flying men – to shake the morale of the bomber crews.

However, a minority did not accept this explanation and refused to believe in Scarecrows. Did they really exist? In the course of my research I was often asked this question and I attempted to find the answer. In the first place it is unlikely that the Germans would have put so much effort into sending up this sophisticated firework-display when a conventional shell would have achieved more direct results. Then, in spite of my asking several night-fighter pilots, one fighter division commander, two historians – one English and one German – who are both experts in this field and, finally, the German Flak units' old comrades' association, I could not find anyone who could confirm that the Scarecrow had existed. This is not conclusive evidence but I believe that the explosions were the sudden end of bombers that had been hit by a lethal burst of *schräge Musik* cannon shells that did not contain tracer.

Bomber Command obviously accepted the Scarecrow story and a report dated April 1944 warned crews of 'the well-known use by the enemy of Scarecrow flares and other pyrotechnic displays'.* The Scarecrows were also freely reported in the British press. It is ironic that the Scarecrow was officially accepted but the real danger of *schräge Musik* remained unknown for so long. Such are the fortunes of war.

In early 1944 the night-fighter force comprised about 15 per cent of the Luftwaffe's aircraft strength but, because the Russians never built a strategic bomber force, the night fighters could be deployed to face Bomber Command at all times except for a small force detailed to cope with the Middle East Air Force night raids.

The chain of night-fighter command went Korps–Division–Geschwader–Gruppe–Staffel, but only two of these, Division and Gruppe, are important here. The fighter division defended a given area of German-occupied territory and had both day and night fighters. The Gruppe was the standard operational unit, normally based on one airfield and operating a single aircraft type. With around forty aircraft it was bigger than an R.A.F. squadron, but the literal translation of 'group' is not suitable either so the original German 'Gruppe' will be allowed to remain untranslated. There were five full-strength fighter divisions in the West, each containing an average of four twin-engined Gruppen for Tame Boar work and two single-engined Wild Boar Gruppen.†

When Bomber Command set out for Nuremberg the Luftwaffe had 361 serviceable twin-engined night fighters complete with crews and about 150 Wild Boar aircraft. The main strength lay in the old Messerschmitt 110 fighter, burdened now with too much weight and of insufficient endurance, but with the almost priceless advantage of its un-jammed SN-2 radar. An unknown proportion of these, possibly between a quarter and one third, also had the unsuspected and deadly *schräge Musik*.

---

* Public Record Office AIR 14/365.

† The full Air Order of Battle of the night-fighter units is given in Appendix 3.

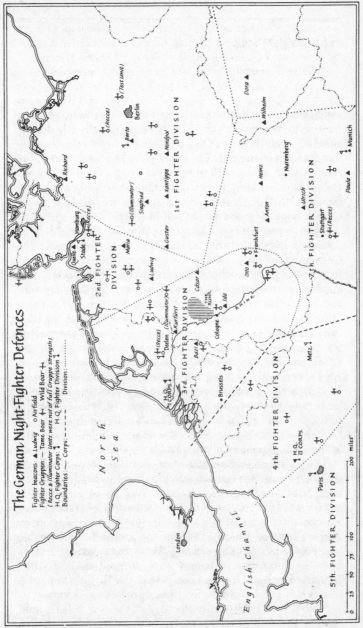

The German Night-Fighter Defences

Fighter Beacons: ▲ Ludwig ○ Airfield
Fighter Gruppen: — Tame Boar + Wild Boar +
(Recce & Illuminator units were not of full Gruppe strength)
H.Q. Fighter Corps: ⌥ H.Q. Fighter Division: ⌥
Boundaries — Corps: ······ Division: ┄┄┄┄

North Sea

English Channel

London

Paris

Brussels

Cologne

Metz

Stuttgart

Frankfurt

Nuremberg

Munich

Hamburg

Berlin

RUHR

RHINE

2nd FIGHTER DIVISION

3rd FIGHTER DIVISION

4th FIGHTER DIVISION

5th FIGHTER DIVISION

1st FIGHTER DIVISION

7th FIGHTER DIVISION

H.Q. I CORPS

H.Q. II CORPS

Richard

Quelle

Stade

Maria

Ludwig

Siegfried (Illuminator)

Gustav

Xantippe

Nordpol

Berta

Dora

Wilhelm

Heinz

Anton

Paula

Ulrich

Otto

Ida

Cäsar

Kurfürst

Basta

Dodon (Illuminator)

Test (Init.)

25   50   75   100   200 miles

Map 2

5

30 March 1944

By March 1944 the people of Britain were emerging from their fifth winter of war. The whole population had long since adjusted their lives in a dogged manner to see the conflict through to the end. The crisis years had now passed; the country was packed with troops from every Allied nation and the invasion of German-occupied Europe was obviously not far away. Although there would still be set-backs, it was a time of hope. The end was at last in sight.

Good news was coming from Russia where Marshal Zhukov's latest offensive was making steady progress. The German garrison at Odessa was about to surrender and Russian troops would soon enter Czechoslovakia. The Americans, too, were doing well in their Pacific campaign and had recently invaded the Marshall Islands. But, on two other battle-fronts, Allied troops were in difficulties. In Italy the Battle of Cassino was going badly. In spite of the monastery there having been bombed to ruins, the latest ground attack had been repulsed and the troops who had landed at Anzio were still hemmed into an uncomfortable beach-head. In Burma the Japanese were making surprising advances in what was to prove their last desperate offensive and the bitter siege of Imphal had just begun. On top of this came the further bad news that Major-General Orde Wingate, the leader of the famous Chindits, had been killed in an air crash.

The people of London and south-west England were again suffering from German air attack. After the Battle of Hamburg Hitler had ordered a bomber force to be prepared for retaliation. It is a measure of how the balance of power in the air had swung in Britain's favour that it had taken from August 1943 to January 1944 for the Luftwaffe to assemble just 200 bombers. The ensuing 'Baby Blitz' lasted for four months. 2,000 tons of bombs were dropped causing 2,673 civilian casualties. In the same period the R.A.F. dropped a tonnage of bombs twenty-five times greater on Germany.

Newspapers published on the day of the Nuremberg Raid contain the following fragments of domestic news. Three quarters of a million tons of coal had been lost in recent strikes and in the Tyneside shipyards apprentices were reported to be in 'an aggressive mood'. The defendants in a case at the Central Criminal Court were found guilty under the Witchcraft Act following seances at a psychic centre. A target of £165 million for National Savings in the 'Salute the Soldier Week' was only £20 million short with one day to go. In a by-election at North Camberwell the Labour candidate had held the seat for his party but with a record low poll. The Government had promised to encourage the development of jet propulsion and to raise pensions. The Irish Republican Army was reported to be helping the Germans.

The most frequently requested songs in the Forces Favourites were, 'If I Had My Way' sung by Bing Crosby and 'Kiss Me' by Vera Lynn; Anne Shelton singing 'You'll Never Know'; 'Pistol-Packin' Mama' and 'Always in My Heart' followed close behind. Longer-established favourites were reported to be Deanna Durbin singing 'Ave Maria' and the 'Warsaw Concerto' from the film *Dangerous Moonlight*. This beautiful piano piece had been written by Richard Addinsell. Few airmen at the bomber station at Coningsby knew that this man was serving there as a navigator with 619 Squadron under his real name of F. L. Chipperfield. He was to fly on the Nuremberg Raid and return safely.

A few minutes before nine o'clock on the morning of Thursday 30 March, Sir Arthur Harris walked down the steps into his underground operations room. Some twenty officers had already preceded him. The Commander-in-Chief's morning conference was about to begin.

Within forty minutes Harris was back in his own office above ground. The conference had ended with a decision that the city of Nuremberg was to be attacked that night. So that I could answer the question, 'Why Nuremberg?' I determined to establish what had happened at this conference and what had led to this decision. I set out to trace as many people as I could who had been present.

Sir Arthur Harris failed to answer my letter. For this I do not blame him; he is an old man who spends much of his time abroad and he must have been plagued with numerous similar requests since the war. However, I was fortunate enough to meet or correspond with seven officers who took part in the proceedings.* The difficulty turned out to be more one of stimulating memories after so many years rather than of tracing retired officers for there was a similar conference every morning of the war and that concerning Nuremberg was not, at the time, exceptional. No record was kept of the conference but, with the help of these officers and many documents, I am satisfied that what follows is an accurate record both of how this decision was taken and the subsequent planning of the operation.

To understand the reasoning behind the decisions taken that morning, it is necessary to look again at the Battle of Berlin in which Harris had engaged his bombers with such high hopes five months before. Nuremberg was destined to be the last raid of the battle. In fact 1 April 1944, the day after the Nuremberg Raid, was the date by which Harris had anticipated 'a state of devastation in which surrender is inevitable'. Alas, in spite of his own determination and leadership and the courage of the bomber crews, this was one battle which had gone to the Germans.

Since the main offensive had been opened at the end of November 1943, Harris had dispatched thirty-four major raids on Germany, sixteen of which had been against Berlin. Initial progress appeared to have been good – the missing rate was less than 4 per cent and there were encouraging estimates of damage in Berlin. Unfortunately these could not be checked as the frequent presence of cloud made both bombing photographs and photographic reconnaissance poor sources of information. When optimistic reports appeared in the British Press, Goebbels who was both *Gauleiter* of Berlin and Minister of Propaganda made no attempt to correct them, thinking that the sooner the R.A.F. thought it had destroyed Berlin the sooner the raids would cease. In fact, the raids had not caused decisive damage.

The battle continued all through the winter months. The

---

* The seven were, Air Marshal Sir Robert Saundby (Deputy Commander-in-Chief), Air Vice-Marshal H. S. P. Walmsley (Senior Air Staff Officer), Air Commodore H. A. Constantine (Deputy S.A.S.O.), Group Captain – but usually called Mr – M. T. Spence (Senior Meteorological Officer), Group Captain W. I. C. Inness and Wing Commander G. A. Carey-Foster (Operations Officers) and Wing Commander F. A. B. Fawssett (Intelligence Officer, Targetting). Some of these officers later achieved higher rank.

repeated attacks on one target helped the defending Germans. To avoid the fighters the routes grew less direct, with smaller bomb-tonnages but more fatigue for the bomber crews, and a higher proportion of the raids had to be directed onto other cities in Germany. Despite all this, the missing rate climbed and 953 bombers were lost between 18 November 1943 and the eve of the Nuremberg Raid. On 19 February a grisly record was established when the bomber-stream reached its target, Leipzig, twenty minutes early due to an unexpectedly strong following wind and seventy-eight bombers were lost, most of them in the enforced wait in the target area for Zero Hour. It was the heaviest loss of the war to date.

The Air Ministry, which had earlier backed Harris's desire to force a decision with his offensive against Berlin, had begun to lose confidence in Area Bombing. They felt now that more success might be achieved by attacking the smaller targets that contained the selected industries – ball-bearings and aircraft – originally contained in the Pointblank Directive which was still officially in force. Early in 1944 Harris was urged to attack Schweinfurt which had become almost the point of principle in this dispute. Harris was reluctant to divert effort from Area Bombing but, after many letters had passed between Air Ministry and Bomber Command, he was formally instructed to attack Schweinfurt. On the night of 25 February, one attack on that town was carried out.

The month of March, ending as it did with the Nuremberg operation, deserves to be looked at closely. Early in the month Bomber Command received a new directive, or rather a further variation to the target priorities of the old Pointblank Directive of June 1943. Six towns, all associated with either the ball-bearing or aircraft industries, were given as Bomber Command's primary objectives:

1   Schweinfurt
2   Leipzig
3   Brunswick
4   Regensburg
5   Gotha
6   Augsburg

The six targets had all been in the previous list but Gotha and Augsburg had now changed places in the order of priority. The document also ordered that 'the foregoing priorities supersede all previous instructions on this subject'. *

Having received such specific orders, one might expect these six towns to figure prominently in the list of major attacks made during March but this was not so. The actual targets during that month had been: Stuttgart (twice), Frankfurt (twice), Berlin and Essen.

The Berlin raid, on the night of 24–25 March, had been costly with seventy-three aircraft lost. It was thought that three quarters of this loss had been caused by adverse winds taking the bombers over the Ruhr Flak defences. If the high loss was adjusted to allow for this factor, then losses for the month so far had averaged an acceptable twenty-one aircraft per raid or 2·7 per cent of those dispatched. On the other hand the results achieved by these raids conformed to an old familiar pattern. Even in non-cloud conditions the bombing results on Stuttgart, Frankfurt and Berlin had been poor – in the second Stuttgart raid, bombing photographs indicated that not one aircraft released its load within the city's limits! The difficulties of accurate target-marking beyond the range of Oboe had not yet been solved. By contrast, the Essen attack, Oboe-marked, had been a huge success. Records from Essen show that forty-eight factories and an impressive list of other establishments were hit although the city had been completely covered by cloud. The sudden switch to a Ruhr target had also caught the Luftwaffe unprepared with the resulting loss of only nine bombers.

Here was the reason for the apparent refusal by Harris to comply with his directives. If his bombers could not hit Stuttgart, Frankfurt and Berlin consistently, then effort expended on Schweinfurt and the other five priority towns, all much smaller targets and beyond the range of Oboe, would be wasted. Harris refused to lose men and aircraft in this way. A few days after the Nuremberg Raid this old problem was to be solved in a dramatic manner but it would be premature to describe it here.

There had been a Commander-in-Chief's conference each morning for as long as anyone present could remember. After a formal 'Good morning gentlemen', Sir Arthur Harris took his seat at a small desk and immediately lit a cigarette – usually one of his favourite American brand, Camels. The

* Public Record Office AIR 14/780.

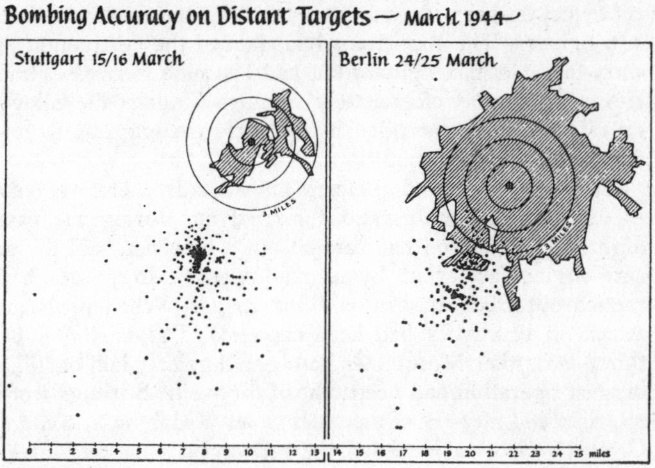

Bombing Accuracy on Distant Targets — March 1944

Diagram 2

These diagrams show the results of attacks on targets beyond the range of Oboe using the Pathfinder marking techniques available at that time. They are extreme examples but neither target was completely cloud-covered. The diagrams are based upon the 'Final Plots of Night Photographs' prepared by Bomber Command's Operational Research Section, now in the Public Record Office, AIR 24/269.

officer representing the American Eighth Army Air Force, whose headquarters were nearby and whose bombers were stationed alongside Bomber Command in East Anglia, was the only other person to be seated and was also the only other smoker. He lit up a large cigar. The officers of the Bomber Command Air Staff stood in a respectful and attentive group behind their chief. The meeting proceeded briskly.

Firstly, the Commander-in-Chief read a report which showed briefly the results of the operations carried out during the previous night. There had been no major raid during the three nights since the Essen attack of 26–27 March. On the first night after this there had only been a few Oboe Mosquito sorties to the Ruhr and on the second night fog had grounded the whole of Bomber Command. The previous day's conference had resulted in the decision to mount a major raid on Brunswick, one of the targets named in the directive issued at the beginning of the month. The Bomber Command attack was to follow up a daylight raid on Brunswick planned by the Americans for that day. This had subsequently been carried out by 236 Fortresses escorted by 438 fighters. The Americans had claimed the destruction of sixty-four German fighters but had lost nine Fortresses and eleven fighters. Unfortunately Bomber Command's follow-up raid had been cancelled in the early evening due to unfavourable weather conditions.

The paper presented to Harris gave details, therefore, only of various smaller operations carried out during the past night. 617 Squadron had carried out a precision raid on an aero-engine factory at Lyons and twenty Mosquitoes had carried out Oboe attacks on Ruhr targets. When the main attack on Brunswick had been cancelled, a raid on Kiel by thirty-two other Mosquitoes had been hurriedly laid on. The biggest operation had been that of forty-nine Stirlings from 3 Group and fifty-six of the older types of Halifax in 4 and 6 Groups which had attacked the railway junction at Vaires, near Paris, with eight Oboe Mosquitoes providing their usual accurate marking. This was one of the experimental raids in preparation for the full-scale attack on French railway targets before the invasion. In all, 184 aircraft had been dispatched during the night, all targets had been hit and only one Halifax from a Canadian squadron was missing from the Vaires raid. *

It was now the turn of Mr Magnus Spence, Harris's principal weather forecaster. Spence had already been in touch with the Central Meteorological Office at Dunstable and prepared a preliminary weather chart. For a successful attack the following conditions were all required: suitable weather for take-off, no heavy convective cloud on the route which might produce icing conditions, good visibility over the target for marking if beyond the range of Oboe and, above all, no fog and a reasonably high cloud base for landing. To forecast a combination of all these for a period of time twelve to twenty hours ahead without the benefit of detailed

* Unknown to Bomber Command, thirteen German troop trains carrying part of the 10th S.S. Panzer Division – the Frundsberg Division – from Lisieux to Russia, had been at Vaires and Resistance men among the French railway workers, who knew of the coming attack, had placed a train loaded with sea mines among these. The bombing had been accurate and the mines had exploded with satisfactory results. Six days later the Germans had collected the identity discs of 1,200 dead S.S. men. Fourteen French railway workers had unfortunately been killed. These details are from a French Resistance report which reached Mr C. E. R. Sherrington of the Ministry of Economic Warfare, who devised the railway bombing plan prior to the invasion of Normandy.

weather observations from the very areas of German-occupied Europe over which the bombers would fly was the difficult problem that Spence was faced with every morning. A further complication on this occasion was the fact that, in the coming night, the moon would be exactly one quarter through its full cycle. There would be a half-moon which would be at its maximum elevation an hour before sunset and would not set until the early hours of the next morning, 31 March. Any bomber operation planned before that time would be subject to the influence of this half-moon.

There were two main features of the weather situation that were important and a comparison of the Meteorological Office weather charts of that day with German charts shows that the information available to Mr Spence was reasonably accurate. A low-pressure area over Norway was causing cumulus cloud to flow into the North Sea and any aircraft flying north of a line from the Humber to northern Holland would face the risk of icing. Secondly, a complex cold front extended eastwards from beyond Ireland through northern France, southern Germany and the Balkans before swinging north to its source in a deep depression centred in Russia. This front was not very active and its slow movement south had been watched for the past three days.

Operationally, the cold front had three implications – its leading, or southerly, edge would probably contain low cloud that would cover a potential target; its trailing, or northerly, edge would possibly contain high layered cloud and there would be steady winds in the upper air paralleling the alignment of the front. Elsewhere over Germany there were only shallow troughs of low pressure with little cloud and extensive clearances.

After Mr Spence came the representative of the Eighth Army Air Force. It had been planned that twelve combat wings of their heavy bombers would make a major raid on aircraft factories in Berlin that day, but this had been cancelled. The American officer could, however, offer that three groups of Thunderbolt fighter bombers were to carry out a sweep over German airfields in Holland and just across the border into Germany that afternoon.

Sir Arthur Harris now considered his options. It was immediately obvious that a raid on any target in northern Germany could not be considered on account of the cloud coming down the North Sea and the large clear areas inland that would expose the bombers to fighter attack in the moonlight. Under most conditions it would have been too late in the moon period for operations at all, but the possibility of high cloud behind the cold front, which might provide some concealment for the bombers, drew his attention to the south.

We can only guess at what went through Harris's mind as he sat and assessed the possibilities. He probably thought with some regret that, except for Essen, the bombing results of his command for that month had been poor. Most of his squadrons were well rested after three nights without a major raid and soon it would be too late in the spring to go deep into Germany. The Americans, now equipped with the long-range Mustang fighter, had resumed their deep daylight raids with much loss to the Luftwaffe day fighters; these operations may have also involved and affected the night-fighter force. Harris's own recent losses had not been heavy if allowances were made for the Leipzig and Berlin missing totals incurred in what were believed to be exceptional circumstances. In the last week alone, his squadrons had flown 1,270 sorties for a loss of only ten aircraft. On top of this, the American sweep that afternoon was bound to help. Had the German night-fighter force shot its bolt for the time being?

Harris decided that he would mount a major attack that night.

In deciding on what target that attack would be made, Harris had to consider, first, the six priority targets of the latest directive, despite the fact that he disagreed with the policy behind the directive. Brunswick, Leipzig and Gotha were all too far north and could soon be dismissed. Augsburg was too far south and might be covered by the frontal cloud. But Schweinfurt, with its ball-bearing works, and Regensburg, with a Messerschmitt factory, were in the general area that Harris was considering. He had attacked three of the directive targets in February – Schweinfurt, Leipzig and Augsburg – and had at least twice in March ordered raids on Brunswick but had been forced to cancel them due to unsuitable weather conditions. There seems no reason why Schweinfurt or Regensburg should not have been chosen as that night's target. Harris, however, probably felt that he had complied sufficiently with the priority directive recently. He was also aware of the shortening nights and the increasing demands being made on his force for pre-invasion bombing. He turned from the priority list. These were not the targets he was seeking.

The next list he consulted was that of the Area Targets – those major industrial cities that had not yet been seriously damaged. Immediately one name became obvious – Nuremberg, a large city lying, ironically, half-way between Schweinfurt and Regensburg. Wing Commander Fawssett, the officer in charge of 'targets', quickly produced his file on Nuremberg. It showed that the city contained several important industrial concerns believed to be making tanks, armoured cars, diesel engines, electrical goods and much more. Apart from a few Mosquito attacks it had not been seriously bombed for seven months. None of the previous major attacks had caused decisive damage there.

Here was a large, virtually intact, industrial target in just the right place. It did not take long for Harris to make his decision – the target for that night would be Nuremberg.

Harris proceeded to outline a tentative tactical plan. The bombers would take off late, follow as far as possible the estimated line of any high cloud there might be at the rear of the cold front and attempt a swift passage into southern Germany using the tail wind. In this way the time spent over enemy territory while the moon was up would be kept to a minimum. Nuremberg could be bombed by the light of the last of the moon and the return journey could be made in the dark when the moon had set.

Not everyone was happy. Some thought that it was too late in the moon period for an attack on a target so deep in Germany. The Deputy Commander-in-Chief, Sir Robert Saundby, was definitely one who expressed doubt and Mr Spence was probably unhappy about the reliance on the high cloud which might prove non-existent if the front moved unexpectedly or the cloud itself broke up.

But the decision was made. It was, to a certain extent, a gamble on the weather and on the reactions of the German night-fighter controllers but so was every raid that Bomber Command attempted to carry out. If the weather conditions changed for the worse during the next twelve hours, then the raid, as were so many, could be cancelled. The conference ended.

What sort of city was Nuremberg, the intended victim of this decision?

Before the war Nuremberg had been a fine example of the beautiful old cities of southern Germany. In the centre was the medieval Altstadt, with its turreted walls, gateways and a moat. Here were churches and museums and many fine old gabled buildings. The Nurembergers boasted that their Altstadt was the most beautiful town-centre in Germany, but perhaps the city's greatest claim to fame was that it had been the birthplace of Albrecht Dürer, the famous painter and the master of etching, and his house was preserved in the Altstadt.

The city, by 1939 joined with the neighbouring town of Fürth, lay on the River Pegnitz in northern Bavaria. Unlike most of Bavaria, Nuremberg was predominantly Protestant rather than Catholic. Peace-time heavy industries include machinery, motorcars and chemicals, but the world knew Nuremberg mostly for its toys, its carved wood and ivory and for pencils. There was a large hop market and five breweries. In size it was roughly comparable with Bristol.

When the National Socialist Party came to power Hitler turned his eyes on Nuremberg. He called it 'the most German of German cities' although it was probably no more than average in its support for the Nazis. Hitler planned to build a vast complex of buildings on the south-east edge of the city for the annual Party rallies which produced such impressive and dramatic spectacles in the 1930s. A young Nazi architect, Albert Speer, was appointed for this task. His design included three huge arenas for up to 400,000 people, a sports stadium, the Kongress Halle, the Märzfeld where army units could carry out manoeuvres before the public and finally a wide, paved avenue, the Grosse Strasse, one-and-a-half kilometres long and 100 metres wide along which vast phalanxes of troops and tanks could parade. These massive structures were designed to last for the 1,000 years that Hitler claimed would be the minimum lifetime of the Third German Empire. Thousands of Germany's large numbers of unemployed were set to work and vast sums of money were allocated, but when the war started much of the work had not been completed. The Kongress Halle, the Grosse Strasse and one of the arenas still remain – useless monuments to Nazism, too expensive even to demolish.

Nuremberg's population in 1944 was estimated by the R.A.F. at 426,000 of whom 200,000 were potential workers. The key to an extremely accurate War Office map of 1944 shows that Nuremberg, with Fürth, contained fifty factories, forty-six other commercial plants, twenty-eight military and sixteen Nazi Party establishments including a huge S.S. barracks near the Kongress Halle. It was also a major administrative, commercial and communications centre. The main industries were the M.A.N. (Maschinen Augsburg-Nürnberg) heavy engineering works, the two Siemens-Schuckertwerke electrical factories and a small aircraft repair factory on the eastern outskirts of Fürth. These, with the many smaller factories, were making a valuable contribution to the German war effort. In addition, a Bomber Command document of 1943 refers to Nuremberg not only as an important industrial target but 'also a political target of the first importance and one of the Holy Cities of the Nazi creed'. The same report also says that 'morale was always particularly shaky in Nuremberg'.*

This was Nuremberg, typical in every way of an Area Bombing target – important industries, uncertain morale and the added attraction of its association with the hated Nazi Party. If the bombers did their work well in the coming night, it would be one less name on the list of such cities still requiring Bomber Command's attention.

When the conference ended, the Commander-in-Chief and some of the other participants left the operations room and returned to their offices and other work. There remained about ten officers who were responsible for the planning of the night's operations. This team was headed by Sir Robert Saundby who sat at the central desk recently vacated by his chief while his subordinates worked around the underground room in little groups, with Saundby co-ordinating their activities. In preparing this plan these men were pitting their skill directly against that of their German counterparts who would that night have to assess the moves of the bombers and the night fighters accordingly. The decisions made in the next hour would be of vital importance second only to the decision just made by Harris.

* From the 'Immediate Assessment of Results of the Bomber Command raid of 10–11 August 1943', loaned privately.

Those responsible for planning the route had the most important task of all. The decisions they reached were always a matter, literally, of life or death for the aircrew. For this reason, the thinking behind the selection of the Nuremberg route must be examined fully.

There were, broadly speaking, two philosophies about routeing – the 'straight in, straight out' principle and that of the indirect approach. There were several advantages in the use of relatively direct routes: the small number of turning-points led to easier navigation; the shorter flying times allowed a higher ratio of bombs to fuel in the aircraft loads and meant less fatigue for the crews and finally less time spent over enemy territory. But there was one great disadvantage to this method of routeing; the longer the bomber-stream flew a steady course over enemy territory, the more chance the Germans had to plot that course and intercept the stream. The alternative was the multi-leg indirect route, the constant course-changes of which often foxed the Germans, but which took away the advantages of the more direct route. There were many vigorous advocates of both philosophies and most of Bomber Command's routes at this time failed to suit one party or the other.

The task facing Saundby and his assistants was a formidable one. Nuremberg lay just three times further into German-held territory than did a Ruhr target. It was as far from the average bomber base as was Berlin yet, because of the shape of the European coastline, no great part of the flight could be made over the sea as it often could with a Berlin raid. The moon would not set at Nuremberg until 01.48 next morning and there was no guarantee that the helpful frontal cloud would be in the right place at the right time or that it would be present at all. * The navigation and operations officers started pinning up their thin coloured ribbons on the large wall map, constantly advised by Squadron Leader Varcoe, the expert on the German defences. It is not known how long it took to produce the route shown on page 89 but the reasoning behind that route is known.

---

* Astronomical details were kindly provided by H.M. Nautical Almanac Office at Herstmonceaux Castle, Sussex. Times will usually be given on the 24-hour clock system as used by the R.A.F. at that time. Fortunately the British time coincided with that used by the Germans at the time of the raid so no adjustments need be made.

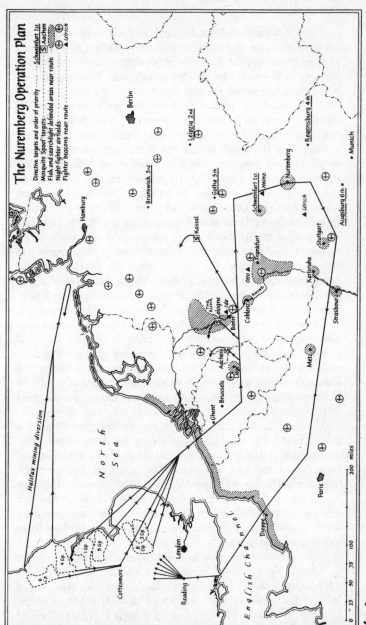

The Nuremberg Operation Plan

Directive targets and order of priority ----- Schweinfurt 1st
Mosquito Spoof targets
Flak and searchlight defended areas near route.
Night-fighter airfields ⊕
Fighter beacons near route ....

⊞ Aachen
⊞ Ulrich
▲ Ulrich

Map 3

The main factors affecting the eventual choice of the outward route were the need to avoid the Ruhr and Frankfurt
Flak defences and the desire to conceal from the Germans the
identity of the target for as long as possible. The late take-off
would help the bombers miss the worst of the moon and the
first leg, from the assembly of the bomber-stream over the
North Sea as far as the turning-point over Belgium, was
uncomplicated. The next leg, 265 miles long, across the
German frontier south of Aachen, skirting the Ruhr defences
south of Bonn and then deep into Germany before turning
south for Nuremberg, was an interesting one. It was an
unusually long leg passing very close to the Ruhr defences,
to the Ida and Otto fighter beacons and to many night-
fighter airfields. It came to be known as the 'Long Leg' and
this is what we shall call it but, although it appears long on
a map it was only sixty-two minutes' flying time because of
the strong tail wind. To the Germans the first part of the
Long Leg was a potential approach to the Ruhr or to any of
the important targets in the Frankfurt, Mannheim or Karls-
ruhe areas. The later stages of the leg could lead anywhere.

At the end of the Long Leg the route made a sharp turn
almost due south only seventy-nine miles or nineteen minutes'
flying time from Nuremberg. This leg passed close to
another fighter beacon – Heinz. The towns of Bamberg and
Erlangen would show clearly on the H2S screens of the Pathfinders and provide them with essential 'fixes' on the final
run into the target.

The whole outward flight in the potentially dangerous
moon period was, thanks to the strong westerly winds, only
100 minutes' flying time from the Belgian coast to Nuremberg. The Long Leg was something of a gamble but it was
hoped that the bombers' passage would be so swift that they
would be well into Germany before the Germans realized
what was happening. If caught on this part of the route, then
there might be some high cloud to protect the bombers from
the German fighters.

The return route was not expected to pose any great
problems. There would be no moon and the long southerly
withdrawal was clear of major Flak areas and also of the
bulk of the night-fighter airfields. The final flight over the
English Channel would avoid the heavy cumulus cloud
coming down the North Sea and also permit the American

bombers in East Anglia to assemble their formations if they wished to make an early start for one of their daylight raids next day. The only disadvantage to the return trip was expected to be the flying time. The head winds would result in a long, boring, five-hour slog for the returning crews.

This route can be said to be a good example of the 'straight in, straight out' route. For a target as far distant as Nuremberg to be raided in these conditions, it was as good a route as any, provided that the risk of fighter interception on the Long Leg in moonlight was appreciated. 6 Group aircraft from north Yorkshire would have the longest flight with 1,580 miles and an eight-hour flying time while those of 3 Group had the shortest with 1,300 miles and one hour less in the air.

The proposed route, however, immediately met opposition. The details of it were passed first to the headquarters of 8 Group for the comments of the Pathfinders. Air Vice-Marshal Bennett had the route plotted on his map but did not like what he saw. The Pathfinders usually favoured the indirect approach with many 'jinks' which confused the Germans and Bennett did not like the look of the Long Leg. He called Saundby on the telephone, stated his objections and asked that the route be changed, suggesting four shorter legs on the outward flight instead of the three proposed. Such counter-proposals were not unusual but Saundby said that on this occasion he wished to consult the other group commanders first. This did not please Bennett who felt that the Pathfinders, as Bomber Command's navigation experts, should have the final say.

Saundby then raised all the other group commanders on the shared telephone-line and stated the two options – the more direct route proposed by his own staff or the indirect one of Bennett. The resulting alignment of personalities and opinions is interesting. Rice of 1 Group, Harrison of 3 Group and Cochrane of 5 Group, with their fast, reliable Lancasters, immediately chose the direct route. They were not prepared to sacrifice bombs for fuel; they did not want too many turning-points with risk of collision and strain on navigation. Carr of 4 Group supported Bennett for two reasons. His more vulnerable Halifaxes wanted every assistance they could get over enemy territory and, knowing Bennett from the days that he had served under Carr in

4 Group, he deferred to Bennett's opinion in such matters. McEwen of the Canadian 6 Group was initially undecided. Like Carr he wanted the best possible chance for his Halifaxes but his aircraft already had the longest distance to travel and he did not wish to make it greater. In the end, he fell in with those who wanted the shorter route. Bennett tried to sway the opposition, but in the end Carr was his only supporter. Saundby did agree to refer the matter to the Commander-in-Chief for a final decision. Harris was informed of the position and, after some thought, decided that the original route should stand. It was a rebuff for Bennett; the acknowledged expert on navigation had been overruled but it was more a tactical matter than one of navigation.*

This disagreement about the route had delayed the finalizing of the plan, but its resolution enabled Saundby and his officers to dispose rapidly of the remaining matters.

The Aiming Point in Nuremberg had already been chosen. As the raid was to be a standard area attack, this was selected so that the bombs would fall in the very centre of the city, that is in the Altstadt and the surrounding residential areas, rather than in the southern suburbs where the main factories, main railway yards and the Nazi Party buildings were situated. As the bombers were to approach from the north and bombing usually crept back from the markers and the markers themselves tended to move slightly with the wind, the Aiming Point was automatically selected south of and upwind from the city centre. After the necessary calculations had been made a railway goods depot near the passenger station was chosen and a note made that the Aiming Point was 1,300 yards on a bearing of 210 degrees from the centre of the Altstadt. Although the goods depot was only 800 yards from the Siemens factory and 2,000 yards from the M.A.N. factory, these buildings were not to be targets.

Zero Hour for the main attack was timed to be 01.10 the

* There is no official record of the above incident and it is one where I have reconstructed the events from the memories of several people. I have to state here that, although none of the contributors differ on the disagreement and the eventual manner of the decision, Bennett disagreed with the sequence of events. He feels that Pathfinder Headquarters produced an indirect route first, that this was objected to by the Main Force commanders and then the simpler eventual route was substituted. Although the planning of routes between High Wycombe and Pathfinder Headquarters was an almost simultaneous process which probably accounts for Bennett's version, I am satisfied that what I have written is an accurate account of the incident.

Nuremberg and the Aiming Point

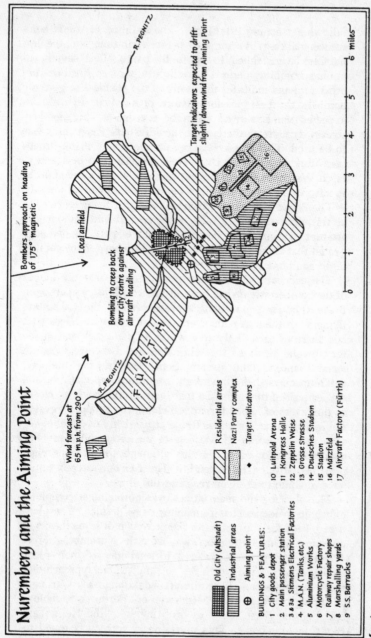

Wind forecast at 65 m.p.h. from 290°

R. PEGNITZ

FÜRTH

Bombing to creep back over city centre against aircraft heading

Bombers approach on heading of 175° magnetic

Local airfield

R. PEGNITZ

Target indicators expected to drift slightly downwind from Aiming Point

0   1   2   3   4   5   6 miles

Old City (Altstadt)

Industrial areas

⊕ Aiming point

Residential areas

Nazi Party complex

♦ Target indicators

BUILDINGS & FEATURES:
1 City goods depot
2 Main passenger station
3 & 3a Siemens Electrical Factories
4 M.A.N. (Tanks, etc.)
5 Aluminium Works
6 Motorcycle Factory
7 Railway repair shops
8 Marshalling yards
9 S.S. Barracks

10 Luitpold Arena
11 Kongress Halle
12 Zeppelin Weise
13 Grosse Strasse
14 Deutsches Stadion
15 Stadion
16 Märzfeld
17 Aircraft Factory (Fürth)

Map 4

following morning, 31 March. The Pathfinders would commence marking five minutes before that time and the last bombers were timed to bomb by 01.22. This seventeen-minute bombing period was slightly shorter than on any other raid and indicates the desire of the planners to give the bombers the best possible chance of survival. In case unexpected winds slowed down or speeded up the bomber-stream en route to the target, the adjustable Zero Hour was to be used. This was a very recent refinement of the Broadcast Winds system which allowed a decision to be taken at High Wycombe during the outward flight and a coded order to advance or retard the Zero Hour to be sent to all aircraft.

The Master Bomber technique was still being developed at this time and many raids were carried out without any attempt to control the bombing at the target. No one suggested that there should be a Master Bomber for the coming night and none was appointed.

The concentrated bombing period meant that the length of the bomber-stream had been shortened slightly. Apart from the Pathfinder primary-marker aircraft and the Lancasters flying with them as supporters, the groups were allocated a fair share of each of the five waves of the attack and of the four height bands so that Halifaxes and Lancasters had an equal chance in the stream. Some time during the day, 1 Group queried the moonlight conditions especially on the earlier part of the flight. So that their aircraft could be closer to the layers of hoped-for frontal cloud, the group suggested flying at least as far as the Rhine at heights 4,000 feet lower than the 20,000 to 23,000 feet of the command plan. The group was allowed to do this although the other groups remained at the greater heights. The 1 Group aircraft would have to climb to these on reaching the Rhine.

The plan for the main attack was now almost complete, only minor details of it remaining to be decided. The planners turned their attention to the provision of some means of directing German attention away from the Nuremberg force. 4 and 6 Groups were ordered to send fifty of their older Halifaxes across the North Sea to simulate the approach of a much larger force. These aircraft would approach Germany as though threatening Hamburg or Berlin but, before crossing the coast, were to drop mines in the Heligoland Bight and fly home. This diversionary force was timed to approach the German coast at exactly the same time as the main attack was approaching the Belgian coast 260 miles to the south-east. It was hoped that the approach of two widely separated but apparently major attacks would induce the Germans to split their fighter force.

8 Group planned to mount three spoof raids, using Mosquitoes, on Aachen, Cologne and Kassel. Each of these three forces would carry large numbers of target indicators to simulate the opening of a full-scale attack on the three towns. The Aachen and Cologne spoofs were aimed to keep the German fighters in the Ruhr area while the bomber-stream flew deeper into Germany, and that on Kassel was designed to represent a major course change by the Main Force again threatening Berlin.

Maximum support was also being arranged by the Mosquito fighter squadrons. 100 Group were to send every available Serrate aircraft with the bomber-stream and the Intruders would operate as normal in the low-level role over German airfields.

Fighter help was also forthcoming from an unusual source. The U.S.A.A.F. had recently sent four long-range fighters – two Lightnings and two Mustangs – to operate with 100 Group in an experimental Intruder role and these were now stationed at the Mosquito airfield at Little Snoring. They had recently flown to Berlin with Bomber Command and were to fly that night to Nuremberg. It is unlikely that any of the R.A.F. bomber crews knew that American fighters were flying with them in this manner.

It is a measure of how much effort was being devoted to assisting the bombers that 162 aircraft would be operating in diversionary or bomber support roles, not one of which would drop a bomb on Nuremberg.

In addition to all these operations connected with the Nuremberg raid, various other activities were being organized, some by Bomber Command but some by others whose aircraft also had business over the Continent that night: Oboe Mosquitoes utilizing the Oboe beams that would not reach to Nuremberg; mining operations in Dutch and French coastal waters; leaflet raids over France and, making use of the moonlight, the dropping of supplies and agents to Resistance groups in the occupied countries. In all, 1,009 aircraft – 570 Lancasters, 274 Halifaxes, 117 Mosquitoes,

20 Stirlings, 10 Albemarles, 8 Wellingtons, 6 Fortresses, 2 Lightnings and 2 Mustangs – would be flying over German-held territory. 6,493 airmen would be called upon to risk their lives yet again so that the end of the war could be brought just a little closer.

By about 11.30 Saundby's team had completed their work. The final plan had been seen and approved by Harris and was ready, as the Command Operational Order, for transmission by teleprinter to the groups. Nuremberg was not mentioned by name, only by its code-word 'Grayling'. Saundby, the keen fisherman, had code-named all German targets with the names of fish. The intention, according to the orders, was 'to cause maximum damage at the Aiming Point' and the bomb loads were code-named 'Arson'.*

For the men who were to fly to Nuremberg the day had started like any other. Due to the Brunswick raid having been cancelled the previous evening the men in most squadrons had had their third consecutive full night's sleep and, as the moon was almost half full, they did not expect any major raids for some time. Many of the senior crews were preparing for leave; newer arrivals being left to cope with any mining operations or short raids that might be ordered.

On two squadrons the day started with funerals. At Waterbeach, a 514 Squadron Lancaster had been badly hit on the Frankfurt raid a week earlier. The navigator and bomb-aimer had baled out and the pilot came home with a wireless operator, a flight engineer and two dead gunners. A small party went from the squadron to the funeral of one of these.

An Australian pilot was having breakfast at the Canadian station at Leeming when the adjutant told him that two of his fellow countrymen and a New Zealander had been killed when a Wellington had crashed nearby on a training flight.

As I was the only available Australian on the squadron I was to attend as a pall-bearer for one of the bodies. I objected strongly to this, pointing out that in the event of being briefed for a raid I would not be able to air-test our aircraft although I did not really expect there would be any operations because of the moon. I went to Harrogate and helped to bury the R.A.A.F. and N.Z. aircrew; a cold and bleak morning. I remember noting the names of three Australians I was at O.T.U. with on the headstones of the services'

* Public Record Office AIR 14/3115.

section of the cemetery a long way back from the graves we had just filled. (Pilot Officer K. H. Bowly, 429 Squadron)

This was Bowly's last day at Leeming. He was shot down that night.

The squadrons had known since before 10.00 that there would be operations that night. The decision to mount a major raid had been immediately passed to groups and from there through bases and stations to the squadrons. Very few people knew the name of the target yet but this was not important. It was enough at this stage to know the number of aircraft required, the approximate length of the flight and the type of bomb-loads required. Group commanders had spoken on shared lines to their subordinates urging them to prepare every possible aircraft for the traditional 'maximum effort'.

The aircrew had been hanging about their flight or section offices waiting for the telephone to ring with one of two messages, 'We have a target' or 'It is a stand-down.' There was surprise and some dismay when the former came through. It was not long before they found out that the operation would be a long one and the dismay deepened – every instinct told them that such a trip was 'not on' in the existing moon conditions. From that moment, there was that peculiar atmosphere of suspense before every raid that would not lift until the last bomber had returned in twenty hours' time.

Early in the morning W.A.A.F. petrol bowser drivers circulated their usual, accurate 'Poop from Group'. Tonight's raid was to be a maximum effort and fuel loads clearly indicated a Berlin-length trip. Our enthusiasm was something less than ecstatic. This was to be our fifth op and the previous four – to Frankfurt twice, Berlin and Essen, all within eight days – had left us, to say the least, edgy. Number five was to be no different. (Sergeant W. J. Blackburn, 12 Squadron)

Inquiries revealed a light bomb-load and a heavy petrol-load – ergo a bloody long trip. Those characters with more wind than courage went sick if they could get away with it – and they quite often did. Frankly, the general feeling was one of quiet dread following Lord Trenchard's remarks. He had visited our airfield and, in all solemnity, warned us that our expectation of life was to be greatly reduced due to the fact that an all-out effort was to be made against the Reich. (Flight Sergeant M. C. Coughlan, 103 Squadron)

This man's squadron had just emerged from a depressing seven-month spell during which no crew had survived to the end of a tour.

Although the ground crews had much to do, there was not the frantic rush associated with the preparation of many raids. The late cancellation of the previous night's raid had left most aircraft fully ready for operations and in most cases only a thorough check was now necessary. Those aircraft which had just become available from major repair or servicing and new aircraft recently delivered were the only ones requiring intensive work by the ground crews. There were few night-flying tests.

The intensive operations in the middle of March and the heavy loss of the Berlin raid six nights earlier had reduced the Lancaster and Halifax III force available from a peak of 860 to just over 700, but the lull of the past few days had allowed a recovery so that the daily availability had gradually risen. Early that morning the groups had 'offered' 785 aircraft, an improvement of twenty-five on the previous day. It was a matter of intense pride that every unit should fulfil or exceed its pledged effort. 5 Group was easily the strongest and would 'put up' 201 Lancasters that night. Waddington would provide the greatest contribution by one station, the two Australian squadrons there providing thirty-five Lancasters, while the biggest individual squadron effort would be that of 101 Squadron at Ludford Magna which would send twenty-six of its A.B.C. Lancasters on the raid. The only fully operational Bomber Command squadron not involved in some way or other was 617 – the Dambusters. They had been out the previous night and had no part to play in the events of the coming one.

The late cancellation of the Brunswick raid had resulted in most of the bomb loads being left untouched in the aircraft overnight, only the fuses being removed. As the Nuremberg route was some 400 miles longer than the one planned for Brunswick, it was a case of unloading bombs and adding fuel. The four-engined bombers used a gallon of high-octane petrol for every mile flown and each aircraft would require between 1,750 and 2,040 gallons depending on the distance of their airfields from the target. The average Lancaster would burn seven-and-a-half tons of fuel to deliver a four-and-a-half ton bomb load to Nuremberg.

The routine area-attack bomb load was to be carried and over 2,600 tons would be needed on this night, more than half of which were incendiaries. The Lancasters mostly carried mixed high-explosive and incendiary loads, much of the high-explosive being in the form of 4,000-pound Blockbusters one of which formed the basis of most Lancaster loads. The biggest bombs on this raid were the seven 8,000-pounders being loaded in the specially modified bomb bays of the Lancaster IIs of 115 and 514 Squadrons. The Halifaxes carried all-incendiary loads which, being loaded in containers, were bulky rather than heavy so that their full load weighed only about one third of a Lancaster load. This all-incendiary Halifax load had been used for some time and was a concession to that aircraft's poorer performance.

The heaviest bomb-loads were probably carried by the Lancasters of 1 Group whose policy was to carry at all times the greatest bomb-tonnage. One mid-upper gunner at Elsham Wolds found that the ammunition trays for his two machine-guns were being left more than half empty. Mid-upper turrets were not often used and someone had decided that bombs were a better payload than machine-gun ammunition.

The Pathfinders were loading the usual combination of pyrotechnics for a Newhaven marking and the seventy-five marker aircraft would carry 120 clusters of illuminating flares and 336 target indicator bombs. 116 skymarkers were added to these loads in case Nuremberg turned out to be covered with cloud and the Wanganui method was needed. These markers still left room in each Pathfinder bomb bay for a useful 8,000-pound load of ordinary bombs.

While the aircraft were being prepared, squadron and flight commanders were selecting the crews to take part in the raid. In some cases this was a difficult task as there was a shortage of experienced crews and some of these had already gone on leave. Although there were plenty of new crews and there was an average of three crews for every two aircraft, Nuremberg was not the ideal target for the introduction of new men to operations. Men about to go on leave were stopped at the last minute and others who had gone on local leave were hurriedly recalled; but many untested crews had to be detailed for this raid.

Nine squadron commanders put themselves down for the

raid. These had to fly at least once a month and hard-bitten aircrew often judged their commanders according to whether they chose the difficult raids for this quota. Forty-one pilots, newly arrived on squadrons, were detailed to go with experienced crews as 'second dickeys'. Half of these were in 6 Group which appears to have ordered a maximum effort for such men on this night. Spare aircrew members were used to fill temporary gaps caused by sickness and often men whose own crews were not due to fly had also to be detailed.

We were on spare crew that night and the flight engineer and myself had to fly with two other pilots. I recollect being a bit bloody-minded about flying as a 'spare bod' as this put me seven trips ahead of my Skipper and I had visions of doing a tour plus seven. I noted in my diary that the Skipper and his female companion at that time went to the Gliderdrome in Boston, the lucky so-and-so. (Sergeant R. I. Hudson, 57 Squadron)

Two men turned up at stations asking to fly as passengers. At Coningsby a wing commander, who was due to take over a squadron of his own soon, was given a place as second pilot in a Lancaster and a flight sergeant, who was a pilot instructing at an Operational Training Unit and had never been on operations, was given a seat in the front turret of a Lancaster at Kirmington. The future squadron commander returned, a very chastened man, but the flight sergeant was to die in his front turret.

As the success of each raid depended on the weather over the routes and the target, every effort was made by the Bomber Command meteorological staff to keep check on weather developments. The forecast given at the morning conference was only of a preliminary nature, the main forecasts being made later in the day. It was in the light of these that proposed raids were frequently cancelled.

The only way of getting reliable information from enemy territory was to send reconnaissance aircraft out over that territory. For this purpose Bomber Command had the Meteorological Flight based on the Pathfinder airfield at Wyton, near Huntingdon. One Mosquito had flown out over the North Sea during the morning inspecting the route that the diversionary mining force would take that night. The crew found broken cumulus cloud, mostly below 9,000 feet, decreasing as they flew east. Much cumulo-nimbus could be seen well to the north. These conditions would permit the mining operation to proceed providing the aircraft involved took off early and returned before the cumulo-nimbus came too far south down the North Sea as this cloud could cause severe icing.

This information was available at High Wycombe soon after the Mosquito landed back at Wyton at 12.35. Mr Spence now had a detailed conference by telephone with the Meteorological Office at Dunstable and with his colleagues at the group headquarters. As a result of this he was able to present the following forecast to the Air Staff at High Wycombe at 13.00:

Bases fit for take-off with only a possibility of a few scattered showers. Over North Sea, broken convection cloud mainly below 12,000 feet but there may be some isolated tops to 15,000 feet or above. Over Continent convection cloud is expected to break up considerably. *

It is significant that the forecast now contains no reference to high cloud over Germany.

Mr Spence had already asked for a second Mosquito flight, this time to have a look at the vital outward route of the Nuremberg force.

At about noon, Flying Officer T. Oakes and his Canadian navigator, Flight Lieutenant R. G. Dale, who were at the top of the duty roster at Wyton were called to Flying Control. The navigator jotted down details of the route to be taken and of the specific weather features to be investigated and, at 12.20, their Mosquito was airborne and heading for the Dutch coast. The routes for these flights had to be discreetly planned so as not to disclose proposed targets to the Germans who could of course plot the whole flight by radar. The Mosquito crossed into Germany near Osnabrück and then flew a wide circular route around the Ruhr and out again to the south over Belgium.

The crew found the weather much the same for the whole flight. Flying between 25,000 and 30,000 feet their Mosquito left a long vapour trail in the clear air. Well below them, at no more than 10,000 feet, they could see between 6/10ths and 8/10ths of what they correctly assessed as

* This and the later forecast are from Public Record Office AIR 24/269.

cumulus-humilis – fair weather cumulus that would probably disappear in the cooler air of night. As they turned for home at the limit of their flight they looked carefully in the direction of Nuremberg 100 miles away to the south-east. They could just see large banks of what they took to be strato-cumulus and some thinner cloud higher up. Other than this, there was no high cloud.

At 15.25 the Mosquito landed at Wyton having flown 950 miles in just over three hours. The navigator ran straight to the telephone at Flying Control and described what he had found on the shared line to Bomber Command and all the group headquarters.

The results of Flight Lieutenant Dale's report were of the utmost importance. Not only did it confirm that the outward flight in the moonlight had little chance of cloud cover but, if the cloud seen over Nuremberg persisted, it would rob the Pathfinders of the ability to mark visually by moonlight. The main attraction of this otherwise unattractive operation appeared to have been lost.

Mr Spence prepared a further forecast:

Nuremberg. Large amount of strato-cumulus with tops to about 8,000 feet and risk of some thin patchy cloud at about 15–16,000 feet.

At 16.40 this was handed to Sir Robert Saundby. It is not known whether he held a discussion with the group commanders but he certainly showed the forecast to his chief. 'I can say that, in view of the met. report and other conditions, everyone, including myself, expected the C.-in-C. to cancel the raid. We were most surprised when he did not. I thought perhaps there was some top-secret political reason for the raid – something too top-secret for even me to know but now I do not think that this was so.'

This letter was written to me on 14 September 1971 in rather unhappy circumstances. Sir Robert died eleven days later.

The two weather reconnaissance Mosquitoes were not the only aircraft to be flying over enemy territory during the day. The sweep by exactly 100 American Thunderbolt fighter bombers over Holland and into Germany went ahead as planned. Five aerodromes, several railway engines and other targets were attacked. Two German aircraft were claimed as destroyed and two damaged. One Thunderbolt was lost to Flak near Venlo but the pilot was seen to escape by parachute.

There was only little R.A.F. activity. A small offensive sweep by Spitfires and Typhoons was carried out over northern France but no success was claimed and one Spitfire was lost near Rouen. Three photographic-reconnaissance Spitfires from Benson flew on routine tasks over northern Germany and various aircraft were active in the North Sea and the Channel, mostly hunting for enemy shipping, although one, a 100 Group Wellington, was flying up and down off the coast between Dieppe and Le Havre trying to plot the frequencies of German coastal radar stations in that area. Further north there was a sharp action off the Norwegian coast when eighteen Coastal Command Beaufighters attacked a large German merchant ship with torpedoes. Two hits on the ship were claimed and a Messerschmitt 110 of its air cover was shot down, but two Beaufighters were lost.

In all, however, it was a day of only light Allied air activity that would not seriously test the Luftwaffe.

Back on the bomber airfields events were running their normal course. The ground staffs were busy carrying out the final tasks to ensure that every possible aircraft was on 'top line'. It was a bright but cold afternoon with occasional snow showers. The Canadian squadrons in north Yorkshire were warned of freezing rain before take-off and their aircraft were sprayed with anti-freeze every hour. There was little for the aircrew to do at this time. Many tried to sleep or to take their mind off the coming raid with billiards, cards or chess, but the thought of what was to come was never far away and those difficult hours were hard to fill. At Leeming, a bored Canadian air gunner passed the time by shooting at a row of milk bottles with a service revolver.

There were sundry moves during the afternoon. Air Vice-Marshal McEwen travelled south from 6 Group; he was due to make a visit to both Bomber Command and the headquarters of the R.C.A.F. in England. Group Captain Carey-Foster, one of the operations officers who had taken part in the planning of the Nuremberg operation at High Wycombe that morning, flew himself in a light aircraft from Halton to a 4 Group airfield. There had been complaints that the squadrons saw little of those who planned their operations so this officer would show the flag at Breighton that night. Others to arrive in 4 Group, this time at Snaith, were newspaper correspondents and a photographer who were to cover the activities of a typical bomber station preparing for a raid.

Among the increasing numbers of people whose business it was to know the target and route there were many who were not happy with what they saw. Bennett's morning objection seemed to be echoed by others in 8 Group because approximately half of the station and squadron commanders rang Pathfinder Headquarters querying the route. An officer at Upwood was surprised that, although a raid had been announced, people were still allowed to leave the station and outside telephone calls had not been cut off. He, and many others, expected to hear at any time that the operation had been cancelled.

One of the more experienced of the Serrate pilots found that the proposed route passed very close to a German visual beacon that he had often observed and knew to be an assembly point for night fighters.

We immediately informed 100 Group H.Q. that such a track would be disastrous for the bombers and couldn't it be changed? They contacted Bomber Command H.Q. but a change of track would not be contemplated. We then asked 100 Group H.Q. if one of us could fly straight to this beacon some time before the bombers reached it. This was also turned down. Because of this, our station commander specially exhorted all of us on this particular night not to abort for radar failure, which was permissible, but to press on, as even one solitary Mosquito might distract a Hun night fighter from the bombers. (Flight Lieutenant R. G. Woodman, 169 Squadron)

In fact, a document dated 23 February 1944 shows that the exact location of twenty-one beacons and even their German code-names were well known to Bomber Command but it was difficult to plan a route that avoided all the beacons as well as the Flak-defended areas.

Late in the afternoon the waiting period ended for at least some of the airmen when the navigators and, on many squadrons, the pilots and bomb-aimers reported for pre-briefing. This was primarily to enable the navigators to prepare their charts and flight plans, a two-hour task at least. Then, after the operational meal invariably composed of bacon and eggs, the aircrews assembled in a large room for the ritual of the main briefing.

This commenced with the adjutant calling the crews to attention for the entry of the squadron and station commanders. Immediately, one of these senior officers, who had been designated as Briefing Officer for the raid, walked onto the platform, picked up a billiard cue, had the curtains covering the map drawn back and opened the briefing in the time-honoured manner, 'Gentlemen, your target for tonight is Nuremberg!'

The intelligence details and meteorological information had all come down through the usual channels from Bomber Command but the way this information was presented to the crews depended on each briefing officer. One wing commander remembers, 'In my squadron briefing I passed down all pertinent information to my crews but clearly slanted it in a way which would have the best possible effect on morale. No doubt after a few briefings the crews developed a competence to interpret my information.' What follows is a synthesis from the briefings carried out on many stations.

The main stress was laid on Nuremberg's importance as an industrial and transportation centre. The tank and electrical factories were mentioned and one squadron was told that railway yards were believed to hold materials destined for the Russian Front. It was pointed out that the Aiming Point was in one of the railway yards and that if the bombing crept back over the Altstadt the medieval buildings there would burn well. This theme and the high incendiary content of the bomb loads was repeated many times. To new crews, it 'seemed a little cold-blooded but logical' but the old hands were quite used to this form of bombing. Canadian crews at Leeming were told that Nuremberg's pre-war toy industry had been turned over to war production and 'every home was now a potential factory'. Much too was made of the city's association with the Nazi Party and the expectation that its destruction would be a major blow to German morale. Many were told that the Nazis always had a big rally at Nuremberg every March but this is not true and it is only a coincidence that it was raided in March of 1943, 1944 and 1945.

The briefing officers now had the difficult job of explaining the Long Leg which passed so close to the Ruhr and Frank-furt defences, the night-fighter airfields and the beacons. Many expedients were used to make light of this. At Conings-by there was a strong reaction when the route was revealed and loud shouts of 'Jeezus!' The crews here were told that the Germans were known to have moved their fighters to the coast in readiness for the shortening raids of the less deep spring nights and would not be expecting a deep penetra-tion. Lissett crews were told that the defences covering southern Germany were weak and the gap near Cologne would be 'virtually unprotected'.

At least three stations were told that the Americans had been out during the day and inflicted heavy casualties on the German fighter force. There was a humorous moment at Snaith when the crews were told that the Americans had been operating during the day and had 'shot down every goddam German fighter in the region'. But the experienced Path-finder men at Bourn did not find it funny and a statement by the embarrassed briefing officer that the Americans had met black-painted night fighters and that this would reduce the risks for the night bombers 'was met with the derision it deserved'.

Details were given of the spoofs and diversions, the Path-finder marking and the method of attack at the target.

The briefing officer outlined the target area with his pointer on a large-scale map of Nuremberg. As he did so (whether by accident or design I do not know) he said, 'You will see that the target area is roughly the shape of an axe.' Someone among the aircrews immediately remarked in a loud voice, 'Chop! Chop!' and everyone in the room joined in a terrific roar of laughter. (Sergeant D. Guard, 115 Squadron)

Next came the station meteorological officer, also with an unenviable task. I have studied carefully just what the crews were told on this subject. The command meteorological staff had made no reference in their afternoon forecasts to high cloud but, at station level, every effort was made to keep from crews the unpleasant fact that they were to fly a constant course for 265 miles through a well-defended part of Germany in bright moonlight with but little chance of cloud cover. On at least eleven stations, the crews were given specific forecasts that there would be cloud cover at opera-

tional height on this outward flight. No change was made to
1 Group's plan to fly at lower heights as far as the Rhine and
several crews in its squadrons were very unhappy when they
were allocated the 16,000 feet-height band – 7,000 feet
below the best ceiling of their Lancasters. No one, not even
the Pathfinder squadrons, who would have to mark the target
was told of the 'large amounts of strato-cumulus with tops to
8,000 feet' now forecast for Nuremberg. The conditions
found by the second Mosquito weather-reconnaissance flight
were not passed down to the stations.

The rest of the briefing was routine. Each section leader –
navigation, gunnery, bombing, signals and engineering –
made his few remarks. The commanding officer of 50 Squadron at Skellingthorpe liked to close his briefings by selecting
a gunner from one of the new crews to come to the front and
repeat the main points of the briefing. Poor Sergeant Frank
Patey, on only his fourth trip, made a hash of it, much to
the dismay of his pilot and the annoyance of the wing commander. Sergeant Patey would die that night.

At East Kirkby the commander of 630 Squadron named five
crews to go on leave the following day. He had not been
known to do this at a briefing before and the crews considered it a bad move on his part. There was a distinct hush.
Of the five due for leave, two crews would abort, two would
be shot down and only one would complete the raid without
trouble.

The crews had mostly listened to the briefings quietly and
attentively. They knew they could do nothing to influence
the course of events but the prospects were not to their liking.
One squadron commander remembers that 'at this period the
crews appeared to have developed a far more sensitive collec-
tive nose for the really dangerous raid than the hierarchy at
Command and Group'.

A few men, usually the inexperienced, were not concerned; Nuremberg did not create an immediate reaction of
unease as did Berlin or the Ruhr and they still had faith in
the meteorological briefings. But such men were in a
minority.

Our navigator and I had a macabre routine that we followed
during nav. briefings. We studied, intensely, the faces and reactions
of the other navigators and bomb-aimers in the room predicted

which crews would get the chop that night. Sadly, our predictions were astonishingly accurate. Uncertainty and plain simple terror permeated the stuffy briefing room that time. Those long, long legs into the heartland of Germany just begged for fighter activity. We finally decided that two of our relatively senior crews appeared to be showing the greatest amount of strain and would likely 'buy it' that night. When we got back we found we had been correct. (Sergeant W. J. Blackburn, 12 Squadron)

There we were, 112 of us each with our own private thoughts but all thinking along similar lines, such as 'Will our crew be one of the lucky ones?'; 'Is this it?'; 'Will I ever see the wife again?' and so on but all around the same theme being 'Will I live or die?' It was obvious that we were all of the same mind because a noisy and jocular dispersal was the norm after briefing but on this occasion we just sat and looked at each other – no words passed but the message was clearly conveyed through an atmosphere that was electric. (Flight Sergeant L. Nugent, 78 Squadron)

Three of these crews would be shot down and Nugent would be the only one in his aircraft to survive.

And so the final preparations were made. At Ludford Magna a young 101 Squadron pilot, Pilot Officer Jimmy Batten-Smith, was friendly with a W.A.A.F. equipment officer and, as usual, he gave her the writing case containing letters for his parents, who lived in India, if he went missing. 'Think of me at one o'clock, will you,' he added on this occasion and before she went to bed that night the W.A.A.F. set her alarm for that time.

The airmen went next to the crew rooms to put on their flying kit and then by bus to their aircraft which were at the dispersals around the perimeter track. Five of 138 Squadron's Halifaxes at Tempsford had been detailed for secret operations. Where these involved the dropping by parachute of agents the crew member who acted as dispatcher went in a closed van to the Garden Hotel on the Great North Road near Peterborough to collect his passengers. These were never seen by other crew members but taken directly to the aircraft standing at the end of the runway ready for take-off. Coded messages had been sent by the B.B.C. in its evening transmission to the German-occupied countries warning certain Resistance groups that men and supplies would be dropped to them.

At the bomber airfields the crews were carrying out the final checks on their aircraft; the pilots running up their engines, other members checking their own equipment. Even at this late hour defects were found and faults were hurriedly rectified or aircraft withdrawn. Two crews on the Australian squadron at Binbrook found their Lancasters unserviceable. There was a race round the perimeter track in crew buses to the spare aircraft.

We won! But I thought later that if we had known of the trip ahead we might not have been so keen to get there first. Of course, a crew, and especially the navigator, has put so much preparatory work into a trip that it is an anti-climax not to go. The spare aircraft was G for George on its eighty-seventh op; an aircraft with a dreadful vibration. I was driven to utter desperation on the flight with this vibration with my navigation instruments spread all over the table continually working their way onto the floor. (Flight Sergeant W. A. Gourlay, 460 Squadron)

This famous Lancaster, W4783, did three more operations and was then flown to Australia where it is now preserved in the War Museum at Canberra.

At Skipton-on-Swale, a bomb-aimer carrying out his checks on a Canadian Halifax pressed the bomb release when the safety bar was not in position. The bomb doors were still open and the entire load fell to the tarmac. There was no damage or casualties, only one load less of incendiaries for Nuremberg.

Another bomb-aimer noticed that

the perspex through which I used to peer for most of the trip was very dirty with oil and dust. It may be a measure of my tension that I flew into a rage and ordered one of the ground-crew sergeants to send the rigger responsible to me. I severely reprimanded the man but also explained that our lives could depend on having good vision. I often wondered how that airman must have reacted when we failed to return. (Flying Officer H. G. Darby, 514 Squadron)

Bomber Command had asked the groups to provide 785 heavy bombers for Nuremberg – 557 Lancasters and 228 Halifaxes. The Halifax groups had failed by sixteen aircraft to fulfil their quota but thirteen extra Lancasters had been found. 5 Group had produced twelve of these. The force now ready to take off was only three bombers short of its planned strength.

There remained one last period of waiting of up to half an hour as the crews climbed out of their aircraft and stood around, smoking, talking quietly among themselves or with the ground staff. They enjoyed a last cigarette and performed the traditional pre-operational custom of urinating together against the bomber's tail wheel. They looked up at the sky, with only a little cloud and the half-moon shining brightly. Many still felt that the raid must surely be cancelled and they looked for the red Very light that would indicate a last-minute decision not to go.

A Halifax crew at Leeming relieved the tension in a novel way.

I remember that at the dispersal point the ground crew had made a giant catapult with the forked limb of a tree and bunjee cable and we used it for target practice on a construction of petrol tins some thirty yards away. I remember lobbing a few half bricks myself and very satisfying it was. (Flight Sergeant J. Robson, 429 Squadron)

At Spilsby, a W.A.A.F. in the Station Engineer's office was friendly with a Canadian pilot of 207 Squadron and she normally stood with the crowd at the beginning of the runway to wave his aircraft off. On this night he had begged her to come out to the dispersal to see him off. This was considered absolutely taboo but he had insisted and she had gone out there with another W.A.A.F.

I even went into their Lancaster and stood behind Jack as he ran up the engines. I told him to drop that little lot – the bombs – for me; I had lost a brother at Dunkirk. When we got out of the aircraft I noticed the whole crew were nervous. Four of them had already started eating their flying rations and the young flight engineer kept taking his helmet off and putting it on again. His face was covered in perspiration. I have no doubt at all that they had a premonition that they were for the chop that night. (Leading Aircraftwoman E. M. Butler, R.A.F. Spilsby)

Pilot Officer Jack Thornton's bomb load was to play an important and unusual part in the night's operations.

The last few minutes ticked away. There was no cancellation. The airfields had gone perfectly quiet. No one seemed to have anything to say now.

The green Very light shot up from the control tower. The

crews climbed back into their aircraft. A pilot started his starboard-inner engine, then the starboard-outer. Gradually, other aircraft would start up until the whole airfield was filled with noise and it was time for the first bomber to move off around the perimeter track. The raid was on.

6

The Outward Flight

At exactly 21.16, Lancaster JB736 of 103 Squadron lumbered down the runway at Elsham Wolds and became airborne. It was the first bomber to take off for Nuremberg.

This Lancaster was up nine minutes before any other. It was a comparatively old aircraft with almost 200 flying hours to its credit but its crew were only on the third operation of a tour that had started badly. They had been forced to turn back from one raid and then twelve nights ago their aircraft had been badly damaged over Frankfurt. The Lancaster had been fitted with a new mid-upper turret and two new engines and was only just ready for Nuremberg but it had not been air-tested. The pilot, Flying Officer Guy Johnston, a Scot, was keen to get on with his tour and was still bitter at having to abort from the earlier raid. As it was a maximum effort raid, his aircraft had been bombed up and fuelled and he was to take off early, fly a short air test and, if all was well, set course for Nuremberg. We shall meet Flying Officer Johnston and his crew again.

It was soon time for the Yorkshire-based groups to start the main take-off, they having the greatest distance to fly to the concentration point over the North Sea where the bomber-stream would form. Gradually the other groups joined in but it was not until almost an hour after Flying Officer Johnston had taken off that the most southerly groups started.

This was the fifth year of the war and a well established, traditional ceremony was observed at every take-off. At the end of the runway from which the bombers would start, a small crowd of onlookers would assemble – W.A.A.F.s with boy friends on the raid, ground crews, clerks, anyone not otherwise occupied. Each bomber took its place at the end of the runway and waited for a 'green' from the controller's lamp. The engines were then run up to full boost, the brakes released and the bomber slowly rolled off down the runway to the accompaniment of cheers, waves and many a silent prayer.

It being a fine night there were many to see the men off to

Nuremberg. At Dunholme Lodge, the station commander formally saluted each aircraft as it moved off; 'a mark of respect from the top brass to a humble sergeant-pilot that always caused a surge of emotion and brought a lump to my throat', remembers one man. The retired general who lived near Waterbeach was in his usual place waving off the 514 Squadron crews and among those at Skellingthorpe was the local 'chop girl'.

There was a certain cheery W.A.A.F. sergeant on the camp and we had been informed that she was a jinx. Apparently every chap who had dated her had failed to return from operations. At tea in the Mess she came up and spoke a few words to me for no particular reason. I remember thinking, 'That does it! We are in for it.' My last impression of Skellingthorpe was of the small knot of non-flying personnel who regularly gathered at the end of the runway to wave off the lads. The W.A.A.F. sergeant was well to the foreground. (Flight Sergeant D. G. Gray, 50 Squadron)

Gray's Lancaster did not return.
And at Mildenhall,

As we turned onto the runway at the take-off point, I noticed a group of W.A.A.F.s and ground crew waving to us and laughing. I learnt later that my rear gunner was waving a pair of W.A.A.F.'s 'blackouts', as their pants were then termed, to the assembled crowd. He told me it was the finest material for cleaning the perspex in the turret. (Sergeant S. Fisher, 15 Squadron)

All through eastern England from Northallerton to Newmarket the March night was filled with the thundering of over 3,000 engines straining to haul the bombers into the air. Many aircrew say that the moments between releasing the brakes and reaching the 'unstick' speed of 105 m.p.h. seemed an eternity and was the moment of greatest fear, sitting as they did amidst twelve tons of petrol and explosives. The failure of an engine could result in a highly spectacular end to a tour.

On this night there were two accidents. At Coningsby the flaps of a Lancaster crept up as it accelerated along the runway. Pilot Officer Hallett noticed too late to brake and was forced to attempt the take-off with insufficient 'lift'. The aircraft did leave the ground but would not climb and it struck a marker post just beyond the runway. The petrol tanks in one wing and a tail-plane were ripped open but by good fortune and the pilot's skill the aircraft did not crash and it landed safely back at Coningsby after all the other aircraft there had left.

An Australian pilot, Flight Sergeant Bucknell, had an even more amazing escape at Skellingthorpe when his veteran Lancaster burst a tyre half-way down the runway. The bomber slewed sideways off the runway and one engine and part of the wing was ripped out but there was no fire or explosion and the badly shaken crew were unhurt. Four Lancasters still waiting to take off had to use another runway.

The only other take-off incident occurred at Breighton where an insecure escape hatch above a Halifax pilot's head was torn off. No harm was done but the aircraft was out of the raid.

Within an hour of the commencement of the main take-off the bulk of bombers had gone. The airfields fell silent; the spectators dispersed; the seven-hour vigil before the bombers returned had begun. Here and there the usual stragglers took off after attention to last-minute faults and hurried on to catch up the others. The honour of being last off on this occasion fell to a 619 Squadron crew. Their aircraft had failed its final check and they were switched to the spare Lancaster of 61 Squadron also based at Coningsby. Flight Sergeant John Paterson, another Scot, finally got away at 22.54 with a delay of at least fifteen minutes to make up. *

A combination of good work by the ground crews and the perfect flying conditions had given the raid a happy start. 779 bombers were set for the first stage of their long flight to Nuremberg.

Directly we had taken off I would, figuratively speaking, cut myself off from the rest of the crew and offer to God a very simple prayer for all of us. I have never disclosed this before – whether any of the others did the same I don't know, but the words I have always remembered. 'Oh Lord, please take us safely to the target, safely through the target and bring us safely home again and, please God, keep us from trouble.' No doubt there are those who would scoff at this prayer and the faith behind it but we survived one tour as a complete crew! (Sergeant P. Bailey, 51 Squadron)

* Of the crews involved in these take-off incidents, Pilot Officer Hallett's survived safely but Hallett was killed on a motorcycle soon after the war; Flight Sergeant Bucknell and his crew later went to the Pathfinders but were all killed when shot down near Paris in August 1944 and similarly the crew of Flight Sergeant Paterson all died while raiding Stuttgart in July 1944.

It would be dramatic to be able to record that as each bomber left the runway it lifted its nose towards Germany but it was not as simple as that. To start with, every aircraft had taken off as near as possible into the light north-westerly wind and was therefore heading away from Germany and even so they could not set course until sufficient height had been gained to be well clear of other aircraft taking off.

Round and round the hundreds of lumbering bombers circled in conditions that no present-day air traffic controller would tolerate and it was, indeed, another of those potentially dangerous parts of the flight but the absence of enemy Intruders, which enabled the bombers to use navigation lights, and the clear, moonlight conditions of this particular night kept the bombers in safety and there were no accidents. The pilots maintained full power up to 2,000 feet and then throttled back to standard climbing power for the remainder of the half hour that it took to gain the required 10,000 or 12,000 feet before setting course.

The exact speed, height and position of every aircraft was pre-determined for the whole flight. The broad outlines of this plan had been laid down by Bomber Command that morning and individual aircraft had been fitted into it by more detailed planning at group, station and squadron level. If all went well there would be no collisions, a tight bomber-stream, concentrated bombing and a safe return. In practice the plan was subject to all the pressures of weather conditions, enemy action and human frailty, for as soon as each aircraft had taken off it was subject to the control of no one but its own crew. There was always a gap between the operation as planned and the execution of it. However, most of this is in the future and as each aircraft reached that precise time and height ordained for it, the navigator advised his pilot to set course towards the bomber-stream's assembly point.＊

＊ This is an appropriate place to explain two points.

The direction and strength of the wind was always a major factor affecting navigation and were of particular importance on this night. It is impossible to state exactly what winds existed at all stages of a flight lasting up to eight hours. I have spent a great deal of time, however, in calculating the actual winds encountered, using many sources: Meteorological Office charts; winds 'found' by the Windfinders and winds broadcast from England during the raid – both based on a study of logs kept by eight navigators during the night; German meteorological documents later captured; the position of crashed aircraft;

For most, the first stage was a direct flight south-east from their bases but the squadrons of 4 and 6 Groups had first to fly almost due south as far as Cottesmore airfield so as not to interfere with the take-off of the Lincolnshire-based squadrons although one Canadian crew of 429 (Bison) Squadron decided to better their chances by flying direct from Leeming to the assembly point and so placed themselves in the first wave of the bomber-stream instead of in the last wave to which they had been allocated.

This part of the flight was without great tension and mainly spent doing routine duties. The I.F.F. (Identification Friend or Foe – a signal emitted by the bomber which identified it as 'friendly') had been switched on before take-off so they were safe from attack by R.A.F. fighters and the wireless operators had wound out their trailing aerials. The navigators were working hard to get the vital accurate fixes that would tell them how the actual winds compared with those forecast. Their Gee boxes were giving a succession of good positions but this aid would become jammed soon after the English coast was crossed. Some navigators were using their H2S sets, unaware that the Germans could pick up the device's impulses even while the bomber was over England. The aircraft had settled to a steady climb of around 100 feet per minute; the pilots could relax a little now and many had engaged 'George', the automatic pilot. Before 17,000 feet was reached the crews had to switch on their oxygen supply. If this failed for more than two minutes at any time in the next six hours they would become unconscious and then die.

The first aircraft crossed the Suffolk coast at around 23.00, a vertical searchlight at Southwold giving its navigator a last visual fix. As the bombers flew out over the North Sea the guns were tested in bursts kept as short as possible, the gunners unwilling to waste a single round of ammunition more than was necessary. The bombs were fused and navigation lights switched off. There was a noticeable increase in alertness and in tension.

---

the position of the bombs dropped on the raid. I am satisfied that wind details quoted are reasonably accurate.

Secondly, aircraft and wind speeds will be quoted in ordinary miles per hour as this was the method used at that time although knots (nautical miles per hour) became standard soon afterwards.

From the English coast to that point over the North Sea chosen as the assembly point was only a short flight of fifty miles or fourteen minutes' flying time. This was completed without incident and the bomber-stream began to form when the leading aircraft reached the position 51° 50′ north, 2° 30′ east. There was no question of the bombers flying in formation in the darkness; they simply came together into a loose stream as each flew over the assembly position at its allotted time and height.

In theory the stream on this night was sixty-eight miles long, a length that would allow it to pass over Nuremberg in the planned seventeen minutes of the raid. There were only ninety-seven aircraft in the first twenty miles of the stream. These were the 'openers', the initial Pathfinder element of twenty-four Blind Marker-Illuminators * and six Visual Markers and the sixty-seven Lancasters of 8 Group and 5 Group carrying high-explosive loads which would act as supporters to these marker aircraft. Following these would be the five waves of the Main Force, each occupying just under ten miles of the bomber-stream although the term 'wave' is misleading as there was no separation between waves and often some overlapping.

The average wave contained 138 bombers made up of nine Pathfinder Backers-Up, five A.B.C. Lancasters with jamming equipment, seventy-eight ordinary Lancasters and forty-six Halifaxes. As every group had been given an equal share of the waves a 3 Group Lancaster from Mildenhall could easily be keeping company with a Canadian Halifax from one of the Yorkshire airfields. It was normal for the more experienced crews to be sent with the earlier waves and the 'new boys' to bring up the rear. The only 'strangers' in the stream were two Halifaxes of 192 Squadron from 100 Group. Taking advantage of the protection afforded by the bomber-stream these aircraft would seek to establish, with their electronic equipment, the latest frequencies being used by German radar. Two Mosquitoes were also performing this important task but their superior speed and ceiling allowed them to roam more freely.

This, then, was the theory of the bomber-stream forming over the North Sea. However, the force was already depleted as many aircraft had succumbed with technical trouble and turned back. The question of these 'early returns' had always been a vexed one. There were the unavoidable cases where to proceed was impossible; but there was also the in-between position where the defect was such as to allow the aircraft to carry on if in the hands of a 'press-on' crew but a less resolute one could return with a reasonable excuse. Early returns failed to count as an operation towards the tour unless bombs had been dropped on some enemy target but many crews were quite happy to forgo this in exchange for the release from a particularly difficult raid. Every effort was made to keep these aborted operations to a minimum and crews that returned in this manner had to undergo a tough interview with the squadron or station commander.

Aircraft had been turning back since just after the take-off and would continue to do so until the force was well into Belgium. The usual reason for the return was engine failure but among other causes recorded on this night are oxygen supplies, intercoms and Gee sets becoming unserviceable, several navigators suffering from airsickness and a wireless-operator's parachute opening accidentally.

The following account by an Australian pilot on his second operation describes a typical early return.

The navigator came up on the intercom and said he was having oxygen trouble. Being a new crew we had not been allocated our own aircraft and we had not used this one before. I sent the engineer back to help. After a few minutes he reported that he could not find the cause of the trouble but the navigator was showing signs of distress. Since he was the only one having difficulty, the fault was either in his mask or in the oxygen point to which he was connected. A spare piece of oxygen tubing may have solved the problem but we had none on board (or so we believed). I ordered him forward to another point and began a descent to below 10,000 feet.

Well, we didn't solve the problem and we had lost too much time and height to continue with the operation so I turned for home. This decision worried me because I reasoned that there would be those who would connect our early return with the leave roster. Charges of L.M.F. loomed in my mind.

The next morning I had to confront the Old Man in his office. He tore me off one hell of a strip because a length of spare tube had been found in our aircraft. I tried to defend myself with the fact that I had never even been in that aircraft until take-off and therefore had no way of knowing the spare tube was on board. This had no effect; he went up one side of me and down the other, digging his toes in all the way up and his heels all the way down. (Flight Sergeant L. N. Rackley, 630 Squadron)*

The total number of aircraft to turn back from the Nuremberg force was fifty-two. This may seem a high figure but at 6·9 per cent it is average for the period. The performance of the different aircraft types reflects accurately the technical superiority of the Lancaster, 4·7 per cent returning early, over the Halifax with 14·2 per cent, while the extremes of morale and efficiency within groups are shown in the 18·5 per cent of 4 Group aircraft returning and the 1·8 per cent of the Pathfinders.

Two of the aircraft in difficulties managed to bomb Ostend, whose docks had been selected as a secondary target, and another dropped its load on an airfield at Flushing but the remainder dumped some 120 tons of bombs in the North Sea so that they would not have to land with a load of live bombs. From the original force of 782 heavy bombers that had taken off for Nuremberg, 725 remained at this stage.

Some mention should be made of those crews who pressed on to Nuremberg in spite of having defects in their aircraft that would have justified their turning back. A Blind Backer-Up aircraft of 35 Squadron refused to climb above 14,000 feet but its pilot kept going to ensure that his markers were delivered to Nuremberg and an Australian crew completed the entire flight with a dud radio set. Another Australian pilot found that

on the climb out of England it became quite obvious why S–Sugar was the spare aircraft. It was as sluggish as a dray load of bricks and to make things really cosy a fuel cock vibrated to an incorrect position and we lost about 100 gallons. We eventually made it to 20,000 feet only to find, on setting the cruising controls, that Sugar sank to 18,500 feet. To conserve our fuel we stayed there and I often think now that perhaps it was lucky, as the future activity by Jerry seemed to be above this height. (Flying Officer T. J. Foster, 463 Squadron)

While the last waves of the stream were still assembling,

* Rackley concluded his operational tour in a peculiar way. When returning rom a raid on Wesseling on 22 June 1944, he was forced to abandon his badly damaged aircraft over England and was injured when he came down by parachute onto an express train.

the leading aircraft were heading for the Belgian coast only ten minutes' flying time away over this narrow part of the North Sea. There was some convection cloud well below but a thin and very broken layer of strato-cumulus was all that was to be found of the high cloud cover that many had been promised and for which all were hoping. Otherwise, visibility was excellent with the half-moon lower in the sky but still shining brightly in the north. In these favourable flying conditions the bomber-stream was able to form without difficulty.

In the heavy bombers everyone was fully alert for the enemy could now be encountered at any time although it was unusual for more than an occasional fighter to appear so early in the flight. Pilots had mostly taken the controls back from 'George', ready to react instantly if an enemy appeared or if there was danger of collision. The aircraft were still climbing slowly but would soon reach their operational height. Slight adjustments to the four engine throttles would keep the air speed indicator showing a steady 155 m.p.h. although, in the thinner air through which they were flying, the true speed in still conditions would have been 204 m.p.h. and the favourable wind was actually carrying the aircraft along at about 240 m.p.h. Occasionally one bomber would run into the slipstream of another without warning; the sudden turbulence would cause a wing to drop and the loss of a little height, and the pilot would have to haul back on his control column to regain his position. This sensation was a little frightening to new crew members but they soon realized that it meant that their aircraft was well tucked into the bomber-stream and they took comfort from it. Close to the pilot, the flight engineer was helping to keep the four engines synchronized, monitoring the engine instruments, calculating fuel stocks and changing tanks when necessary. When not engaged on these tasks he spent as much time as possible acting as a look-out.

Down on his stomach in the nose of the aircraft the bomb-aimer was a busy man for not only was he trying to help the navigator by map reading but he was in charge of the Window and had to unpack the brown paper parcels that cluttered up his compartment and push the metal strips down a small chute at the prescribed rate of one bundle per minute, a laborious and much-hated chore.

The hardest thing was to read the maps as no lighting was allowed in the nose and the only source of light was a very dim flashlight. I started to undo the brown paper parcels of the Window and it wasn't long before maps, brown paper and string and myself began to get mixed up as the blessed chute wasn't large enough to push the brown paper out as well. (Sergeant D. G. Patfield, 61 Squadron)

The navigator definitely had the best job on night ops. He could not see what was going on outside, unless Flak was very close, and, providing he had enough sense to carry out the standard ten-minute cycle of getting a fix, checking wind, track and E.T.A., he was working like stink and had no time to worry about what was happening. (Flying Officer H. B. Mackinnon, 57 Squadron)

Most navigators preferred to cut themselves off completely from what was happening outside and immerse themselves in their work.

Not far from the navigator sat the wireless-operator. A long trip for this crew member could mean many hours of intense boredom for he was not a look-out man and his duties, unless his crew was a Windfinder, were few.

Our wireless operator was no doubt reading the book he took on every trip, *The Amazing Adventures of Doctor Syn*. He read more feverishly when the action started and I don't think he ever finished the book or knew what he read. (Sergeant E. Wilkins, 626 Squadron)

The two gunners were also bored but could not afford to relax as they swung their hydraulically powered turrets from side to side, each searching his allotted area of sky. There was plenty to be seen on this particular night. Visibility was so good that one Halifax tail gunner counted fifteen bombers at one time all keeping the same steady course in relation to his own aircraft. The gunners were in the unheated section of the bomber and extreme examples of the discomforts suffered by the poor air gunners, even without the hazards of enemy action, are demonstrated by two events of that night. The electrically heated suit of one man developed a fault early in the flight which burnt a large blister on his leg so severe that he later received a pension for the injury. Another gunner found it so cold that he finished the flight with a long icicle hanging from his oxygen mask. When he handed his parachute in after landing he also gave a startled W.A.A.F. a piece of ice nine inches long.

After the bombers had taken off the commanders in England were almost completely out of touch. Although every wireless-operator could contact his base by Morse there was no question of relaying back to England details of a massive enemy reaction or of dangerous weather conditions. Once the bombers had taken off they were irrevocably committed to the operation. At this stage of the operation, aircraft only used their transmitter if they were Windfinders or if they were coming down in the sea and there was a chance of the crew being saved. On this night there would not even be a Master Bomber to exercise his slender control when Nuremberg was reached. Both the commanders at home and the crews approaching Germany were now powerless to influence the course of events.

We must leave the Nuremberg-bound bombers just before they cross the Belgian coast to see how other operations were progressing.

The first to operate that night had been the Oboe Mosquitoes of 105 and 109 Squadrons making the most of the Oboe beams before these were needed to assist the spoof raids on Aachen and Cologne. Seventeen aircraft had attempted precision bombing attacks. In yet a further attempt to help the heavy bombers, thirteen of these had bombed five German airfields in Holland and France. The remaining four Mosquitoes had attacked factories in the Ruhr.

These Mosquitoes suffered a variety of misfortunes. Because of technical troubles five could not use their Oboe equipment and had to bomb blindly and a sixth brought its bomb load home when the bomb release failed. One Mosquito was damaged by Flak over the Ruhr – the first aircraft casualty of the night – but the crew were unhurt and it returned without difficulty.

There is no information on the effect of the airfield attacks, but the result of the only attack by a Mosquito to use Oboe successfully on a Ruhr target is known. Flying from north to south, Flight Lieutenant I. O. Breckon, a New Zealand pilot of 109 Squadron, and his navigator Flying Officer K. L. Pring, made their bombing run on the Guttehoffnungshutte

A.G. works at Oberhausen. This was a typical Ruhr heavy industrial firm making tanks, gun barrels and shells and it actually had two factories in Oberhausen only 600 metres apart. In the gap between the two factories was the workers' housing estate of Eisenheim.

So swift was the approach of the Mosquito that the air-raid alarm only sounded four minutes before Breckon's 4,000-pounder bomb was released. As the people of Eisenheim were running to their air-raid shelter, the Blockbuster exploded just outside it. Twenty-three people were killed instantly and thirty-two were injured – the first human casualties of the night.

Less lethal were the activities of eight Wellingtons, with crews making the short semi-operational flight with which they finished their course at Operational Training Units, and six American Fortresses of the 422nd Bomb Squadron based at Chelveston in Northamptonshire. These aircraft had dropped several million leaflets over Paris and nine other cities and towns in northern France. An inquisitive Junkers 88 had followed one of the Fortresses for some time without making an attack and another Fortress was coned for ten minutes by searchlights over Doullens. The Fortresses all returned safely, but one Wellington was hit by Flak although no one was hurt and its crew brought their aircraft home without difficulty.

The most important of these preliminary operations was that of the Halifax mining force that was intended to draw enemy fighters to north Germany. Out of fifty obsolete Halifaxes detailed for the diversion, forty-nine had taken off – twenty from 4 Group and twenty-nine from 6 Group. The barrage balloons guarding the Imperial Chemical Industries works at Billingham had been hauled down to allow the Canadians to fly out over the mouth of the River Tees while the 4 Group aircraft had left from Flamborough Head. One Halifax had aborted but the remainder completed the 380-mile crossing of the North Sea in safety despite much icing when they climbed through heavy cloud. The two forces had met at a point mid-way across the North Sea and from there approached Germany on a heading that pointed straight at Berlin, Windowing heavily in an attempt to hide their small numbers.

Five aircraft of 419 (Moose) Squadron first got an H2S

fix on Heligoland and then acted as markers by dropping parachute flares over the designated mining areas. The Halifaxes were engaged by Flak both from Heligoland and from the Friesian Islands but neither this nor a near collision in the mining area resulted in any casualties. The force then turned back behind its own screen of Window and made for home having completed its part in the night's plan. As the Halifaxes had crossed the 7° east line, the crews could count this as a full operation towards their tour.

The 112 mines sown here just as the Nuremberg bombers were reaching the Belgian coast were obviously incidental to the hoped-for diversionary effect. Some fighters were seen as the Halifaxes left the area but it remained to be seen whether the ruse had been successful.

At 23.22 the head of the bomber-stream crossed the Belgian coast at Knokke only a short distance from the frontier with Holland. Once more, air space claimed by Hitler's Germany was being invaded in strength, but this latest intrusion was greeted by only a little light Flak which failed to reach the 19,000 feet or more at which most of the bombers were now flying.

Nuremberg was still 420 miles away but such was the help that the raiding force was receiving from the following wind that this only represented 103 minutes of flying time and, with the passage of every one of these minutes, the hated half-moon sank further to the horizon. Had the German night fighters been drawn north by the mining diversion? And, if they had not, could the raiders speed through the gap south of the Ruhr and along that long straight leg before the German controllers reacted? Those next hundred minutes would provide the answers.

Still pursuing their south-easterly course the bombers flew inland, over Ghent where Flak failed to cause harm, by-passing Brussels and on to the first turning-point. There was understandably a great deal of apprehension among the crews at this point.

I recall shortly after crossing the coast seeing another aircraft with its navigation lights on, it was a Halifax, and of our being beset by doubts and helplessness in either warning the crew of their mistake or of being tricked ourselves. We were all very conscious of the possibility of Q-aircraft, that is Halifaxes or Lancasters repaired by the enemy and carrying a great deal of armament which, by mingling in the bomber-stream, could create havoc. Sufficient to say that any aircraft coming close was viewed with suspicion. (Flight Sergeant J. Robson, 429 Squadron)

A long ribbon of white fire splayed out on the ground as a sluggish Canadian Lancaster that would not climb jettisoned the incendiaries in its bomb load. There were other, un-explained, lights on the ground; one man claims to have seen the street lights of Brussels although that city was fully blacked out. There were odd bursts of tracer as nervous bomber gunners fired at imaginary attackers but there was no return fire.

One incident can be explained. A Halifax from the secret operations airfield at Tempsford was relying on the presence of the Nuremberg-bound bomber force to distract the Germans' attention. There were ten men aboard – the regular seven-man crew, a second pilot being initiated to this work and two Belgian Resistance agents who were to be dropped at a lonely spot south of Antwerp. These last were already sitting by the circular hole cut in the fuselage floor with their parachute release straps fastened to the interior of the aircraft.

The Halifax was flying inland, just above one of the estuaries of the River Scheldt when it was suddenly fired upon by two alert Flak positions, one on either bank of the river. The aircraft was immediately hit in the nose and in two engines. The pilot hauled the Halifax round in an attempt to make for home and the tail gunner fired off one defiant burst. But two engines were on fire and the aircraft had only a few seconds to live. With some skill the pilot landed on the river and the rubber dinghy inflated automatically but only five men escaped. The three crew members in the nose of the Halifax had been killed by the shell bursts and the two agents, strapped to the interior of the fuselage, had drowned when the water flooded up through the hole by which they had hoped to parachute back to their native country. It was a far better death than the one they could have expected if they had fallen into the hands of the Gestapo. Two English-men, two Belgians and a Canadian were the first Allied deaths of the night.

There was another reason for the nervousness of the bomber crews. The layers of high cloud which had never been very thick now dispersed completely. There was no fog on the ground, no low or medium cloud, no high cloud. The air was so clear that one crew assessed the horizontal visibility at 200 miles and a gunner vividly remembers watching the reflection of the moon in a river 18,000 feet below.

Twenty minutes after crossing the coast the leading bombers reached the first turning-point, a little north-east of the coal-mining town of Charleroi, the exact turning-point being over the old battlefield of Ligny where Napoleon had won a last success before his defeat at Waterloo, although the bomber crews had no time for such historical reminiscences.

The bombers were now beginning to lose their compact formation and, if the veil of darkness could have been lifted, the stream would have appeared somewhat ragged with a preponderance of aircraft to the north of the correct track. There were two factors causing this northward drift – one a product of nature and the other of man.

The upper winds were running parallel to the old cold front but, unknown to most of the bomber crews, this had changed its alignment. That part of the front that was lying over north-eastern France had moved south faster than had the part over Germany. This had two effects – it had drawn what little high cloud there had been south leaving the bombers without any cover and it had caused the winds to flow from almost due west instead of from west-north-west. The strength, too, of the wind had changed, having decreased slightly.

It was precisely these changes that the Windfinder aircraft at the front of the bomber-stream were supposed to discover. They had been transmitting their 'found winds' back to England every half hour since the flight had started. In theory, the group radio stations had sent this information to Bomber Command H.Q. where the meteorological staff were to average it out and send it back to groups who would transmit the new winds, now known as 'broadcast winds' to all the bombers. If these new winds were used by the whole force, the bomber-stream should remain compact. If they were not, and each crew attempted to find its own winds, the stream would disintegrate.

On this night, however, the Windfinder system had already broken down. Just after the Belgian coast had been crossed, the bombers had received the first wind broadcast from England, each from its own group transmitter but the broadcast had differed from group to group. For example, the 23.30 forecast for the next stage of the flight had been 300°/50 m.p.h. (a fifty miles per hour wind from a direction of 300 degrees) for 1 Group aircraft, while 5 Group were transmitting 290°/55 m.p.h. Some groups were not to receive a wind at all for another half hour.

The clue to what had gone wrong may be found in a document published by 8 Group after the raid for distribution among the Pathfinder squadrons. Having many crews at the head of the bomber-stream, all of high navigational ability, the Pathfinders were to provide a high proportion of the Windfinders. The 8 Group document complained that the wireless-operators in these aircraft had failed to 'listen out' properly to ensure that no one else was using their wave-length before transmitting their short message to the group receiver. If two messages went back to England simul-taneously, neither was received. 8 Group had expected to receive winds from thirty-six Pathfinder aircraft but had only received thirteen usable reports. In addition, those thirteen received had contained a spread of wind velocities over a 44 m.p.h. range and the wind directions had been spread over 48 degrees. All this had happened on a peaceful outward flight before a single bomber had come under attack. There was little wonder that Bomber Command H.Q. was unable to put out a common forecast and the groups had to make up their own.*

With Gee now jammed, none of the crews could get really reliable fixes. The better crews, especially those who had H2S and were skilled in its use, were able to detect the changing winds and remained on track but the forecasters in England, faced with conflicting or insufficient reports, never recognized that the wind had changed so that those crews relying on the broadcasts gradually drifted to the north of their track and also fell behind time. These winds were to bedevil the night's operations.

As the bombers flew due east away from the Charleroi turning-point with only eighteen minutes' flying time to the

* The document is the 8 Group Summary of Events, Public Record Office AIR 14/540.

German frontier, there came the first signs of German fighter activity. The bombers' route passed between two of the regular night-fighter airfields at Saint-Trond and Florennes and the visibility was so good that some of the bomber crews could see runway lights there. The German-speaking special operators in the 101 Squadron Lancasters had warmed up their radio receivers before crossing the Belgian coast. Soon after turning near Charleroi the familiar blips began to appear on their oscilloscopes showing that a German controller was talking to night fighters that had taken off. The operator tuned one of his three A.B.C. transmitters onto the frequency and pressed the key switching on the curious warbling sound over the German voice. If the Germans started on a new frequency, the operator had two more transmitters available. In spite of the attentions of twenty-six such aircraft the voices continued to break through – but were the fighters close by or hundreds of miles away in the north?

There are several reports that the first fighters sighted were single-engined Messerschmitt 109s although it is not clear from which unit these came or what they were doing over Belgium. However, only one combat developed when one of the 109s attacked an Australian Halifax of 466 Squadron flying at the rear of the stream. The fighter was driven off, claimed by the Australians as damaged, and the Halifax was unharmed.

Soon after came evidence that twin-engined fighters were also in the area.

We saw below us several Junkers 88, first two together and then three single ones. We banked to starboard and lost height as the pilot wanted to have a look at them. The navigator didn't like him doing this and there was a little argument which ended with the pilot saying, 'Leave it to me. I'm going to get rid of those b—s!' The mid-upper wanted to have a go but the pilot wouldn't let him.

We lost those Germans and were regaining height when the mid-upper got very excited. 'Look out Skip, there's one to the starboard' but the tail gunner had also seen it, 'Take it easy, it's one of ours.' We all had a look as it came closer and saw from its letters – GT – that it was one of our own squadron but we didn't know which crew it was. It formated on our wing tip and we flew for a long time together. It was a very comfortable feeling. (Sergeant L. Wooliscroft, 156 Squadron)

These two Pathfinder crews were in fact close friends. Wooliscroft's pilot was Warrant Officer Jack Murphy, an Australian, and the other pilot was Captain Finn Johnsen of the Royal Norwegian Air Force.

It was just after midnight when the first bomber was shot down but it did not fall to the German fighters. A Lancaster, drifting north of the correct track, had flown over the Liège Flak defences.

There goes the first one down. A faint golden glow, then a trail of fire until 'plop', and another of our bombers was glowing red on the ground. This sickening blood-red fire belching black smoke – our own boys were in that! Wonder who will be next. (Warrant Officer G. C. Notman, 550 Squadron)

When Notman referred to 'our boys' he did not know how true this was, for the Lancaster was from his own squadron. Only three men, all injured, escaped by parachute.

At about the same time as this incident, the leading bombers were crossing the German frontier south of Aachen. There remained a mere 270 miles to Nuremberg – just over one hour's flying time.

7

The Long Leg

The life-style of the German night-fighter crews conformed closely to that of the men of Bomber Command. Just as the bomber men had slept soundly for three full nights and had been preparing for leave that morning so too had the Germans. The night-fighter men were in good heart just then. They felt that they had more than held their own over the winter from which they were emerging and only six days earlier had achieved what they thought had been their greatest success of the war when the R.A.F. had raided Berlin. The German radio had announced the destruction of 112 of the 'terror bombers' of which the fighters had claimed eighty-eight. In fact, Bomber Command had lost seventy-three aircraft from all causes that night.

One German unit had not had a restful time. II/NJG 1 had been bombed out of their airfield at Saint-Dizier in northern France by an American daylight bombing raid three days earlier and eight of their twelve Messerschmitt 110s had been hit. The remaining four fighters had since been ordered from one airfield to another, first to Athies near Laon, then to Saint-Trond in Belgium and then, on this afternoon, back again to Athies. The crews landed there in the early evening, looked at the clear weather and the moon and decided they would not be flying again that night.

Every day and night Luftwaffe officers at various levels had to make a series of decisions based always on incomplete or conflicting evidence and in the face of every effort by the R.A.F. to mislead. Late that afternoon, reports from the German radio listening stations travelled their daily path up the chain of command until all were consolidated and placed before the duty operations officer of the I Fighter Corps at Zeist in Holland. At about the same time as Sir Robert Saundby was showing Sir Arthur Harris the reports of the Mosquito weather flights and expecting his chief to cancel the raid, the commander of I Fighter Corps, Generalleutnant Josef Schmidt, a Bavarian who only a year earlier had commanded the Hermann Goering Panzer Division in Tunisia, was being shown these radio reports.

No record exists of what was decided but, in view of what followed, it is reasonable to assume that the Germans concluded that the R.A.F. was likely to operate in strength that night but, because of the thick cloud in the North Sea, the raid would be to the centre or south of Germany and because of the moon the penetration would not be a deep one. The Ruhr was a likely target as it had been for the last raid four nights earlier.

At Chantilly near Paris, Generalleutnant Werner Junck's II Fighter Corps, with only four night-fighter Gruppen, agreed with the assessment and that his corps would conform with the plans of its more powerful neighbour. The code word *Fasan* (pheasant) then travelled back down the chain of command – 'Enemy raids expected tonight'.

The first decision had been safely taken. The assessment was accurate except for the expected penetration of the raid.

While the British heavy-bomber crews had been attending their briefings the German fighter-operations rooms had plotted the Mosquitoes that had flown in during the early evening to carry out the Oboe bombing attacks. But the German fighter units had ignored the Mosquitoes completely. These fast, high-flying raiders were left to the Flak.

It was not long after this that the Germans were informed by their monitoring service that a force of aircraft had taken off from bomber airfields in the north of England. Soon the radar station at Texel, which was proud of its record of being the first to detect approaching raiders, confirmed that these were flying across the North Sea on a course threatening Hamburg or Berlin. This was the Halifax diversionary mining force. Following close on these reports came news that more bombers had taken off and were flying south-east after assembling in the Norwich area. So, at about 23.00, the Germans had identified the two forces approaching their territory, each of which could be expected to cross the coast in about thirty minutes but at points 300 miles apart. A second decision had now to be made by the Germans – one that was of vital importance to the men flying to Nuremberg. Which was the main attack?

Two Luftwaffe generals had a hand in answering this question. Both bomber forces had been approaching the area of Josef Schmidt's I Fighter Corps but on courses that would threaten the areas covered by two different fighter divisions. Not far from Schmidt's H.Q. at Zeist was situated the operations room of the 3rd Fighter Division at Deelen near Arnhem, a town that would become famous just six months later. Here, the commander was Generalmajor Walter Grabmann, a tall Prussian officer only thirty-nine years old, but a veteran of the Condor Legion that had fought for Franco in Spain and also of the air fighting in Poland, France and the Battle of Britain. Grabmann had had no hesitation in deciding that the bombers approaching his area represented the main threat and that the ones flying towards north Germany were a diversion. He had immediately ordered every night-fighter Gruppe in his division to take off and had chosen radio beacon Ida, south-east of Cologne, as their assembly point.

Grabmann had then spoken with Schmidt, his corps commander, telling him of his appreciation of the situation and of the action he had taken. Without any discussion whatever Schmidt approved what had been done and went straight on to contact the other three divisions of his corps and ordered these also to comply. In addition, II Corps agreed to send its four Gruppen to join in. Those Gruppen whose aircraft could not reach Ida in time were ordered to fly to a second beacon, Otto, just north of Frankfurt. These orders went out just as the first bombers were flying out over the English coast for the North Sea crossing.

These decisions had been taken extraordinarily quickly and with a minimum of consultation. The Germans' excellent technical intelligence had helped them to identify the main attacking force. The vital factor had been the ability to detect the bombers' H2S transmission while they were still in the Norwich area. This had enabled the Germans to assess the size of the bomber force to within fifty of its exact strength and the subsequent plotting of the H2S transmissions had revealed the bombers' south-easterly course towards the Belgian coast.

The choice of the Ida and Otto radio beacons was a happy one for the Germans. The bombers' route passed close to both beacons.

Swift action followed these orders. Before a single British bomber had even crossed the Belgian coast, night fighters were taking off from airfields as far apart as the Berlin area,

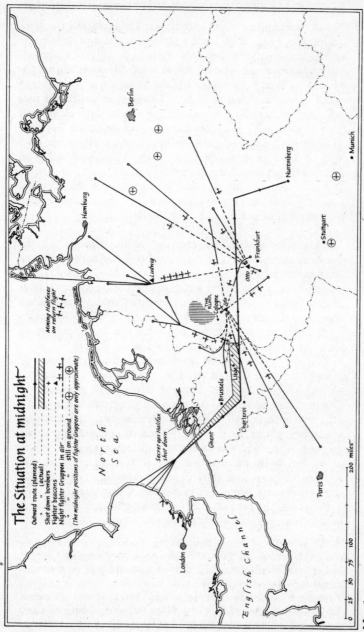

The Situation at midnight

Outward route (planned)	━━━▶
" " (actual)	━━━
Shot down bombers	━━━
" " fighters	✠
Fighter beacons	▲
Night fighter Gruppen in air	━ + ━
" " " still on ground	— + — + —
(The midnight positions of fighter Gruppen are only approximate)	⊕

Mining Halifaxes on return flight ✠✠✠

Secret gas Halifax shot down

North Sea

English Channel

London

Paris

Brussels
Ghent
Charleroi
Liège
THE RUHR
Cologne
Frankfurt
Otto
Ida
Ludwig
Hamburg
Berlin
Nuremberg
Stuttgart
Munich

0   25   50   75   100   200 miles

Map 5

Westerland on the island of Sylt near Denmark and Coulom-
miers near Paris. The accompanying map shows their paths
to the beacons. Out of twenty-eight night-fighter Gruppen,
only five remained on the ground – the Messerschmitt 110s
of II/NJG 6 at Echterdingen (now Stuttgart airport) which
was fog-bound, three Wild Boar Gruppen in the Berlin area
and another near Nuremberg. These single-engined fighters
were as yet too far away, but the commitment by the Germans
of four other single-engined Gruppen this early in the raid
will be used as evidence later in the book to counter an
unusual theory about the Nuremberg raid.

As the head of the bomber-stream reached the German
frontier a minute or two after midnight, over 200 German
night fighters were flying to Ida and Otto.

Simultaneous with the crossing of the frontier by the
bombers came the first of the three Mosquito spoof raids, on
Aachen, twenty miles to the north. Six Mosquitoes, using
Oboe, dropped red target indicators and 500-pounder bombs
in an attempt to delude the Germans into thinking that Aachen
was to be the main target. The bomb doors of one Mosquito
were frozen and it could not bomb but the others performed
their task satisfactorily and returned without loss.

The meticulous Aachen town archives show that four out
of twelve bombs did not explode; the remainder damaged a
variety of buildings and brought down some tram cables.
One hundred and fifty-seven people were bombed out but
only one soldier and a civilian were injured. All this was
secondary as far as the R.A.F. was concerned; the main
purpose of the raid was to induce German fighters to remain
at Aachen while the bombers flew further inland. The ruse
appears to have been only partly successful. A few single-
engined fighters were seen in the area a little later.

However, the path of other German fighters flying towards
beacon Ida crossed the bomber-stream's route into Germany.

We were flying from Laon and had been told by the running
commentary that the bombers were about five minutes away. I
hadn't even switched on the SN–2 set when the gunner poked me
in the back and pointed, 'There he is up there, the first one!' As
we came round we saw another straight away, about 200 metres
directly above. I switched on my SN–2 but we had dropped 2,000
metres behind in the turn and had lost them. When the set warmed

up I saw three targets on it at once. I headed for the nearest and Drewes [the pilot] picked it up at 600 metres. Weather was marvellous – clear sky, half-moon, little cloud and no mist – it was simply ideal, almost too bright. It was a Lancaster flying nicely on a steady course so that, when we were comfortably positioned underneath and from about fifty metres, Drewes opened fire with the upward firing cannon at one wing which immediately caught fire. We followed the Lancaster for five minutes until it crashed below with a tremendous explosion. (Unteroffizier Erich Handke, III/NJG 1)

The Lancaster, from the Australian 467 Squadron, was the first fighter victim of the night. The action of Major Martin Drewes in following the burning bomber without firing again gave Flight Lieutenant Bruce Simpson and all his crew the opportunity to bale out safely. Simpson had instinctively turned and headed for home when hit and the bomber had actually flown back across the frontier. It crashed and blew up near Spa in Belgium.

The encounters which took place between the German frontier and the Rhine seem to have been marked by a certain confusion almost as though both sides were surprised to have met each other so early in the flight. Some of the German fighters still had their navigation lights on, thinking they were merely on the preparatory flight to a beacon, but finding to their surprise that they were in the middle of a bomber-stream. The bomber crews had been nervous for a long time and the fear that they were doomed to be caught by fighters in the bright moonlight was obviously being confirmed.

This probably led to the following incident described by Sergeant Don Brinkhurst, mid-upper gunner of a 101 Squadron Lancaster.

A Halifax came right over the top of us; he was about 300 feet up, crossing from starboard to port. He was roughly ten o'clock from us when I last saw him and, just as he disappeared, I saw one long burst of tracer come down at us from that direction. German tracer was bluish but this was the pink and red that we used. It caught us all down our port side and we were soon on fire. At the time we were weaving and I expect that to a gunner who was on edge and jumpy we could have looked like a fighter making an attack.

I tried to contact the skipper on the intercom but got no joy.

I got out of my turret; the rear gunner was already out of his and sitting on the Elsan – he was not using it – only resting. I indicated to him to get his parachute on but he didn't seem to take any notice. I got mine on and managed to reach the door by pulling myself upwards for we were going down steeply. I could feel the 'special' (the A.B.C. operator) holding on to the back of my harness and I felt sure he would follow me out.

This tragic mistake cost the lives of five men in a crew on the last but one operation of their tour. Brinkhurst and two others parachuted safely but the special operator, probably injured by the machine-gun fire, was found two days later hanging dead by his parachute harness from a tree. The identity of the Halifax is not known.

Another peculiar encounter took place a few miles further along the route. A Junkers 88, one of the first to be factory-fitted with the *schräge Musik*, was flying down from Quackenbrück.

Just before Aachen, I got an SN–2 contact at a distance of about five kilometres. I remember quite clearly that this blip on my radar had a strange, unusual shape. In night operations there were often confusing situations and I naturally discussed my peculiar contact with the crew and asked them to be particularly vigilant.

We worked ourselves literally metre by metre closer but we didn't sight him until we flew into a patch of clearer sky where, to our amazement, the strange target blip resolved itself as two planes flying in close formation. They were Lancasters and we assumed they were Pathfinders. We flew very carefully under the left hand plane and fired from roughly eighty metres. The first burst hit at once and our opponent caught fire in the left wing. We peeled off to the right and a few seconds later were sitting under the second machine. Strange as it may seem, it continued flying in the same direction. We acted quickly and our slanting cannons spoke again.

Everything happened exactly as before and we were now able to see two enemy planes flying close together and on fire but still maintaining their old course. We could not see the crews bale out, although in our opinion they had sufficient time and our bursts had hit them in the wing. It was some considerable time before the two planes hit the ground with terrific explosions and for some seconds it was as bright as day even up to our height. The explosions showed us the visiting cards of our opponents. Coloured cascades and Christmas trees burnt on the ground for some time, so they had been Pathfinders after all! It was particularly rewarding to have shot them down. (Oberfeldwebel Walter Heidenreich, II/NJG 2) *

What Heidenreich described as 'Christmas trees' were the target indicators of two Pathfinders. They were the 156 Squadron Lancasters that had met earlier and flown on together. Nothing can illustrate more clearly the deadly effect of the unsuspected *schräge Musik* on fully laden aircraft whose crews failed to realize in time how badly their aircraft had been hit. Of the fifteen men in the two crews there was one survivor. Sergeant Wooliscroft, the wireless-operator in Warrant Officer Murphy's crew, was blown out of his aircraft and came down by parachute.

This preliminary skirmishing in the forty-five-mile section of the route from the German frontier to the Rhine cost the British ten Lancasters and two Halifaxes. All had fallen to German fighters except two Lancasters of 101 Squadron, the one hit by a Halifax and a second which had strayed south and been promptly shot down by the Coblenz Flak. Two more bombers had been damaged; one, a Pathfinder, pressed on, but the other had to turn back with two men wounded. The fights had not been all one-sided. Bomber crews claimed one Messerschmitt 109 destroyed (confirmed by several other crews), two Junkers 88s probably destroyed and five other fighters damaged.†

* From an account in the German magazine *Jägerblatt*, November/December 1963. I wish to thank the editor for his permission to reproduce this extract. Oberleutnant Köberich who captained this successful Junkers 88 crew was killed by American bombing at his home airfield less than a week later and the gunner was wounded. Heidenreich, the radar man, had just left for Easter leave and missed the bombing.

† It would be advisable here to write something on the subject of sources of information. R.A.F. squadron records contain full details of all aircraft and crews involved and a résumé of the debriefing report of every crew that returned from the raid. After the war the R.A.F. Missing Research teams compiled a report on every aircraft that was lost throughout the war and those of this raid were made available to me by the Ministry of Defence. These give precise details of where aircraft crashed, what happened to each crew member and often how the aircraft was shot down. Details given here of R.A.F. losses in both men and aircraft are, therefore, reliable. Appendix 4 contains full details of R.A.F. aircraft and crews lost in the Nuremberg Raid.

German records at unit level are non-existent. The only reliable German document is the War Diary of the I Fighter Corps which does contain much useful material, but about the activities of units rather than of individuals. (I am indebted to the Historical Research Division of the United States Air Force for providing the full text of this document.) For this reason, British claims of German fighters destroyed or damaged cannot be confirmed by documentary

By examining the British losses on this section it is possible
to be quite precise about which part of the bomber-stream
had been hit. The head of the stream with its early Pathfinders and Supporters had slipped through and crossed the
Rhine unopposed (the two Pathfinders shot down had both
been Backers-Up). The losses had mostly been among Main
Force crews with many operations to their credit. Such crews
usually flew well up the bomber-stream and it must have
been the first and second of the five Main Force waves that
had clashed with the German fighters. It was on this section
of the route that the 1 Group aircraft had been ordered to
fly between 16,000 and 19,000 feet. But the cloud which it
had been hoped would provide shelter there had been missing
and the objections of the 1 Group crews to flying so low had
been justified. Five of the twelve aircraft shot down had
been theirs.

Seven hundred and twelve bombers flew across the Rhine.

The planners at High Wycombe had routed the bombers
through the narrow twenty-mile gap between the southern-
most part of the huge Ruhr Flak and searchlight system and
the smaller defended area around Coblenz. Bomber Command had often had to make use of this gap – it was known
as the Cologne Gap – and the Germans had covered it with
the fighter beacon Ida. The flashing light for the single-
seater fighters was on Hangelar airfield near Bonn and the
radio beacon was a little distance away, but both were only
fifteen miles north of the planned route to Nuremberg.

Just five minutes before the leading bombers were to fly
through the gap south of Ida, the second spoof raid was due
to be carried out on Cologne fifteen miles north of the
beacon. Eight of the nine Mosquitoes allocated for this task
performed it on time and dropped green target indicators and
Blockbusters hoping to pull the fighters at Ida north to
Cologne, while the bomber force slipped through the gap to
the south. German records show that the Oboe-marked

evidence. German civil records are usually scrupulously kept and details
quoted of casualties on the ground can be taken as accurate.

Successful German aircrew often kept much detail of their combats and it is
sometimes possible to compare British and German versions of a combat.

Finally, I hope the reader will excuse my expedient of describing one section
of the route at a time although, with a bomber-stream seventy miles long,
action may have been simultaneous in more than one section.

bombing was remarkably accurate and much damage was done in the area of the main station near the famous cathedral. At least ten trains were hit, railwaymen and passengers were killed, but once again the success of the spoof was not to be measured in material damage.

The night-fighter Gruppen of two divisions and part of a third had been ordered to fly to Ida. Some of these, possibly fifty fighters, had stumbled upon the bomber-stream while on their way to the beacon and had started scoring victories. It is possible that another nine Gruppen, or 100 fighters, had won the race with the bombers and were at the beacon. Most of these were twin-engined fighters well used to the Tame Boar tactic of finding the bomber-stream and fighting in it.

The waiting Germans were flying in gentle circles, usually standing off a little way from the beacon and showing navigation lights for safety but easily keeping in touch with the beacon's radio signal. The single-engined fighters had to keep the flashing light in sight. The fighters were now in the area of Generalmajor Grabmann's 3rd Fighter Division which was probably the most experienced in Germany as many raids passed through its area and the huge underground operations room at Deelen airfield had been the first one built. It was to this division's running commentary that the fighter crews at Ida were now listening intently. To their amazement, just as the Mosquito markers and bombs started going down to their north on Cologne, the running commentary told them that the main bomber-stream was heading straight for them. This was a most unusual event; the fighters had usually to go chasing all over Germany to find the bombers. Now the British had obliged by flying right into their arms. The slight northward spread of the bombers in the unrecognized wind had been sufficient to take many of them, not through the gap, but north of it and on a collision course with the fighters.

The German fighter crews prepared to give battle.

It was also a great shock to the bomber crews to meet the German fighters in such strength so early in their flight and apparently waiting dead on track. The horrible suspicion entered the minds of several men that the enemy somehow knew of their route and had laid an ambush. The poor British bomber crews could not have found themselves in a more desperate position; every possible factor in night fighting was in favour of their enemy. German fighters were at hand in great strength, with unjammed radar and the unsuspected *schräge Musik*, with two hours fuel in their tanks and in the clearest weather conditions under the brilliant half-moon. To all this was now added one more hazard. Due to some unusual and unforeseeable quirk of the weather, vapour or condensation trails, not usually found below 25,000 feet, had started to appear behind each bomber. The dead-straight streams of pure white cloud could not have given away more clearly the path the bombers were taking.

Until this moment, nearly every crew had been faithfully attempting to follow the planned route and any straying had been unintentional, but now this tight discipline began to falter and the stream disintegrated. The first to leave were definitely the experienced men who recognized immediately that the bomber-stream was no longer a place of safety. Wing Commander Pat Daniels, a Pathfinder squadron commander, was flying with one of his new crews.

When you were experienced and had seen so much trouble you worked your aircraft up and used every inch of sky you could find. The crew I was with saw so many going down that I told them that they were probably those new Scarecrows we had just heard about but I knew they weren't. I'd never seen so many at once and I'd done seventy-six trips before this one. I thought it was getting a bit dangerous and it was time I packed it in.

Many pilots 'worked their aircraft up' in this manner. One 76 Squadron crew flying a brand new Halifax were delighted to find that their aircraft reached 26,000 feet at which height they flew on in complete safety. These crews found an added bonus when their vapour trails disappeared as they climbed.

We started leaving contrails at the height at which we had been ordered to fly, 19,000 feet. We were an experienced crew and I decided to disobey orders and get as much height as possible. We got up to about 22,000 feet which was as high as we could get fully loaded. From there I could see a mass of contrails below us; they were like a formation of American daylight bombers.

I watched a Lancaster flying about 2,000 feet below and about two miles off to my starboard. It had a dirty great contrail out at the back. I watched, fascinated, as a twin-engined German type overtook him, approaching just under the contrail. I could see everything perfectly clearly but we couldn't help. The German got underneath the Lancaster and fired straight into his belly with an upward-firing gun. The bomber took no evasive action at all. There was an explosion and it blew clean in half. There were no parachutes. My stomach turned over and we tried to get even higher. By then, I was feeling very cheesed off with the powers that be for sending us out on a night like that. (Flight Lieutenant D. F. Gillam, 100 Squadron)

Undoubtedly several crews now got rid of part of their bomb loads to gain height. One Halifax, struggling along lower than the rest, dumped its entire load, turned back and flew home but a Pathfinder pilot who could not get his Lancaster higher than 14,000 feet pressed on in true Pathfinder style at that height. Many of the victims of the battle above them came crashing down past them 'like a blazing inferno, some too close for comfort', remembers the tail gunner, but they were never attacked and carried out their marking on time.

Other crews sought safety by flying off to one side or other of the stream.

In two tours, it was the only moonlight trip we did, apart from mine laying. We went in south of Cologne and were immediately met by the German fighters, I could say hundreds. It was a fantastic sight in the clear moonlight, aircraft going down in flames and exploding everywhere. We went north and ended up in the Flak and in sight of Cologne. It was much healthier there. (Squadron Leader G. D. Graham, 550 Squadron)

The crews who deliberately left the bomber-stream were undoubtedly wise to do so. There was nothing that one bomber could do for another in such circumstances and the stream itself had obviously become a death trap where the Germans were to reap a rich harvest. Those who remained in the stream were the conscientious crews who were prepared to obey orders at all times and the new men without the experience or initiative that would have helped them to act otherwise. Gamely these flew on, doing their best to keep to the correct track and height, streaming their tell-tale vapour trails behind them.

This air battle was a perfect example of Tame Boar fighting. The choice of beacon Ida as the fighters' concentration point had brought a considerable number of German fighters into the bomber-stream. Some of these were from special reconnaissance units whose crews' first duty was to report the progress of the stream to the divisional control rooms. Bomber gunners often had to watch helplessly as these aircraft formated on them but remained just out of range while plotting the bomber's course, speed and height.

A Gruppe from a Junkers 88 bomber unit had been trained in a special 'Illuminator' role for the night battles. Their aircraft flew high above the bomber-stream and every time they saw evidence of the bombers' presence a cluster of parachute flares was dropped. Conditions for these 'fighter-flare' tactics were ideal on this particular night. The Illuminators could fly with little difficulty above the British vapour trails and their flares, visible from a great distance, brought many more fighters to the scene.

The British bomber men hated these pale red flares which they had often seen before. Their effect that night has been described as 'like a six- or eight-lane highway', and 'like flying along a very long runway with a lane of flares on either side; they seemed to burn for minutes and minutes and minutes'. Another man had 'the impression of being on a well-lit main road and being shot at from unlit side streets'.

Once they were in the stream, the Tame Boar fighters used their SN-2 radars to pick up a bomber and then their eyes for the final visual contact. The freedom from interference to their radar sets and the outstanding visual conditions of the moonlit night made this especially easy for those experienced Germans who had the *schräge Musik* and few of them failed to find targets. The following descriptions are typical of this type of attack as seen by both victor and victim.

The running commentary had brought a Messerschmitt 110 into the bomber-stream from Parchim, 220 miles away to the north and almost on the Baltic coast:

Normally our biggest problem was to find the bomber-stream but on this night we had no trouble. I found the enemy at a height of 6,000 metres (nearly 20,000 feet). I sighted a Lancaster and got underneath it and opened fire with my slanting weapon. Unfortunately it jammed so that only a few shots put out of action the starboard-inner motor. The bomber dived violently and turned to the north, but because of good visibility, we were able to keep him in sight. I now attempted a second attack after he had settled on his course but because the Lancaster was now very slow, we always came out too far to the front. I tried the Slanting Music again and after another burst the bomber fell in flames. Our plane stalled but I was able to regain control, 2,000 metres lower. The crash showed that we had caught a Master of Ceremonies, for the resulting fireworks on the ground were red, green and white colours. I had never seen anything like it. (Oberleutnant Helmut Schulte, II/NJG 5)

It was not unusual for Germans to describe a shot-down aircraft that had carried a large pyrotechnic load as a Master of Ceremonies. Schulte's victim was, in fact, a Blind Marker Illuminator of 635 Squadron. There were no survivors. Schulte went on to shoot down three more bombers and when he landed it was found that his two *schräge Musik* guns had used only fifty-six cannon shells.

Leutnant Wilhelm Seuss had also found the bomber-stream having flown in from his airfield at Erfurt in the east. He quickly dispatched two Lancasters from underneath but had trouble with a third. He fired once and the bomber immediately went into a violent corkscrew. He had to wait for three minutes while his radio operator fitted a fresh drum of ammunition to the *schräge Musik*. During this time Seuss flew beneath the Lancaster, skilfully matching every movement of his opponent so as to remain unseen. When the cannons had been re-loaded he fired again, but instead of striking between the engines of one wing, which was his usual method, the bomber's corkscrew caused Seuss's shells to splay right across both wings and the fuselage. The wings burst into flame and the incendiaries in the bomb bay caught fire as well. The Canadian pilot, Flight Sergeant Clyde Harnish of 101 Squadron, made a desperate last attempt to put out the flames by diving for 7,000 feet but it was too late. Harnish perished but four men survived including the flight engineer, whose account of the combat confirms that of Leutnant Seuss in every detail. At no time had the Lancaster crew seen the Messerschmitt.

Eight minutes later Seuss found his fourth Lancaster but again he hit the bomb bay in error and only by diving violently did Seuss escape the massive explosion as the bomber blew up. The radar operator reported a fifth contact but Seuss was completely exhausted by his four successful combats and especially by the narrow escape from being engulfed by the last of them. He could face no more but flew home to Erfurt still with ammunition and fuel unused.

76 Squadron flew Halifaxes from Holme-on-Spalding-Moor in Yorkshire. Three of the fourteen bombers it sent on this raid were shot down, all by *schräge Musik*. The first was near beacon Ida and its pilot, Flight Lieutenant Henry Coverley, survived to describe his aircraft's end.

I was humming 'Paper Doll' to myself when trouble started in the shape of air-to-air firing ahead of us and to our starboard. A lot of aircraft were going down; I thought they must be the Scarecrow shells that the Germans were reputed to be using. The first attack came very suddenly – I think one of the gunners identified the enemy aircraft as of the Ju 88 breed – but the gunners drove him off although he had made a mess of one of our starboard engines and also started a fire somewhere amidships.

The next thing I remember was cannon shells ripping through the aircraft, setting fire to the starboard wing, the rear gunner shouting that he had been hit – I think he meant his turret – and the aircraft refusing to answer to the rudder and elevator controls. The fighter, identified as a Me 110, had taken up a position directly underneath us in such a position that our mid-upper gunner was unable to bring fire to bear, and there he stayed while he pumped shells into us at short range. There being nothing more that I could do, I gave the order to abandon, while the aircraft, in spite of my efforts, went its own way persisting in a nose-up attitude and approaching the stall. . . . My own aircraft had been unserviceable so I was flying the one used by the squadron commander. It was known as the Royal Barge, and the C.O. must have been a bit sick when I failed to return it to him.

Coverley's low-key account of what must have been a terrible experience does not reveal that he remained at the controls of his burning Halifax for some time while all his crew baled out. Unfortunately the flight engineer's parachute had caught fire, probably as he left the burning Halifax, and he fell to his death.

Thirty miles further east the aircraft of Squadron Leader Kenneth Clack was attacked. Here the description is by the mid-upper gunner, Flight Sergeant Guy Edwards.

We were attacked from immediately below and it was obvious that we had encountered for the first time some form of aircraft that could fire vertically upwards with extreme accuracy because, from my position as mid-upper, I saw the tracer in the cannon shells pass vertically upwards through all four engines and the wings.

I can recall feeling the heat through the perspex as the flaming petrol from the engines passed alongside the turret and, for a few seconds, the aircraft maintained its flying position with four engines completely on fire, spilling four streams of burning petrol back as far as the tailplane. The Skipper told us to prepare to bale out. As I clipped the 'chute onto the harness, the aircraft stood on its nose and began to dive almost vertically. I would think that from the first shells hitting the aircraft to the point of it going into a dive would be no more than ten seconds.

A few moments later, the Halifax exploded and Edwards was blown, shoulders first, through the metal side of the aircraft. He was the only survivor. Among the crew was a Canadian second pilot who had only arrived at 76 Squadron two days earlier.

The third Halifax to go down from this squadron was captained by Flying Officer Gordon Greenacre, described by one of his friends as 'a tenacious and gallant pilot' and surprise was shown that he was only a flying officer and without a decoration at the time of his death. His crew had been over a year on their tour with many set-backs including a bad crash which had removed two members with serious injuries and also a two-week spell at the disciplinary centre at Sheffield for 'beating up' a training airfield to which they had once been diverted – hence no medals for the pilot.

Greenacre's Halifax had survived an earlier attack by a pair of single-engined fighters without being damaged, but then without warning it was hit in the port wing from beneath. A fire started which rapidly spread to the fuselage. The pilot ordered 'For God's sake get out', but only the wireless-operator was able to do so before the Halifax went into a dive and exploded. One more man, the flight engineer, survived this. The 'tenacious and gallant' Greenacre died with the remainder.

The shooting down of these three 76 Squadron crews has been highlighted to show how even experience was no shield against the unsuspected *schräge Musik* attack from underneath. Coverley, Clack and Greenacre had between them carried out a combined total of 105 successful operations before they took off for Nuremberg.

The Germans without the advantage of the upward-firing guns had to make their attacks in the older, conventional method *von unten hinten*. These combats usually lacked the swift execution stroke of the *schräge Musik* and the odds were slightly less balanced in favour of the attacker. Sometimes the fighter could creep up unseen and one good burst, especially if it hit the tail gunner, would decide the issue. If the fighter was spotted or failed to score decisively with his first burst, a long duel could develop with the bomber pilot desperately corkscrewing and the fighter trying again to get into a firing position. Hosepipes of red and green tracer crossed in the night as German pilot and British air gunner tried to deliver the final burst. If the German was a novice he might follow clumsily for some time before losing his quarry or being hit by return fire but the experienced German would often break off the combat to look for a less watchful victim.

One of these stern attacks can be seen through the eyes of the German pilot. He was Oberleutnant Fritz Lau who had taken charge of the four Messerschmitt 110s of II/NJG 1 that had survived the bombing of Saint-Dizier and had since flown from airfield to airfield finally landing at Athies near Laon that evening.

Against all our expectations we were ordered into action. I hurried with my crew to our plane, but we found that they had forgotten to refuel it so, while my comrades were taking off, we went looking for the fuel lorry. It was so late that I wondered if it was worthwhile taking off at all but then I decided to go in the hope of catching the bombers on their return flight.

After half an hour, I saw the first planes being shot down. Whenever we burned, we burned bright white; when our opponents burned, it was dark red. I remember on this night I only saw two white fires but many red ones. The radar operator reported a contact. I flew towards this and recognized a four-motored bomber. It was flying a defensive, snake-like path which we called a *Webeflug* [literally 'a weaving flight' – the bomber was probably doing a gentle corkscrew].

I tried to put myself in position to attack, but, whenever I thought I had got him in my sight, he had gone again and so it went, to and fro, for several minutes. My intention was to get within fifty metres and then shoot. Gradually, however, I got the impression that he would escape from me unless something happened quickly. I decided to attack at the next opportunity even if it was not completely suitable. The moment came when the bomber, somewhat higher than we, was in a gentle curve to the right. The distance was 100 to 150 metres; I raised the nose, took aim and fired. Within seconds, the bomber burst into flames, banked to the left and lost height quickly. I flew above him and we were able to see one man jumping out by parachute. The bomber broke into two burning parts which soon afterwards hit the ground.

Lau's radar operator plotted a bearing from the Ida radio beacon to the site of the Halifax's crash. On a map, this leads exactly to where a 158 Squadron aircraft came down. It was being flown by a mainly Australian crew on their first operation. As Lau says, only one man escaped by parachute. He was Flying Officer Shanahan, the bomb-aimer. Unfortunately Shanahan sustained head injuries which led to his death after the war.

The biggest score of bombers destroyed during the night was achieved, not by the crew of a *schräge Musik* fighter, but by one using the conventional forward-firing armament. Oberleutnant Martin Becker of I/NJG 6 had flown night fighters since 1941. He was an exceptionally skilled pilot who was often allowed to fly against the bombers when weather conditions were so bad that other fighters remained grounded. Only eight nights earlier, when Frankfurt had been raided, he had shot down six of the thirty-three aircraft lost by Bomber Command.

Against the Nuremberg raiders, Becker had taken off in his Messerschmitt 110 from Finthen airfield near Mainz and been ordered to Ida. Before reaching the beacon, however, he ran into the bomber-stream and started scoring at once. Becker's technique was to pull away to one side as soon as he made visual contact with a bomber ahead, then approach his target, still keeping as much to the side as possible in the hope that the bomber's tail gunner would not spot him. Then, at the last moment, Becker would slide across into the *von unten hinten* position and attempt to dispatch the bomber with one accurate burst.

Becker's first contact was a Halifax of 432 (Leaside) Squadron and the attack was probably made in his normal manner. The bomber's mid-upper gunner was the first to report a fighter behind; immediately, the tail gunner announced on the intercom that he had been watching it for some time presumably before Becker had slid across into his final attacking position. The delay in reporting the fighter had been fatal for the Canadian crew. A burst of cannon fire struck the Halifax before either of the gunners opened fire or the pilot could take evasive action. Only the three men in the nose of the bomber – navigator, wireless-operator and bomb-aimer – survived.

In the half hour from 00.20 to 00.50, Becker found and attacked three Halifaxes and three Lancasters between the Rhine and the end of the Long Leg. He claimed them all as destroyed and the Luftwaffe organization whose task it was to match bomber wrecks with night-fighter pilots' claims credited him with the six.

As no raid had developed on Aachen, Cologne or the Ruhr, many of the single-engined Wild Boar fighters had followed the bombers and attempted to join in the battle. Normally their lack of radar would have rendered them useless over the open country where the air battle was taking place, but the excellent visibility encouraged them to take part. There are many reports of bombers being attacked by these Focke-Wulf 190s and Messerschmitt 109s and one experienced Pathfinder pilot records that 'it was one of only two occasions when I saw single-engined fighters at night and the only occasion when I saw them doing "curve of pursuit" attacks as if they were operating in broad daylight' (Flight Lieutenant C. B. Owen, 97 Squadron). Several of the reports mention that the small fighters hunted in pairs.

Despite their efforts, these Wild Boar pilots did not achieve much; their training and equipment was just not up to the sophisticated business of successful night interception away from a target city, even in moonlight. Most of the attacks consisted of one quick pass at a bomber; after that, neither bomber nor fighter saw each other again. There are only two confirmed instances of bombers falling to single-engined fighters on the outward flight. During the same period, on the other hand, four such fighters were claimed as destroyed by the British bombers.

The first of the two bombers shot down by the Wild Boars was observed by an Australian pilot who recorded the combat in his diary two days later.

South of Cologne we were flying fairly close to another Lanc which we could see clearly in the moonlight. A single-engined fighter attacked him but apparently he did not see it because he took no evasive action at all. He was hit in a fuel tank and the flames seemed huge in comparison to the size of the aircraft, like a great white torch in the sky. To protect my own and the gunner's night vision I told them not to look at it and, after a brief glance, did not look at it myself but told the flight engineer to watch it to see if any parachutes came out. He did not see any. (Flight Sergeant H. J. Whittick, 460 Squadron)

Almost immediately, Whittick's own Lancaster was attacked by two single-engined fighters but he evaded them.

The second such combat was also seen and the report was later recorded in a Bomber Command summary by an unknown crew but the location mentioned in the summary identifies the victim as an Australian Lancaster which came, like Flight Sergeant Whittick, from 460 Squadron. The crew was a veteran one, nearing the end of its second tour. The pilot was Squadron Leader Eric Utz, D.F.C. and Bar, a grazier from the 'New England' district of New South Wales. He was, in fact, Flight Sergeant Whittick's flight commander. Another pilot on the squadron describes Utz as 'a quiet chap but a very efficient and confident pilot who seemed to be as certain as anyone could be of finishing his tour. His loss was taken very hard by the squadron.'

The *Bürgermeister* of the small village of Obernhausen, near Fulda, who also witnessed the crash, counted six bursts of fire as the small fighter attacked again and again. The Lancaster exploded in the air and only one man, the navigator, was blown out and managed to open his parachute.

Some bombers, of course, sustained serious damage but, due either to the skill of the pilot and gunners, the clumsiness or faintheartedness of the German or just plain luck, managed to escape the final attack that would have finished them off. The bombers themselves were capable of withstanding a great deal of damage; it was fire reaching the heavy loads of fuel and bombs that caused most of the crashes on the outward flight. If there was no fire or if the fire could be quickly extinguished, if the pilot was not seriously hurt and managed to evade the fighter, the bomber stood a good chance of reaching safety. The bombs were immediately dumped, for they were now over Germany and discretion in this matter was unnecessary. The bomber then hauled out of the stream and set a course for home.

Some bombers were attacked over and over again and still survived. The Lancaster of Pilot Officer D. Paul of 61 Squadron ran into the German fighters near beacon Ida. The navigator, Flight Sergeant R.A.F. Griffin, came out of his position and

looked out and saw two German single-engined fighters wing tip to wing tip about 100 feet above us; they whizzed over our heads and disappeared. Then we were attacked. I saw this one pulling away above us. It was a Ju 88. I distinctly remember seeing a stream of tracer bullets, probably from our mid-upper turret, going straight into his belly but with no apparent effect. We heard that they had armour plating and our ·303 bullets could not damage them.

The Lancaster fought off two more attacks in the next fifteen minutes by vigorous corkscrewing and good work by the gunners but finished up at only 10,000 feet and with two engines stopped. The pilot decided to get rid of his bombs and turned back. The gunners claimed two German fighters damaged and one probable.

Another Lancaster, this time from 9 Squadron, was also hit near beacon Ida. The tail gunner, Sergeant B. Pinchin, describes the attack.

We were attacked first from the starboard quarter but we cork-screwed and, after one full corkscrew, I reported to the captain that the attack had been broken off and we resumed flying straight and level again. We had done ten trips and felt that we knew what it was all about. I felt we had lost him but only a few seconds later there was a hell of a clatter. We had been hit by another fighter that we hadn't seen. He had sprayed the area between the rear door and the end of the bomb bay. The hydraulics to my turret caught fire and the whole of the fuselage up to the mid-upper turret was in flames. Through these I could see the mid-upper gunner getting down from his turret and he started to crawl up to the front of the plane. The pilot decided to drop all our bomb load and dive the flames out. I didn't think the fire would go out and was expecting to be ordered to bale out but, at 13,000 feet, the fire did go out.

The wireless-operator was sent back to see to the other gunner but found him dead. Pilot Officer Forrest decided to stay with the stream and later flew right over Nuremberg with empty bomb bay. When the dead gunner was removed from the aircraft on landing at Bardney, he was apparently unmarked but the medical officer found that a small fragment of cannon shell had entered his stomach and cut the small intestine.

Several pilots, like Forrest, stayed with the stream after they had jettisoned their bombs, believing that there was more safety in the company of others than in attempting a lone flight to England. In this, they were probably wrong; the Germans had sent their whole strength against the stream and solitary aircraft were usually quite free from further attacks.

Sergeant R. C. Corker, a flight engineer in a 578 Squadron Halifax, describes another attack.

We were obviously going to be busy so I decided to crib and make my log up for the next thirty minutes. I was bending over and writing it up on the floor when, without any warning at all, we were attacked from underneath. There was an enormous bang as a cannon shell exploded in the starboard-inner engine and four or five pieces caught me in the fleshy part of the bottom. I let out a yell and the Skipper responded in commendable fashion and went into a corkscrew. The fighter shot across our nose and attacked another Halifax about eleven o'clock high from us. It blew up. He had made the two attacks in about twenty seconds.

After a burning engine and a smouldering load of incendiaries had been dealt with, the wireless-operator attempted to dress Corker's wound.

He said, 'Drop your trousers' but I declined, it was too cold for that. I felt something down my legs and my feet squelching in my flying boots. I had thoughts of bleeding to death and in the end took a torch and had a look at my boots. It was only hydraulic fluid. I was able to carry on and we got home alright.

We last met Sergeant Patfield in his bomb-aimer's position, with maps, brown paper, string and bundles of Window all around him. His aircraft had flown through the air battle until, near the Otto radio beacon, they were attacked simultaneously by no less than three fighters, two Junkers 88s and a Messerschmitt 110. Patfield again:

We heard the gunners firing like mad and a yell from the rear gunner 'Look out Skipper. Three of them coming in.' At the same time there was a terrific explosion and, all around, things whizzing about. A sickly smell of smoke and cordite and I was almost thrown on my back as the aircraft tilted at a crazy angle and went into a steep dive. My first impressions were of flames around me and my face very wet and sticky. Blood! But I felt no pain and seemed to be in one piece. This sticky mess turned out to be the hydraulic oil from the gun turret just above my head, as a considerable part of the turret had disappeared and the severed pipes spewed out their contents over me.

To do justice to the remainder of Patfield's account would require a small book of its own. One engine had been hit; there were small fires in the cockpit and the nose; the astro-dome and pilot's windscreen were both smashed and the main hatch had disappeared. Four men – navigator, flight engineer, wireless-operator and one gunner – were injured, the first three seriously. The injured were attended to and then Patfield tackled the navigation, finding the chart table 'a shambles with torn maps, quite a bit of blood and no pro-tractors or any other navigating instrument to be seen anywhere. This wasn't a bit like the navigation exercises I had done during training and the crew hoping I would get them home!' He worked out a rough course for the pilot but, then, concentration became more difficult. He slid from his seat and spent the rest of the flight under the navigation table. His oxygen mask had been damaged in the attack.

And so this Lancaster found its way home, with two wounded men under morphia, two more wounded but still at their posts, one man out through oxygen failure and only the pilot and tail gunner properly fit. Sitting in an icy gale which lashed through his smashed windscreen, the pilot, Pilot Officer D. C. Freeman on only his third operation, managed to reach England and crash-landed at Foulsham. *

The experiences of a Canadian Halifax crew, who were attacked head-on by a fighter, show how exceptional was the visibility.

At briefing we knew the trip would be rough going, just how rough became apparent with a beautiful clear night and lots of fighter activity – easy to see the tracer, then the ball of fire and scratch one of Bomber Command. I began to think that what I saw could not be bombers going down but some German scare tech-nique but I soon realized that it was the real thing and that Bomber Command was taking some terrible punishment.

---

* Two men in this crew were decorated for their actions on this night; by a coincidence they were both Lincolnshire men. Pilot Officer Freeman of Gains-borough received the D.F.C. and the wireless-operator, Sergeant L. Chapman from a village near Spalding, was awarded the rare Conspicuous Gallantry Medal for remaining at his set despite serious injury. The crew never flew together again and unfortunately Freeman, Chapman and the two gunners were killed in later raids.

The fact that I was hit head-on gives some indication of the visibility; all I saw was white tracer getting nearer, then *Bang!* It all happened in one or two seconds. The aircraft was on fire and I knew we probably had about ten seconds to get out. A small panic developed among the boys trying to get the hatch open but there always seemed to be at least one guy standing on it. We were hit again from above and behind and the flames were shot right out by this second burst, so I ordered 'Hold everything' and no one jumped. We were hit a third time and had lost a lot of height. We jettisoned the incendiaries and continued on our happy way with the main stream across Nuremberg. The aircraft would only fly at just above the stalling speed and so we rapidly fell behind. We were sharpened up by Flak several times and only by the grace of God reached England. (Flying Officer F. F. Hamilton, 424 Squadron)

One feels that a less calm and resolute pilot than Hamilton would never have brought this aircraft home.*

There were two instances where aircraft returned with incomplete crews. It is understandable that if, as Flying Officer Hamilton says, a bomber might have only ten seconds to live once it had been set on fire, some men should jump first and ask questions later. Indeed, many survivors of crashed bombers owe their lives to such swift action but, in those instances where the bomber recovered and returned home, such premature parachute escapes could be acutely embarrassing to the men concerned.

A 166 Squadron Lancaster with a mixed crew of three Canadians, three Englishmen and a Northern Irishman was attacked by a Messerschmitt 110 which came so close that the tail gunner 'could not focus on the whole wing span'. There were two short, almost simultaneous bursts of fire – one from the German, which set the Lancaster alight, and the tail gunner's return fire, which caused the Messerschmitt to blow up. The combat had lasted for perhaps three seconds.

The bomber had been seriously damaged and the fire, mostly in the tail, had good hold so the Canadian pilot ordered his crew to prepare to bale out, but first dived hard in a last attempt to save the Lancaster by blowing out the fire. Sergeant Ben Wilkinson says,

* Flying Officer Hamilton also received a D.F.C. for his action, adding it to a D.F.M. awarded earlier. He survived two tours and returned safely to his home in Regina, Saskatchewan.

I got out of the mid-upper turret, put my parachute on and went to the rear door. We were on fire right back to the rear turret. I found the tail gunner standing there too, with his intercom plugged into the point there. He gave me a thumbs down signal which I took to be the signal to bale out. The mid-upper was supposed to go first, so out I went.

In fact, the pilot had decided to delay the bale out and try to save his Lancaster. The tail gunner, Sergeant 'Paddy' Manuel, put out the fire, being badly burnt on the face in the process, then manned the empty mid-upper turret until he collapsed. After more adventures, the Lancaster landed safely at Kirmington.

The gunner who had parachuted was eventually captured and, not meeting any of his fellow crew members, assumed that his aircraft had blown up and they had all perished.*

Almost certainly the narrowest escape and the most adventurous return flight was that of a 578 Squadron Halifax. For reasons which will become obvious later, a closer look should be taken at its captain, Pilot Officer Cyril Barton. Although only twenty-two and with the face of a boy, Barton had already flown his crew on seventeen operations including five to Berlin. He was completely untypical of the average bomber pilot, being a quiet-living and intensely devout Christian who pressed his crew into attending the village church, at Burn near Selby, and confessed that he had to screw up his courage to kneel and pray each evening in the presence of the two officers who were his room companions.

Barton's Halifax was well into Germany before being attacked. Within a few seconds, the aircraft had sustained terrible damage – all turrets were out of action, one engine had failed, the radio and the intercom were damaged and two fuel tanks were leaking. Fortunately there was no fire.

Bombers were fitted with an emergency signalling system for crew members to communicate with each other by means of button-controlled lights. Barton had an arrangement with his gunners that, in the event of intercom failure, they would

* Sergeant Manuel from Belfast received the D.F.M. for his bravery. Sergeant Wilkinson, from Sheffield, did not discover the details of what had happened that night until I re-introduced him to four members of the crew in 1972. The pilot, Pilot Officer P. J. Wilson of Edmonton, Alberta, received the D.F.C. and, with two new gunners, went on to complete a tour with the Pathfinders.

signal for evasive action on this system and this is what they did. Unfortunately, the three men in the nose of the Halifax took these signals as the order to abandon the aircraft. The fighter was shaken off but Barton found himself with a crippled aircraft and without a bomb-aimer, navigator or wireless-operator. The key men in his bomb-aiming and navigational team had baled out.

Bomber crews had always been told that two things were expected of them: they were to find and bomb their targets if at all possible and they were to do their utmost to get their precious bombers home. Even so, none would have blamed Barton if he had given up and baled out with the remainder of his crew or, at the very least, if he had dumped his load of incendiaries and turned for home. But he took neither of these courses of action. They were not too far from the target so he decided to fly on and attempt to deliver his incendiaries to Nuremberg. There surely cannot have been a better example of the 'Press on regardless' spirit of Bomber Command. We shall pick up the story of Cyril Barton and his depleted crew later.

There were other crews who only narrowly escaped with their lives. The Lancaster of Flying Officer E. R. Penman of 106 Squadron survived repeated attacks by two night fighters working together. First one turret and then a second was put out of action and an engine caught fire but Penman managed to shake off the fighters and struggle back to England. When he touched down at the emergency airfield at Manston, the undercarriage collapsed. Pilot Officer J. R. Dickenson of 49 Squadron also survived all his turrets being put out of action and escaped only after a desperate cork-screwing session that went on for eight minutes during which Dickenson later reported: 'the gunners' patter throughout the attack was highly commendable'. The skilful gunners who saved this crew were Sergeants E. Ellenor and R. H. Hudson. An Australian, Pilot Officer D. A. Woods of 514 Squadron, brought his Lancaster back for an emergency landing at Woodbridge after five fighter attacks. His rear turret had frozen and a defect in the mid-upper turret prevented it firing more than four rounds at a time.

No more details of these engagements can be given. Penman, Dickenson, Woods and all their crew members were killed on later raids.

Most bomber operations were carried out in complete darkness and the crews rarely saw much of other aircraft, friendly or hostile; only an occasional burst of tracer or anti-aircraft shell and the explosion when one of their fellow crews went down. So intense and concentrated was the action on the Long Leg, however, and so good was the visibility, that many hundreds of the bomber men witnessed clearly the terrible sight of their comrades meeting sudden death. Their own words describe best what they saw and what they felt.

Suddenly our pilot pulled up the kite almost on its tail and a black shadow passed below, too near to identify except that it was one of theirs. Trying to get back on an even keel and on course took a little time but, when we did manage it, the sight to the rear, of aircraft on fire and parachutes opening, was a fearful sight indeed. We became extra alert. The bomb-aimer took his place in the nose at his bombing station, the wireless-op climbed into the front turret, the two gunners kept their own stations and I, as flight engineer, was on the starboard side bubble. For the first time for days, I took the wakey-wakey pills prescribed for long trips. (Flight Sergeant H. Sutcliffe, 15 Squadron)

I was in the nose of our Halifax and no matter in which direction I looked I could see tracer fire and balls of flame falling, which I believe were aircraft going down. We were in the middle of all the activity so I put on my parachute as I envisaged a short career in Bomber Command. Incidentally, on only one other occasion during my tour did I deem this action necessary. (Flying Officer C. E. Willis, 640 Squadron)

Our first encounter was with a Ju 88 which we avoided successfully by rapid and continuous corkscrew tactics. That same fighter was observed to attack a Halifax from close on our starboard side, the attack taking place as usual from astern and below. The Halifax took no evasive action whatsoever and apparently was hit in the bomb bay which triggered an amazing fireball. (Flight Lieutenant G. A. Berry, 61 Squadron)

The tail gunner was reporting endlessly that aircraft were going down in flames – it was his duty to do so. The pilot, feeling that morale was falling, particularly among those of us who couldn't see outside, told him to shut up. A bomber blew up only about two hundred yards away on our port side. The blast from it threw us nearly onto our back and I thought we were going down too. Then, a little later, the tail gunner told us that a Junkers 88 was hovering just above us. He didn't fire and, then, suddenly he was whipped away by our slipstream and we didn't see him again. (Flight Sergeant S. Welch, 427 Squadron)

One of the strangest attacks I saw was on a Lanc flying straight and level about a mile away. She was being repeatedly attacked from dead astern but took no evasive action and there was no answering fire from her guns. I concluded that all on board were either dead or wounded and watched until she disappeared, still flying a level course. (Sergeant F. V. Shaw, 12 Squadron)

Sergeant Shaw's own aircraft was attacked over Nuremberg and Shaw suffered an eye injury. He never flew again.

I particularly remember seeing a twin-engined night fighter, with navigation lights on, approximately 1,000 yards dead astern and above my aircraft. He was firing rapid bursts of cannon fire at numerous bombers with no serious results to my knowledge. A rear gunner of an aircraft some distance astern of us fired a burst from his Brownings at this particular fighter but the range was too great and I could see his tracer falling short. (Sergeant R. S. Cripps, 158 Squadron)

I saw the light of tracer fire and an aircraft hit and going down on fire. Its markers must have been jettisoned for I saw them burst below. I identified the markers as belonging to those of the aircraft which had taken off just before me and was sure then that it was my friend Len Hyde. (Flight Lieutenant C. S. Chatten, 97 Squadron)

Flight Lieutenant Hyde's aircraft, a Pathfinder Blind Backer-Up, was shot down in this area. There were no survivors.

I recall an attack on a Lanc about 400 yards on our port beam, level. It was hit by a fighter and a stream of burning petrol poured back from the starboard inner as one of the crew baled out of the starboard entry door. He was hit by the petrol, pulled his rip cord and the parachute went up in a flash. He probably had about 22,000 feet to fall. (Sergeant E. Wilkins, 626 Squadron)

Our navigator gave up logging aircraft shot down. We arbitrarily decided *if* they were decoys it was a waste of time and *if* they were for real we had better get on the ball, get to Nuremberg and safely home. For the first time, I think my nineteen-year-old mind grasped the fact that operations were NOT a 'piece of cake'. (Sergeant W. J Blackburn, 12 Squadron)

When we got right into this area where lots of aircraft were going down, I looked back out of the blister at the side of the cockpit towards England, towards Plymouth where my girl friend, Elsie, lived. I said out loud, with the intercom off, 'Goodbye Elsie, Goodbye Elsie.' I quite reconciled myself to getting killed and after that I felt a great calm. (Sergeant H. W. Hudson, 106 Squadron) *

It was obvious that losses were going to be high – one could navigate on the blazing wrecks below – and this was one occasion when I was really convinced that we had 'had it' as there was still a long way to go. Others evidently thought the same as another Lanc practically formated with us for quite some time for moral support. (Flying Officer L. Young, 103 Squadron)

I will state that, in all the trips I had been on, and this was number forty-eight, I have never been so frightened. I was nearing the end of my second tour and this, of course, added to the anxiety. It was also my twentieth birthday and I honestly thought I would never see another. (Flying Officer J. D. Routledge, 405 Squadron)

I had never been a deeply religious person, yet in times of danger when I was operational, I always imagined myself repeating the 23rd Psalm *The Lord is my Shepherd*. That night, I didn't imagine it. For hours on end I repeated it out loud, for that was how much I was afraid. I had never before seen parachutes descending at night, but that night I did. (Flight Sergeant F. A. Taylor, 626 Squadron)

This kind of pressure we suffered, as a rule, for minutes; in this case it was for hour after hour. I do not think there were many moments when some aircraft somewhere was not under attack. Maybe you can put into words a memory of fighter flares shedding light from above, aircraft burning on the ground illuminating us from below. The sight of short bursts of red and green tracer which nearly always resulted in the explosion of the bomber being attacked. Tired eyes searching the sky with a desperation born of terror, looking for the unseen enemy. The emotional shock and physical shock each time another machine hit the ground or were torn to pieces in the air. Of sitting, as it were, on a platform overlooking the end of the world. Watching a Lancaster blazing from end to end and flying straight and level for what seemed like forever. The night, which seemed empty and was obviously not, and, from which, at any moment may come the end of everything. (Flight Sergeant R. Rhodes, 35 Squadron)

* This flight engineer later married his girl friend. The crew returned safely from Nuremberg which was the last operation of their tour. Five members of the crew are now business associates in a London company.

Review at 00.45

At 00.45, the leading bombers reached the end of the Long Leg and started to turn towards Nuremberg. It is a suitable time to leave detailed descriptions of the battle and turn to the factual progress of it and the activities of some of the less obvious of its participants.

The head of the bomber-stream – the leading Pathfinders and their Supporters and the first of the five waves of the Main Force – had managed to slip through the gap south of Bonn almost unmolested, probably helped by a higher than average standard of navigation which had kept them on track and away from the German fighters waiting at the Ida radio beacon. It was when the aircraft behind the leaders had strayed north between Bonn and Cologne and into the arms of the German fighters that the main clash had erupted.

An analysis of the losses suffered by the various elements making up the bomber-stream, the debriefing reports of returned crews and the memories of men involved, all enable a quite precise picture to be given of which parts of the stream were suffering. The main blow at Ida had fallen on the centre and rear, that is on the third and fourth waves of the Main Force, and had slowly moved forward through the stream to involve the second wave and some of the first. The leading Pathfinders and the Supporters retained their blessed immunity at the front of the stream and were never under fighter attack at any time. The tail of the stream, usually reckoned to be the most dangerous place, also did not suffer heavily.

However, it would be misleading to talk too much of waves as though the bomber-stream was still compact. There had been much scattering when the German fighters struck at Ida but the winds too were responsible for a further dispersal. In spite of the fact that those Windfinder aircraft at the front of the stream were not under serious attack, the Broadcast Wind system was functioning even worse. The Pathfinder papers, which had complained of only receiving thirteen usable wind reports instead of the expected thirty-six earlier in the flight, show that from the Long Leg only nine were received. Group winds, broadcasts from England at 00.33, contained variations of up to 20 m.p.h. In addition, the 290 degrees estimate which appeared in all the broadcast winds was incorrect; the wind was probably blowing exactly from west to east, that is from 270 degrees, on the whole of the Long Leg. These variations in wind speeds and the error in direction resulted in the stream becoming progressively longer and spreading even more to the north of the correct track.

And so the battle had raged four miles up in the night sky above the Rhine Valley and the wooded country of the Westerwald, past the towns of Wetzlar and Giessen and on over the hills of the Vogelsberg to beyond Fulda. Soon after crossing the Rhine, a thin sheet of cloud had appeared many thousands of feet below the height at which the bombers were flying, but this had brought more danger rather than help to the bombers for, as one Pathfinder pilot noted, 'aircraft lower than ourselves stood out like flies on a tablecloth. It must have been a night-fighter pilot's dream.' The treacherous vapour trails had continued at certain heights and there was never any high cloud on the outward flight in which the bombers might have sheltered.

Not all the shot-down bombers had been the victims of night fighters. Besides the secret-operations Halifax shot down by Flak into the Scheldt, three of the Nuremberg-bound force had strayed off track and had fallen to the guns of Liège, Bonn and Coblenz and more were to fall in this way.

The small town of Westerburg lies in the heart of the sparsely populated, wooded area of the Westerwald which stretches for forty miles east from the Rhine. It was a country town like many others in Germany with no industry and it contained nothing more important than a railway bridge which, if destroyed by bombing, would have disrupted local communications. There was however talk of there being a secret factory in the nearby woods, reputed to be making parts for V-weapons, and a British airman shot down near Westerburg that night saw his first jet aircraft taking off from a small local airfield before he was captured. Westerburg was just three miles north of the bombers' route to Nuremberg and it was not marked on the crews' Flak map as being a defended town.

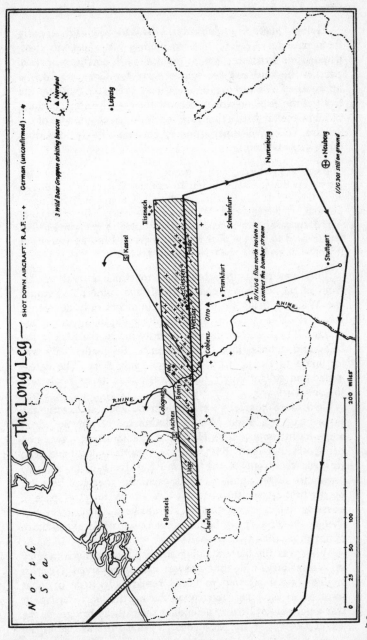

The Long Leg — SHOT DOWN AIRCRAFT: R.A.F.···+   German (unconfirmed)····✱

3 Wild Boar Gruppen orbiting beacon

✱ Nordpol
▲

✕

North
Sea

• Leipzig

• Brussels

RHINE

Charleroi

Liège

Aachen

Cologne

Bonn

Lahn

RHINE

Coblenz

• Kassel

Eisenach

Giessen

Wetzlar

Otto

Fulda

• Frankfurt

Schweinfurt

II/NJG6 flies north to
contact the bomber stream

• Nuremberg

• Stuttgart

U/IO 301 still on ground
⊕ • Neuburg

0   25   50   100   200 miles

Map 6

Flying Officer Guy Johnston, who had taken off so early from Elsham Wolds, had concluded his short air test, decided his Lancaster was in good enough condition to take part in the raid and set course early for Germany. As he approached Westerburg he must have been still flying at the front of the bomber-stream because the crew had seen nothing at all of the air battle that had developed in the middle of the stream. The mid-upper gunner, Sergeant Fealy, describes what happened next.

I was in my turret, facing astern, when I saw a salvo of Flak bursts on the starboard beam. It was the first thing I had seen since take-off. It was distant enough to look pretty but not danger-ous and I didn't report it. Within a few seconds, another group of bursts appeared 50 per cent nearer. I started to get worried then and decided to tell the pilot to start weaving. I had no sooner got my hand to my mike, than the aircraft was hit.

This was radar-predicted Flak, to which aircraft at the front of the bomber-stream were always vulnerable because the Window being dropped by all bombers only developed into a sizeable cloud in time to protect the main part of the stream. The Lancaster had been badly hit by the Flak in the belly and it burst into flames at once. Sergeant Fealy was fortunate to escape with both legs badly hurt. The deter-mined and gallant Guy Johnston was not so lucky. Fealy was the only survivor.

Two more bombers were caught by Flak at exactly the same place – a Blind Marker-Illuminator of 635 Squadron and a flight commander's Halifax of 158 Squadron – two men being killed in each. Both of these aircraft would have been towards the front of the stream. Survivors from the two crews are of the opinion that in each case they had been hit by the first salvo aimed at their aircraft. Within the space of possibly five minutes, this highly efficient Flak battery had shot down three heavy bombers for the possible expenditure of not more than twenty shells.

What was the battery doing there? Despite much inquiry in Westerburg, a definite answer cannot be given. German civilians were allowed to know remarkably little of what went on in their neighbourhood during the war. Perhaps it was a permanent battery defending the railway bridge, or the secret factory, or the jet airfield. Perhaps it was one of the mobile railway batteries that chance or good judgement had placed in a siding at Westerburg station. Sergeant Fealy was told by the Germans on his capture that his aircraft had been shot down by guns manned by women. Whoever it was had served the Fatherland well that night.

Few of the several thousand men flying in the British bombers realized that, while their own aircraft were being attacked with such terrible effect by the German night fighters, there was also a considerable number of friendly fighters in the same area attempting to protect their bomber comrades. Fifty-five Mosquitoes and four American fighters had been dispatched on Intruder or Serrate operations. Much of the Intruder effort over the German airfields took place later in the night and will be described in another chapter but the Serrate fighters had been around and even in the bomber-stream while the German fighters had been making their heaviest attacks. What had these Serrate crews been able to achieve?

The Mosquitoes carried two electronic devices – the Serrate set which could pick up the impulses of the older Lichtenstein radar set with which the German night fighters had been equipped in 1943. The Serrate could home upon these from as much as sixty miles distance under certain conditions but it was no good for close work and the final stage of the chase had to be carried out with the second device – an ordinary radar set, named the A.I. This operated in much the same way as the sets being used by the Germans. Even in normal times, the task of the Serrate men was far more difficult than that of a German night-fighter crew but, now that the new German SN–2 radar set which was unknown to the R.A.F. was in use, the Serrate sets could not home on to the enemy radar impulses.

100 Group had ordered a maximum effort by its Serrate squadrons but so short were they of crews qualified in this difficult art that only nineteen Mosquitoes had taken off from their airfields at Little Snoring and West Raynham. Two turned back with technical trouble and the remainder flew on to join this unequal battle. They would patrol where the Germans were expected to be found using their radar sets – over the fighter beacons and around the bomber-stream. They could not operate effectively in the bomber-stream

itself because their A.I. radars could not distinguish friend from foe and they were in great danger in the stream from the bombers' gunners. The bomber crews considered any twin-engined aircraft as an enemy.

In spite of the most determined efforts by their crews, the Serrate aircraft could do little to help the bombers. Not surprisingly the Serrate sets picked up few real contacts and many of the Mosquito crews reverted to using the A.I. set only, but, as the bomber-stream had become so scattered, only a few of the many contacts they picked up in this way turned out to be Germans.

A 239 Squadron Mosquito which was patrolling well ahead of the bomber-stream picked up an A.I. contact and intercepted a German fighter which resulted in the two fighters having an old-fashioned dog-fight in the brilliant moonlight. Round and round they went for twelve minutes, each trying to get into a killing position on the other's tail, until the two finally lost each other in the haze near the ground.

Another Mosquito from the same squadron, with an all-N.C.O. crew – Flight Sergeants Campbell and Phillips – picked up a Junkers 88, again on A.I. not Serrate, near beacon Ida. They attacked once but missed and lost their contact. A few minutes later they again found and attacked a Junkers 88, possibly the same one for its rear gunner was alert and put just seven bullets into the Mosquito, setting an engine on fire. But this time Campbell and Phillips had not missed. One engine on the German aircraft blew up and the Mosquito crew were able to see it fall all the way to the ground where it crashed and exploded only a short distance from the Ida beacon. The Mosquito's engine fire was extinguished and the fighter nursed safely home on one engine.

Flight Lieutenant Woodman, who had protested to 100 Group H.Q. about the route being too near to the German fighter beacons, became so frustrated that he went right into the bomber-stream in the hope of catching a German fighter there. His radar operator, Flying Officer Kemmis, started picking up contacts at once. Woodman describes the results:

Twice we tried to turn Serrate contacts into A.I. contacts but, with all the bombers there, it was odds of twenty to one against it being a Hun. Twice I came up under bombers but turned away before the rear gunners saw me. 100 Group Mossies were Huns to the bomber boys. The third time, the rear gunner spotted me, gave me a burst but, at the same time, warned his pilot. The bomber did a turning dive to port and the fire went over my head. Kemmis, his head glued to the radar – he never once raised it in spite of my lurid description of the slaughter going on outside – tried hard to pick out two contacts close together, possibly a Hun after a bomber. We could have got very close to a Hun in this way but the bomber suddenly became a sheet of flame across the night sky only a mile or so ahead and the Hun had quickly switched to another bomber and become just one of the twenty or so other blips on the A.I.

There were to be no victories for Woodman and his radar operator on this night despite further efforts.

Another Serrate crew, patrolling south of the Ruhr, kept getting repeated contacts on their Serrate set which always led them to the same spot near Cologne. Here, they found that each chase became a tight orbit with the contact always below them. The Germans appear to have been transmitting decoy signals in an attempt to lure the Mosquitoes down to be shot at by Flak. The ruse did not work with this aircraft which escaped unharmed but another Serrate crew, who had several abortive chases in the same area and were trapped three times in cones of searchlights, were probably victims of the same trap.

The first time was momentarily frightening, because one minute all is blackness, then suddenly, the night becomes mid-day in full sunshine. One feels very naked and exposed, more so with the knowledge that many muzzles are pointing in your direction! It is at this time that one's ability for evasive tactics comes to the fore. Having managed to evade the cone of lights, we then had to establish our position and continue the operation. On the second illumination I was more prepared, having survived the shock of the first episode. I must say that the Germans were quite good search-lighters. It was their third and last coning that resulted in some damage from Flak. Having felt the impact and seen a hole appear in the wing and, being near the end of my patrol time, I decided to return to base, hoping that no main structure had been damaged. With a few prayers, a lot of luck and a detour round the Flak-infested Hook of Holland we returned safely.

Once again a calm account, this time by Pilot Officer Rolfe of 141 Squadron, does not do full justice to this crew who

were caught time and time again by searchlights and became
the target for all the Flak in the area and still kept returning
to their patrol area.

The entire 100 Group effort had resulted in only seventeen
aircraft reaching the vital area and the switch by the Germans
from Lichtenstein to SN-2 had resulted in only two Mosquitoes even firing their guns. One German night fighter
had been destroyed at a cost of two Mosquitoes damaged.

Another effort by Mosquito aircraft to help the heavy
bombers – the attempted spoof bombing raid on Kassel – had
also come to nothing. This was the final and largest of three
such raids carried out by 8 Group aircraft and was an interesting little operation. Twenty Mosquitoes had taken the
same route as the Nuremberg force where, flying well
above the heavies, their crews had had a grandstand view of
the air battle. They left the main route where it crossed the
Rhine near Bonn and flew north-east, dropping German-type
fighter flares to draw the enemy fighters and also Windowing furiously in an attempt to make themselves look like a
large force of heavy bombers. The route they were taking
represented a threat either to Kassel 110 miles away or to
Berlin some distance further on. The Bomber Command term
for this type of diversion was 'side-stepping'.

This well-planned operation was executed perfectly and
every aircraft performed its allotted function. Much Window
and a long line of flares were dropped all the way to Kassel.
There, two loads of green and yellow target indicators were
accurately placed by H2S and thirty-six 500-pounder bombs
dropped around them. Two civilians were killed and twenty-
six injured but little material damage was done in a city that
Bomber Command had already claimed as 'virtually destroyed' in 1943. The Mosquitoes turned west and flew home
without loss, reporting on their return that the Kassel Flak
could be considered 'very poor'.

In their operations rooms, the Germans plotted the flight
of the Mosquitoes to Kassel but otherwise ignored it completely. Their reconnaissance aircraft had easily remained in
visual touch with the real bomber-stream.

The sophisticated operations room of the German fighter
divisions had been operating at full pressure. The vital
decisions as to when the night-fighter Gruppen should take
off and to which radio beacons they should fly had been taken

earlier and the fighters had become heavily involved in the battle. The main effort was now concentrated on plotting the progress of this battle on the huge screen in each operations room and attempting to forecast which city or town would become the bombers' target.

In every room there were several rows of seated Luftwaffe girls each of whom wore a telephone headset linking her directly to one particular source of information. Every radar or radio report, every visual sighting from the ground or from an aircraft actually in touch with the bombers immediately reached one of these girls. She controlled a torch which projected a thin but powerful beam onto the screen. As soon as her informant sent in fresh information, she moved her distinctive symbol a little further along the screen. These girls were known as *Lichtspucker* – 'light spitters'. All reports were sent simultaneously to each of the five operations rooms so that every divisional commander and his staff could tell exactly what was happening 'with about one minute's delay' as General Galland was later to write. A photograph was taken of the screen every five minutes for the division's war diary and also so that a post-mortem could later be carried out on the decisions taken and tactics employed.

The Germans had obviously expected that the raid would not involve a deep penetration on this moonlight night but, as the bombers had flown past the Ruhr and then past the Frankfurt area without deviating from their straight easterly path, the Germans had to think afresh where the eventual target would be. Their Tame Boar aircraft were already in successful contact with the bombers but there remained four Wild Boar Gruppen, as yet still on the ground, which might be brought into action over the target if this could be guessed in time for the single-engined fighters to take off and reach it. For this to happen, a forecast would have to be now made as to which way the bombers would turn at their next turning point. Would it be north or would it be south? It was the next of the important decisions that the Germans had to take.

Although there are no documents recording the choice made, a study of the eventual disposition of the Wild Boar Gruppen and the clear memory of a German pilot who can recall the running commentary at this point shows that, for once, a mistake was made. Three single-engined Gruppen near Berlin were ordered to take off, not for a flight south, but to assemble over the Nordpol beacon south-west of Berlin and convenient for Wild Boar action over Berlin or any of the cities in this area. 1/JG 301, the Messerschmitt 109 Gruppe at Neuburg, only fifty-five miles south of Nuremberg, received no orders. The fighter-pilot listening to the running commentary remembers being told that the bombers were expected to turn north and that Berlin or Leipzig were possible targets.

Despite this error, the Germans had already achieved their greatest concentration of night fighters at the right time and place. Something between 200 and 250 night fighters had reached the general area of the battle.

However, in spite of the impressive numbers of the German fighters reaching the right area the bomber crews could count themselves fortunate that several factors were operating in their favour and the execution could have been much greater. A high proportion of the German pilots, although they had the right aircraft and radar and had been sent to the right beacons, were never a menace due to the low average of competence from which the Luftwaffe's night-fighter arm was suffering. Probably half of the Germans stumbled around in the night sky and never once got behind a bomber. At least one third of all bombers shot down by fighters on this night were accounted for by just eight successful German crews. One of these, which shot down three bombers, found next morning that they were the only crew from their Gruppe to have scored. Many of the others had been milling around beacon Ida long after the battle had passed on, unable to take advantage of the running commentary or unwilling to fly too far from their own airfield. Other unsuccessful crews came from the more distant Gruppen that did not arrive in time and could only struggle along in the wake of the battle without ever catching up.

Then there were the plain unlucky crews who were among the bombers but on whom fortune did not smile. Major Wilhelm Herget, commander of 1/NJG 4, who had forty-nine confirmed night victories to his credit, had flown from Florennes in Belgium to Ida.

I got into the bomber-stream and I could see bombers going

down to my left but I could not find a bomber of my own. My navigator was trying all the time on his radar and I was weaving from side to side and up and down trying to find the slipstream of a heavy bomber, but on this night I didn't see one. I could have kicked myself; it was obvious that other fighters were doing well. Then we were ordered to fly on to Otto and soon I saw four exhausts and the shape of a plane so I tried to get it with my 110s top speed. After twenty minutes I caught him up when he turned and I cut the corner. I positioned myself thirty or forty metres underneath him and prepared to attack with my *schräge Musik*. First, I thought it was a Short Stirling because it only had one tail fin. I could easily have shot him down but, then, I saw he was a Ju 88. *'Verdammte Scheisse.'* I was furious. I nearly put a few rounds in front of his nose to wake him up.

Herget had to wait another four weeks before achieving his fiftieth victory.

The R.A.F. had a radio station at Kingsdown in Kent which listened into the German radio traffic whenever the bombers were over Germany. After each raid it sent a report of the night's activities to Bomber Command and that of this night contains some interesting details of how the Germans were transmitting their orders to the fighters and the results of the British effort to jam them.

Broadcasts were heard from all five fighter divisions. Not all of these would be the running commentary, some would merely be preliminary orders to fighters to proceed to a beacon. In all, the Germans used nine different speech channels and two Morse channels often switching rapidly from one channel to another. During the period when the main air battle was taking place, the running commentary itself was being broadcast on five different channels. The A.B.C. aircraft of 101 Squadron, flying in the bomber-stream, found and jammed all of these but the German transmitters had become so powerful and the use of so many channels caused the jamming to be spread so thinly that the commentary came through clearly at all times.

In addition, the Germans used a new method to avoid the jamming. They had discovered that the A.B.C. operators turned off their equipment for a short time every half hour so as not to interfere with the regular broadcasts from England of the wind forecasts. The Germans used these jamming-free periods to change all their frequencies. When the A.B.C. operators switched on again, they had to find afresh the frequencies which required jamming. This small new development in the continuing radio counter-measures war gave the Germans several minutes every half hour of completely un-jammed broadcasting.

The Kingsdown unit could also hear many of the German fighter pilots announcing their victories. As soon as they had shot down a bomber, the successful crew made a short trans-mission which consisted of the Nazi greeting, *Sieg Heil!*, followed by the aircraft's call sign. This provided valuable information for the plotting of the bomber-stream, which went via the Luftwaffe girls' torches onto the screens at the operations rooms, and was also the basis of the crew's claim, which would be later checked by a ground organization that allocated each crashed bomber to one fighter, that is if the Flak did not put in a counter-claim. On this night, the flood of claims gave the first indication to anyone in England that the bombers were in serious trouble.

The bombers' path over the 220-mile route from Liège to the end of the Long Leg was now clearly marked by the blazing remains of fifty-nine bombers. These aircraft – forty-one Lancasters and eighteen Halifaxes – had been shot down within the hour following midnight. It is unlikely that a single hour, before or since, has seen a greater rate of aerial destruction.

It is easy to record these bomber losses statistically but let us return again to the air battle, this time to look closely into these doomed aircraft. Let us try to visualize, with the aid of some of the pitifully few survivors, what suffering and anguish, what fortunate escape or mercifully swift death, lay behind these statistics.

The odds were heavily laden against the bomber crews from the very start. None wore parachutes save for a few lucky pilots who had a seat-type pack as a cushion. Most men had the chest packs which were so bulky that they interfered with the crew member's work and so were not clipped on to the parachute harness until the pilot decided that his crew should prepare to leave the aircraft. There was a carefully planned and often rehearsed drill for abandoning a bomber, but when that aircraft was heavily laden with bombs and fuel and being struck by explosive cannon shells, it became a desperate race to beat the resulting explosion or the spinning or diving descent to the earth nearly four miles below, with men imprisoned in their machine by centrifugal force or jammed hatches. Of all the aircraft shot down on the outward flight, there was only one where the entire crew survived.

Fire was the greatest danger and with justification the most feared by the crews. The Lancaster of Sergeant Luffmann, a 101 Squadron flight engineer, was hit in the bomb bay and the incendiaries started burning.

We had about fifty bundles of Window stacked all along the floor and these caught fire too. We went down about 7,000 feet before the pilot started pulling out. The crew were all shouting over the intercom but the pilot hadn't said a word from beginning to end. The navigator got his parachute and was gone like a shot. I couldn't find mine; there were these bundles of Window all on fire and the floor itself burning away so I gave up completely. I thought, 'Well, this is it!' I sat down and there was the parachute over my foot. Where it had come from I couldn't tell you. I tried to put it on but it wouldn't fit; the lead to my helmet was burnt into the clip on my harness. I tore the helmet off and threw it into the fire. Then I went and sat astride the wing spar and started clipping the parachute on.

I looked back and the pilot was climbing out of his seat but he slipped and fell through the floor which had burnt away. His harness had caught in the arm-rest of his seat and he was trapped in the flames over the bomb bay.

I reached the door and the special operator was stood leaning against it. 'What are we doing, junior? Are we baling out?' I sat on the ledge, pulled the rip-cord and rolled out, all in one action. I didn't count at all and this saved my life.

I have often worried since, that I didn't turn back and attempt to save the pilot but I am certain I couldn't have done anything. It all happened so quickly.

Luffmann was only in the air for a few seconds. He had jumped just in time. The A.B.C. special operator who had followed him out was badly injured when he hit the ground with a partially opened parachute and died later.

Many men owe their lives to the pilot's devotion in remaining at the controls to the very end in order to give his crew every chance of escaping. Two men in a 166 Squadron Lancaster did even more. This aircraft was crippled after a

long combat near the Rhine and settled into a gentle glide.
Pilot Officer Walter Burnett ordered his crew out and kept
the Lancaster steady while five men went, including the
injured flight engineer who was thrown out by the navigator.
All came down safely. The tail gunner had reported himself
trapped in his turret and, although the pilot and the mid-
upper gunner, Sergeant Peter Brown, were both seen with
parachutes on and with ample time to jump, they did not do
so. It is probable that the two men went back to help the
trapped gunner for the bodies of all three were later found
with the wrecked aircraft.

Pilot Officer Albert Lander, a New Zealand pilot on only
his second operation had better luck.

After I told the crew to abandon the aircraft, I tried to keep the
plane straight and level as long as I could until the flames entered
the cockpit. I covered my face with my left arm but lost control of
the aircraft which went into a spin throwing me out of my seat
into a position with my back against the cockpit window. Many
thoughts flashed through my mind as I lay there. Anyway, things
were getting bloody hot in there and my clothes were starting to
burn, so I put my feet against the pilot's seat and, by straightening
my legs, I managed to push myself out through the window and
flipped out over the wing. How quiet and cool everything was then.
I realized I still had a chance and felt for the rip-cord.

Unfortunately, only one other man in Lander's crew had
been able to get out.

There are many stories of narrow escapes. Sergeant Fealy
was the only survivor when Flying Officer Guy Johnston's
aircraft had been hit by Flak near Westerburg.

There was a great hole in the floor and a fire all around my
turret. I dropped down and had difficulty finding any of the floor
left to stand on. I was frightened to death. I couldn't bale out in the
orthodox manner because there was a wall of fire between me and
the door but the H2S had disappeared so I started to ease myself
through the hole it had left in the floor. As soon as I got my feet
through, my legs were blown back in the airstream and my boots
came off. Then my 'chute got stuck one side of a beam in the floor
and I was wedged the other side. I struggled but couldn't release
myself. I decided then that I had had it and gave up. I don't know
how long I was like this but the aircraft was going down very
steeply. I had one more go and, this time, I managed it.

Flight Sergeant Nugent of 78 Squadron was another sole

survivor when the Halifax of Flight Lieutenant Harry Hudson, an American pilot, was raked from end to end by cannon fire.

I realized the plane was doomed and, in all probability, the rest of the crew were already dead. I was on my knees becoming weaker and weaker without oxygen and started to feel for the escape hatch situated mid-way between my own turret and the rear turret. Next thing I knew was that I was hard up against the rear turret. I had no control over my actions but something guided me back and unwittingly my hand felt the door handle. One twist and I was out, spinning through the air like a top. I didn't need to jump – the air rushing past plucked me out like a mammoth vacuum cleaner picking up a fragment of dust.

Six nights earlier, Flight Sergeant Tom Hall of 106 Squadron and his crew had flown to Berlin on the first operation of their tour. This was the night when unexpectedly violent winds had caused Bomber Command much trouble and seventy-three bombers had been lost. Hall, like many others, had arrived at Berlin too early, but, while others bombed and made for home, Hall did a complete orbit over the heavily defended city before bombing. On the return flight the winds took them, again like many others, over the Ruhr where his Lancaster was hit by Flak and two engines took fire. Hall brought his crew home after a desperate flight, although the Lancaster was written off.

Now Hall was on his second operation. On the Long Leg his aircraft was hit in the bomb bay and petrol tanks. Sergeant Dack, the wireless-operator, describes what happened.

The Skipper said, 'It's time to get out. Get out everyone.' I was a careful sort of bloke and I always kept my parachute underneath my seat. I put it on but then she went down with all four engines flat out. It went through my mind that it was just like a scene from one of those American films with the aircraft going screaming down out of control. Once that started, I knew we couldn't get out. I was thrown on top of the navigator and we were rolling about together. I remember my face being pressed against two dials which I remembered were in the roof so I knew we were upside down. I tried to prod the navigator up towards the front to get out of the front hatch. There was all the time the awful thought that we had a Blockbuster on board which went off on impact. I forgot that we wouldn't have survived the impact ourselves.

Then there was an almighty explosion and I was sent spinning.

I thought we had hit the ground but it eventually dawned on me that I was in the air. Then, something whooshed past my face and I was sitting nice and peacefully up in the sky under my parachute. I remember shouting for my wife – I was apologizing because I had promised to be home on Saturday.

Only Dack and the flight engineer survived this explosion. The body of the pilot was found near the wreckage. This brave young man's operational career had lasted less than a week. He never knew that he had been awarded the D.F.M. for his good work on the Berlin raid.

By contrast, Squadron Leader Philip Goodwin was on his forty-seventh operation, flying as pilot of a Pathfinder Visual Backer-Up aircraft. His Lancaster was probably the sixth victim of the high-scoring Oberleutnant Martin Becker. It burst into flames after one long burst of cannon fire which probably killed the rear gunner. In the nose, Flying Officer Isted, the specially trained visual-marker bomb-aimer, obeyed Goodwin's order to dump the bombs but not the target indicators in case these misled following bombers.

The aircraft was on fire further back and it started to dive. I was thrown forward into the perspex nose, hitting my head on the bombsight. I was held there and could not get back to the escape hatch. I remember watching through the perspex; the world was spinning round and round and I thought that if this was the way I was going to die, it was an easy way to go. It'll all be over in a few seconds.

Then, the perspex broke; possibly one of the target indicators had exploded. I pulled myself up through the nose and dragged myself out.

Three more men survived when the aircraft broke up, including Goodwin who had been pressed flat against the roof of his cockpit watching the trees and snow on the ground revolving as the aircraft spun. Like Isted he thought he was to die and felt sad for his wife whose marriage would only have lasted six weeks. Goodwin owes his life to the seat-type parachute pack that he was wearing for the very first time.

Another who thought his end had come was Pilot Officer Tony Monk, the flight engineer in a 76 Squadron Halifax.

I reached the escape hatch which was already open but the G was terrific, pressing the whole of one's body down. I couldn't move. I thought 'This is it. This is the end.' I had been brought up in a religious family and I put my hands together and prayed. I seemed to relive the whole of my life in a few seconds. Then, there was a terrific roar in my ears and the next thing I knew I was somersaulting over and over in the air.

In a similar situation, a Halifax of 51 Squadron with a crew of five Australians and two Englishmen on their first operation was badly hit by a night fighter. Some of the crew were killed in the attack and only the navigator managed to bale out before the Halifax went into a vicious and uncontrollable spin which trapped those still alive in the aircraft. The pilot, Flight Sergeant Geoff Brougham, a New South Wales man, calmly called off the heights at each thousand feet that they passed from their operational height down to 4,000 feet, in the hope that others might still get out but, when the Halifax broke up at that last height, only two more men escaped to tell this sad story.

Perhaps nothing can illustrate more clearly the horror of being in a shot-down bomber than the story of the last moments of a 640 Squadron Halifax which was caught by a single *schräge Musik* burst. As the Halifax was weaving at the time, the explosive cannon shells hit the nose section as well as the starboard wing and engines. The Canadian pilot received terrible injuries to his legs and just had time to order his crew to bale out before he died. The flight engineer was either killed outright or, like his pilot, mortally wounded. The navigator, also badly injured, fell across the forward escape hatch and prevented others using it. Three men managed to leave by the rear hatch but the seventh man in the crew, Flying Officer Martin Corcoran, an Australian from a little town in Queensland, refused to leave the injured navigator and, although he had time to escape, was last seen by the side of his dying comrade.

These stories of death, horror and heroism are those from bombers out of which at least one man escaped. But from one crew in every three of those shot down on the outward flight there were no survivors at all. Their stories can never be told.

9

Nuremberg

At approximately 00.45, a Lancaster at the head of the bomber-stream reached the end of the Long Leg and its pilot turned on to a new heading towards Nuremberg, now just seventy-five miles away. Because the wind was no longer on the bomber's tail, it would take twenty minutes to cover this distance.

In theory this unknown Lancaster pilot had turned at 50° 32' north, 10° 38' east and, as he was probably a Pathfinder with a good navigator, the turn should have been accurate. However, for the less skilled who were to follow, the turning-point was not an easy one. The spot chosen was above a remote part of the Thüringer Wald with no easily recognizable physical feature or large town anywhere nearby. Because route-markers had started to attract German fighters, Bomber Command had discontinued their use at turning-points so no target indicator went down to mark this important position. For many navigators, the last accurate fix had been on crossing the Rhine 150 miles back and the broadcast winds they had been receiving from England since then had been unreliable. The average bomber turned well to the north of the correct point and slightly short of it.

Although the moon was lower in the sky now, with just over an hour to go before it finally set, the visibility was good enough for the German fighters in the stream to follow the turn. Back went the reports of the new course to the operations room of Hajo Herrmann's 1st Fighter Division which was now controlling the fighters and, within seven minutes of the first Lancaster turning, the running commentary was telling every German fighter of the new path being taken by the bombers. Nuremberg was mentioned for the first time but only as being in the area towards which the bombers were now flying.

The turn did little to save the British from the attentions of the German fighters. On the first half of that short leg to Nuremberg ten more bombers went down – nine Lancasters and one Halifax. Two of the Lancasters were Pathfinder

1. *Air Chief Marshal Sir Arthur Harris, Air Officer Commanding-in-Chief of Bomber Command, 1942–45.*

2. *The Handley Page Halifax Mark III flown by 4 Group and part of 6 Group in March 1944. LV857 was photographed when new before delivery to 51 Squadron at Snaith. Sergeant Jack Binder and his all N.C.O. crew, on their third operation, set out for Nuremberg in this aircraft but were all killed when it was shot down near Fulda.*

3. *The Lancasters, flown in March 1944 by 1, 3, 5 and 8 Groups. These are Marks I and III of 50 Squadron, based at Skellingthorpe.*

4. A Messerschmitt 110, the main German night fighter at the time of the Nuremberg Raid. This particular aircraft landed in error on an airfield in Switzerland in March 1944. The Germans feared that its presence in neutral Switzerland would lead to its secret new SN-2 radar becoming known to the Allies. In return for a squadron of brand new Messerschmitt 109s the Swiss agreed to blow up the 110.

5. The Junkers 88 was a heavier, faster but less manoeuvrable night fighter than the Messerschmitt 110. Only a few Gruppen were equipped with it at the time of the Nuremberg Raid but it came into more general use later in the war. The aircraft in this photo is another that 'went astray'. Its pilot, from 111/NJG 2, set a wrong course on his compass and landed the aircraft intact at Woodbridge in Suffolk in July 1944 thus presenting the R.A.F. with the secrets of the SN-2 radar which had defied both Window and the Serrate Mosquitoes in the early months of 1944. This aircraft was also fitted with a Flensberg homing device (the aerials are just visible on the port wing near the engine) which could pick up the signals of Monica, the tail-warning device fitted to British bombers.

6. *Bomber crews relax. Wing Commander John Voyce, a flight commander of 635 Squadron at Downham Market, and other officers. Their song refers to a toilet in danger of burning down. Voyce returned safely from Nuremberg and survived the war.*

7. *An operational crew. Canadian F/O Jimmy Wilson and the crew of 429 Squadron's F-for-Freddie. Wilson was drowned when his Halifax ditched in the Channel returning from Nuremberg.*

8. *A Lancaster of the Australian 463 Squadron at Waddington being bombed up with high explosives (not for the Nuremberg Raid). Flying Officer Joe Foster of Mascot, New South Wales, flew this aircraft, DV280, to Nuremberg, returning safely. It was lost with another crew on a raid to Gelsenkirchen in June 1944.*

9. *A 4,000-pound Blockbuster being loaded in a 692 Squadron Mosquito at Graveley. This type of bomb was really no more than a steel cylinder packed with explosives and was designed to blow in roofs and windows so that incendiaries could start fires.*

10. *Briefing. Squadron Leader F. P. Hill briefs the Halifax crews of 51 Squadron at Snaith for this raid on Nuremberg. Twelve hours later, thirty-five of these men (including Hill) would be dead and seven would be prisoners of war.*

11. *German night fighter crews of I/NJG4, at Florennes in Belgium, receive a weather briefing from their Met. Officer. The Gruppe commander, Major Wilhelm Herget, one of the German aces, watches from his position on the table.*

12. *The usual crowd of well-wishers waves off a Halifax Mark III of the Australian Squadron 466 at Leconfield. The target on this occasion in January 1944 was Berlin.*

13. *The pilot of a Lancaster runs up his four Merlin engines before taking off for a night raid.*

14. *The old centre of Nuremberg which was the target for the area raid of 30/31 March 1944. Little damage was done on this night but the city centre was destroyed by 514 Lancasters on 2/3 January 1945, when nearly 2,000 people were killed for the loss of only four Lancasters.*

15. *A raid being plotted in a German fighter control room. The crayon markings and the lights being shone onto the back of the frosted-glass screen indicate that operations are under way between Liege and Frankfurt but it is not known on which night this photograph was taken.*

16. A British target indicator bursts and cascades for a German cameraman to photograph. The Pathfinders could drop dozens of these in a raid to mark the Aiming Point but they were of no use if thick cloud covered the target.

17, 18 (above opposite) and 19 (below opposite). Only 'light' damage was in-flicted on Nuremberg on 31 March 1944 because of the unexpected cloud cover. The worst casualty incident was at the apartment block in Kesslerstrasse (left) where nineteen people died. The Railway Parcels Depot (top right) has suffered mainly blast damage. Similar damage at the peace-time Zoo, now used as a fire station (bottom right), shows how 4,000-pound blast bombs could remove the tiles from buildings and allow showers of small incendiary bombs to penetrate buildings.

20. Pilot officer Michael O'Loughlin and his crew are interrogated by an intelligence officer at Snaith on their return from Nuremberg. Their aircraft had been slightly damaged.

21. Major Herget presents the Iron Cross Second Class to members of a crew whose first victory (not on the Nuremberg Raid) has just been confirmed.

22. *A German officer inspects the tail unit of a burnt out Lancaster; 3,431 Lancasters were lost during the war.*

23. *The 115 Squadron Lancaster which F/Sgt Fogarty crash-landed near Stuttgart after giving away his parachute.*

24, 25 and 26. Three of the 47,268 Bomber Command aircrew lost on operations during the war.

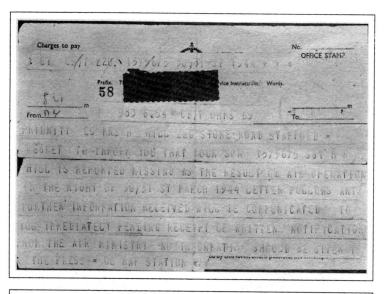

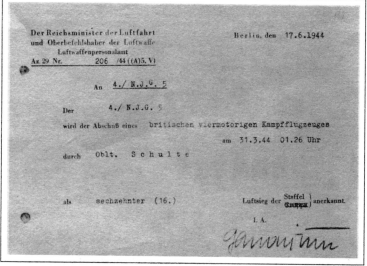

27. *The telegram sent by the station commander at Waterbeach to Mrs Hill of Stafford informing her that her son, Sergeant Roy Hill, a tail gunner in Pilot Officer Crombie's crew, was missing. Sergeant Hill was killed when his Lancaster blew up on the way to Nuremberg and has no grave.*

28. *The certificate awarded to the 4th Staffel of NJG/5 for the destruction of an R.A.F. bomber in the Nuremberg Raid. It was the sixteenth success credited to the relatively new night-fighter unit.*

29 and 30. The cost of taking the war to the German homeland. The British War Cemeteries at Durnbach, in Bavaria, and at Berlin. More than eighty per cent of the men buried in these cemeteries were from Bomber Command. Both cemeteries contain many graves from the Nuremberg Raid; the three graves nearest the camera are from 630 Squadron crew shot down on the way to Nuremberg.

Backers-Up and another was an A.B.C. aircraft, the fifth loss by 101 Squadron. One of the shot-down Pathfinders was that of Flight Lieutenant Desmond Rowlands of 97 Squadron. His crew were mostly second-tour men who had only just started operating with the Pathfinders. Their aircraft was found near Coburg by the Messerschmitt 110 of Major Martin Drewes. The German positioned himself under the Lancaster and fired just one burst of cannon shells into the starboard wing. There was no return fire and the bomber went straight down and burst apart with a brilliant red explosion as its bombs and the four red target indicators blew up.

Six bodies were found near the main fuselage on the edge of a wood. The tail came down some distance away and the body of the rear gunner was found in his turret. This was Flight Lieutenant Richard Trevor-Roper; D.F.C., D.F.M., who had flown as tail gunner in Guy Gibson's Lancaster on the famous Dams Raid. This veteran gunner and his crew had finally fallen to the unsuspected *schräge Musik*.

The bombers reached Bamberg, a town only forty miles from Nuremberg. They were greeted by thirty searchlights and much Flak but this did not reach to the bombers' height where fighters had been given priority.

The deadly approach flight was now almost over and the bomber crews were preparing for the added hazards of attacking one of Hitler's major cities. The last broadcast from England had informed them that the Zero Hour was unchanged and the wireless-operators had then wound in their trailing aerials. The bomb-aimers had switched on the gyros in their bomb sights and the heaters on the camera housed in the bomb bay. The rate of Windowing was doubled to two bundles per minute; it would be doubled again when Nuremberg was reached.

Despite those that had turned back early with technical troubles and despite the fierce onslaughts of the German fighters, 643 bombers, four out of every five that had taken off, were poised ready to attack Nuremberg. If the Path-finders could find and mark the target, if the bombers could defy the Flak and fighters on their bombing runs, then the city of Nuremberg could still be dealt a heavy blow.

At about the time that the tail of the bomber-stream was

turning at the end of the Long Leg, the first bombers reached Nuremberg. These leading aircraft, most of which were Pathfinders and the best that 8 Group could provide, were the Primary Marking Force commonly called the 'Openers'. It was their duty to ensure that Nuremberg was adequately marked for the Main Force. For the last 100 miles, their navigators had been calculating their E.T.A.s not just to the city of Nuremberg but to the small railway goods depot that would be the night's Aiming Point. The plan that they would follow, although a complicated one, was the product of nearly two years of operational trial and error by 8 Group. Upon this plan and the skill of the Pathfinders would depend the success of the attack.

TIME-TABLE FOR PRIMARY MARKING FORCE

Marking Method: Newhaven with Emergency Wanganui.

01.00   9 Mosquito Window Openers drop large quantities of Window.

01.05
- 24 Blind Marker-Illuminators drop flares and markers by H2S.
- 62 Supporters fly in with Pathfinders to divert radar-predicted Flak.

01.07   6 Visual Markers attempt to mark the Aiming Point visually.

01.10   Zero Hour for Main Force.

Total Aircraft: 92 Lancasters and 9 Mosquitoes.

Total Pyrotechnics: 120 clusters of hooded flares.

        156 target indicator bombs – 126 greens, 30 reds.

        24 release point flares – red with yellow stars (called skymarkers in text).

Total Bombs: 383 tons of high-explosive, no incendiaries allowed before Zero Hour to avoid confusion between fires and primary marking. All Pathfinder aircraft carried bombs which were dropped with markers.

As this force, hardly touched by the German fighter attacks, flew past the searchlights of Bamberg only thirty miles from Nuremberg, they suffered a critical setback – not from the Germans but from the bomber's old enemy, the weather. Below them appeared the well-defined edge of a thick sheet of cloud. The weather reconnaissance Mosquito had seen and reported cloud in the direction of Nuremberg and Mr Spence had included this in the late afternoon forecast that had been shown to Harris. The cloud had been given as 'strato-cumulus with tops to about 8,000 feet' and was obviously believed to be the remains of the cold front moving south that had yet to clear Nuremberg. In fact, the cloud was nimbo-stratus moving northwards. A convenient German report shows its base to have been 500 metres (1,640 feet) and that it extended up to 3,500 metres (nearly 11,500 feet).

What had happened was that, although the cold front had moved well away to the south from the earlier part of the bombers' route, here the warm air being pushed along ahead of the front had become compressed and had spilled back over and behind the front, forming great chunks of cloud as it did so. The air was in the process of occluding, or of forming what in 1944 would have been called a V-shaped depression but now would be known as a wave-depression. Such a weather occurrence was impossible to forecast and it was the cruellest of luck for the bombers and particularly for the Pathfinders that, on a cold front that stretched from beyond Brittany all the way to Moscow, the warm air should have chosen the Nuremberg area as the place for its rebellion. Not only had the wave-depression covered Nuremberg with cloud but the winds, still blowing from the west, had suddenly increased in velocity.

Several thousand feet above the cloud, the leading bombers flew on in the deceptively clear sky. Although they had often marked a cloud-covered target, the Pathfinders were now faced with the worst possible combination of conditions in which to carry out the vital marking. Their pyrotechnics had been loaded for the visual Newhaven method but the target indicator bombs they carried would burst just above the ground and would not be seen through cloud that was nearly two miles thick. True, some carried small numbers of release point flares, usually known as skymarkers, for an Emergency Wanganui marking but skymarking was rarely accurate beyond the range of Oboe especially in strong wind conditions.

When the Pathfinders crossed the edge of the cloud sheet they had only eight minutes in which to appreciate the changed conditions, find the new winds, change their plans

from Newhaven to Wanganui and then mark the target.
Many never managed the adjustment.

At exactly 00.58, Flight Sergeant Jim Marshallsay, pilot
of Mosquito N-Nan from 627 Squadron, opened the attack on
Nuremberg. Three of his four 500-pounder bombs would
explode on hitting the ground 25,000 feet below; the fourth
had a time delay in its fuse. Where these bombs fell cannot
be stated with any accuracy for Marshallsay's navigator,
Flight Sergeant Ranshaw, had been on dead-reckoning since
crossing the Belgian coast.

Seven more Mosquitoes bombed soon after this but the
four bundles of Window each was releasing every minute
were of far more importance than the 500-pounders. This
Window would help to disrupt the 100 radar-predicted Flak
guns defending Nuremberg before the first Lancasters
arrived five minutes later. In fact, these Mosquitoes bore the
quaint name of 'Window Openers'. Two H2S-equipped
Mosquitoes were to have dropped a green 'floater', a target
indicator set to cascade well above the ground, but the H2S
set of one of these aircraft had broken down and it retained its
marker. The other H2S Mosquito was occupied elsewhere.
We shall meet it later.

At 01.05, five minutes before the Main Force's Zero Hour,
the serious marking and bombing was due to open as
twenty-four Blind Marker-Illuminators and sixty-two Supporters all bombed at once. As their title suggests, the Blind
Marker-Illuminators had a dual role. In a Newhaven, each
would drop their bombs, four green target indicators and
five clusters of hooded flares. These flares were to flood the
whole area with light for the Visual Markers who would
follow. However, on this night, the only effective marker
these aircraft were carrying was just one skymarker each for
the Emergency Wanganui.

The Blind Marker-Illuminators aimed their loads, not
visually, but by H2S. They had no conventional bomb-aimers
but two navigators, one doing the normal position-plotting,
the second sitting alongside him working the H2S set. The
two, known as Nav 1 and Nav 2, worked as a team. The
H2S set in use at that time always had a 'mush' of ground
returns in the middle of the screen so that accurate fixing of
one's present position was difficult. It was easier to see

where the aircraft had been and where it was going by working from the more clearly defined echoes on the edge of the screen. The Blind Markers were to have made a timed run from Bamberg and got a final 'fix' at Erlangen, which is why the stream had been routed over these two towns.

Of the twenty-four Pathfinder crews acting as Blind Marker-Illuminators, three had been shot down en route, two had got themselves lost, one had a dud H2S set and three arrived late. The remaining fifteen all marked before Zero Hour and they should have been sufficient to perform the primary marking.

But some of the Pathfinders had failed to detect the sudden increase in wind velocity and had been blown sideways to the east while making their timed runs from Bamberg. Instead of flying over Erlangen and on to Nuremberg, they had crossed another small town, Forchheim, and at the end of the timed run were near the town of Lauf, much smaller than Nuremberg but with similar H2S characteristics, being situated on a river and surrounded by woods. Some of the H2S operators realized their mistake and did not release markers here but at least four aircraft did. Only the small skymarker was of any use in the cloud conditions but most of the Pathfinders dropped their entire load. The green target indicators burst unseen below the cloud but the skymarker parachutes opened soon after leaving the aircraft and the pretty red flares with their yellow stars floated in the wind still further to the east.

Another element in the force opening the attack were the Supporters who had been ordered to bomb at '01.05 precisely'. Their main purpose was to give protection to the Blind Marker-Illuminators on their marking runs by making it more difficult for the radar-predicted Flak to single out and engage individual aircraft during that critical period before the increasing clouds of Window stopped the radar Flak completely.

Sixty-two Lancasters had been detailed as Supporters – thirty-two were 8 Group crews not yet qualified as markers and thirty were provided by 5 Group. All had to bomb blindly by H2S and without the benefit of markers. The Supporter force had also been depleted by aircraft turning back, being shot down or suffering H2S failure and only nine of the sixty-two bombed 'at 01.05 precisely'. Of the 8 Group crews, twenty-four did manage to bomb somewhere in the Nuremberg area before Zero Hour but only eleven of the 5 Group Supporters were there before that time.

The last of the Openers were the six Visual Markers who were due to place their large loads of mixed red and green target indicators on the Aiming Point by the light of the Illuminators' flares three minutes before Zero Hour. Although all arrived on time, their task was hopeless. Flying as low as 16,000 feet among the Flak, their specially selected bomb-aimers could see nothing through the dense cloud. These aircraft carried no skymarkers for the Emergency Wanganui. Their sixty target indicators which should have formed a clear and vivid target for the Main Force bomb-aimers either burst uselessly below the clouds or were taken back to England.

The Openers had done the best they could in the difficult conditions but all that could be seen of their marking efforts was one group of skymarkers over Nuremberg and a smaller group ten miles to the north-east near Lauf, both being blow eastwards and falling towards the clouds.

There was one bright aspect. The Openers usually suffered higher casualties than the Main Force but no German fighters had been seen; the searchlights had been unable to penetrate the cloud; the Flak had soon succumbed to the Window and its fire was now erratic. Not one aircraft of the sixty-five that had passed over the area had been shot down.

The scene, just before Zero Hour, was unlike that of most raids. Sergeant H. Maxwell, a flight engineer in one of the Pathfinder aircraft, has described it.

There was usually a certain grandeur about the scene with the markers, the Flak, the searchlights and the night fighters, even though there was always the death and destruction – it was a spectacle. But on that Nuremberg do it was eerie. It was as though we had no right to be there. I suppose we hadn't really.

Zero Hour was due. Five hundred and fifty-nine Main Force bombers should have been ready to attack.

The critical time, 01.10, arrived but did not bring with it the expected climax of the whole operation. Even allowing for the casualties suffered by the Main Force, Nuremberg should now have been receiving bombs at the rate of forty-seven aircraft loads or 160 tons per minute but this main attack opened with only a whimper. In that first minute, only three aircraft bombed and in the first five minutes only thirty-three did so. Where were the Main Force aircraft?

There were two reasons for their non-appearance. The first is a simple one. The expert crews of the Openers, untroubled by fighter attack and carrying out their own navigation, had mostly arrived in the Nuremberg area at the correct time but the majority of the Main Force, navigating on the broadcast winds, had been carried well north of their correct track on the Long Leg. When they turned on the new heading for Nuremberg they were about three minutes' flying time further from the target than planned. There was thus a well defined gap between the Openers and the Main Force.

Provided Main Force crews could get themselves to the general target area their navigational problems ceased as soon as Pathfinder markers were spotted. Such crews did not have to find the Aiming Point in the centre of Nuremberg. They had simple instructions – to fly at 165 m.p.h. on a heading of 175 degrees magnetic and bomb onto the centre of the largest group of red target indicators. If these target indicators were invisible because of cloud, crews were to bomb the centre of all red and yellow skymarkers. It was for the Pathfinders to place these markers in such a way as to ensure that the Main Force Blockbusters and incendiaries fell into Nuremberg. If the Pathfinders were accurate, all were accurate. If the Pathfinders were wrong or confused, then the carefully planned attack would fail. Such was the essence of night bombing tactics in March 1944.

Because of the cloud, the thirty-three bombers that had arrived on time had seen no target indicators but only the two groups of skymarkers several miles apart. Some chose to aim their bombs through the middle of one or other of these groups while the remainder compromised and bombed into the dark gap between the two. The choice made by this small number of aircraft is not important. The main body of bombers was about to arrive.

The task of renewing the vital skymarkers was that of the Blind Backer-Up crews. There were twenty-two of these flying in with the Main Force and the duty of each was to re-mark the target with four skymarkers. Only one Blind

Backer-Up had been shot down on the way; another had probably got himself well lost but the remainder were all present.

When the approaching Main Force crews saw the first skymarkers several miles ahead, they were confused – there was not one but two well-defined groups of such markers in the distance. Four Blind Backers-Up had arrived just before Zero Hour. One probably re-marked accurately the group of skymarkers over Nuremberg. The second had H2S failure and dropped bombs but no markers. The other two had failed, like some of the early Pathfinders, to appreciate the new strong wind and were near Lauf and the earlier, wrongly placed markers. They re-marked this group. This clarified the situation for the approaching bombers – the skymarkers near Lauf were now the most prominent group.

It was at this moment that a good Master Bomber would have been invaluable. Provided he had been able to establish his own position accurately by H2S he could have broadcast instructions to the Main Force bomb-aimers to ignore the skymarkers near Lauf and would have called upon the Backers-Up to re-mark the correct ones over Nuremberg. Instead, each Main Force crew would have to make its own decision. The vast majority headed for the larger group of markers to the east ignoring the smaller group over Nuremberg.

Every bomber crew had its own style when preparing for and making the dangerous two-minute bombing run. Many had gained as much height as possible before reaching the target and would bomb while diving through it; their navigation logs might record the regulation bombing speed of 165 m.p.h. but this would be a false entry. One Halifax navigator, who was regarded as something of a comedian, carried out his own routine drill. After giving his pilot the final course to the target, he folded up his table, clipped on his parachute and sat next to the escape hatch ready for a quick getaway if his aircraft was hit.

The pilot could not even see the target underneath the bomber's nose and it was the bomb-aimer, flat on his stomach, who now took over direction of the aircraft, trying hard to guide his pilot in such a way that the skymarkers, themselves moving in the wind, ran up the centre of the bomb sight. A bomber crew was very vulnerable while this was happening. It was a time of great danger and tension.

Bomb loads were normally released over a ten-second period. The actual order of release was carefully calculated so that the bomber's centre of gravity was not unduly disturbed. As the bombs fell away the bomber surged up in the air with the sudden decrease of up to five tons in its weight.

A photoflash was automatically released from the aircraft at the same time as the bombs fell. The pilot had to hold his aircraft steady for a further thirty seconds before this flash would automatically go off over the approximate place where his bomb load would hit the ground. At the end of the run, a camera housed in the still-open bomb bay took eight photographs in rapid succession and, in theory, one of these would show the photoflash and the resulting ground details. This became the important bombing photograph which would show where the aircraft had bombed. Even though Nuremberg was cloud-covered, the hated photograph had still to be taken although none of the several hundred photographs taken would show anything but cloud and skymarkers.

At last, the bomb doors could be closed and the pilot could put down his aircraft's nose still further and speed from the danger area. The doors of one Halifax refused to close at this point, resulting in the long return flight being 'rather draughty'.

Most bomb-aimers were content to aim their loads at whatever markers they could see but a 101 Squadron special operator, who had done several operations with other crews, was very impressed by the conduct of the new all N.C.O. crew, most of whom were from Newcastle and Co. Durham, with whom he was flying for the first time. He heard on the intercom the bomb-aimer refuse to bomb on his first run because he was doubtful about the position of the markers and the pilot, Flight Sergeant Davidson, hauled the aircraft round in a wide orbit to start again. They bombed on the second run but had the frustration of finding that the heaviest bomb in their load, a 2,000-pounder, had stuck and, despite all efforts to release it, had to be carried back to England.

There was much danger on the bombing run of being hit by bombs released from higher flying aircraft. Warrant Officer Jack Broadley of 420 (Snowy Owl) Squadron was horrified to look up straight into the gaping bomb bay of a

Lancaster only a few feet above his head. 'Needless to say I immediately took the necessary action.' The brand new 622 Squadron Lancaster of Pilot Officer Lunn was struck heavily on a wing by what was probably a 30-pound incendiary bomb but, despite the fact that the main spar was cracked, Lunn got home safely. It was not unusual for bombers to be destroyed by 'friendly bombs' but, fortunately, none was lost in this manner over Nuremberg nor any from collision, another hazard over the target.

When the Main Force started bombing the skymarkers near Lauf, prompt and accurate re-marking over Nuremberg by the remaining Blind Backers-Up would have rectified the mistake but no markers at all were dropped in the next three minutes between 01.11 and 01.14. The majority of the Main Force had been happy to bomb near Lauf for as long as the skymarkers there lasted and they continued to bomb here during the gap in the backing-up after the markers disappeared into the clouds.

At 01.14 fresh markers were dropped and, for the next ten minutes, more red and yellow skymarkers continued to appear regularly. Alas, the damage had been done. Some of these later Pathfinders placed their markers accurately over Nuremberg but, again, other markers continued to appear to the east. Soon, there was a ragged line of skymarkers ten miles or more in length. Some of the Main Force crews with H2S realized the error and bombed the correct markers at Nuremberg but there is ample evidence that most crews continued to bomb well to the east of the correct position. When plotted on a map, the wreckage of the eight Main Force bombers and one Blind Backer-Up shot down on their bombing runs would form a long line leading directly from Bamberg to beyond Lauf.

Another fault – the creep-back – now started to occur as bombs started falling short. It was only human nature that a bomb-aimer should press his bomb release button just a second too soon to help shorten the tension and the dangers of the bombing run. Every effort by Bomber Command to eliminate this had failed and the planners had now to allow for it by placing the Aiming Point beyond that part of a city they wanted bombed. The creep-back on this night started early and developed quickly. The scattered marking and

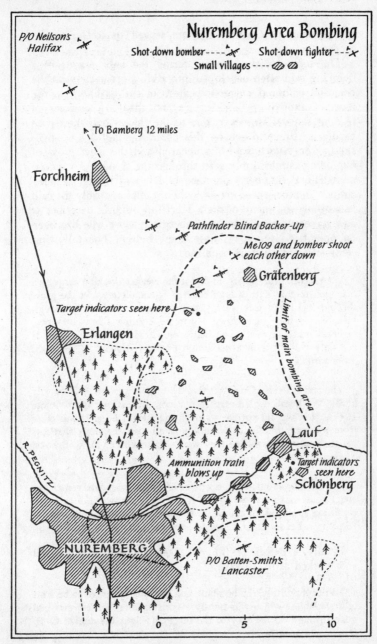

Nuremberg Area Bombing

Shot-down bomber ---- ✕ Shot-down fighter --- ✕

Small villages ---- ⬭ ⬭

P/O Neilson's Halifax

To Bamberg 12 miles

Forchheim

Pathfinder Blind Backer-Up

Me109 and bomber shoot each other down

Gräfenberg

Target indicators seen here

Erlangen

Limit of main bombing area

Lauf

Target indicators seen here

Ammunition train blows up

Schönberg

R. PEGNITZ

NUREMBERG

P/O Batten-Smith's Lancaster

0   5   10

Map 7

the presence of German fighters served to accelerate the process.

The scene on the ground during the later stages of a bombing raid often developed into a vivid spectacle with the beautiful coloured target indicators of the Pathfinders, the flash of exploding Blockbusters and the fiery outlines of blazing streets. However, due to the thick cloud there was hardly anything to see on this occasion, only a few small skymarkers which soon disappeared and the brief glow of exploding bombs dimly seen through the cloud. As a 'maximum effort' Bomber Command raid it was indeed an anticlimax. Inexperienced crews could not tell how badly the raid was going and many of their debriefing reports described it as a successful attack on Nuremberg but those who had been on operations for some time knew better. The following comments are all from such men.

We reached Nuremberg to find it the weakest looking target we had seen to that date. Cloud covered it completely and the glow through the cloud was weak, small in area and white, as though incendiaries had gone down but were burning themselves out, whereas other targets, even below cloud, rapidly showed red. It certainly did not look a maximum effort. (Sergeant H. Hannah, 9 Squadron)

The target itself, if in fact it was the target, was not well marked at all. We bombed on a marker that appeared at our approximate E.T.A., but we did not see much in the way of fires. It was clear from the way the bombs were falling all over the place that few people really knew where they were. (Pilot Officer O. V. Brooks, 15 Squadron)

It was without a doubt the worst night that I can ever remember and I could not recall when the R.A.F. was thrown into so much confusion resulting, of course, in bombs being scattered anywhere. (Squadron Leader L. D. Leicester, 640 Squadron)

Finally, a Pathfinder Blind Backer-Up pilot who bombed and marked at 01.19 says,

To put it politely, the bombing and marking appeared to be a bit of a shambles, which was hardly surprising after what crews had gone through on the way to the target. (Flight Lieutenant C. B. Owen, 97 Squadron)

Up at 20,000 feet, other crews were more concerned with the scene immediately around them. There were masses of vapour trails, spasmodic Flak over Nuremberg but not elsewhere, the tracer fire of combats, exploding aircraft.

There was certainly plenty of stuff flying around and it was so like a good firework display that I called the navigator and wireless-operator to come up and enjoy the sight, which offer was promptly declined. (Squadron Leader R. W. H. Gray, 625 Squadron)

We were late getting to the target and I don't think we got a photo for we were chased by a fighter and then a very twitchy Lancaster gunner tried hard to shoot us down. (Flight Lieutenant W. D. Marshall, 467 Squadron)

I could see black silhouettes of other bombers passing in front and to our side slightly below us. Above, I caught a glimpse of a radial-engined Halifax with bomb bay doors open, about 2,000 feet up. I remember wondering what part of his bloody load was going to drop right through us. I called the usual chant 'bomb doors open, left – left – right – steady – left – steady – bombs away – bomb doors closed – let's get out of here!' As I was about to check the bombing panel for hang-ups, I saw a Ju 88 less than 100 yards below us and, flying in the same direction, slide from under our port wing. It was so close I could see the illuminated instruments in his cockpit. For a second, I had the heroic thought that I could blast him out of the air with the two ·303s in the front turret but I remembered they had been faulty when I had test-fired them over the sea. Discretion became the better part of valour and we slipped out of the target area into the friendly darkness. (Sergeant A. W. Brickenden, 625 Squadron)

Another bomb-aimer who encountered a German fighter over the target was Flight Sergeant Hill-Smith of 101 Squadron.

I looked through the bomb-sight window and there, not more than 100 feet below and climbing slowly, was a Ju 88. By the time I got into the front turret it was only about ten feet below and fifty yards in front. My advice from the rear gunner was 'Leave the bastard alone. He's not harming us.' The skipper was saying 'Have a go.' Regardless of what either of them said, I was determined to get him – we were so close that the ring sight covered from about a foot on the right side of the starboard engine and the complete cockpit. I pulled the trigger and nothing happened. The guns, which had been tested over the sea, were frozen up.

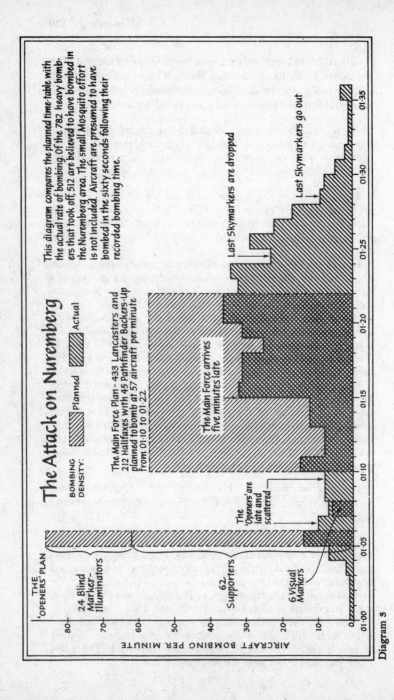

The Attack on Nuremberg

BOMBING
DENSITY: [Planned]   [Actual]

This diagram compares the planned time-table with the actual rate of bombing. Of the 782 heavy bombers that took off, 512 are believed to have bombed in the Nuremberg area. The small Mosquito effort is not included. Aircraft are presumed to have bombed in the sixty seconds following their recorded bombing time.

THE 'OPENERS' PLAN

24 Blind Marker-Illuminators

62 Supporters

6 Visual Markers

The 'Openers' are late and scattered

The Main Force Plan – 433 Lancasters and 212 Halifaxes with 45 Pathfinder Backers-up planned to bomb at 57 aircraft per minute from 01·10 to 01·22

The Main Force arrives five minutes late

Last Skymarkers are dropped

Last Skymarkers go out

AIRCRAFT BOMBING PER MINUTE

80 — 70 — 60 — 50 — 40 — 30 — 20 — 10 —

01·00   01·05   01·10   01·15   01·20   01·25   01·30   01·35

Diagram 3

The chart opposite shows how the progress of the bombing compared with the planned time-table. At 01.22, when the raid should have been finishing, it was still in full swing. It is probable that at about this time the Blind Backers-Up stopped marking to the east of the city and concentrated a good group of skymarkers over Nuremberg. Unfortunately this development came too late to influence much the course of the bombing. The Main Force continued to bomb in the open country well to the east of Nuremberg and the creep-back now measured fifteen miles. The fresh skymarkers over Nuremberg were eight miles to the west of the average aircraft's bombing run, and it required a considerable effort by a bomber crew to abandon its run and start a fresh one. Many regarded these accurate skymarkers as German decoys and some debriefing reports record them as such. A detailed time-table of events from Nuremberg contains no mention of bombs falling in the city after 01.21 although 186 aircraft bombed in the Nuremberg area after that time.

At 01.28 the last skymarkers went out and the aircraft that were still arriving had to bomb without the benefit of any Pathfinder marking at all. A Canadian pilot, Pilot Officer Greenwood of 514 Squadron, arrived two minutes after the markers had ceased. He was carrying one of the rare 8,000-pound Blockbusters. Beneath the clouds, his bomb-aimer could see the glow of two large fires estimated to be twenty miles apart. He chose the more easterly glow and released his huge bomb on to it.

Straggling bombers continued to arrive for several minutes. The doubtful privilege of being last fell to a 467 Squadron Lancaster that had been delayed by a long combat. Flight Sergeant McDade, its Australian bomb-aimer, released a 4,000-pounder and 984 incendiaries. The Lancaster hurried away.

At least three Mosquitoes and several German fighters remained over the city, sightseeing and eyeing each other suspiciously, but no fights developed and these, too, departed.

An hour earlier, at the Ida radar beacon, the Germans had achieved the perfect Tame Boar fighter interception. A successful follow-up to this by the assembly over Nuremberg of the single-engined Wild Boar fighters would have added still further to their success but this had not happened. Many of the Wild Boar fighters had been committed too early in anticipation of the raid being on the Ruhr, but if the Germans had been able to forecast the target correctly four fresh Gruppen might still have been brought into action over Nuremberg. Three of these, the Messerschmitt 109s of JG 302, had been ordered up from their airfields in the Berlin area and sent to the Nordpol beacon south-west of the capital, but the unexpected turn south of the bomber-stream at the end of the Long Leg had left these stranded too far to the north and they landed without attempting to engage. The remaining Gruppe, 1/JG 301 with possibly twenty Messerschmitt 109s stationed at Neuburg, only fifty miles south of Nuremberg, could have done a great deal of damage as the bombers ran straight and level for their two-minute bombing runs over the target but the Gruppe never took off. The reasons are not known – possibly the airfield was affected by bad weather or was fog-bound; probably the 7th Fighter Division at Schleissheim, near Munich, had also been unprepared for the bombers' turn south.

The bombers over Nuremberg were protected from radar-predicted Flak by Window, from the searchlights by the cloud, and from a concentrated Wild Boar fighter attack by the German failure to anticipate the bombers' turn towards Nuremberg. But the bombers continued to be exposed to a fourth danger – the Tame Boar fighters who had been in the bomber-stream for over an hour. Many of the Germans had fallen out with failing petrol supplies or empty ammunition trays but enough of them remained to cause further loss to the bombers. The running commentary had not definitely confirmed Nuremberg as the target until 01.13 but the 101 Squadron special operators could now clearly hear the German broadcaster urging his fighters 'Nach Nürnberg. Nach Nürnberg.'

The Halifax of Pilot Officer Chris Neilson, the 'Mad Dane', was caught south of Bamberg just as he was preparing for his bombing run. Not much is known of what happened except that his aircraft was shot down by an attack from underneath – the *schräge Musik* again. Neilson came down by parachute into a village churchyard and was promptly captured. Two more of the crew, the wireless-operator and the tail gunner, also became prisoners but the remainder, including a new pilot making his 'second dickey' trip and Flight

Sergeant Chris Panton, the young Lincolnshire flight engineer who had hoped one day to become a pilot, were killed. Neilson's crew had needed only two more operations after Nuremberg to complete their tour.

Flying Officer R. A. Marshall, a Lancaster navigator, watched the destruction of another bomber.

As we approached the target, heading for the P.F.F. flares, I went up forward and kept watch. I reported a Lancaster about 100 yards to starboard and slightly above and Bill [Squadron Leader Whamond] told me to keep an eye on it. Without any warning it suddenly exploded and nothing was left except a ball of dirty smoke and odd flashes as either ammunition or flares went up.

But not all the German attacks were successful.

We had just started our bombing run when I saw him, an Me 110, before he started popping off at us. I gave the pilot instructions to start evasive action and, just as we dived, the German fighter opened fire on us but our action caused him to pass over the top of us. I returned his fire but, just then, the pilot pulled up in the corkscrew manoeuvre; my stomach went down to the bottom of the turret; my guns went up in the air and I missed him. He hadn't hit us and we didn't see him again. It was the only night fighter I ever saw in my tour of operations. (Flight Sergeant D. R. Chinery, 61 Squadron)

Papers attached to the War Diary of the German I Fighter Corps contain an account of how an unnamed Feldwebel (sergeant) pilot, who had already shot down two bombers, found a Lancaster in the target area. The Feldwebel was a *von unten hinten* attacker and was spotted by the Lancaster's tail gunner. A vicious exchange of fire ensued. The German hit and badly damaged his intended victim but was hampered by the dense contrails of the corkscrewing bomber and by oil which splashed over his cockpit. He fired again and saw the bomber catch fire, a large piece of wing fly off and, then, the bomber disappeared earthwards. The Feldwebel claimed it as destroyed.

The Lancaster was that of Flight Sergeant Ray Lemoine of 115 Squadron and it was, indeed, in serious difficulties. The cannon fire had caused extensive damage and also set fire to a canister of incendiaries that had failed to drop over the target. Damage to the starboard wing had released the rubber dinghy stowed there and this flew back and wrapped itself around the tailplane, jamming the elevators and flapping violently against the rear turret. The mid-upper turret was jammed and it was hydraulic fluid from its broken power lines that had covered the German fighter's cockpit.

The wireless-operator tried to put out the burning incendiaries by forcing the nozzle of an extinguisher through a small hole in the floor but the fuselage continued to fill with choking smoke. Then the pilot opened the bomb doors in an effort to get fresh air into his aircraft and by good fortune the incendiaries burnt through their container and fell away. The dinghy finally freed itself so that the pilot was able to regain control of his very battered Lancaster. The dinghy falling away was probably the Feldwebel's 'large piece of wing'.

This inexperienced crew, only on their second operation, had performed very well in the emergency and they survived being coned by searchlights later in the flight and a very shaky landing on a strange airfield in England.

Several crews report seeing a combat over the target area between a bomber and a Messerschmitt 109 that had probably followed the stream all the way from the Ida beacon. An exchange of tracer resulted in both aircraft catching fire. The Messerschmitt was seen to explode and fall in pieces and the bomber also went down.

A sad loss was that of the sixth 101 Squadron Lancaster to go down. The reader will remember Assistant Section Officer Patricia Bourne at Ludford Magna being told by her boy friend to 'think of me at one o'clock'. She had been awakened by her alarm at that time and had thought for a few moments of him as he had requested before sleeping again. At about 01.30, Pilot Officer Batten-Smith's Lancaster was caught by a German fighter as it flew out of the target area and became approximately the eighty-third bomber shot down during the course of the night. Jimmy Batten-Smith died with all his crew and the wreckage fell beside the big clover-leaf *Autobahn* junction six miles east of Nuremberg.

In all thirty-nine bombers were shot down on the final approach and over the target area – probably all by fighters. The bomber force had now lost seventy-nine aircraft, a total exceeding the record seventy-eight on the Leipzig raid six weeks earlier. The encounters over the target had not been completely one-sided – three German fighters were claimed as destroyed, one as a probable and three damaged. Another is reported by a German pilot to have been hit by its own Flak, the pilot escaping by parachute, but there are no records that can confirm these German casualties.

This was the sixth major air raid suffered by the people of Nuremberg. The previous attacks had also been by night, one in 1942 and four during 1943. In the last two raids, in August 1943, there had been unexpectedly heavy loss of civilian life when 656 people had died. Since then there had been a seven-month lull but Nuremberg knew that as a major industrial city still largely intact its turn would come again. The Flak and civil-defence units had been strengthened and drilled; there was now a place in a proper air-raid shelter for every citizen. Nuremberg had been as ready as it could be for the R.A.F.

Germany did not have a black-out quite as rigid as that imposed in Britain during the war. Railway yards, factories and other establishments important to the war effort were allowed to carry on normally as long as no enemy aircraft were in the vicinity. The first event of the night for Nuremberg had been the receipt just before midnight of an order cancelling this black-out relaxation but the bombers were still more than 200 miles away and this was a routine precaution that had been taken on many other nights. Soon after this, the sirens sounded for the preliminary *Öffentliche Luftwarnung* – another precautionary measure. However, at 00.38, just before the bombers turned at the end of the Long Leg, the more urgent *Fliegeralarm* was sounded. This warned Nuremberg that the city might be the target for a major attack.

It was now compulsory for everyone not on duty to take cover. The older houses all had cellars or basements which had been adapted as air-raid shelters with emergency access to the street above or to neighbouring cellars in case the house collapsed. The four huge towers at the corners of the Altstadt with walls two metres thick provided shelter for many other people and the inhabitants of the more modern houses in the outer residential areas trooped off to their recently built communal shelters. Reserve policemen, firemen, rescue workers and ambulance personnel all hurried to their places of duty.

If the air raid had been on a British city, these units would have been supplemented by women volunteers but in Germany this was not so – the female population was not expected to play a major role in the war. Instead, it was the young men of the Hitler Youth who provided the additional manpower for these air-raid services. Every 'pure' German boy joined the highly organized *Hitler Jugend* at his fourteenth birthday and served in it until the age of seventeen when he was conscripted into the armed forces.

When the British turned and flew almost due south to their city, those responsible for the defence of Nuremberg received minute-by-minute reports of the bombers' progress. At 01.00 the sounds of many aircraft could be heard to the north and east of Nuremberg and two minutes later the local Flak went into action when the first bombers were heard overhead. A detailed time-table kept at the time by the city air-raid centre and several reports compiled immediately after the raid enable an accurate picture to be given of subsequent developments.

Although Flight Sergeant Marshallsay's Mosquito had bombed at 00.58 the first bombs did not fall in Nuremberg itself until four minutes later. There was never a heavy concentration of bombs at any point but the early reports mostly tell of bombs falling in and around the Altstadt. These bombs were mainly high explosive and would be dropped by Pathfinders or Supporters bombing on H2S.

This type of bombing – high-explosive bombs falling at various points around the centre of a city – was the normal preliminary to an Area Bombing attack. It was designed to crater roads, topple buildings into the street and force the German fire-fighters to remain under cover while the Pathfinders marked the Aiming Point ready for the arrival of the Main Force who would then set the city alight with the combination of Blockbuster and incendiary bomb. As has already been told, however, this intended programme of destruction went wrong on this night. With the early high-explosives came green and red target indicators duly recorded over the centre of the city, but these were seen only by the few Germans on duty above ground and certainly not by the bomber crews flying above the thick cloud.

The bombs that fell into the Altstadt failed to cause either serious damage or fires despite the many ancient buildings there. In the Castle were stationed 160 Hitler Youth boys commanded by a *Wehrmacht* sergeant. Six boys were on lookout duty in the Castle tower while the remainder were in the safety of the large cellars beneath. As soon as any hits were spotted among the buildings in the Altstadt, teams of boys were despatched to deal with these as quickly as possible in an attempt to extinguish or contain the fires until the regular firemen arrived. A few fires broke out near the Castle itself and also in the vicinity of the famous St Lorenzkirche but were soon brought under control and neither of these historic buildings was damaged. The main incident in the Altstadt was the destruction of the Norishalle, a favourite dance hall. Although many people lived in the old city centre, not a single person was killed there.

More serious, however, was the effect of the bombs that dropped just outside the Altstadt. Some damage was caused to railway buildings near the main station and three main railway lines out of Nuremberg were cut. Several houses, the head post office and the local labour exchange were hit and also the Maximilian Augenklinik, a small private hospital for eye patients, but no one was hurt there. A large fire broke out and burnt for several hours among houses near the Christuskirche right on the edge of the main Siemens-Schuckert factory but neither Siemens nor the important M.A.N. factory received a single bomb.

The most serious incident occurred in the Kesslerstrasse just outside the Altstadt walls when a single heavy bomb exploded either in the street or inside a large apartment building which collapsed. A fire started in the ruins.

First on the scene was Johann Völkel, a fifteen-year-old Hitler Youth member. He went down into the cellar of the next house in an attempt to reach the basement of the wrecked building. Watched by the anxious inhabitants of this cellar he started to remove the bricks blocking the connecting aperture but as soon as an opening had been made hot smoke billowed out and he was forced to replace the bricks. The boy ran back up to street level to find that a light fire engine had arrived and a desperate attempt was being made to rescue the people believed to be in the cellar. Völkel, the smallest present, was doused with water, given a breathing mask and sent down through a basement window with a water hose. He succeeded in getting into a first cellar and, though he

could hear a woman's voice call *'holt uns raus'* ('get us out')
from further along the smoke-filled cellar, he could not
reach them because the smoke concealed a fierce blaze.
Völkel was ordered out – choking and vomiting from the
smoke he had inhaled.

It was almost two days before the fire was put out, the
debris cleared away and the bodies of the nineteen inhabitants
of the building recovered – all had died by fire in their cellar.
In the city archives there is a record of every victim by name,
age and occupation – dentist, businessman, representative,
art dealer, retired decorator, an elderly widow and her
daughter, five housewives, a secretary, two domestic servants,
four schoolgirls.

Across the street stood the Postcheckamt in which was
located Nuremberg's main telephone exchange which also
served as the city's air-raid reporting centre. The blast from
the bomb blew in the front of the building and a rumour was
later spread of thirty telephone girls having been killed
here, but this was not true. They may have been trapped for
some time but the stout construction of this modern building
saved them.

The civilian deaths in the Kesslerstrasse were regrettable
but, if the raid had developed properly, the damage to the
telephone exchange might have seriously affected Nuremberg's air-raid defences.

When the bombing later moved away eastwards from the
city centre many of the bombs fell into open spaces near the
River Pegnitz although some exploded in the built-up
suburbs. The main object of the raid – the setting alight of
the city centre – failed and none of the scattered bombs hit
the main industrial area south of the city centre. However, the
eastwards drift of the bombing did achieve some accidental
success. There were two smaller industrial areas situated in
the residential outskirts – one on the north bank of the Pegnitz and another further north in the suburb of Herrnhütte.
Both of these suffered severely from the bombing. Large fires
were started in a motor-cycle factory and an iron foundry and,
at a margarine factory, the administrative block was completely wrecked and stock later valued at 1·5 million Reichsmarks (£150,000) was destroyed. The heaviest damage was
at Neumeyers, a large factory where 6,000 workers made
electrical cables. Few details are available but in a secret

Nuremberg City Bombing

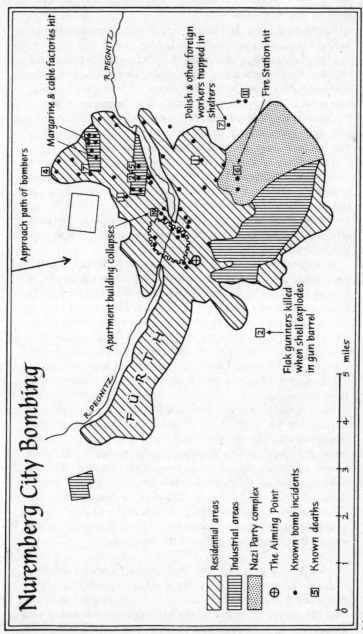

Approach path of bombers

Margarine & cable factories hit

Polish & other foreign workers trapped in shelters

Fire Station hit

Apartment building collapses

Flak gunners killed when shell explodes in gun barrel

R. PEGNITZ

FÜRTH

Residential areas
Industrial areas
Nazi Party complex
⊕ The Aiming Point
• Known bomb incidents
5 Known deaths

0   1   2   3   4   5 miles

Map 8

report to Berlin this important target was later classified as having been 50 per cent destroyed.

Many houses were also hit in this north-eastern part of the city and there were more casualties. Among these was the Schmidt family who lived in the street adjoining the burning motor-cycle works. Herr Schmidt was an engineer who had married an English woman; they now had a son, Colin, who was four years old. Both parents were badly hurt when a bomb struck their house. The little boy was killed.

The effects of the bombing in the south-eastern suburbs was entirely different. Here were situated among large open spaces the buildings designed by Albert Speer and built for the Nazi Party. Several bombs fell near the S.S. barracks and the unfinished Kongress Halle but are unlikely to have caused serious damage to these massive structures although the S.S. probably lost some of their windows.

Not many bombs fell in this area at all but those that did were responsible for three incidents involving the deaths of twenty-four people. Between the Kongress Halle and the S.S. barracks were the buildings of the old *Tiergarten* (zoo) in which were stationed two of Nuremberg's ten fire brigades and a rescue team. A bomb fell here and destroyed most of the fire engines and rescue vehicles. Six men were killed, three of whom were Ukrainian prisoner-of-war volunteers. Again, this would have been a useful bomb-hit if the city had been set alight.

Not far away had once been another of Hitler's creations – a camp for his *Kraft durch Freude* (Strength through Joy) organization. The wooden huts, now the home of forced labourers and families bombed-out in earlier raids, were blown to pieces by more high-explosive bombs. The inhabitants had all taken shelter but by a rare stroke of misfortune bombs also scored direct hits on two air-raid shelters. The reinforced concrete roofs of both had collapsed. Seven people, probably all Germans, were killed in one shelter and eleven Polish workers perished in the other.

Map 7 on page 187 shows that bombs eventually fell over a huge area roughly the shape of a lop-sided triangle. Nuremberg was at the western end of the triangle's base and was the target for many of the early bomb loads but it was the skymarkers dropped near Lauf at the eastern end of the base of the triangle that drew most of the Main Force crews.

Lauf itself, a small and attractive old town, was badly hit. The blast from at least two Blockbusters smashed windows and removed tiles from the old houses and many fires developed from the incendiaries that followed. Twenty-two fire engines were rushed in from other places but ten properties near the market square – two small breweries, two pubs and six houses – were completely burnt out and many more damaged. A factory producing insulators and other ceramic goods for the war effort was also gutted but one of the largest radio stations in Germany situated just outside the town was not touched.

In the woods south of Lauf stands the small village of Schönberg. Early in the raid a load of brilliant and beautiful target indicators cascaded over the woods between the village and Lauf. Although these were invisible to the Main Force bomb-aimers, the skymarker also dropped by this unknown Pathfinder who was eleven miles from his correct Aiming Point would be seen. Frau Hilde Gregori later wrote this eye-witness description of what happened.

The 'Christmas trees' which marked out the area to be bombed stood threateningly near to our village. Even then, many did not seriously believe that now it was to be our turn. What sort of military target could Schönberg offer and what value could the destruction of a village have for the enemy leaders? This is what the optimists said. But whoever had still to cross the road to reach his air-raid shelter would learn a different lesson and would experience on the way the beginning of a bombardment which, God willing, would not be repeated.

It literally rained incendiary bombs. In the meadows around Schönberg there were lights everywhere which looked like large torches and, already, from this roof and that roof, flames were pouring. All hell was let loose. The fires crackled as they spread; tiles snapped in the heat. The whole of the village was a single sea of flames. An observer who lived ten kilometres away later said that he assumed that no house could have been left standing in Schönberg.

When the bombing was over everyone feverishly worked to put out the fires. The village fire brigade could not tackle the fires in a proper manner because each man went first to look after his own property. The animals were set free and had to remain out in the snow for many hours. As soon as this had been done we fetched all the furniture outside and only afterwards did we criticize ourselves for not having selected the important things first, for it soon became too dangerous to do much about the household possessions. It deserves to be mentioned that children and women helped most courageously and accomplished things which now seem hardly possible.

Towards the end of the raid there had been 'an ear-splitting explosion' when a particularly heavy bomb fell just outside Schönberg. One of the firemen working there remembers that 'the blast literally swept a nearby farmhouse from the ground'. This was probably the 8,000-pounder dropped at the end of the attack by the 514 Squadron bomb-aimer who had dropped his bomb onto a large glow seen beneath the cloud.

Sixty-five houses and barns were burnt out in Schönberg and ninety-five people became homeless but, because of the high proportion of incendiary bombs in the loads of the Main Force aircraft responsible for the bombing in this area, neither Lauf nor Schönberg suffered any deaths during the night.

As the raid had progressed the bombing, which had started in the two corners of the triangle, became more scattered. Soon bombs were dropping all along the base of the triangle and then crept back rapidly northwards to beyond Gräfenberg twenty miles from Nuremberg. Within this area were numerous small villages, open farmland and dense woods. It is recorded that twenty-one villages sustained bomb damage. There were some serious incidents and an unknown number of deaths but in many cases only a few barns were burnt out and most of the bombs fell in fields and woods.

An indication of the Pathfinders' confusion is a report by several people in Etleswind of target indicators seen falling near their village which was fourteen miles north-north-east of Nuremberg. These, probably the load of a Backer-Up, could not have come from a shot-down bomber as no Pathfinder came down near here.

One lucky bomb load hit a military train at Behringersdorf, just east of Nuremberg, and set it alight. There was a large explosion when a wagon loaded with ammunition blew up. This would probably account for the report in 460 Squadron's Operational Record Book of a tail gunner seeing a large flash as his aircraft flew away from the target.

Other bombs hit a prisoner-of-war camp situated in the woods near Nuremberg. An unconfirmed report says that twelve huts were burnt out and some Russian prisoners killed. The Germans described the event in one of their propaganda broadcasts to England and ridiculed the R.A.F. for bombing their own comrades although the camp contained no British prisoners at that time.

Back in Nuremberg the civil-defence workers had had a comparatively easy time; indeed so light had the raid been that many of the fire and rescue units had seen no action at all. The Flak batteries had fired steadily throughout the raid and later claimed one-and-a-half victories but it is unlikely that they actually destroyed any bombers. A misfire had occurred in the barrel of one 10·5-centimetre gun. The gun crew waited as long as they could but were finally ordered to unload it so that the gun could be brought into action again. As they did so the shell exploded killing four men – a soldier, a schoolboy auxiliary and two Russians.

It was difficult for the authorities to judge exactly when the raid finished because aircraft continued to be heard overhead for some time, although these were almost certainly German fighters. It was not until 02.52, well over an hour after the last bombs had dropped, that the *Entwarnung* (final All Clear) sounded.

Area Bombing was a direct conflict between the bomber crews who sought to overwhelm a city's defences and set it on fire and the citizens of that city who would attempt to put these fires out before they could take good hold. On this night the lack of concentration in the bombing and the work of Nuremberg's fire teams had saved the city from destruction. The good work by the fire-fighters can be attributed to careful organization and training but it had been the unexpected movement of a pocket of warm, moist air bringing with it strong winds and thick cloud that had really saved the historic city and its inhabitants from fire and death.

10

The Other Targets

In the previous chapter it was stated that there were two answers to the question 'Where was the Main Force?' when Zero Hour at Nuremberg passed without the prompt opening of the main attack. The first answer was given in that chapter: due to navigational difficulties the bombers were five minutes late. But the table showing the progress of the attack on Nuremberg shows that only 512 aircraft eventually bombed in that area although 631 could have done so. This chapter will give the second answer to the question of where the Main Force was at Zero Hour and shows where the missing 119 bombers had got to.

At 01.00 Flying Officer Ted Jackman was lost. His Pathfinder Mosquito was one of those due over Nuremberg at that time to drop Window, one green target indicator and three 500-pounders. Like everyone else his Gee navigational aid had been jammed early in the flight by the Germans but then his new H2S set had also ceased to work due to technical trouble and Flying Officer Button, Jackman's navigator, had been forced to rely on dead-reckoning.

At the time that the Mosquito should have been approaching Nuremberg, a large concentration of searchlights and Flak did appear directly ahead. These were defending a built-up area which appeared to be covered by haze. Jackman, an experienced pilot on his fortieth operation, presumed that he was at Nuremberg, flew across this target at 25,000 feet and released his load. As there was no high cloud, his brilliant green target indicator remained visible for several minutes.

Jackman's difficulties were not over. Unknown to its crew, the Mosquito's V.H.F. radio was jammed on transmit – a defect they did not discover until attempting to call their airfield prior to landing. Every word said between pilot and navigator could be heard by the Germans, although it is unlikely that anything serious was divulged. On landing, the two were placed under open arrest until an examination of the Mosquito proved that they were not to blame for the fault nor been aware of it.

Flying Officer Jackman was not the only one anxious to bomb on time. The 5 Group Supporter aircraft had instructions to release their loads at 01.05, five minutes before Zero Hour. At 01.03, Pilot Officer O'Leary of 106 Squadron, probably drawn by Jackman's target indicator, bombed the same target and within six minutes six more Lancasters had done so, all but one of them being these 5 Group Supporters.

These two events – the accidental green target indicator and the seven Lancaster bomb loads – were not necessarily sufficient, on their own, to trigger off further bombing and in fact there followed a small lull. But the activity had attracted bombers of the Main Force, many of whom had little idea of their exact position as Zero Hour approached.

Hauptmann Gustav Tham had taken off in his Messerschmitt 110 from Erfurt and had already shot down a Lancaster on the Long Leg but then his SN-2 radar had packed up. After half an hour of visual searching, Tham spotted the four glowing exhausts of another Lancaster only 150 metres ahead and he immediately opened fire. With its fuselage and port wing ablaze, the bomber went down in a flat spin being followed by the searchlights of the defended target as it fell. There were no parachutes.

Flight Sergeant Hawkins, bomb-aimer in a Main Force Lancaster, was watching too.

At a time when we felt that we should have been near Nuremberg, a Lancaster was shot down ahead of us and spiralled down in a brilliant orange glow illuminating the whole of the countryside below. In the light of this, we saw an industrial town ahead and assumed it to be Nuremberg, although we had no positive identification. We continued our run towards the assumed target and bombed visually from the light sent off from the flaming Lancaster.

The bomber shot down by Hauptmann Tham was that of Pilot Officer Jack Thornton, the Canadian pilot whose W.A.A.F. friend at Spilsby had gone into his Lancaster at dispersal and exhorted him to 'drop that little lot' in return for a brother killed at Dunkirk. His blazing Lancaster and the 4,000-pounder which exploded was the final signal for many bomb-aimers like Flight Sergeant Hawkins that they had arrived at the correct target.

The absence of thick cloud resulted in many of these crews

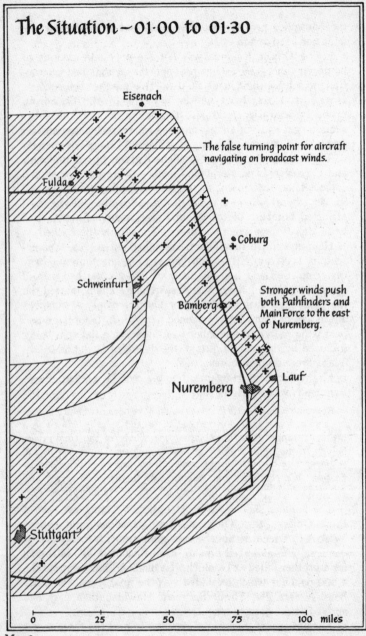

The Situation – 01·00 to 01·30

Eisenach

The false turning point for aircraft
navigating on broadcast winds.

Fulda

Coburg

Schweinfurt

Bamberg

Stronger winds push
both Pathfinders and
Main Force to the east
of Nuremberg.

Nuremberg

Lauf

Stuttgart

0   25   50   75   100   miles

Map 9

bringing back clear bombing photographs. They were at Schweinfurt, fifty-five miles north-west of Nuremberg and home of the German ball-bearing industry. It is ironical that this unplanned attack should fall on a target that Sir Arthur Harris had often insisted was not suitable for the aims of the bomber offensive and not within the capability of his command to find and bomb effectively.

There was a simple explanation as to why so many bombers were at Schweinfurt thinking it to be Nuremberg. The incorrect winds broadcast to the crews while flying the Long Leg had led most of them to a false turning-point at the end of that leg. The bearing and distance of the run from that false position to Schweinfurt was approximately the same as the run from the correct turning-point to Nuremberg.

Jackman's green target indicator had burned for about four minutes. After it had gone out aircraft bombing at Schweinfurt could only guess at an Aiming Point in the absence of further markers and the bombs dropped at this time were well scattered. After the trials these crews had undergone earlier in the flight, there is little wonder that they released their loads on this unmarked target without worrying too much where they were. One could always blame the Pathfinders for being late.

This account, by Warrant Officer Claud Notman, an Australian bomb-aimer in 550 Squadron, is probably typical of such crews.

Max, the navigator, said we should be there in five minutes. A glow on the right. I'm sure it's an attack. More incendiaries; big ones. There it is! 'Max, there is a decent prang over on our right. Could that be Nuremberg?' 'Yes, could be,' says the navigator cryptically. Still no Pathfinder flares but this must be Nuremberg. We went in on the others, held her straight and level and old R-Roger took a very important photoflash. We held to a new course away to the south for a while and then we saw activity over Nuremberg. It appeared only a poor prang while, behind us, our own target had gained in intensity. Christ, what will Butch and his men say? We, of all crews, on our twenty-fifth operation and bombing the wrong target! Silence was supreme on the way home. We were humbled by our mistake.

Many crews reaching Schweinfurt refused to bomb immediately and they orbited, waiting for Pathfinder marking.

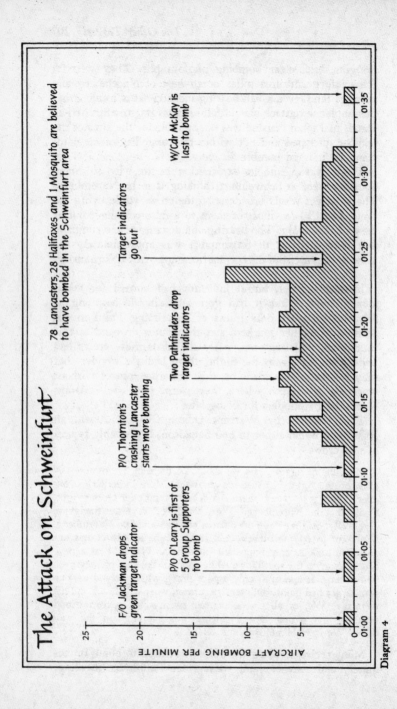

The Attack on Schweinfurt

AIRCRAFT BOMBING PER MINUTE

78 Lancasters, 28 Halifaxes and 1 Mosquito are believed to have bombed in the Schweinfurt area

F/O Jackman drops green target indicator

P/O O'Leary is first of 5 Group Supporters to bomb

P/O Thornton's crashing Lancaster starts more bombing

Two Pathfinders drop target indicators

Target indicators go out

W/Cdr McKay is last to bomb

Diagram 4

Their patience was rewarded when, at either 01.16 or 01.17, fresh target indicators were seen going down backed up two minutes later by even more. These vivid cascades remained in sight for seven minutes in the cloudless skies over Schweinfurt.

Who dropped these target indicators? Due to lack of evidence it is impossible to answer this question precisely and indeed some of the evidence that does exist is conflicting. There is no record of a Pathfinder aircraft bringing back a Schweinfurt photograph although at least one of their crews produced a photograph showing ground detail, but its position could not be plotted – they were certainly not at Nuremberg. Could the markers have been German decoys? This is unlikely because the debriefing reports of eight crews whose photographs later showed Schweinfurt say that they bombed onto markers and one Halifax photo contained what appeared to be a target indicator burning on the ground within three miles of the centre of Schweinfurt. The Germans were unlikely to have had a decoy so close to such a vital target and men serving with the Schweinfurt air defence organization at that time confirm this.

The target indicators appeared to have been greens backed up by reds; red and yellow skymarkers also figure in some reports. No single Pathfinder aircraft carried all such markers, but there are several combinations of two aircraft that could have done. An Australian Main Force pilot, Squadron Leader 'Bluey' Graham, on his fortieth operation writes 'I am sure that a couple of Pathfinders at least were with us and marked Schweinfurt.' Perhaps the best witness was Flight Lieutenant Poulson, a crew member of a Pathfinder aircraft that had an unserviceable H2S set. It dropped no markers but bombed what was later found to be Schweinfurt. Poulson clearly remembers seeing at least two loads of markers going down – 'reds on greens'.

The aircraft bombing at Schweinfurt were not all flown by new crews. A 101 Squadron Lancaster had as its navigator Squadron Leader Rosevear, a flight commander on his second or third tour and probably one of the most experienced navigators in the Main Force. Flying away to the south after bombing Schweinfurt, he had the mortification of seeing the attack on Nuremberg, thirty miles away on his aircraft's port beam. Pilot Officer Cotter, a Halifax pilot on his thirtieth operation, carried the experienced Base Bombing Leader as his bomb-aimer but his navigator was only on his first or second trip.

With the heavy fighter attacks, the navigator could not have had a more unfortunate introduction and eventually he was unsure of his position. Before we were due at Nuremberg we saw Path-finder markers going down just off our track. We had not been briefed on any diversionary target here and I immediately assumed we were at Nuremberg. I just thought we were lucky that, with minimum navigational assistance, we had got to Nuremberg and bombed. Not one of us queried the target. I still believe that the markers had been put down by the Pathfinders. When you fly over a city which is marked, is apparently being bombed heavily, where you see several combats in progress, you assume it is your target.

There was much coming and going among the bombers over Schweinfurt. Some of the luckier crews who had H2S took a good look at the town, realized it was not Nuremberg and flew on further south. At least two crews, however, having flown past Schweinfurt, found the attack at Nurem-berg so unspectacular that they turned and flew back to Schweinfurt, not realizing that the thick cloud at Nuremberg was concealing most of the action there. Others continued to orbit Schweinfurt while bomb-aimer and navigator argued. The bomb-aimer had a good target in sight which was marked and upon which many bombs were falling. The navigator felt sure that, in spite of all the activity, they were not over the correct target.

There was one major difference between conditions over Schweinfurt and Nuremberg. The absence of cloud over Schweinfurt allowed the searchlights there to reach to the bombers' height and the strong Flak defences of this vital industrial target were, for most of the raid, given priority over night fighters. It was, therefore, these ground defences and not the night fighters that were the greatest danger to the bomber crews. Although the official Bomber Command post-raid report refers to the Schweinfurt defences as being 'inaccurate', the Flak did claim two victims. Herr Alfred Popp, now a dentist in the area, was then a schoolboy helper on a Flak site on the eastern outskirts of the town which was later credited with the shooting down of two Halifaxes.

Herr Popp is sure that one was a Lancaster and he is probably correct. Its destruction was observed by several mèn including Sergeant Rowlinson, a wireless-operator, whose own aircraft almost suffered the same fate.

We could now see other Lancasters silhouetted against the sky and one poor devil was coned. He was twisting and corkscrewing to try and shake off the searchlights but we could see Flak bursting close by and then there appeared a flicker of flame from one of the wings. Then we were coned ourselves. What an experience! Chas [Flying Officer Startin, the Australian pilot] immediately dived just like a fighter; we lost hundreds of feet in a few seconds. Due to the sudden loss of gravity thermos flasks, pencils, charts and various other items were floating about in the cabin. I grabbed my flask as I did not want to lose my hot drink. Then we pulled out of the dive and away to port, then a sudden turn to starboard, the light suddenly faded and we had lost them.

The records of 50 Squadron show that Flying Officer Startin eventually made his bombing run at only 8,000 feet!*

The Lancaster seen in the searchlights by Sergeant Rowlinson was that of New Zealander, Flight Sergeant Charles Foster, of 550 Squadron. This and the other Flak victim, a Canadian Halifax of 424 (Tiger) Squadron, both came down south of Schweinfurt. There were no survivors in either aircraft. Late in the attack, German night fighters made a belated arrival and the Flak was ordered to stop firing but no more bombers were shot down.

When the Pathfinder markers went out at about 01.24, the raid was still attracting aircraft from the tail end of a very confused Main Force and a further twenty-seven aircraft bombed after that time. Some of the latecomers realized that they were at Schweinfurt but it was now too late for them to go further as the attack on Nuremberg would be closing down also.

Wing Commander McKay, the Canadian commander of 432 (Leaside) Squadron, had orbited Schweinfurt for nineteen minutes trying to make some sense of the confused situation and hoping for more markers but, at 01.34, he

---

* Two months later Chas Startin's crew was lost. It took off to raid Brunswick without Rowlinson who was sick. Nothing was heard of them again until the bodies of two men were washed ashore, one on the island of Borkum and one on the Dutch coast.

decided to bomb. His load of incendiaries was the last to fall on Schweinfurt.

The town of Schweinfurt, with a population of around 40,000 in 1944, was similar in size to the English towns of Guildford or Mansfield. Situated on the north bank of the River Main, it would give the appearance of being a pleasant market town in this rural part of Germany but for the existence of three large factories in the eastern part of the town. A Swedish firm had built two of these, the Vereinigte Kugellager Fabrik factories (known as V.K.F. No. 1 and V.K.F. No. 2) and the third was a German concern, Kugel-fischer A.G. The Ministry of Economic Warfare in London estimated, quite accurately, that these factories produced approximately half of Germany's roller-bearings and ball-bearings which is why Schweinfurt figured so prominently in the directives issued both to Bomber Command and the 8th U.S.A.A.F. Any bomber failing to find its correct target could not have stumbled upon a better place to bomb than Schweinfurt.

The Germans had recognized the vital importance of the bearings industry here and, as soon as the American attacks had commenced in 1943, they had started to disperse the industry to smaller towns. Meanwhile the defences of Schweinfurt were strengthened and its population well drilled in preparation for further raids.

As early as midnight, when the bombers were still 180 miles away near Aachen, smoke generators had started putting the usual smokescreen over the town. This was the cause of many reports by bomber crews of haze or fog over the target. Then, about half an hour later, the regional air defence system warned that Schweinfurt might be attacked and the civilian population either went down into their cellars or were taken by bus and lorry to shelter in woods out in the country. However, the factory workers were not allowed to leave their work until the last moment. This applied particu-larly to the many foreign workers deported to Germany from the occupied countries. In a subsequent Bomber Command attack two weeks later, forty-eight of the fifty-one fatal casualties were among these foreigners forbidden to take early shelter.

If Schweinfurt had been like many other towns its Flak

and searchlights would have kept quiet when the bombers first flew over, to avoid attracting attention, and Flying Officer Jackman's Mosquito and the Supporters might never have started bombing here. But Schweinfurt was a lively, aggressive target and its defences opened up with everything they had when the first raiders were heard overhead.

Schweinfurt's records say that ten *Luftminen* (Blockbusters), 300 other high-explosive bombs, 1,500 of the 30-pound incendiaries and 15,000 stick incendiaries were dropped on the town. These bombs fell in all parts of Schweinfurt but the heaviest damage was in the old town centre near the river. This area would be the natural target for the early Supporters bombing on H2S. The buildings in the Fischerrain, an old street near the river, and the nearby municipal abattoir were almost completely destroyed by high-explosive bombs. Among several buildings here caught by incendiaries and burnt out was the much-treasured church of St Salvator. The thousands of incendiaries caused many small fires in the outer residential areas, but these never joined to form a serious blaze. It is recorded that the fire brigade had more difficulty finding these small fires in house roofs, due to the dense smokescreen, than in actually putting the fires out.

The R.A.F. men who bombed Schweinfurt that night will be pleased to know that at least some damage was done to all three of the ball-bearing factories, in particular a large fire was started in the grading department of the V.K.F. No. 2 works. Unfortunately, no high-explosive bombs appear to have fallen here and the incendiaries caused damage to buildings but none to the vital machinery. The ball-bearing companies later claimed compensation of 406,602 Reichmarks (nearly £41,000) from Berlin for damage to their factories. A report sent direct to Albert Speer by his special commissioner in Schweinfurt says that 'in contrast to the heavy damage caused by the attacks on 24–25 February [a U.S.A.A.F. raid on 24 February followed by a Bomber Command raid that night], the effect on production is not so great and it is not expected that there will be any damaging effects on deliveries'.*

The first four raids on Schweinfurt – this was the fifth on the town – had caused the death of 841 people but the

* The report to Speer is now the Bundesarchiv Koblenz document R 3/1586.

214 of The Nuremberg Raid

stringent air-raid precautions since introduced and the light-
ness of this attack had resulted in only one death, that of a
child. Sixteen people were injured, many being men who had
remained at work in the ball-bearing factories.

Many bombs had fallen in the country areas near Nuremberg because the Pathfinder marking had, for much of the
attack, been over those areas. The majority of the bombing
in the Schweinfurt area was also in the country areas but for
different reasons. The training of the bomber crews, the
bomb loads they carried and the tactics employed were
wholly intended for attacks on large, built-up areas. Schweinfurt, being a small, compact target, would not have been easy
to hit even if properly marked. In the absence of continuous
Pathfinder marking, many crews could only bomb 'the
approximate centre of the defended area', a phrase that often
occurs in debriefing reports. It was the standard practice of
Schweinfurt's searchlights to form themselves into a line
across the approach path of the bombers which were, on that
night, mostly coming in from the north-east. To the bomber
crews 'the centre of the defended area' would, in fact, be
slightly north-east of Schweinfurt. This, and the usual ten-
dency to bomb a little short in the face of fierce Flak, produced the usual creep-back. The map opposite shows the
limits of the area into which the bombs fell.

Seven villages found themselves in the area bombed but
five of these escaped lightly with only a few farm buildings
being burnt out. Some crews actually aimed at the base of the
searchlights in the absence of markers and a military report
tells of barracks and tents hit and two German soldiers and
two Russian volunteers being killed on one site.

It may have been the presence of such a searchlight and
Flak position on a hill-top near Schonungen that drew bombs
to this village nearly four miles to the east of Schweinfurt. At
least two Lancaster loads hit the village, the two Blockbusters
missing the Flak position by 200 and 300 metres respectively.
Many incendiaries also fell and the report of the village's
Catholic priest, written in 1966, records that there were eight
large fires in houses, warehouses and other buildings, and
forty-six small fires. The regular village firemen were
helped by eighteen women auxiliaries and by brigades from
other villages. The fire-fighters had a difficult time working

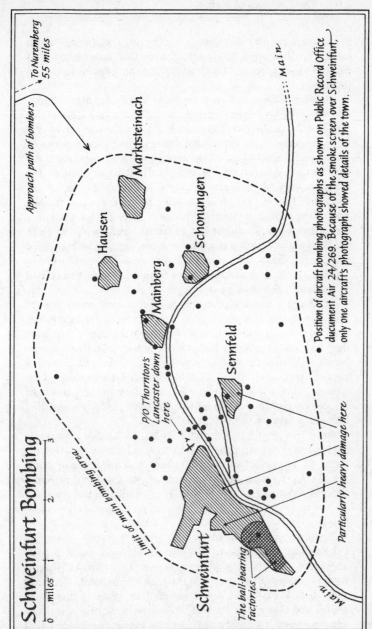

Schweinfurt Bombing

Map 10

miles
0   1   2   3

To Nuremberg
55 miles

Approach path of bombers

Limit of main bombing area

Marktsteinach

Hausen

Schonungen

Mainberg

Main

P/O Thornton's
Lancaster down
here

Sennfeld

Schweinfurt

The ball-bearing
factories

Main

Particularly heavy damage here

● Position of aircraft bombing photographs as shown on Public Record Office document Air 24/269. Because of the smoke screen over Schweinfurt, only one aircraft's photograph showed details of the town.

in a temperature of minus 15 degrees centigrade which caused their soaked clothes to freeze like boards, but the priest ends his report, 'by good fortune, no lives were lost in the raid'.

Another village had an even more terrifying night. Sennfeld lies only two miles from Schweinfurt. It was hit early in the raid by a Blockbuster which fell in the centre of the village square. The Protestant church, the priest's house, a school and the 300-year-old town hall were all destroyed. All that remained intact at the town hall was the oven of the parish bakery. A favourite lime tree in the square, known as the Adolf Hitler Tree, was uprooted by the blast and thrown 150 metres over a block of houses. Incendiaries started a large fire which soon got out of control and, being so close to Schweinfurt, attracted many more bombs as the raid progressed. Soon, houses and barns were well alight throughout the village and fire appliances from Schweinfurt itself had to be sent to Sennfeld's aid.

Once again strict air-raid precautions saved heavy loss of life. Ten firemen sheltering in a cellar were trapped when the house collapsed in ruins above them but they were later dug out unhurt and, at the priest's house, a high-explosive bomb fell only three metres from a cellar in which twelve people were sheltering. The bomb failed to explode. One woman, almost ninety years old, was slow getting down to her cellar. Her house was hit and the poor old lady was killed – the only fatality in the village.

An interesting little report tells how a soldier serving in Finland was given three weeks' special leave because his home in Sennfeld had been bombed. One of Bomber Command's aims was to give indirect help to the Russian Army fighting on the Eastern Front. This small incident resulted in one soldier being temporarily removed from duty on that front.

Because of the clear bombing photographs taken at Schweinfurt it has been possible to be even more precise about the way the bombing progressed there than at Nuremberg. Forty-eight crews brought back photographs showing that their loads went down within five miles of the town centre and many more would have done so but for the dense smokescreen. Two different German reports estimated that 150 bombers raided Schweinfurt but, after a close study of every crew's de-briefing report, my estimate is that approximately 107 aircraft had bombed here. 5 Group were best represented with thirty-two aircraft, the remainder being spread evenly through the Main Force. The high 5 Group total is not a reflection on 5 Group's navigational skill. On this night, Cochrane's squadrons had to provide the Supporters whose crews had the difficult job of finding a target to bomb five minutes before Zero Hour. The green target indicator dropped by the erring Mosquito provided that target.

Some crews bombed neither at Nuremberg nor at Schweinfurt. A bomb-aimer in a Canadian crew describes a typical experience.

Our H2S became unserviceable shortly after we reached the enemy coast and we were aware that we had drifted off course. The navigator had absolutely no navigational aids and, when we reached our E.T.A. at the target area by dead reckoning, I could not see the ground nor could I locate the Pathfinder markers. I reported this to my captain and he ordered me to release the bombs so that we could 'get the Hell out of here'. Afterwards, we talked about this raid as being the most futile and frustrating of the entire tour (Flying Officer M. H. Albers, 427 Squadron)

At least thirteen aircraft bombed in this manner. Where most of these bombs fell will never be known but the destination of one of the few 8,000-pounder bombs carried on the raid is more certain. Again, the bomb-aimer describes:

During the fighter attacks we had been corkscrewing for at least an hour. We circled what we thought should be the target area and I bombed what was probably a stick of jettisoned incendiaries. It was our first 8,000-pounder and this was the only time I saw my own bomb explode. It went off with a bright orange flash surrounded by white shock waves, a bit like a large poached egg. About two minutes after bombing we saw the target about twenty miles ahead. No sense going over that lot, so we did a dog-leg and came home. (Flying Officer F. J. Parker, 514 Squadron)

The town archives of Bamberg, thirty miles north of Nuremberg, refer to a few incendiaries and one heavy bomb which hit the premises of a building contractor causing much damage but no casualties.

A Pathfinder Supporter brought back a photograph showing clear ground detail. Its H2S had been no good since leaving England but the bombs were released at the correct time at the end of the long, dead-reckoning flight. The photograph showed a small town sixty miles north of Nuremberg! The crew did not fly again with the Pathfinders, probably because of this incident; they returned to the Main Force and were all killed soon afterwards.

Undoubtedly the most tragic incident resulting from the bombers' work that night had occurred some time earlier and nearly 400 miles from Nuremberg. Crews were given a 'last resort' target in case they had to turn back before reaching Germany and, for this night, the docks at Ostend on the Belgian coast had been selected. Two Lancaster crews had taken advantage of this, a Pathfinder of 7 Squadron with technical trouble and a 50 Squadron aircraft whose navigator was badly airsick. The Ostend town archivist writes, 'The bomb-aimers missed their target, for their bombs dropped into a densely populated quarter of the town which contained no barracks or military posts. There were no deaths among the Germans.'

The archivist's records are very detailed and show that eighteen houses were completely destroyed and a further 391 damaged in an area one mile from the docks. Thirty-six Belgian civilians, ranging from an old lady aged sixty-eight to a baby girl of six months, were killed.

11

Other Operations

As the bombers fly into the darkness, away from cloud-covered Nuremberg or from the fires of Schweinfurt, we will leave them and turn to an examination of other aerial activities, some on the fringes of the bomber battle but others taking place several hundred miles away.

The Intruder Mosquitoes operated on most nights but, when Bomber Command was flying a major raid, their effort was directed as much as possible to the support of the bombers. The presence over an airfield of just one Intruder could delay the take-off of a complete night-fighter Gruppe and completely disrupt the German plans to intercept the bomber-stream. How were the Intruders faring?

Thirty-seven Mosquitoes had taken off and none had turned back with technical trouble. The greatest effort had been by 418 and 605, the two regular Intruder squadrons of Fighter Command. To these had fallen the task of patrolling the most important of the German night-fighter airfields, some of which were deep into enemy territory. 'Bud' Miller, an American pilot flying with 605 Squadron, flew low-level all the way to Stendal airfield near Berlin while one of the Canadian crews of 418 Squadron was detailed to go as far as Czechoslovakia. The American found no 'trade' at Stendal and the Canadians never reached Czechoslovakia because of bad weather but they found alternative airfields to patrol.

The Intruder effort had been augmented in recent weeks by three of the Mosquito fighter-bomber squadrons of the 2nd Tactical Air Force. After the invasion of Normandy, these would operate by night behind the enemy lines and, partly to gain experience and partly to help Bomber Command, the best crews from these squadrons were sent out as Intruders. The squadrons involved were an interesting selection: 21 Squadron, which six weeks earlier had carried out the famous low-level bombing attack on the walls of Amiens prison in an attempt to release French Resistance men under sentence of death; 487, a squadron of New Zealanders, and 613 (City of Manchester), another of the pre-war Auxiliary squadrons. Their crews were allocated the nearer German airfields. On arrival, they were to bomb runway intersections and then remain on patrol in the vicinity for as long as their fuel allowed.

The final Intruder participants were the two Lightnings and two Mustangs from the American contingent in 100 Group. One Lightning had to turn back early but the remainder completed their patrols although without recorded success.*

The Intruder crews were fully conscious of the importance of their work when the heavy bombers were flying. Their reports illustrate both the difficulty of the task and the devotion with which the Intruders persisted with their efforts. There are many accounts of crews patrolling more airfields than ordered and staying out to the limit of their aircraft's endurance. Flight Lieutenant Jim Connell, one of the Canadian pilots, had been ordered to patrol an airfield at Bonn, near the route of the bombers' Long Leg. He had arrived just as the bomber battle had broken out many thousands of feet above him.

We patrolled there for over an hour but we didn't see a single light from the airfield. We tried to be as inconspicuous as possible and attempted the old trick of de-synchronizing our engines in an attempt to imitate the 'hum-hum' of the German engines. At each end of our patrol line there was the burning wreckage of a bomber which made things easy for my navigator. There was a group round one of these and we debated whether to have a go at them but decided not to in case the crew of the bomber were there.

Connell then flew down the Rhine to have a look at two more airfields, at Coblenz and Wiesbaden, but found nothing there. He describes it as an 'interesting trip' because a faulty petrol connection caused trouble to both engines on the return flight and he only just made the emergency airfield at Manston.

Flight Lieutenant John Pengelly's patrol area covered the airfield at Nuremberg and he was able to observe the bombing 'as from a low-level ringside seat. Having witnessed several major attacks of this sort, I can only describe them as

---

* The American Intruder experiment soon ceased. One of the Lightnings was later shot down making a second run over a German airfield; experienced Intruders rarely made more than one such attack. The remaining Americans left 100 Group on 27 April 1944.

large-scale, sinister November the Fifths'. Nuremberg airfield produced no activity but soon afterwards fighters could be seen landing at Ansbach, twenty miles to the south-west. Pengelly went after these but was unable to get into an attacking position before the airfield lights went out.

Flight Lieutenant Peter Garner of 605 Squadron had patrolled Erfurt for over an hour before he saw German fighters starting to land there. He managed to line himself up behind one of these but its pilot must have been warned of Garner's presence because the German switched off his lights and overshot. Garner and his navigator, Flying Officer Duncan, could see a hangar on the airfield with doors open and lights on inside. 'We had been hanging around the district for a long time and being very frustrated, we virtually flew into the hangar to give them something to remember us by!'

The crew's combat report shows that eighty-nine cannon shells and fifty-four machine-gun bullets were fired and strikes were seen on two fighters in the hangar. Garner and Duncan flew home. When I visited Germany in 1972 and interviewed former Leutnant Wilhelm Seuss in Frankfurt, he complained that, after shooting down four Lancasters and returning to his home airfield at Erfurt, a Mosquito shot a hole in the propeller of his Messerschmitt 110 which was in that hangar.*

Another 605 Squadron crew was patrolling an airfield near Mainz. Flight Lieutenant 'Dicky' Bird describes his encounter with the Germans.

I saw a chap with his lights on above me. I thought, 'if he keeps those lights on long enough, we've got him'. I opened up and climbed but, as we got level with him and started closing, he switched everything off. Then, some searchlights came on and the industrial haze provided a backcloth of light like the effect of headlights in the fog. I found I was right on top of him. It was a Dornier 217 and I had to pull out before I crashed into him. Then a Focke Wulf 190 flashed past over us. I realized, then, that the first aircraft was a decoy or else they were carrying out some training exercise.

I never saw either aircraft again nor any other aerial activity so we went off to have a look at the city of Mainz. I found some

---

* Flight Lieutenant Garner was killed at Yeovil in 1948 while flying as a test pilot on the Westland Wyvern.

trains in the marshalling yard there; you could see the steam and smoke quite easily. I went down and attacked two locomotives. We hit one at least.

In all, the Intruders visited forty-four German airfields but only three German aircraft plus Flight Lieutenant Bird's locomotives were claimed as damaged. The Intruders rarely achieved startling success; theirs was a war of steady attrition and harassment. But on this night the early take-off of the German night fighters had obviously frustrated the Intruder plans. One of the Intruder pilots said that there was some surprise among the crews of his squadron at finding so many airfields dormant. 'The Germans were not in their normal lairs.'

A 21 Squadron aircraft had been detailed to bomb and then patrol Handorf airfield near Munster, the home airfield of one of the German Illuminator units. Another crew reported encountering the Mosquito near Handorf but it was never seen or heard of again. Out of all the R.A.F. aircraft lost in the operations of that night, this is the only one of whose fate absolutely nothing was ever discovered. The Canadian pilot and his English navigator were the only Intruder casualties of the night.

Another sizeable Allied activity was completely unconnected with the Nuremberg operation. It was that which officially came under the heading of 'secret operations' – the parachuting of supplies and agents to the various Resistance groups who would come into the open after the invasion in ten weeks' time and fight behind the German lines. This work was carried out by single aircraft flying at low level, and moonlight conditions were essential because navigation over much of the route was dependent upon map-reading.

Exact details of these operations are not available because they are still classified by the Ministry of Defence as secret. However, it is known that at least forty-one aircraft were detailed for this work, the aircraft coming from three different types of squadrons. The specialist squadrons at Tempsford flew the really difficult sorties, the remainder being performed by 3 Group Stirlings which were no longer on Main Force raids and the transport squadrons of 38 Group based in the West Country which would take the airborne divisions to Normandy on D-Day. The American squadrons which normally helped with this work were in the process of changing airfields and were not available.

Most of these supply-dropping flights appear to have been intended for the French Resistance groups in the Haute Savoie area between the River Rhône and the Swiss border. At least six sorties were cancelled before take-off due to unsuitable weather forecasts for the dropping zones and many of those who did go encountered cloud which prevented low-level navigation and forced them to turn back. Others carried on but could not find the coded torch signals of the 'reception committees'.

The following account by Flight Sergeant A. M. Miller, a New Zealander flying as second pilot in a 149 Squadron Stirling, shows how difficult this work could be in bad weather. The Stirling crew was trying to find a dropping zone in the foothills of the Alps.

We ran into low cloud and snow and we searched for the drop-ping-point lights for some time without success. The pilot said he would try once more and, if we didn't find them, we would go home. We were approaching a ridge higher than we were – I wanted to yell at Tommy [Flight Lieutenant T. C. Danvers, the Australian pilot] to tighten the turn but realized that any mis-understanding might cause him to fly straight into the hill. I held my breath and waited for the crash – the wing tips and props must have brushed the tree-tops as we cleared the ridge. The bomb-aimer had a better view than I and considered that we had actually swept through the trees. Today, Danvers probably lives in ignor-ance of how close we came to eternity. We brought our load home.

The German air defence system appeared to have turned its attention exclusively on the bombers attacking Nurem-berg and these solitary aircraft were unmolested by fighters. The 138 Squadron Halifax shot down into the Scheldt by Flak, an incident already described, was the only casualty of the night among the secret operations aircraft but bad weather had caused more than half of the sorties to be abandoned. The Albemarles, Stirlings and Halifaxes of 38 Group had the least success – only three of fifteen aircraft managed to deliver their loads to the waiting Resistance men.

The only other Allied operation of the night was the dispatch of more 3 Group Stirlings to drop sea mines off Texel and in the mouth of the Seine. This was tactical mining not a diversion and was part of the little-publicized participation by Bomber Command in the sea war. Eight aircraft from 75 (New Zealand) and 149 Squadrons navigated by the accurate Gee to the mining areas, dropped thirty-two mines and returned safely; but it was a long-winded way to complete a tour. These flights only counted as one third of an operation.

The aerial activity was not confined to the skies over Germany and the occupied countries. The Luftwaffe sent three raiding forces against England. In the early evening British radar had plotted twelve 'hostiles' coming in over south-east England. Only three of these reached London where a few bombs caused minor damage but no casualties. This small raid was part of the Baby Blitz, Hitler's reply to the destruction by fire of Hamburg eight months earlier. These 'hit-and-run' raiders were too fast for Fighter Command and no interceptions were made.

In the early hours of 31 March, while the British bombers were flying home from Nuremberg and Schweinfurt, two more forces appeared on the British radars, this time off the coasts of Lincolnshire and Norfolk. The first of these, estimated at twenty-five aircraft, probably never crossed the coast but a few Junkers 88 fighter bombers came in, hoping to catch tired Bomber Command crews over their airfields. But the Germans were too early; the bombers were not yet home.

One Junkers dropped two bombs on the runway at Metheringham and others dropped bombs near two American airfields but without causing serious damage. At the fighter airfield at Coltishall a Mosquito of 25 Squadron crewed by two Fleet Air Arm officers had landed after a patrol and was taxi-ing from the runway by the lights of a lorry. The activity attracted one of the Germans who made an attack, hitting the Mosquito and damaging it in both engines but unfortunately the two Fleet Air Arm men were unharmed.

These small incidents illustrate one aspect of the air war very clearly. Even before 1939 R.A.F. leaders were determined that their aircraft should be primarily weapons of attack rather than of defence. Even though the bombers raiding Nuremberg were suffering fearsome casualties on that particular night, another aim of the R.A.F. was being achieved. The aerial war had been carried firstly by Bomber Command and then by the Americans to their enemy and the Luftwaffe forced back onto the defensive. The Germans could only mount these puny efforts over England while over 1,000 British planes had taken off to fly over Hitler's territory. It was the German civilians who cowered for their lives in cellars and shelters while the English slept safely in their beds.

12

The Return Flight

When bombers flew away from Nuremberg they were pursued for a short way by the German fighters and several more combats took place. But the odds were not so heavily in favour of the night fighters now – the Germans were tiring and their aircraft would soon be running out of fuel, while the bombers, having dropped their bombs, were more manoeuvrable. At least five bombers were attacked immediately south of the target but the only aircraft to go down was a Junkers 88 shot down in flames by the gunners of a 57 Squadron Lancaster.

Two of the other encounters are of interest. The reader may remember how the Canadian 433 (Porcupine) Squadron had been formed a few weeks previously around a nucleus of five crews who had all been in trouble of some sort at their former squadrons. Three of these did not survive long and the American, Chris Neilson, had been shot down on his bombing run just short of Nuremberg. The last of these five crews was captained by Pilot Officer Ronald Reinelt, an English pilot whose 'crime' on his previous squadron was that, having had to divert to an aerodrome near his home, he took a day off. This resulted in his being charged with 'misappropriating one Halifax aircraft while on active service'.

Reinelt's crew had a short fight with a German fighter soon after leaving the target and just one cannon shell hit his starboard outer engine and set fire to the nearby fuel tanks. Reinelt tells of how the mid-upper gunner 'thought it a huge joke when a large piece of wing went sailing past his turret'. The attack left the Halifax with a windmilling propeller and a long streamer of flame from the holed tanks. The crew prepared to bale out but decided to remain with their bomber for as long as possible.

Unknown to the bomber crew they were now being watched over by friends. Flight Lieutenant Woodman's Serrate Mosquito was in the same area.

I saw an odd orange light crossing the sky. We intercepted it, then flew in formation a quarter of a mile away, keeping a radar look-out for German fighters. It was a Halifax on fire. The fire gradually died away and he flew on in the dark with our best wishes for a safe return to England. 'Good luck, chaps' I called out aloud, although they did not know we were there.

The Mosquito men would have been pleased to know that Reinelt nursed his Halifax safely home.

The second combat in which we are interested also had a happy ending. Oberleutnant Helmut Schulte had already shot down four bombers but his *schräge Musik* had now jammed and when he found another Lancaster south of Nuremberg he had to attack this with his forward firing guns. Schulte had no experience of attacking from the rear and was a little frightened of the bomber's tail gunner. His first attack came to nothing because he had forgotten to arm the nose guns then, as soon as he got into position again, the bomber went into a corkscrew. Schulte followed for five minutes and, when the Lancaster settled to a steady course again, took up a position behind the bomber.

At first, he didn't object to this formation flying and he must have been watching me as I got into position again. As soon as I opened fire he dived away and my shells passed over him. I thought that this chap must have nerves of steel; he had watched me formate on him and then had dived just at the right time. He had been through as much as I had – we had both been to Nuremberg that night – so I decided that was enough. I would like that pilot to know that I deliberately let him go.

This encounter coincides with the experiences of a 115 Squadron crew captained by Warrant Officer Howard Hemming. The tail gunner responsible for directing the corkscrew was Sergeant John Carter, who thought the attack had been carried out 'in a half-hearted manner, possibly by a fighter flown by a pilot from a training unit'. The Lancaster gunners had deliberately not fired, relying on evasion and escape into the dark.

The night fighters that had fought all the way to Nuremberg and over the target had been those who went into action earlier in the flight at Ida and Otto; but they had not been reinforced during the later stages of the battle due to the expectation by the Germans that the bombers would turn north instead of south at the end of the Long Leg. German pilots, like Oberleutnant Schulte, had now to break off the pursuit and land.

The only Gruppe so far unaccounted for in the whole of the German night-fighter force was II/NJG 6 with its Messerschmitt 110s at Echterdingen near Stuttgart. The return route from Nuremberg passed within twelve miles of this airfield. Major Rolf Leuchs, the Gruppe commander, tells how fog had earlier kept his aircraft on the ground and then,

after much to-ing and fro-ing we received orders from the 7th Fighter Division to take off. We flew north, to beacon Otto, and then followed the bombers all the way to Nuremberg. We could see ahead of us in the distance a large number of fires in the air but we never caught up and, as far as I can remember, none of my crews shot down a bomber on this night.

This Gruppe had thus been sent north and committed to an unprofitable stern chase to the target. After the British left Nuremberg, they flew right past Major Leuchs's empty airfield – a fortunate escape for the bombers.

It would be useless now to write of a 'stream' for the bombers were spread over a huge frontage. Many aircraft had started the return flight from Schweinfurt, thinking that the town they had bombed was Nuremberg, and they navigated accordingly. The broadcast winds failed to reveal that the wind was still carrying the bombers to the north and there were also many pilots not even attempting the planned return route – badly damaged aircraft and those with captains who always cut corners. The Pathfinders were probably the biggest offenders here; their greater experience enabling them to avoid trouble spots and reach home early for an hour's extra sleep. The navigation logs of such crews never revealed this practice. As one Pathfinder pilot says, 'Bennett would not have approved.'

The friendly wind that had carried the bombers from the Belgian coast to Nuremberg in just over 100 minutes was now basically a head wind and, for most, the flight back to the French coast near Dieppe would be a long, boring drag of three hours. Many pilots lost height and flew in the thick cloud which now stretched all the way to Dieppe – the very cloud they had hoped for on the outward flight. Others preferred to stay above the cloud and retain the advantages of visibility. These still left thick vapour trails but the moon finally set at 01.48 and the greatest period of danger was obviously over.

The bomber force lost two more aircraft before it left Germany – both near Stuttgart, a heavily defended area north of the route over which many aircraft flew in error. It was the Stuttgart Flak that probably accounted for the first of these losses, that of the Halifax piloted by Squadron Leader Hill of 51 Squadron (see Plate 26). The second crash was that of a Lancaster whose captain was an N.C.O. pilot of 115 Squadron. Tom Fogaty, D.F.M., has been described by another man in his crew as 'a brave man but in a sense a very ordinary one, just a level-headed man from Devon'. Fogaty's Lancaster had been hit much earlier in the raid, first by a fighter and then by Flak. For the last 150 miles it had been losing height steadily and, near Stuttgart, it went into a shallow dive to starboard which the pilot could not correct. There was a discussion among the crew as to whether it was best to attempt a landing, which Fogaty wanted, or to bale out. In the end, the latter course was chosen. The flight engineer could not find his parachute so Fogaty pressed his own upon him. Six men jumped safely and the pilot was left to attempt his landing – in a crippled plane, alone, at night and in an enemy country!

The six who had baled out were soon captured and taken to the local police station. They were most surprised to be joined later by their pilot. At 500 feet he had put down full flap, switched on the landing lights, found a convenient field and set his Lancaster down on its belly. Fogaty had been knocked out and came to lying in the snow surrounded by farm workers. He had a bump on his head, a grazed leg and was, not surprisingly, 'very dazed'.

The crew of Squadron Leader H. W. Trilsbach, who had come from Brazil to fly with the R.A.F. and was now a flight commander in the Canadian Pathfinder squadron, were more fortunate when they flew over Stuttgart.

They waited until we were directly overhead and then opened up with searchlights and some really good Flak. Our starboard-outer engine was hit and caught fire. My flight engineer, a replacement for my regular one, was new and very shaken, and when told to press the fire extinguisher, did so but for the *starboard-inner* instead.

Subsequently he did press the correct button but it did not put the fire out or have any effect on the blaze. As a last resort to getting the crew to bale out, I put the Lancaster into a very steep dive down to something like 6,000 feet and this put the fire out.

We proceeded home on the two port engines at, of course, a much reduced speed and height. I did not report the fire extinguisher incident at interrogation and, as the ground crew covered up, the flight engineer did not get into trouble. Poor chap, he went missing shortly afterwards.

Sergeant D. A. Kelley was one of the very few Canadian flight engineers in Bomber Command. He was killed while flying with another pilot over France three days before D-Day.

Just over an hour after leaving Nuremberg, those aircraft that were following the planned route flew over the Rhine north of Strasbourg and on into France. For the crews it was an important psychological landmark; they were finished once more with the sinister dark skies of Nazi Germany. If they were forced down now, at least they would find themselves among friends.

For most crews the flight had become an event of anti-climax, boredom and increasing fatigue. The bomb-aimers continued to push out Window with even less enthusiasm than before, the wireless-operators to receive the half-hourly wind broadcasts, the gunners to search for fighters. Many gunners could still see, for some time, the glow behind them of the fires their bombs had started and different squadron records contain statements that this glow could be seen from sixty miles, one hundred miles and one even from the French coast. Near Château Thierry, a 44 Squadron crew were delighted to have a succession of Vs for Victory flashed to them by the torch of some unknown Frenchman.

The navigators remained busy as always and one of them upset the remainder of his crew.

There was only one time in my tour that I knew time to go slowly. This was the very long leg coming home. We had a terrific head wind and even I thought it would never end. I remember, about half-way along, I was asked how long it was to the coast. These requests always came as you were immersed in some calculation and, rather stupidly, I replied that it was only about an hour. Some hour-and-a-half later, the same questions. This time I gave the correct answer which I think was just over an hour. Even over the intercom I could feel the icy-cold reception of my news. I am sure the crew never really forgave me. (Flying Officer H. B. Mackinnon, 57 Squadron)

The German running commentary had now ceased and one of the A.B.C. special operators found time dragging.

It was very cold and the return journey seemed to go on for days. I do remember that I passed quite a lot of the time on the way back recalling the score of Wagner's *Die Meistersinger von Nürnberg*, an opera for which I had, and still have, considerable affection. I had always wanted to visit Nuremberg and it seemed an ironic situation that this should be my first visit. (Sergeant A. H. Grainge, 101 Squadron)

The pilot was faced with the usual problem of relieving himself without leaving his seat and the empty tin was passed to him. One pilot filled this and his flight engineer was carefully handing it down to the bomb-aimer who would dispose of it.

At that precise moment my rear gunner suddenly shouted 'Corkscrew starboard GO!' I flung the aircraft into a diving turn to starboard and had lost about 200 feet when the gunner said 'Sorry Skipper. It was one of ours,' followed by a loud guffaw. The bomb-aimer pushed his head into the cockpit and I saw that his face and the upper part of his body had taken the full force of the urine. We at the front just refused to have him near us for the rest of the journey because of the odour. You may not find it as amusing as I did. (Sergeant S. Fisher, 15 Squadron)

But the bombers were still not completely out of danger. Damaged aircraft and those with technical troubles were often suffering from accumulating difficulties as one thing went wrong after another. A Canadian crew, in which the navigator outranked the pilot and was therefore the aircraft captain, suffered first one engine failure and then a second, both on the port side. This left their Halifax both unable to manoeuvre or to maintain height.

I polled my crew – Switzerland or home? They said it was up to me. I then gave a course for the shortest route home and also a rate of descent to maintain speed. No sooner done, than a German fighter, possibly a Junkers 88, came up on our starboard side practically at our wing tip. I ordered the gunners to leave him alone. He flew with us for perhaps three quarters of an hour then he came underneath and up on the port side. He flew thus until nearly at the French coast, then he left us. (Flying Officer N. Dubeski, 427 Squadron)

Dubeski is sure that his shadower was not a Mosquito. It may have been a German fighter that had expended all its ammunition and was returning to its airfield.

By the time the bombers had all left Germany, the aircraft that had been to Nuremberg and Schweinfurt had spread out to such an extent that the two groups had merged again to form a stream so wide that the Germans were unable to plot a definite route. For this reason, and also because most of their fighters had landed, they ceased to broadcast the running commentary and gave up the Tame Boar type of interception. However, the German defence system was very flexible and they took advantage of the wide dispersal of the bombers which lessened the effectiveness of Window. A few fighters were still in action and the Germans found it possible to revert to the close control of these from ground radar stations, directing them onto individual bombers. Other Germans were freelancing, hoping to find a bomber with their own radar sets.

The first of a renewed series of combats involved Oberleutnant Martin Becker who had earlier shot down six bombers before landing near Mainz.

There was a large number of fighters there from different units. This was not bad for me; I could quietly take on gasoline and fresh ammunition. We were told that the bombers were going back between Stuttgart and Mannheim. I took off again and this time I was in a 'room' [part of the old box system of ground-controlled interception] and the officer on the ground said 'I have a target for you' and gradually directed me on to it. 'You should see him now. *Pauke machen! Pauke machen!* [Attack! Attack!]'. Then I saw it, flying quite fast.

The bomber was a Halifax of 429 (Bison) Squadron and Flying Officer J. Dougall, the Scots bomb-aimer, describes the effect of Becker's attack.

We had flown over Saarbrücken and were engaged by Flak but this suddenly stopped and we should have realized there was a fighter about. The first thing I knew was the aircraft being hit by cannon fire. The gunners had not seen it but I looked out and there was this twin-engined fighter passing just beyond our wing tip. It was so near that I could almost have reached out and shaken hands with its pilot.

The Halifax was on fire in one engine and the almost

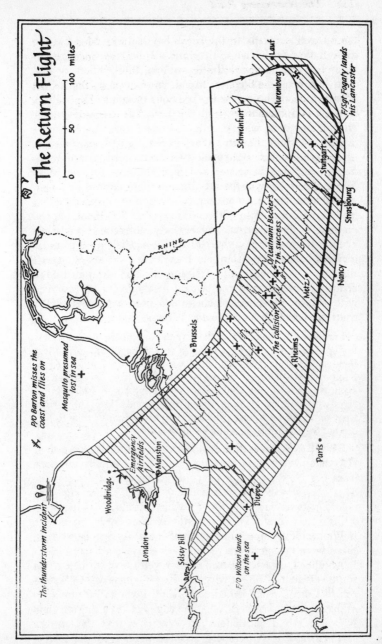

The Return Flight

100 miles
0   50

The thunderstorm incident

P/O Barton misses the coast and flies on

Mosquito presumed lost in sea

Woodbridge

London

Emergency Airfields

Manston

Selsey Bill

Dover

F/O Wilson lands on the sea

Dieppe

Paris

Brussels

RHINE

Rheims

Metz

Oberleutnant Becker's 7th success

The collision

Nancy

Strasbourg

Stuttgart

Schweinfurt

Nuremberg

Lauf

F/Sgt Fogarty lands his Lancaster

Map 11

empty overload tank in the bomb bay had exploded but the aircraft flew on for some time and all the crew managed to bale out. The pilot was the Australian, Pilot Officer Bowly, who had been detailed to attend the funeral of one of his countrymen at Harrogate the previous morning. His Halifax crashed in Luxembourg and the Luftwaffe credited Becker with its destruction.

This was Becker's last victory of the night. If my research is correct, he had destroyed two Lancasters of the Path-finders and one Lancaster and four Halifaxes of the Main Force. Thirty-four of the fifty men in these aircraft had died.

The next bomber to be caught by a fighter was also piloted by an Australian, Pilot Officer Haste of 61 Squadron, but the method of interception was entirely different. Nachtjagd-gruppe 10, the night-fighter test unit, had taken off from its forward base at Hangelar near Bonn with a variety of aircraft testing new equipment. Its commander, Major Rudolf Schoenert, was one of the last off in a Junkers 88 equipped with Naxos, a device which homed onto a bomber's H2S transmissions from underneath the bomber-stream.

I followed the bombers all the way to Nuremberg and kept pick-ing up signals on my Naxos but was very disappointed to find that these suddenly stopped each time I tried to find the bomber. Again I followed the bombers for a long way back from the target and eventually picked up a Lanki which was flying home. I hit it in the right wing with my slanting cannon and started a fire. The bomber went on flying for a long time and they had plenty of time to bale out but they didn't and eventually it went down.

The R.A.F. navigators had been warned not to keep their H2S sets switched on for long periods over enemy territory in case a Naxos-type device could home upon their signals. This was why Schoenert's contacts kept disappearing. The unfortunate navigator in this crew had left his set switched on a little too long. The Lancaster crashed near Namur in Belgium, eighty-five miles north of track. As Schoenert says, there were no survivors.

Another Lancaster to come down well north of the correct route was that of Flight Sergeant Ron Thomas of 115 Squad-ron, a Cornishman. His aircraft, shot down by an unknown night fighter, crashed on the edge of Wellington and Napoleon's old battlefield at Waterloo, exactly on the *outward route* to Nuremberg and 115 miles from his correct return route, an indication of the spread of the bombers at this stage.

Bomber crews were sometimes told that, if they could bomb an enemy target successfully just once, then the cost of their training and of their aircraft would have been repaid. Such an improbable calculation was produced as a morale booster but poor Flight Sergeant Thomas and his crew had fulfilled the conditions. They were all killed returning from bombing the target on their first operational flight.

German fighters were responsible for the destruction of five bombers between the German border and the Channel coast. Another was either a fighter victim or had succumbed to heavy icing – it is only known that a propellor came off and hit the fuselage, causing the Halifax to crash with the loss of its entire crew. Another had been hit by Flak as it flew over Metz and crashed later and a third Halifax was seen by many crews to be hit by Flak and go down into the sea off Dieppe. It is not known whether it was hit by a coastal Flak battery or by a Flak ship. The aircraft concerned was probably a 640 Squadron Halifax which was the only heavy bomber lost on that night not subsequently traced by the R.A.F.'s Missing Research Teams.

We are almost finished with bombers crashing over enemy territory but one tragic incident remains to be described. Squadron Leader 'Turkey' Laird, D.F.C., an experienced Canadian pilot of 427 (Lion) Squadron had been advised by his navigator that he was off-course north of track and had made a slight course alteration to port.

The pilot was the only one to spot the other aircraft as he yelled out 'What the Hell?' and there was a terrific bang as we collided. The other aircraft brushed the top of our's and the only thing that saved me was that my back was to the shock and the rear of my turret was padded. I saw the Lancaster off to my left; he just seemed to nose down. There was no fire. I believe most of the chaps in our aircraft must have been killed instantly.

Pilot Officer John Moffat, remote in the rear turret, managed to escape by parachute and was the only man in either crew to survive the collision.

The Lancaster involved was that of Flight Sergeant Pickin of 622 Squadron. The two bombers·crashed in the south-east corner of Belgium, close to the borders of both France and

Luxembourg. By a coincidence, the navigators of both aircraft were from the same Canadian town of Saskatoon. The
deaths of both men reveal personal tragedies. In the Halifax,
Flying Officer 'Red' Soeder was reputed to be on the last
operation of his tour and Warrant Officer John Merritt, in
the Lancaster, had been married to a Hampshire girl only
ten days previously.

The whole incident was really a piece of appalling bad
luck. Collisions usually occurred over home airfields, over
the target or at route turning-points. These two aircraft were
forty miles off track in the middle of a leg almost 300 miles
in length.

Just before 04.00, the first of the scattered bomber force
reached the coast and flew out over the English Channel.
German radar plotted the departing bombers between Saint-
Valery-en-Caux, west of Dieppe, and the mouth of the
Scheldt in Holland – a spread of 160 miles. It would be
nearly two hours before the last stragglers were clear of the
skies over German-occupied territory.

Ninety-four bombers and their crews were missing.

The crossing of the coast was another psychological mile-
stone in the flight and the crews of aircraft not in difficulties
relaxed. Some had now descended to below oxygen height
and were able to have coffee from their flasks, a bite to eat
or the forbidden cigarette which they felt they deserved on
this occasion. Gunners were never supposed to relax their
search but, after nearly five hours of constant peering into the
darkness, many did so. Gee was now free of jamming and,
for the first time in many hundreds of miles, navigators were
able to fix their position reliably. Some, especially those who
had been to Schweinfurt, were greatly surprised to find they
were up to 100 miles north of their estimated position. The
various devices to jam German radars and radio were
switched off; the A.B.C. special operators ceased their radio
watch; I.F.F. was switched on so that English night fighters
and ground radars could recognize the approaching aircraft
as friends. The worst was over.

The aircraft that were over the Channel set course for
Selsey Bill, the landfall chosen for this flight and one that
experienced crews had often used. Those who had come out
well to the north continued to fly on to the coast of East

Anglia, although one or two crews whose navigation had really been in trouble came in over the Lincolnshire or even the Yorkshire coasts. All kept clear of London over which no sensible bomber man flew intentionally for fear of provoking the city's strong anti-aircraft defences.

The head winds into which the bombers had been flying since leaving the target were decreasing but not by as much as had been forecast and the final part of the flight took longer than had been anticipated. Those aircraft crossing the North Sea faced a further hazard. The thick cumulus cloud had come further south during the night and the returning crews had to descend through this, facing a risk of icing and of severe turbulence. These conditions did not present too much difficulty for most crews but for those with badly damaged aircraft, injured crewmen or in technical trouble, this sea crossing was an anxious time. The sea claimed many bomber crews during the war.

A Halifax of 429 (Bison) Squadron with a crew of four Canadians and three Englishmen had been attacked and badly damaged near Stuttgart and only the presence of an alert gunner in one of 6 Group's newly installed belly-gun positions and immediate evasive action by the pilot saved the aircraft from complete destruction. A violent dive finally shook off the German but damaged hydraulics left the Halifax with wheels and flaps down. The Canadian flight engineer put out a fire by chopping a hole in the side of the fuselage and kicking out two blazing magnesium flares kept there in case of a landing in the sea. The Halifax flew on at considerably reduced speed. When the coast failed to appear on time, pilot and wireless-operator were all for getting a radio 'fix' that would immediately establish their exact position but the navigator was unwilling – his navigation was not that bad! When the coast still failed to appear after a further interval, the pilot ordered the radio fix to be obtained. To the horror of all, they were well south of Paris. The violent dive which had helped put out the fire had probably upset the gyro compass. There was not enough fuel remaining to reach England but the crew were all in favour of flying as far as possible out over the Channel and hoped to be picked up by an Air–Sea Rescue launch.

Eventually the sea was reached near Le Havre but there was now only a little fuel left. The wireless-operator sent out their distress call and then clamped his Morse key down so that the signal would go out to the very end. In the cockpit, the red light came up showing that the last tank was almost empty, and all but the pilot took up crash positions with back to the main wing spar, heads in hands, knees up to chin.

The pilot lined his aircraft up for a landing along the line of the waves but the two starboard engines cut without warning and the Halifax swung into the side of a wave. The whole nose broke off and disappeared at once but the six men behind the main spar were able to walk out along the wing and into their rubber dinghy.

Flying Officer Jimmy Wilson from Moose Jaw, Saskatchewan, had made the sacrifice that every pilot knew he may one day be called upon to make for his crew. His body was never found.

After a complicated rescue operation involving Spitfire, Tempest, Sea Otter and Walrus aircraft, the six men were picked up that afternoon only twenty-five miles off the Normany coast by two R.A.F. launches from Newhaven.*

The only other serious incident of the sea crossing occurred many miles to the north. A 61 Squadron Lancaster, making for Coningsby, was at or near the Norfolk coast when it ran into stormy conditions in cloud. The Australian Pilot Officer J. A. Forrest turned south-east to avoid the turbulence but the aircraft was then struck by lightning on the front turret. The shock passed right through the Lancaster and Forrest, temporarily blinded and stunned, lost control. Thinking he was over land, he ordered his crew to parachute out of the plunging bomber. Only two men, a gunner and the wireless-operator, had recovered sufficiently from the electrical shock to act and out they went.

The pilot did manage to regain control only 1,000 feet from the ground, or rather from the sea, for he had not, after all, crossed the coast. He landed as soon as possible at a nearby airfield and reported the incident. As soon as it was light, a search by both ships and aircraft of the area was commenced but no trace of the two men was ever found.

The extra lease of life that poor Forrest had gained for

* Two of the six men saved died later in the war – Sergeant 'Hank' Glass, just before he was due to receive, from the King, the D.F.M. for dealing with the blazing flares, and Flight Sergeant Cyril Way, the English navigator, on his second tour. The mid-upper gunner refused to fly again and returned to Canada

the other crew members was not a long one. They all died soon afterwards.

There was always rivalry on squadrons as to which crew could land first after a raid. Those who won were usually the 'old hands', more skilled in the air and also more experienced in 'adjusting' their navigation logs. On this night, the first heavy bomber to return from the target was the Lancaster of Flight Lieutenant C. R. Snell, the Canadian pilot of a Pathfinder aircraft that had been over Nuremberg at 01.07. The records of 635 Squadron and Snell's log book show that he landed at his home airfield at Downham Market at 04.10. He must have flown almost directly there from Nuremberg. This fast return flight made against the wind in just over three hours illustrates several points – the skill of an experienced Pathfinder crew, on their thirty-sixth operation, who could pick their way through the defended areas of Germany and reach England in this incredibly short time and the independent attitude of Canadians to what they sometimes regarded as unnecessary route discipline. Another point of interest is that Snell was amazed when, later, he heard of the heavy losses. Here was a crew that had flown to Nuremberg at the head of the bomber-stream and then taken an independent route home. The only action he had seen had been over Nuremberg itself. It was twenty-five minutes before the next aircraft landed, again a Pathfinder at Downham Market.

One of the first of the Main Force aircraft to land was that of Warrant Officer Mervyn Stafford, an Australian pilot, who landed at Binbrook at 04.58. He had decided soon after leaving the target that the bomber-stream was no longer the safest place and had flown straight to Binbrook.

I was the first to return from our squadron. We were met at the aircraft by the group captain [Hugh Edwards, v.c., d.s.o., d.f.c. – a famous Australian airman]. He wanted to know why we had returned early. When I explained what had happened, he did not say much and after he had heard the rest of the crews' reports I heard no more about it, so I assumed he agreed with what I had done.

These crews had all taken the short cut over the North Sea and East Anglia. Those who followed the planned route came in over Selsey Bill, where a searchlight welcomed them, then on to the last turning-point at Reading where the bomber-stream finally dispersed and each aircraft was free to fly direct to its own airfield.

The leading aircraft of those now flying north from Reading were often those who had bombed Schweinfurt in error and had made a surprisingly early return.

As we flew up over Lincolnshire and south Yorkshire we began to suspect that all was not well. When the bomber force was returning from a raid, the flarepaths of the bomber airfields illuminated the countryside. This night, all seemed to be in darkness. When we got to Leconfield, the airfield lights were out; they were not expecting us so soon. We knew then that we had bombed the wrong target. (Pilot Officer J. Cotter, 640 Squadron)

Soon after 05.00, many more aircraft were streaming in over Selsey Bill and making for their airfields. The weather in southern England was good and, thanks to Gee, navigation was no longer a problem. The airfields started to become active as they received home their tired crews. The pilots called the control tower by V.H.F. as soon as they reached their own airfield and were allocated a turn among the waiting aircraft. A good airfield could land aircraft at the rate of one every two or three minutes but, even so, this often meant a long wait if many arrived together. Some crafty pilots reported themselves present before they reached the airfield so that they could beat others in this aerial queue.

The fine weather conditions continued for some time and many crews were able to get down safely, but the ill luck that had dogged this operation had one more card to play. The northerly winds had earlier caused snow and sleet showers over south Lincolnshire and the Fens, where there were no bomber airfields, but, as the landing of the bombers proceeded, this bad weather spread south-eastwards into East Anglia. Soon, the airfields of 3, 8 and 100 Groups became badly affected by these showers and the low cloud they brought scudding along only 200 or 300 feet above the runways. At the same time, many of the airfields further north were also becoming affected by industrial haze or morning mists so that more than half of the bomber airfields were now unusable. Growing numbers of aircraft, many of them low on fuel or damaged, started seeking diversionary landings in southern England. It was a race against time as flying-control officers at every level of command from High Wycombe down to station struggled to arrange emergency landings for possibly 200 of the returning bombers. But this type of situation was not new and the diversion system started well. Aircraft were soon landing at fighter airfields, O.T.U. airfields, American airfields, anywhere where there was a runway long enough to take a Lancaster or Halifax.

The two emergency airfields, at Woodbridge in Suffolk and Manston in Kent, with extended runways for aircraft suffering hydraulic failures and with special medical teams and rescue equipment, catered for the worst hit of the damaged aircraft. A 61 Squadron Lancaster had been badly hit by fighter attack and its navigator, Flight Sergeant Griffin, tells of his return.

Against a strong head wind with two engines out we made only about 80 knots over the ground so we set course for Woodbridge. We opened the rear door and threw out everything we could move – guns, ammunition, parachutes – but we continued to lose height and I thought we would have to ditch. Then, over on the port side, we saw the lights of Manston. The pilot simply said 'Going straight in' and put her down first time.

We were a bit shocked and had a couple of stiff brandies before going to bed. Next morning I woke up and looked out of the window. It was like a grave-yard. There were aircraft all over the place, some smashed up, some burnt out.

At Woodbridge, a 619 Squadron Lancaster crash-landed after flying all the way from Nuremberg on only two engines – a fine performance both by the Lancaster and by the young pilot, Sergeant John Parker, a Northern Irishman, and his all N.C.O. crew. Parker and his men only just managed to get out before the Lancaster caught fire and was completely gutted. Yet again it was only a temporary reprieve for both Parker and his crew.

Another pilot was diverted to Woodbridge because of bad weather at his own airfield. He carefully landed at the end of what he then realized was a three-mile-long runway so, to avoid a long taxi-ing, he took off again and flew a little further before making a second landing on the same runway.

In spite of the efficiency of the diversion procedure, not all the landings were successful. There was no answer to the problem of getting really crippled aircraft down or those whose pilots were injured or even dead. The first crash was at 05.03. A 101 Squadron Lancaster flew into the ground as it tried to get down at an American airfield at Newbury. A few minutes later, a 51 Squadron Halifax crashed into a wood at Stokenchurch in Oxfordshire. This crash may have rattled the windows at Bomber Command H.Q. only five miles away. The reasons for these two crashes are not known for there were no survivors.

A little further north, another Halifax was trying to get down at the O.T.U. airfield at Silverstone (now the motor-racing circuit). Crews that had already landed watched this aircraft coming in on three engines. The pilot could not line up with the runway and the control tower heard him say 'I'll try to come round again. I'll try to.' But the wheels of the Halifax touched the roof of the airfield's fire-section building. It tumbled and exploded across some playing fields for 200 yards. Squadron Leader M. McCreanor of 578 Squadron and six of his crew, including a new second pilot, were either killed outright or died later, leaving the tail gunner, concussed and burnt, as the only survivor.

Pilot Officer E. W. Chitty, an Australian pilot, was making his final approach at Waterbeach when his crew heard the control tower in their earphones. 'Who's that bloody fool making a right-hand circuit?' Another pilot was desperate to get down and had cut in. Chitty had no option but to open up his engines and overshoot but, at that moment, a flurry of snow caused him to lose sight of the ground. A few seconds later there was a horrible shudder as the wheels were torn off and then the Lancaster, in a nose-down attitude, hit the ground hard. Chitty and four more escaped with various injuries. It was some time before the mid-upper gunner could be found and lastly the body of the bomb-aimer, lying crushed under a wing. It was never discovered how he had got into this position.

Another crash had a happier ending. A Pathfinder aircraft, almost out of fuel, was diverted due to bad weather at Oakington and had to land at Feltwell in conditions little better. The navigator used Gee to get them to the Feltwell runway and the pilot side-slipped his Lancaster straight in from out of the cloud-base, but could do no better than touch down half-way along the runway. He swung off this to avoid going over the end but the Lancaster burst a tyre and finally came to rest when it hit a concrete pill-box. The crew tumbled out and up went the Lancaster in a spectacular blaze that was helped on by four target indicators that were still on board.

The navigator, Flight Lieutenant F. Bell, describes the next development.

We stood well back watching the blaze; ammunition and T.I.s were burning and exploding merrily when, from a house just over the perimeter, came two elderly ladies with a small child between them. They had their nighties well tucked into red flannel drawers and went across the field as if the very devil was after them. The poor kid's feet never touched the ground. This incident relaxed the tension.

There are several instances of aircraft being landed in open country. After being lost in thick cloud with his petrol almost exhausted, Canadian Flight Sergeant Jack Ward, a former 'Mountie', spotted open fields below through a gap in the cloud. He ordered his crew to their crash positions and then made them a very bumpy wheels-down landing which ended with the nose of the Halifax buried in the roof of a small farm building. No one was hurt and the next event was the appearance out of the mist of a soldier carrying a bucket of tea and some mugs! Ward had come down three miles from Cranwell airfield.

A similar successful landing was made by an American pilot, Lieutenant Max Dowden from Santa Cruz, California, who had joined the R.C.A.F. before Pearl Harbor, following a broken engagement. He now held an American rank but was completing his tour of operations with Bomber Command. Dowden tried to get down at Silverstone but 'a landing there was refused emphatically' according to the bomb-aimer, Sergeant Brickenden. Doubtless Silverstone was in trouble with Squadron Leader McCreanor's crash. Dowden was given a course to where a vertical searchlight would indicate another airfield but no searchlight was to be found. With his fuel almost gone, Dowden just had to get down. He descended gingerly through the cloud and emerged at 1,500 feet with just enough light to see the ground.

The landing was amazingly smooth with a slight swing to port and an occasional bump. We had touched down in one field, run over a plough, crossed a road and ditch, gone through an iron fence, left the port wing in a tree, swung across another field, through a hedge, demolished a pig pen and had come to rest in the third field.

We stood there, inhaling a welcome cigarette when, across the fields in greatcoat and, believe it or not, long nightshirt, came one of Britain's best Home Guard waving a rifle.

Dowden and his men were given a warm welcome and a ham-and-egg breakfast by the inhabitants of a small town or large village, the identity of which is not known but it is believed to be in the Buckingham area.*

We left Pilot Officer Cyril Barton determined to fly on to the target in his badly damaged Halifax without three crew members who had baled out prematurely. Officially, Barton did reach Nuremberg and dropped his load of incendiaries there, but, from the evidence of Sergeant Trousdale the flight engineer, it is more likely that the bombs fell on Schweinfurt. Barton was now faced with the long return flight with only three engines and having lost 400 gallons of fuel, with no navigator to guide him or wireless-operator to get a radio fix and with no intercom to communicate with his remaining crew. Barton's exact route will never be known but his return to England must surely rank as an epic flight. He calculated rough headings himself and, while it was still visible, the North Star was much relied upon. No trouble was encountered over Germany but, as the sea crossing seemed to go on and on, there were doubts as to whether the fuel would last. All movable equipment went out into the sea.

Barton was probably aiming for East Anglia but his land-fall was nearly 200 miles further north among the balloon defences of Sunderland in County Durham. He had probably flown right up the east coast of England but just out of sight of the land. To avoid the balloons, Barton turned and flew out to sea again but the engineer warned that their fuel was almost exhausted. The coast was crossed again a little to the south, all eyes searching for a suitable landing place.

Ryhope is a small mining town on the Durham coast surrounded by hilly country. As the Halifax flew over this place at about 1,500 feet, its petrol supply finally failed. The

* The following months took their toll of many of the crews mentioned here. Lieutenant Dowden's went in May, Warrant Officer McGown's (see later in chapter) in June, and Pilot Officer Chitty, with a rebuilt crew, in July. There were some survivors but Dowden and Chitty were among the killed.

two gunners and the flight engineer hurriedly took up crash positions by the main spar while Barton, with only diving speed to manoeuvre the sluggish bomber, attempted the landing.

In the path of the Halifax were four rows of miners' cottages and Barton lifted the nose to clear these but the loss of speed robbed him of the last control he had. The bomber flopped heavily onto a hillside, ran over a railway and right into the yard of the local coal mine.

The Halifax was torn to pieces but the three men by the main spar all survived without serious injury. Two coal miners on their way to report for the morning shift were hit – one being killed. In the cockpit of the Halifax, Pilot Officer Barton was also dead.

There are two sequels to this story. The letter left by Barton for his mother in the event of his death was a remarkable testimony to this young airman's Christian beliefs. His mother allowed it to be published and it was widely circulated.

Except for leaving you I am quite prepared to die. Death holds no terrors for me. I know I shall survive the judgement because I have trusted in Christ as my Saviour. . . . All that I am anxious about is that you and the rest of the family will come to know Him. . . . I commend my Saviour to you.

Three months later it was announced that this pilot had been awarded a posthumous Victoria Cross for 'gallantly completing his last mission in the face of almost impossible odds'. Cyril Barton's v.c. was the only one to be awarded to a Halifax crew member throughout the war.

Fourteen bombers crashed or crash landed in England although not all were complete wrecks. There were several smaller accidents and numerous narrow escapes as pilots got their aircraft down on the last of their fuel. One incident, however, was unusual for 1944. Flight Sergeant A. F. T. L'Estrange had taken the short cut over the North Sea and was flying over Norfolk. He had switched on his navigation lights and the crew were preparing for the landing at their home airfield in Lincolnshire. Sergeant A. Davenport, the tail gunner, had switched on the light inside his rear turret and was, no doubt, relaxing after the long flight.

Without warning, two long bursts of cannon fire hit the Lancaster from dead astern. The second of these wounded Davenport and caused extensive damage to the Lancaster. The fire had come from one of the Junkers 88s that had come Intruding earlier in the morning. While the others had flown home, this resolute crew had hung on hoping to catch just such an unwary victim as this Lancaster. There was no return fire and the Junkers escaped safely. L'Estrange managed to get his aircraft home to Wickenby but collided on the runway there with another Lancaster. The collision was not serious and no one was hurt. This was the only instance of a Bomber Command aircraft being attacked over England in the whole of that month.

A book of this nature inevitably leans heavily on a description of the experiences of those aircraft and their crews that had been shot down, attacked and damaged, or had been involved in some other dangerous incident. To keep things in proportion, it should be stated that out of 782 heavy bombers that had taken off just over 500 had reached and bombed either Nuremberg or Schweinfurt without encountering a fighter or being hit by Flak and had landed safely in England. No doubt, many crews had observed plenty of action beyond the confines of their own aircraft and had been very frightened, but, for two out of every three men who flew on this night, it had just been one more operation towards the completion of their tour with Bomber Command.

They were, of course, delighted to reach home.

As we got closer to the relative safety of England, it began to dawn on me that, not only had we not been involved in a combat at all, but I had not had a sighting of an enemy aircraft that was within range. This was quite incredible but it lasted all the way back to Snaith and safety and it was a very, very thankful crew that climbed wearily out of Halifax MH–P on the morning of Friday 31 March 1944. (Sergeant P. Bailey, 51 Squadron)

It was a wonderful relief to reach England and, as we started on the long haul from the south coast to Waddington, I remember leaving my navigation table go to to the Skipper to somehow share this reassurance of being over friendly territory. We landed at base, well overdue, but the welcome from the interrogation officer and everyone else, after what was now realized to have been an eventful occasion, was very heart-warming. (Sergeant J. Wesley, 467 Squadron)

The operation was nearly over. By 07.15 only two aircraft remained in the air. It had been a most difficult night for Sergeant Handley of 50 Squadron and his inexperienced crew on only their second operation. Handley had wandered around for some time in bad weather looking for a place to land and he finally found safety at Winthorpe, near Newark. The tired pilot made a bad landing and ran off the end of the runway. The Lancaster tipped onto its nose, which was smashed in, and the two inboard propellors were bent but no one was hurt.*

It was a Scots pilot, the now-dead Guy Johnston, who had been the first to take off for Nuremberg. It was another Scot, Warrant Officer Bill McGown from Glasgow, who piloted the last aircraft to return. His Lancaster was diverted from Waterbeach, its home airfield, to Stradishall but this airfield was also fog-bound and despite several attempts McGown could not land here.

Time and fuel were running out as the Lancaster was diverted yet again. McGown dared wait no longer and ordered his crew to bale out. Two men did so, an unnerving experience from below 1,000 feet and into fog, but both survived. Before more could jump, the fog cleared and the pilot promptly put his aircraft down in a Hertfordshire field. Although the Lancaster was a write-off, McGown's landing had been good enough, for there were no casualties.

It was 07.25. The Nuremberg Raid was over.

---

* The navigator in Handley's crew was Flying Officer Theodore Archard, who was a close friend of my family and a frequent visitor to our house when I was a young boy. He was a bachelor, a very religious man and he insisted on volunteering for flying duties although he was in a reserved occupation and, at thirty-two, older than most aircrew. I admired him immensely and it was his death, with the remainder of Sergeant Handley's crew in another disastrous raid at Mailly-le-Camp five weeks after Nuremberg, that later aroused my interest in Bomber Command. The result is this book dedicated to my friend 'Theo' Archard

13

The Next Morning

The tired airmen were collected from their aircraft by bus and taken back to the crew rooms. After disposing of parachutes, flying suits and equipment, they went straight into debriefing or 'interrogation' as it was called in 1944. With welcome cigarettes and hot drinks topped up with rum, each crew sat around a table and gave its report to one of the station's intelligence officers. These reports would be consolidated and then sent up the intelligence chain from the station, through base and group, to High Wycombe. This procedure was an integral part of every bomber raid.

Unless in difficulties or acting as Windfinders, the crews had maintained radio silence throughout the raid and those senior officers who had not been flying were now hovering around the interrogation tables, anxious to hear how the raid had gone. It would be the first news they would hear of the dramatic events that had unfolded at beacon Ida six hours earlier.

However, there was little mention at first of the fighter battle and interrogations proceeded normally. The earlier crews had not seen much of the action and, being usually the more cynical 'old hands' on a squadron, they kept their answers as brief as possible so that they could be released quickly. These crews would be responsible for the reports to be found in the Operational Record Books of many squadrons telling of 'a quiet trip' – anything to get off to bed!

But as crews started telling of the massive fighter interception and the sight of many bombers going down it soon became apparent that this had not been a normal operation but a fearful disaster. The exact losses, even at squadron level, would not be known for some time due to the late arrival of stragglers and the many bad-weather diversions.

After the quiet start, these reports were received with caution and sometimes with outright disbelief. A second-tour New Zealander had a brush with an intelligence officer at Breighton.

He asked me how many bombers I had seen shot down and I said, 'Approximately thirty'. He said I must be wrong and nobody had seen so many and that he would put down eight. This made me pretty mad. I didn't argue but said that he would find that this was the worst night Bomber Command had yet had. Unfortunately, I was proved correct. (Pilot Officer J. C. Palmer, 78 Squadron)

Men who forecast that the eventual loss might be as high as eighty or ninety bombers were brusquely told by their commanders to pull themselves together. Before take-off, crews at Kirmington had been told that 795 aircraft would be operating. On his return, a Canadian bluntly told his intelligence officer that Bomber Command could strike off the odd ninety-five – a remarkably accurate forecast.

As more crews went through interrogation it was eventually accepted that losses had been exceptionally heavy. But then another matter arose – there was much conflicting evidence about conditions over the target. Many men reported the presence of thick cloud and that they had bombed on Pathfinder skymarkers but others had bombed a clearly visible target which, they complained bitterly, the Pathfinders had failed to mark properly. It soon became evident that more than one target had been attacked. Several crews at Ludford Magna were accused of failing to bomb Nuremberg and there were angry scenes. A Canadian crew at Linton-on-Ouse, who had long before realized that their bombs had gone down on Schweinfurt, deliberately held back from being debriefed in order to see what other crews said. When they eventually faced the intelligence officer, the pilot immediately stated that they had bombed Schweinfurt. At this, several others, including crews who had already been debriefed, admitted a similar error.

Later, when the bombing photographs were developed, it was soon confirmed that Schweinfurt had been the accidental target and many other crews found, for the first time, that they had been in error by fifty-five miles. Surprisingly little was made of this. A mistake had been made but an important target had been hit, and for most, that seems to have been all that happened. If anything, it was regarded as a bonus and many of the crews involved eventually became quite proud of their achievement. The only rumblings were in the navigators' 'trade union' and there was much back-checking of navigational logs in the following days.

An N.C.O. gunner at Grimsby reported that he had seen

green tracer being fired at an angle of 80 degrees from the horizontal into bombers which had then caught fire. This report of the *schräge Musik* was not taken down and he left with the impression that 'as a simple airman I couldn't possibly have known what I was talking about'. But, at Waddington, the concern of an experienced Australian pilot was noted in 467 Squadron's Operational Record Book:

> The section of the route from Aachen to the target was reminiscent of a battlefield of burning aircraft. . . . very noticeable in the last half dozen trips is the fact that so many aircraft were seen going down in flames from operational height. . . . I would suggest that the enemy are using a new type of ammunition.

This pilot, Flight Lieutenant M. F. Smith, was killed a few weeks later. At the same station, the debriefing report of Pilot Officer Merril of 463 Squadron read:

> Fighter activity from leaving position B [i.e. Charleroi] to the target was such that enemy may have been aware of the route taken by the Main Force.

It was quite normal for group commanders to go out to one of their stations to attend the debriefing. At Melbourne, one crew found themselves describing their experiences to no less than six senior officers – Air Vice-Marshal Carr, two U.S.A.A.F. colonels and the base, station and squadron commanders.

> But, living up to wartime aircrew's tradition, we were not overawed, although we had to contend with a barrage of questions from them. Our pilot was asked for this brief summary of the sortie and I think his reply is worth quoting: 'I did not think we were going to reach the bloody target, let alone return to base.' I think those few words very aptly expressed the feelings of the whole crew. (Pilot Officer J. D. Whiteman, 10 Squadron)

Air Vice-Marshal Bennett, flying his small personal aircraft, visited two Pathfinder stations. At Graveley, he reproved a squadron commander who had flown on the raid for suggesting that a record number of bombers had been lost, and, at Bourn, did the same to another pilot who forecast a loss of 100 aircraft. 'Nonsense. You must be over tired!' However, when the full loss was announced, Bennett himself was furious at what had happened in view of his own protests the previous day about the choice of route. 'I was more than angry.'

On a few stations there were beery celebrations for a crew that had finished a tour, but it was mostly a very sombre scene as crews waited for friends to return, or the telephone call to say that aircraft had landed on another airfield. 101 Squadron, at Ludford Magna, had suffered the heaviest loss of the night – seven of their aircraft and fifty-six men were missing. An Australian, Pilot Officer 'Dutch' Holland, looked for his friends.

We waited and waited and waited. We were an experienced crew and accustomed to losing the odd one or two aircraft and this was the era when we in Bomber Command were losing large numbers on every raid. But, with nearly one third of our squadron missing, this was a big kick in the guts to us all. We waited up until nearly mid-day before going to our huts – stunned, shocked and silent, each crew member wrapped in his own mental anguish.

The previous evening, press correspondents and photographers had watched seventeen Halifaxes take off from Snaith. Sergeant Philip Bailey's crew had been photographed there while being debriefed; now, he had the opportunity to observe the newspaper men.

They watched and waited so considerately whilst the lads were coming in but, as the time went on, they too became aware that there were some losses. I shall never ever forget the faces of two of them – both middle-aged – when it was quietly put to them that six crews were unaccounted for, forty-two lads out of the 119 they had watched set off into the night sky. The notebooks and cameras were put away and their owners quietly left, obviously not wishing to intrude on our feelings.

The two Canadian squadrons at Leeming had sent off twenty-nine Halifaxes and five of these were missing, including those of two popular flight commanders. One man reports that, at debriefing, several of the crews 'got into the rum and told off the group captain'. Leaving aside the anger of the Canadians, these losses have an interesting tactical aspect. The Leeming squadrons had been allocated the highest – reckoned to be the safest – height band in 6 Group. But twenty-six aircraft from Tholthorpe, given the lowest heights in the group, had returned with the loss of only one aircraft.

Not all airfields were places of gloom. 100 Squadron had sent out eighteen Lancasters. None had been lost or diverted; in a little over one hour, all had landed safely at their home airfield near Grimsby. Three aircraft had been damaged but not a man hurt. The crews were able to go off to breakfast together in joyful mood and profoundly thankful to have been spared.

Flying Officer Ted Stone of 61 Squadron had been about to go home to Somerset on leave the previous day but at the last moment had been asked by his C.O. to stay and help make up the squadron's required effort for the raid. In return the C.O. had promised to 'lay on' a Lancaster and a 'sprog' crew to fly Stone home to Somerset as soon as he returned. Stone landed safely at Coningsby and within a few minutes was airborne again bound for Weston Zoyland. By mid-morning he was at home in Bridgwater.*

At Mildenhall, a young flight engineer just beginning his tour had undergone several alarming experiences during the raid. For him, it was 'a quick bit of snogging with the W.A.A.F. girl friend and then off for a good long sleep'.

Later, refreshed after a sleep, officers and N.C.O.s congregated in their respective Messes for a lunch-time beer and waited for the B.B.C. 1.0 p.m. news which usually gave the first reliable details of casualties. Throughout the airfields of Bomber Command and, no doubt, throughout the whole country, there was intense dismay when it was announced, 'Last night our bombers attacked Nuremberg. Ninety-six of our aircraft failed to return.'

I remember thinking, always bloody aircraft missing – never crews. What in hell are we anyway when machines are accorded more importance than human lives? Damn it to hell, didn't they realize that nearly 700 aircrew had gone missing? (Sergeant W. J. Blackburn, 12 Squadron)

It was by far the heaviest loss of the war, exceeding by

* The Lancaster Stone had flown to Nuremberg was ED860, N-Nan. It was the 103rd trip by a famous aircraft that was eventually retired after completing 136 operations. Stone's crew were very proud of this Lancaster which carried them safely through their tour and they agreed among themselves that the first daughter born to the wife of a crew member would be christened Nan. Stone's own wife was first and so, later in 1944, Jennifer Nan Stone received her name. The ex-Lancaster pilot later emigrated to Australia and Nan herself married. In 1971 a grand-daughter was born in Sydney and the wartime Lancaster was again remembered for this baby was christened Nanette!

almost twenty the recent record loss against Leipzig. The total would later be reduced to ninety-four with the rescue of the Canadian crew from the Channel and the discovery of another aircraft that had crash-landed in England. The loss of the Intruder Mosquito and of the secret operations Halifax were never announced. Officers at Wickenby tuned in to a German broadcast and heard the claim that 132 bombers had been shot down.

This broadcast confirmed the worst fears of the men who had flown to Nuremberg. It meant that so many friends made at training units and on the squadrons would never be seen again. It meant that, if Bomber Command tactics and choice of targets remained unaltered, their own chances of survival, already slender, would fade to nothing. In the Sergeants Mess at East Kirkby, a young wireless-operator noticed that 'some of the older N.C.O.s, who thought we had got our stripes too easily and normally didn't care much for aircrew, were not unfriendly', and a New Zealander with the Pathfinders remembers that, at Oakington, 'there was a stunned silence in which nobody moved or spoke for a full thirty seconds. I still think of that silence in the Mess while proceeding nowadays around my farm.'

News had come through that the squadrons were stood down from operations and many more men went off on leave; the 'moon period' had now really started and there would be no more deep-penetration raids for at least a week. The routine of a bomber station carried on just as on any other day following a raid. Telegrams were sent out to the relatives of the missing men; rooms were cleared of personal effects and, within only a few hours, the bright, eager faces of replacement crews anxious to get onto operations took the place of those who had been lost.

Aircraft that had been diverted returned home after their crews had slept and been fed at some strange airfield. One man, whose Halifax had come down at an O.T.U. at Westcott, suffered his first attack of 'crabs' from the bed provided there and then arrived at Snaith to find that a favourite bicycle that he had ridden for many months had been stolen. The captain of a Canadian crew that had landed at another O.T.U. after a difficult flight had to slap two of them across the face when they became hysterical on being awakened.

Those men who had landed in the south with badly

damaged aircraft returned to their home airfields by train. A 640 Squadron crew were surprised that, when they crossed London by Underground, complete with flying suits and parachutes

nobody took the slightest bit of notice of us despite our impedimenta and generally scruffy appearance and, when we reached Beverley, the station master refused to let us use his telephone to ring Leconfield for transport. We couldn't raise tuppence between the seven of us and it was some time before we found a 'phone. All of which went to show that the world did not think us heroes even if we did ourselves.

The crew of Lieutenant Max Dowden, who had crash-landed his Lancaster in open country, had to wait for some time at King's Cross station with the bomb sight and eight machine-guns with belts of ammunition from their aircraft. Dowden and two others found a good fish and chip café, while the remainder of the crew entered the station bar just as the B.B.C. news was telling of the heavy losses. They were well plied with free drinks and just caught their train 'absolutely sloshed'.

In 8 Group a new Pathfinder squadron was formed on that day. The third flights of two other squadrons flew to Little Staughton and immediately became 582 Squadron although C Flight of 156 Squadron arrived somewhat depleted, having lost three crews the previous night.

At the Canadian airfield at Croft, an English wireless-operator decided he had had enough. In the words of the compiler of 434 Squadron's Operational Record Book, 'Pilot Officer — refused to fly and forfeited the confidence of his commanding officer who hoped for an early posting.' Neither this officer nor his squadron had taken part in the Nuremberg operation and it is only surmise that the news of the heavy losses had persuaded him to take this drastic step. The officer's documents would be stamped 'L.M.F.' before he received the 'early posting' desired by the C.O.

Such unfortunate men did not reflect the general feeling among the crews. The initial gloom persisted for some time and there was much grumbling at the met. men, at 'Butch' Harris and at authority in general. However, the morale of these resilient young men did not crack. They realized that the bombing war brought inevitable casualties, sometimes severe casualties. It was enough that, for the moment, they were still alive.

I cannot recall any particular despondency over the heavy losses of this raid but, then, I don't think that I would have noticed it anyway. I was young, alive, and only interested in remaining that way if at all possible. After a trip, as far as I was concerned, the post-operational egg, a few hours' sleep and, then, down to Boston to the dear old 'Gliderdrome' and a few pints in the 'White Hart' was all that I demanded.* (Sergeant R. I. Hudson, 57 Squadron)

The only thing that I can remember about the next day is the shock of the size of the casualty list and the grateful thanks that we gave to Lady Luck, who once again allowed us to go to Grimsby for more beer and to find what we then called a 'popsie'. (Sergeant G. D. Dixon, 100 Squadron)

Although shaken by the losses, I don't remember anyone quitting nor do I remember any blame being laid on 'Butch' or, as we called him, 'Chopper' Harris. In fact, rather a feeling of pity for him and his burden of responsibility. Our crews did what we always did at these times. We got drunk. (Flying Officer F. J. Parker, 514 Squadron)

Only a small staff had remained on duty at High Wycombe during the night. In the Operations Room, the Duty Group Captain, a met. officer and a navigation officer would have been dealing with the reports of the Windfinder aircraft. The War Room at the Air Ministry had only been informed of the target's identity after Zero Hour at Nuremberg had passed. This confinement within Bomber Command of the target's identity was a normal security measure although the information had been common knowledge the previous evening in those public houses and dance-halls of Yorkshire, Lincolnshire and East Anglia frequented by off-duty airmen.

The only people in England to have any idea of what had been happening during the night had been the staff of the Kingsdown radio unit who had been listening to the German radio traffic but their duties did not include the making of immediate reports on what they had heard. It was only much

* Many airmen who served with 5 Group remember with affection the Gliderdrome dance-hall in Boston. After the war it was completely destroyed by fire one night after a Conservative Party rally in 1959. A new Gliderdrome was later built on the same site. The old 'White Hart' still stands.

later, when the station intelligence reports had been for-
warded through the group intelligence channels, that news
of the losses reached Bomber Command H.Q.

Just before 9 o'clock on the morning of 31 March, Sir
Arthur Harris went down into the Operations Room and
commenced his daily conference. He was handed a report
showing that ninety-six heavy bombers had failed to return
from Nuremberg and that preliminary evidence indicated
that the bombing attack on the German city had failed to
achieve any decisive concentration.

One more day in Bomber Command's war had passed.

14

In Germany

As usual, very few of the German night-fighter crews had landed on their home airfields. Most had been forced to quit the battle at about the time the bombers left Nuremberg, but airfields in that area were affected by the bad weather so many of the Germans flew a short distance north-west and landed in the Frankfurt area. Mainz, Wiesbaden and Hanau all received large contingents.

More than forty excited crews came down at Hanau, woke up the cooks and ordered a huge meal to celebrate the obvious success of their efforts. This man, a pre-war Lufthansa pilot, viewed the triumph more calmly however.

A Leutnant was very pleased with his two victories, 'I could stand at attention in front of myself,' he said, but a large number of crews had no success to report. I was, of course, pleased to have shot down at least one but what I said about this was different from what my comrades in general were saying. Because of my age – I was thirty-two years old, about ten years older than most of the others – I viewed everything more soberly. I had seen Nuremberg burning and, although I had seen many bombers shot down and already sensed that it would be an unusually large victory, this seemed to me to be not enough when measured against the destruction of our cities. (Oberleutnent Fritz Lau, II/NJG 1)

Also present at Hanau was the leading ace at that time, Hauptmann Schnauffer. The crews in his Gruppe, from Saint-Trond, had got in among the bombers at beacon Ida and scored many victories. Schnauffer had attempted an even earlier interception by flying out to the coast but he had missed the stream and, although he doubled back, he never caught up with the battle. At Hanau, he had to face pilots who had been more successful. 'How many aircraft can we congratulate the Hauptmann on shooting down?' Schnauffer ruefully had to admit that he had failed to score.

After a sleep in a strange bed, the Germans flew back to their own airfields next morning just as, in England, the diverted bomber crews were returning to their bases. Again, just as the bomber men gathered round their radios at lunchtime, so too did their enemies.

The latest reports of the attack last night on the Reich territory show it to have been a unique catastrophe. Our defences now report that at least 132 four-engined British bombers have been destroyed.

The bulletin went on to hint that the British had been prevented from carrying out their attack on Nuremberg but admitted that 'damage was caused and the population suffered casualties in the Nuremberg area and in several other southern German localities'.

With the possible exception of Nuremberg and these 'other localities', the whole of Germany, especially the Luftwaffe, was jubilant. The preliminary reports of the nightfighter units claimed 101 bombers destroyed and six more probables, although these claims would not subsequently stand up against the more careful allocation of crashed bombers and the counter claims of the Flak.

The congratulations flowed in. At Zeist, I Fighter Corps received two telegrams; the first was from General Martini, chief of the Luftwaffe signals and radar. He spoke of 'the greatest joy and highest admiration of the whole German people, the officers of the High Command and the rest of the Luftwaffe'. The other telegram was from the great Reichsmarschall Goering who referred to 'the admirable bravery of the night-fighter crews that has brought about a new triumph over the British *Terrorfliegers*. . . . The enemy suffered its worst defeat by night so far during its criminal attacks on our beloved Homeland and the German people were given their first revenge through the merciless spirit of the night fighters. *Weiter so!* [Let us have still more!]. *

For the aircrew also, there were congratulations, leave and awards of medals. Some pilots had taken advantage of the perfect conditions to shoot down their first bomber; these received the automatic award of the Iron Cross and the fervent hope of their commanders that this initial victory would be the start of a successful night-fighting career. Oberleutnant Martin Becker's seven victories in the night brought him a telegram ordering him to Hitler's H.Q. in East Prussia where Becker received the coveted Knight's Cross at the hands of the Führer himself.

* The telegram texts are from the War Diary of I Fighter Corps.

That night, the officers of I Fighter Corps at Zeist held a great party, described by the War Diary as a *Sautreiberfest* – literally, a 'boar-beaters' feast'. Luftwaffe officers' messes were famous for their lavish dinner parties throughout the war – even the last days of it. These parties were often named after Goering's beloved sport of hunting. The recent night-fighter victory was obviously a suitable occasion for celebration by the officers at Zeist.

Daylight gave the inhabitants of Nuremberg the opportunity to assess the damage caused by the bombing. The Nurembergers soon realized that they had escaped lightly from an obvious attempt by the R.A.F. to destroy their city when they found that the bombs they had heard the night before had, in most cases, fallen outside the city. There was surprise and some dismay, however, that for the first time in the war they had been raided through thick cloud which, until then, had been thought to be a certain protection against the bombs.

Rescue operations continued in the rubble of bombed houses and the last fires were put out. When the bodies of the dead had all been recovered, the final casualty figures were assessed. These were almost as nothing compared with successful R.A.F. raids on Hamburg, Dresden and other cities but still seventy-five civilians had lost their lives. The Nuremberg archives carefully classify these: sixty Germans had been killed (twenty-eight men, twenty-four women and eight children), but so too had fifteen foreign workers (fourteen men and a woman). The records go on to show that thirty-seven of these deaths were caused by people being buried in bombed houses or shelters, nineteen by falling debris and another nineteen by fire. The number of injured is not known exactly but is believed to be 100–120; 256 buildings had been completely destroyed and a surprisingly high estimate of 11,000 people had been bombed out although many of these would quickly repair their homes with help from prisoners-of-war and from German soldiers under training at the local barracks. The material for the repairs would be provided by the Nazi Party, who were thereby to be seen as the helpers of ordinary people. *

* These casualty details are taken from the report of the Polizeipräsidium Number 7, which is now held by the Nuremberg Stadtarchiv, reference C18. The report only contains details of civilian casualties but it is not thought that

The dead would later be buried at a mass funeral in the city's South Cemetery; their bodies being laid alongside the victims of previous raids. Apparently, there was a small outburst here against the Nazis by grief-stricken relatives but fortunately this was not reported to the authorities.

Perhaps the greatest shock had been among the inhabitants of the country areas to the east and north of Nuremberg who had never expected that their little communities would become targets for the bombers. The worst-hit village had been Schönberg, near Lauf. Frau Gregori describes the scene there on the morning after the raid.

The village presented a picture of terrible destruction. Whole streets lay in rubble and ashes with collapsed walls, burnt beams, shattered glass. In the meadows, the animals were wandering around loose; in the farmyards lay the burnt carcases of pigs; of the poultry there was no trace. People stood with distorted faces, the women weeping and helpless in front of the remains of their possessions.

In view of the load of target indicators dropped near Schönberg by an unknown Pathfinder and the intensity of the bombing there, the inhabitants assumed that the R.A.F. had deliberately chosen their innocent village as a target. One unfortunate man was killed when a heavy beam fell on him while he was helping to clear up a damaged barn and at Bullach, another village near Lauf, a youth was also killed on the day following the raid when a delayed-action bomb exploded.

Schweinfurt, that much-bombed town, soon recovered from its bombing. The inhabitants were relieved to have been let off so lightly by what they thought had been a major raid by the R.A.F. The German High Command soon realized from captured navigation logs, interrogations of aircrew prisoners and from the B.B.C. news bulletin, that the raid on Schweinfurt had been unplanned and no mention of it was allowed in the German press, not even in the local newspapers. A Schweinfurt historian, Ludwig Wiener, writing of this raid after the war, records that 'When one tried to read about the raid in our papers next day, one could only read that spring

---

there were many military ones other than those that occurred when a shell exploded on the Flak site.

was coming and that it was time to fetch "our coloured friends, the flowers, up from the cellars".'*

Schweinfurt had many more raids to come and, eventually, this one became dim among the others in people's memories. It is unlikely that they know to this day that Sir Arthur Harris had never intended his bombers to raid their town on that night.

Most of the shot-down bombers had crashed in open country and caused no damage but a few had blown up over unsuspecting villages or had even crashed into them. When a 12 Squadron Lancaster hit a hillside near one village, the subsequent explosion completely destroyed a house. The R.A.F.'s Missing Research Team was later told that the family living there were all killed but this was an exaggeration; one woman was injured, losing an eye. Another Lancaster, of 101 Squadron, crashed into a village and the explosion of its 4,000-pounder caused considerable damage. One of its crew arrived by parachute only seconds afterwards and was beaten up by the angry villagers. The mid-upper gunner, Sergeant Mike McGeer, son of a Canadian Member of Parliament, sensibly hid in a nearby chicken house and only emerged when the fury had subsided.

The village of Rodenbach, near Neuwied on the Rhine, was more fortunate. A 460 Squadron Lancaster blew up above it and pieces of the aircraft came down all over the village but no houses were hit and no one hurt. Next morning, one villager discovered a Merlin engine just outside his front door and another found that the whole of the Lancaster's tail unit was leaning against the wall of his house. Further searching revealed three bodies of the crew in different parts of the village and a fourth was found by the local policeman hanging by its parachute lines from a tree.

On the other side of the Rhine, three bombers crashed in the parish of Sinzig. Inhabitants of Westum, a nearby hamlet, had watched the air battle above their heads. Heinz Schmalz, a local historian, writes,

But, suddenly, they could see in the east a blazing aircraft that was obviously going to crash. It came down at an increasing speed and would have crashed between Sinzig and Westum but then it reared up and flew on a little. It then looked as though it would

* From *Schweinfurt Sollte Sterben*.

crash into the middle of Westum and engulf our small village. Burning fragments and petrol were falling from the aircraft as it flew overhead and three barns were set on fire. The aircraft flew a complete circle to the south and then, once again, approached the village and crashed close to a roadside shrine.

The identity of this aircraft is known. One man had success-fully baled out; three bodies, including that of the pilot were found elsewhere but the remaining three were never found. Whether the aircraft was under the control of some crew member who was seeking a landing place in this hilly area can only be guessed. The wreckage burnt on for two weeks but no one would go too near because of the smell and the danger from exploding ammunition.

In Westum there were some French prisoners-of-war working on local farms. Schmalz complains indignantly that these stood about without attempting to help when the barns were on fire. In turn, the Frenchmen later told the R.A.F. that they were beaten up when they placed flowers on the communal grave where eleven men from the three air-craft that crashed in this area were buried.

Next morning, the inhabitants of Sinzig streamed out to look at the wrecked aircraft. Rosemarie Bongart, who was then thirteen years old, describes what she saw.

I joined the crowds of curious people but we were kept at a distance by the Hitler Youth. Two machines were totally destroyed and burnt out; of a third, the tail was still intact and through the molten glass we could see the machine-guns. I saw two places where the earth had been pressed down in the shape of a body and splattered with blood. These men's parachutes had been burnt and they had been killed when they crashed to the ground.

Back in Sinzig I saw an airman being taken to the *Bürgermeister's* office. He carried his flying suit over his arm and wore a white pullover. He was a tall, kindly looking man and I was surprised to find myself feeling sorry for him although he was an enemy. He even held open the door to the *Bürgermeister's* office to allow a lady to enter first. That completely surprised me!

Near my house was a barracks and farmers had brought eleven dead in on carts and left them in an empty room there. Through an open window I saw the bodies laid out in a row; they hardly had any external injuries but their limbs were so twisted! One had red hair. Someone said that most of the dead were Canadians. My curiosity was punished, however. For a long time afterwards, I could not sleep at night – I still kept seeing those dead bodies.

Actually there were no Canadians among these eleven dead airmen but there were four Australians. The red-haired man was an English navigator but I cannot identify the polite prisoner who opened the door for a lady beyond narrowing it down to three possible men.

There was supposed to be a death penalty in Germany for the looting of crashed aircraft or the stripping of dead airmen but any food in a wrecked bomber usually disappeared immediately, as did the parachutes and the socks and white pullovers of dead R.A.F. men. The sweaters and socks could often be seen being worn by Germans even after the war. The parachutes were cut up by the women for petticoats and blouses.

The airmen's bodies were usually buried in local civilian churchyards although some were taken by the Luftwaffe and buried in the funeral plots on their airfields and, in France and Belgium, the R.A.F. men were often buried in military cemeteries alongside their dead countrymen of 1914–18. At one German village there developed a macabre wrangle over the burial of one crew involving a Nazi *Bürgermeister*, superstitious villagers and the Luftwaffe. The *Bürgermeister* refused to allow a burial in the churchyard so the men from the village buried the crew by a roadside crucifix close to where their aircraft had crashed and, unknown to the *Bürgermeister*, the local Catholic priest conducted a short service there for them.

Six weeks later, the Luftwaffe rang up and insisted that the dead be reburied in the churchyard. The *Bürgermeister* gave the necessary orders and seven graves were prepared near the church, but the men ordered to transfer the bodies were most unhappy, not wishing to disturb the original grave. After much *schnaps* had been drunk they started digging by the crucifix but could not go through with the job. They replaced the earth over the bodies and also filled in the empty graves in the churchyard, reporting to the *Bürgermeister* that his orders had been carried out. Towards the end of the war the villagers were terrified that the British would take revenge when they found empty graves in the churchyard. The R.A.F. team that eventually arrived were told conflicting stories and had to open both graves before discovering the truth. The Nazi *Bürgermeister* was crushed to death by a bull in his own barn shortly afterwards.

Let us go back now to the experiences of some of those fortunate men who had survived from the shot-down bombers.

Flight Sergeant Robert Hughes, a Canadian second pilot, had accidentally opened his parachute in the aircraft and had gathered the billowing silk in his arms.

I jumped and almost simultaneously let go of the parachute without taking into account that I should have waited several seconds to slow down my forward speed. The parachute straps gave me quite a jolt and the shrouds went up over my face and skinned my cheeks. I thought the parachute had been hooked on to the aircraft. I looked up anxiously and saw the most beautiful flower I had ever seen – a white blossom with orange segments.

Hughes had jumped north of Nuremberg and calculates that he was in the air for over fifteen minutes, being tossed around in the turbulent clouds of the wave depression forming there.

Flight Sergeant Donald Gray had survived the violent explosion of the Blockbuster in his Lancaster.

Immediately, everything was black and silent and I realized with amazement that I was no longer in the aircraft. My relief turned to panic, however, when it dawned on me that I was hanging upside down with the parachute harness tangled around my ankles. I dare not make any move in case my feet slipped out of my flying boots. I locked my ankles tightly together and went through my limited repertoire of prayers.

Fortunately, Gray survived the subsequent head-first landing without serious injury. He found later that he had missed coming down on an *Autobahn* by only a few yards.

There were painful injuries and even deaths when the parachutists landed – an inevitable result of men's first jumps being made by night and over unknown terrain despite 'landing in a manner approved by the Air Ministry' as one man who broke an ankle recalls. Another had the misfortune to come down simultaneously with the cockpit of his own aircraft and fell across it on landing, fracturing his spine. Pilot Officer Albert Lander just managed to get out of his blazing Lancaster and opened his parachute a few seconds before falling into a small river near Dillenburg.

One o'clock in the morning in a river fed by melting snows. Boy, was it cold after the fire! The water was slightly over my head and I was able to push myself up to the surface every time I sank.

Eventually, I drifted into shallower water where I met the radio op who helped me out of the river. He was minus an ear and an eyelid. I had very few clothes left, a badly burnt wrist and my face felt it didn't belong to me because of the burns.

Sergeant Dobbs, a Halifax wireless-operator, found himself lying on some straw in the back of a lorry surrounded by German soldiers. He was badly injured and never did find out whether he had come down by parachute or had survived his aircraft's crash. He was the only man of his crew alive.

For those men who landed safely it was a most emotional moment. A few seconds or minutes earlier they had stared death in the face; now their chances of surviving the war were probably better than the men who would fly back to England.

I was immediately overcome by a feeling of profound relief that never again would I have to run that gauntlet. I experienced a distinctly warm glow, almost of elation. I had done my bit and now, given a shade of luck, I would survive and live to a ripe old age. I swore a solemn oath that I would never go in the air again. (Flying Officer H. G. Darby, 514 Squadron)

I sat down at the foot of the tree I had just come down, looked for my pipe and some Four Square Green tobacco that I had just bought in the Mess. My boots and socks were gone but my pipe and tobacco were there so I sat there and smoked at least two pipefuls, trying to think out what to do next. (Sergeant R. D. Dack, 106 Squadron)

I could hear the roar of the bomber-stream overhead, like the sound of distant city traffic. It was a very lonely sensation but then I had a feeling of tremendous freedom – laws and rules don't apply to me any more. The first thing I did was to pull my Mae West rubber life jacket – a thing everyone wanted to do at one time or another. The perishing thing was broken though; it didn't work. (Sergeant A. R. Luffman, 101 Squadron)

But Flight Sergeant Gray, who had just landed on his head, took a different view.

I had always been keen on flying and I remember thinking, naïvely, what a nuisance this all was, as it would take me two or three months to get back to England and I would be losing all that flying time and probably miss the excitement of participating in the Second Front operations.

Gray set out to find his crew but could not do so. Two men had survived and had come down some distance away but the remainder were dead including the poor young gunner who had been unable to repeat the main points of his wing commander's briefing at Skellingthorpe the previous evening.

When Squadron Leader Utz's Lancaster had blown up over a sparsely populated area, his navigator, Pilot Officer McCleery, badly injured in one leg, had been the only survivor. He would undoubtedly have died if he had not landed in a tree only 500 yards from a village. His cries brought out the inhabitants who took him by sledge to a *Gasthaus*. The local doctor saved him from being finished off by angry people who had been bombed out of their homes in the Ruhr and sent to this village, but one of McCleery's legs had to be amputated. The bodies of Squadron Leader Utz and the other five crew members were recovered from deep snow the following day.

What happened to another badly wounded man, from one of the aircraft shot down by Flak near Westerburg, is described by Walter Zimmermann who was then sixteen years old.

We boys went out with the old men of the Home Guard to look for the aircraft and found it on a railway line. It was burning and the ammunition was exploding. Shortly afterwards, the flares exploded and the forest turned to a firework display of yellow and red. At that time, I was particularly interested in aeroplanes of all kinds and I decided that it was a Handley Page Halifax, probably a Pathfinder. [Zimmerman was only partly correct. The aircraft was a 4 Group Halifax; his 'flares' were probably its 30-pound incendiaries.]

I came upon a group of men who were having an argument. They had found a wounded British airman in a stream. A police officer said, 'Let this criminal die; he dropped bombs on women and children.' But a soldier in a black Panzer uniform, who was on leave from the Russian Front, opposed him and said that a prisoner-of-war had the right to humane treatment.

Eventually they lifted him out of the water and laid him on his parachute. An old farmer, one of the Home Guard, was left to guard him and I remained with him. The prisoner said his name was Harvey. At first, we could not see his injury in the darkness but he was in severe pain. He was very cold – his teeth were chattering – so we fetched some wood and lit a fire. I could hear him murmuring for his wife and child.

And so, the old man and the young boy kept watch with this badly injured airman until dawn. Zimmerman heard later that he had died in hospital but this is not so. The man was Flying Officer R. G. A. Harvey, D.F.M., of 158 Squadron, and he returned to his wife and son in England.

Unfortunately both McCleery and Harvey failed to recover completely from their injuries and died some years after the war. Young Zimmermann was himself a prisoner-of-war in 1945. He was captured by American troops after only two weeks' service with a Flak unit.

The R.A.F. had always impressed upon its aircrew that, for them, being shot down was not the end of the war. They were to make every attempt to avoid capture and return to England, and if this failed, were told that their duty was to escape from their prison camps. There were two motives behind this policy – to cause the maximum inconvenience to the enemy and, secondly, to ensure that these highly trained men could be used again on operations. Every man had received some escape training and carried maps, a compass, food and money. There was a well-established 'escape route' organized by the Resistance movement in the various occupied countries which passed shot-down airmen over long distances into Spain and Switzerland.

The R.A.F. built up a great reputation for its escape activities during the war but by a coincidence the climax had occurred just six nights before the Nuremberg Raid when there had been a tunnel escape by seventy-six Allied air force officers from Stalag Luft III at Sagan, south of Berlin. Three escapers reached England but the remainder were recaptured. This mass escape, coming on top of many other attempts, angered Hitler so much that he ordered fifty of those retaken to be executed. Goering protested but without avail.

On the afternoon of 30 March, while the aircrew who were to fly to Nuremberg that night had been resting, six officers were shot by a German roadside and the next day while so many of the men shot down on the way to Nuremberg were themselves on the run, eleven more of the Sagan escapers were executed. These shootings were not carried out by the Luftwaffe, who were normally responsible for R.A.F. prisoners, but by the S.S. Earlier in the war, Goering had ordered that no R.A.F. man was to be unfairly treated while he was in the hands of the Luftwaffe and thousands of ex-prisoners will testify that these orders were faithfully obeyed.

The attempt to avoid capture could only be a gesture for most of the men shot down on the Nuremberg Raid. They had landed deep inside Germany, in semi-winter conditions, and were either hurt or badly shocked by their recent experiences. However, they gamely hid their flying suits and parachute, cut off the tops of their flying boots, tore off their badges of rank and set out to walk westwards towards Belgium or south towards Switzerland.

Sergeant Wilkinson, of 166 Squadron, came down near Coburg. He found a railway line and started walking along it in the general direction of Switzerland 200 miles away, changing all the points as he went. He was caught after a few miles. Flight Sergeant Keigwin from the same squadron had no chance at all of escaping. His aircraft had fallen in flames onto Giessen airfield. Keigwin landed only a few yards from the Lancaster just as it blew up with a violent explosion which threw debris over Keigwin's head, damaging a nearby Junkers 88. When Keigwin stood up a few seconds later he found himself covered by two armed Germans.

Sergeant McAvoy, flying on his first operation, had been in a 49 Squadron Lancaster that had been shot down in flames. He received terrible burns to his face and feet.

I couldn't see and touched my face and head; there was a hard crust. I crawled around in the snow, bumping into trees, and it was two hours before I was found by some civilians and taken to a village. They put me in a coal cellar and I got the impression that they had left me there to die because I received no attention at all.

McAvoy was left here for twelve hours, very cold and in great pain. Then, he was taken out and placed on a cart with another injured airmen, the navigator in his own crew. This man could not recognize his burnt comrade and went through the names of the crew until McAvoy raised an arm on hearing his own name. Both men were taken to a local hospital where McAvoy, at least, received devoted nursing attention – a certain Sister Annie sat with him for several days. The navigator disappeared and McAvoy did not discover until after the war that he had died, while McAvoy went on to undergo thirty surgical operations for his burns.

Some men walked on for several days, hiding up by day and travelling by night. However, Flight Lieutenant Coverley, who had thought of how annoyed his C.O. would be at losing his favourite Halifax, fell into the mouth of a railway tunnel so he decided to travel by day, finding 'the forests a festive sight, decked in a mass of Window, while there was plenty to read in the way of our propaganda leaflets'. Coverley was captured four days later crossing a Rhine bridge at what he believed to be Bonn, thirty miles from his starting point.

Flying Officer Bowly, who had come down in Luxemburg, hid for some time on the edge of an airfield on which were parked many Junkers 87 dive bombers. He considered the problems of starting a strange aircraft and then the possibility of being shot down by the R.A.F. if he ever reached England and reluctantly abandoned the idea of stealing one. Bowly's dark-blue Australian uniform, without badges, was similar to that worn by some German units. He walked right through the city of Metz, where he was shouted at by a German girl in uniform, presumably for having his hands in his pockets and for being without a hat. Bowly was later picked up on the road to Verdun.

A Canadian gunner, Sergeant Sjöquist, suffered minor injuries on being shot down and then walked for several days without making much progress. Lonely and exhausted, he reached the outskirts of a large town during a snowstorm and decided to give himself up, but had great difficulty in finding someone who would accept his surrender. It was some time before a wounded soldier on leave finally took him over.

Five men had survived when the secret operations Halifax had crashed into the Scheldt and they had split into two parties – two officers in one, three N.C.O.s in the other. The N.C.O.s were soon captured but the officers fell in with the Dutch Resistance and remained with them until September. They were the first of fifteen men shot down on that night who were able to avoid capture although three of them were captured later in the year. Those men who had come down in France, Belgium or Holland had the best chance; nearly half of such men successfully avoided the Germans.

When Flight Lieutenant Bruce Simpson's Lancaster had been attacked by a night fighter near Aachen, he had been

able to turn and fly back over Belgium before his crew baled
out. The Belgian Resistance were able to hide every one of
Simpson's crew from the Germans. Later, two had the misfortune to be with a group of Belgians hoping to avoid being
sent to Germany as forced labourers when the Germans surrounded the woods in which they were hiding, but the other
five all made their way to England.

There had only been one survivor of the collision between
two bombers on the return flight from Nuremberg. The
Canadian crew involved were carrying a second pilot and
when the Germans found the two wrecks with fourteen
bodies they perhaps thought that there was no one else. Pilot
Officer Moffat was never captured and spent five months
with various Resistance groups before meeting up with
American troops. He returned to England classified medically
as 'suffering from malnutrition'.

Every story of evasion and escape is worthy of acknow-
ledgement but the one that will be highlighted here is that
of the only man to reach England after coming down in
Germany on that night. Sergeant Don Brinkhurst had been
in the Lancaster shot down in error by a Halifax and had
landed about ten miles inside Germany. His crew had always
agreed that, if shot down, the survivors would do their best
to get home and contact the relatives of any man killed or
hurt. Brinkhurst started walking towards Belgium through
the heavily wooded country of the Eifel. During the next
four days, he avoided Germans patrolling with dogs, hid
near a German airfield and suffered agonies of stomach cramp
after eating raw potatoes when his escape rations ran out.
Having travelled forty miles in a circuitous, cross-country
route, he eventually approached 'a very fat lady at an isolated
farmhouse who was putting out her washing'.

Brinkhurst was soon given shelter by loyal Belgians at
Visé just north of Liège. In the next three weeks, he was
given a grand twenty-first birthday party and a day out in
Liège but then his presence was betrayed by a young woman
and Brinkhurst only just managed to escape from the German
search. After many more adventures, he reached Switzerland
but soon tired of the idle life there and recrossed the border
into France to find Allied troops who had recently landed in
the south of France.

On his return to England, this resourceful N.C.O. was

commissioned and returned to his old squadron. On 2 January 1945, he took off for the first of another twenty operations – the target was Nuremberg.

After the war, Brinkhurst returned to Visé to thank the civilians who had helped him. To his great sorrow he found that nine Belgians had been arrested after his escape; two of them later died in a German concentration camp. The woman who had betrayed them was sentenced to twenty years in prison.

Several thousand airmen became prisoners during the war and those captured after the Nuremberg Raid were treated, in most respects, no differently from any others. First stop for most was the nearest village, where they were kept in the police station, or in the smaller villages an inn. The captured airmen were the objects of much curiosity and several men report that the entire population appears to have come along to have a look at what the German wireless would call *Terrorfliegers*. Most men captured in these rural areas say they were treated with the natural kindness one finds in most country dwellers. One Canadian pilot was amazed to be given a meal in the kitchen of an inn and offered a choice of beer, wine or *schnaps*. The waitresses took turns to sit on his knee amidst much giggling.

Some men underwent a rudimentary interrogation here, carried out by self-important local officials, policemen or school masters. One such questioning was done by a naval officer who claimed to have been off the coast of England three nights earlier. Occasionally, the questions were accompanied by physical violence and a few unlucky airmen were badly knocked about at this stage.

Luftwaffe airfields were often used as collection points for prisoners. Here, the airmen were treated fairly although several obvious attempts to infiltrate bogus R.A.F. men to pick up information took place. Curious Luftwaffe aircrew came to talk to the prisoners, sometimes claiming to have scored victories against the Nuremberg force. A Canadian crew member, shot down close to Erfurt, the home of a night-fighter Gruppe, met there an English-speaking pilot who said that he had been responsible for shooting down the Canadian – 'your exhausts and the four red-hot manifolds made you a sitting duck'. At Giessen, in the centre of an area where there were many combats, a large number of wounded were sent to the airfield's sick quarters. The R.A.F. men speak highly of the careful treatment they received there.

Those shot down in the Nuremberg area were taken to the prisoner-of-war camp that had been hit in the bombing. One R.A.F. sergeant who wandered among the French and Yugoslav prisoners there found that

without exception, they saluted me with a formality and dignity they could not have bettered for royalty. It was my first indication of the respect in which they held the R.A.F. I suppose we were their only allies visibly attacking the common enemy and represented some hope for their eventual release.' (Sergeant G. E. Watts, 630 Squadron)

All fit aircrew prisoners were sent to the Luftwaffe's interrogation centre at Oberursel, near Frankfurt, before going to the permanent camps. Here each prisoner was put through a set routine. Firstly, they were placed in a one-man, windowless cell for about three days. An outside control gave alternating extremes of hot and cold conditions and the man recived a minimum of food and attention. The prisoner would be visited during this 'cooling off' period by a bogus 'Red Cross man' who invited them to complete a form containing many questions. When the R.A.F. man refused to give more than the 'rank, name and number' required by the Geneva Convention, it was hinted that failure to complete the other questions would result in a long delay in informing the prisoner's family of his safety. When this failed, the 'Red Cross man' would threaten to hand over the prisoner to the Gestapo. All this had been covered in the training of aircrew and many men actually gained confidence from the ritual, feeling that they had only to follow advice given to them in training and all would be well.

Next, would come formal interviews with Luftwaffe officers. The first real shock for the prisoner was the presentation to him of an album containing photographs, press cuttings and much personal information about his own squadron – that is, if the Germans had been able to connect the prisoner with his crashed aircraft. The squadron code letters on every bomber were well known to the Germans.

The German information was remarkably up-to-date and men were amazed to be told the names of their senior officers, of their favourite drinking places and even the identity of crews recently posted to the squadron. A Canadian gunner was told the names of his wife and son, every school he had attended in Vancouver and his home address. Sergeant Wilkinson, whose Lancaster had returned safely to England after he had baled out, found that the Germans knew the names of his own pilot and of nearly every other pilot on 166 Squadron. Wilkinson was so fed up with the extent of the Germans' knowledge that he agreed to fill in their questionnaire. 'I gave a wrong answer to every question. I suppose he realized he'd got another liar on his hands.'

In one respect the interrogation of the Nuremberg prisoners did vary from the normal. They found that their route to and from Nuremberg had been plotted on a wall map. The Germans confidently stated that they had known this route at 4 o'clock in the afternoon on 30 March – over five hours before the bombers had taken off. This, they claimed, was how the night fighters had been assembled ahead of the bombers early in the flight and was the cause of their success. The prisoners realized that this astonishing claim might be false but some, at least, had the sickening feeling that it could well be true after the effective demonstration by the night fighters.

Physical force was never applied at Oberursel and, providing the prisoner stuck to the 'name, rank and number' routine, the Germans soon gave up. Officers, in particular, were hardly asked any questions; perhaps the Germans did not really expect them to co-operate. Those who were kept longest at Oberursel were men whom the Germans could not identify with a particular aircraft or squadron and exceptional people like Sergeant Fealy of 103 Squadron who had worn a complete suit of civilian clothes under his flying suit and had no means of proving he was an R.A.F. man. The Germans were satisfied when he named three men in his own crew who were dead. Sergeant Kimpton, of 138 Squadron, was a member of the crew of the secret operations Halifax and had been carrying a revolver when captured. He was in 'solitary' for forty days as the Germans suspected that he was connected with the dropping of the Resistance agents but he, too, eventually left Oberursel and like his fellow captives went to an ordinary prison camp for the remainder of the war.

We shall return to Oberursel later.

15

The Cost

The Nuremberg Raid has been described by historian Alfred Price as 'the greatest air battle of all time', and it is certain that the intensity of the aerial carnage between the German frontier and Nuremberg, when eighty heavy bombers and possibly ten night fighters were destroyed in the hour-and-a-half after midnight, has never been surpassed.

Nine hundred and ninety-nine British and ten American aircraft had taken off for the night's operations. Of these, eighty had turned back early, 832 had performed their allotted duty and had returned to England, although some of these had been damaged, and ninety-seven aircraft had been lost beyond the coast of England. As fifteen of the missing aircraft are known to have bombed before being shot down, it can be claimed that 84 per cent of the aircraft dispatched had bombed a target, sought out enemy fighters near the bomber-stream or over airfields, parachuted agents and supplies to the Resistance, dropped mines into enemy waters, scattered leaflets over French towns or performed a radio counter-measures function. Whatever may be said of the losses, a positive contribution had been made by the Allied airmen to the war against Germany.

But it is in terms of the force of heavy bombers sent to attack Nuremberg that the balance sheet does not look so good. Ninety-five aircraft were missing; ten were a total loss after crashes in England; and one was written off due to severe battle damage. Seventy more sustained damage ranging in severity from two bombers that were six months being repaired to the many that only had small Flak holes to be covered over.* Bomber Command's own yardstick for casualties was to express them as a percentage of the force dispatched. 13·6 per cent of the Lancasters and Halifaxes sent to Nuremberg were a total loss.

* A heavy bomber was reputed to cost £40,000 and the training of an aircrew member £10,000. If these figures are accurate then over £4 million in aircraft and £7 million in aircrew training had been expended, to say nothing of the cost of bombs, fuel, ammunition and equipment. (A new Tornado aircraft now costs the R.A.F. approximately £10 million!)

The damage caused by the bombs dropped was by comparison minimal. In Nuremberg one factory was half destroyed and three others suffered lesser damage. It is impossible to calculate the exact effect of this on Germany's war effort but clearly it was no more than a pinprick. The accidental bombing of Schweinfurt again hardly affected production of the vital ball-bearings. This and the unconfirmed destruction of ten German fighters was a poor return.

If the secret operations Halifax and the Intruder Mosquito that had been shot down are now included, the total loss in aircraft numbers 108. It cannot be stated with absolute certainty how each of these met its end but the following table is reasonably accurate:

Crashed on take-off	1
Shot down by night fighter	79
Shot down by Flak	13
Hit by both night fighter and Flak	2
Collision	2
Shot down by 'friendly' bomber	1
Crashed or crash-landed in England	9
Written off after battle damage	1

It is possible to further subdivide some of these causes of loss. The Wild Boar aircraft may have been responsible for only five of the fighter victories. The Messerschmitt 110s had claimed the lion's share of those shot down by the twin-engined fighters with possibly fifty or more victories; the Junkers 88s had shot down nearly all of the remainder, although at least one bomber was caught by an old Dornier 217. The German heavy Flak had taken a steady toll as the operation progressed, the successful batteries being in the following areas: Liège, south of Bonn, Coblenz, Westerburg (three successes), Schweinfurt (two), Stuttgart, Metz and, finally, guns either at Dieppe or on a Flak ship just off the French coast. Light Flak was responsible for the loss of the secret operations Halifax over the Scheldt and probably for the Mosquito patrolling the airfield near Munster. Bomber Command estimated that it lost an average of one aircraft through collision out of every 200 dispatched; the two bombers that collided while flying back from Nuremberg were not, therefore, out of the ordinary. The crashes in

England were far higher than average due to the bad weather over the airfields.

The relationship between the losses of the different aircraft types comprising the heavy-bomber force confirms the fears of the Halifax men that they were flying the more vulnerable aircraft. 14·6 per cent of the Halifaxes and 11·2 per cent of the Lancasters that took off had not returned. However, these figures are misleading. A much higher proportion of the Halifaxes had turned back with technical trouble and had never been exposed to the German defences. If the losses are calculated as a percentage of those aircraft that flew on, then 17·3 per cent of the Halifaxes had been lost compared with 11·7 per cent of the Lancasters. Put another way, a Halifax crew member stood half as much chance again of being shot down as did his Lancaster colleague.

In the crew room at the Australian station at Binbrook there hung a large sign: H-E-I-G-H-T spells S-A-F-E-T-Y. Here was the simple answer to the Halifax vulnerability. On the Nuremberg operation, the Halifaxes were loaded with a light all-incendiary load and they were allocated an equal share of the height bands and waves of the bomber-stream. Despite this, the tight stream-discipline failed when the German fighters struck at beacon Ida and many of the Lancasters sought safety at higher altitudes. The Halifaxes could not follow and they suffered accordingly.

There is little point in devoting much space to a comparison between the losses of the heavies and those of the Mosquitoes. One Mosquito was missing and three damaged out of 117 that were operating. This effective little aircraft was so superior that the Germans practically ignored it. There was more profit for them in seeking out the lumbering heavies.

But there is further interest in the distribution of the losses and the general performance of the different groups in Bomber Command.

Among the all-Lancaster Groups, the Pathfinders had done well with the lowest proportion of early returns and of losses and the best bombing figures. This was a credit to the efficiency of Bennett's squadrons but on this occasion they had benefited from the comparative safety at the front of the bomber-stream, a factor that had also helped 5 Group whose turn it had been to provide some of the Supporters.

It had been an unlucky night for 3 Group, half of their eight losses coming from 514 Squadron, and 1 Group's casualties had been inflated by their decision to fly the early part of the route at an altitude lower than the remainder of the Main Force.

Group	Dispatched	Aborted	Missing	Bombed
1	180 Lancasters	8	21 (12·2%)	151 (83·9%)
3	56 Lancasters	6	8 (16·0%)	42 (75·0%)
4	119 Halifaxes	22	20 (20·6%)	81 (68·1%)
5	201 Lancasters	10	21 (11·0%)	168 (82·7%)
6 (R.C.A.F.) {	93 Halifaxes	8	11 (12·9%)	76 (81·7%)
	25 Lancasters	0	3 (12·0%)	22 (88·0%)
8 (Pathfinder)	107 Lancasters	1	11 (10·4%)	94 (87·9%)
TOTAL	781	55	95 (13·1%)	634 (81·2%)

The aborted total includes three aircraft that crashed or were damaged on take-off. The missing percentage is of those aircraft that took part in the operation *after* those with technical trouble had turned back but the percentage bombed is of *all* aircraft that had taken off.

The performance of the Halifax squadrons in 4 Group had been very disappointing. They were operating the same type of aircraft as were the seven Halifax squadrons in 6 Group, yet both in the proportion of aircraft turning back early and in the number being shot down, 6 Group's Halifaxes had done no worse than the Lancaster groups. There are three possible reasons for this superior Canadian performance. Earlier in the war many Canadian pilots had been retained in Canada as instructors for the Empire Air Training Scheme but some of these were now being allowed to come to England for an operational tour. Thus, the Canadian pilots were more experienced than the average Main Force pilot while those of 4 Group may have been slightly below the average level of experience due to the persistent heavy losses in that group. Secondly, a quarter of the Canadian aircraft had now been fitted with the mid-under gun position which must have cut down losses from *schräge Musik* attacks. Finally, the recently arrived Air Vice-Marshal McEwen had somehow been able to instil that higher morale into his men that was so elusive in parts of 4 Group. These three considerations are all valid but a study of 6 Group casualties on other operations in this period shows that the gap between the two groups was rarely as wide as on this occasion. The extra margin on that particular night must be attributed to the erratic fortunes of war. Lady Luck had just not smiled upon the poor 4 Group crews on their way to Nuremberg.

Casualties at squadron level were even more a matter of chance than among the greater number of aircraft in a group. 101 Squadron at Ludford Magna had suffered the heaviest loss, six Lancasters being lost over Germany and a seventh crashed in England out of a total of twenty-six dispatched. It was purely a coincidence that these heavy casualties should occur in the only squadron to be operating the A.B.C. Lancasters and there is no evidence that the Germans were homing onto their special radio equipment. It was in 4 Group, however, that the greatest percentage squadron loss had occurred. 51 Squadron at Snaith had sent off seventeen Halifaxes of which five were missing and a sixth had crashed in England – a 35 per cent loss rate. 514 Squadron at Waterbeach had lost six Lancasters and five more squadrons – 50, 106, 156, 158 and 166 – had each lost four aircraft although in some of these cases, crews had been saved from crashes. At the other end of the scale, seven Lancaster squadrons and two squadrons of Halifaxes had operated without any casualties other than a few aircraft that returned slightly damaged. *

If the men of any single type of squadron could count themselves as being lucky on this disastrous night then it was those who were serving with the four Australian squadrons that had dispatched seventy-five Lancasters and Halifaxes and lost only five – a casualty rate of slightly less than half of that incurred by the average squadron. The records of 467 Squadron at Waddington, which had lost two Lancasters, expressed disappointment. These were their first losses since 25 February. The Australians had hoped for a clear month in March; it would have been their first since the squadron had been formed.

Sadder than the loss of valuable bomber aircraft were the casualties among their young crew members. The full list of dead, wounded and prisoners for the night numbered 723, all but two of whom were from Bomber Command.

The 545 dead represented in every way a cross-section of

* Appendix 4 gives the performance and casualties of all squadrons involved in the raid.

the men who served in the bomber squadrons. The nationalities were distributed as follows:

United Kingdom	369
Canada	109
Australia	47
New Zealand	11
United States	2
Norway	2
Eire	2
India	1
Nigeria	1
Bahamas	1

One hundred and fifty officers, twenty-four warrant officers and three hundred and seventy-one N.C.O.s died. It is not known who was the youngest but the oldest was Squadron Leader Colin Wilson, D.F.C., a thirty-eight-year-old Pathfinder pilot.

A further 152 men became prisoners-of-war, some of whom were badly injured. This was the largest single bag of aircrew prisoners the Germans had ever had. The senior prisoner was Squadron Leader Philip Goodwin, another Pathfinder pilot, and the presence of two U.S.A.A.F. men, Technical Sergeants W. E. Steeper and M. G. Lanthier, added a little variety. Fifteen of the men who had been shot down avoided being captured by the Germans but the R.A.F. was deprived of these men's services for several months. Twenty-six men were injured in aircraft that returned with battle damage or had crashed in England.

It appears that when a bomber was shot down the average crew member had only one chance in four of surviving. The Halifax was reputed to be an easier aircraft from which to escape than the Lancaster and an analysis of the casualties of each type on that night lends support to this theory, although the incendiaries-only bomb loads carried by the Halifaxes would also give their men a better chance. From the seven regular crew members in each type of aircraft, 29 per cent of the Halifax men escaped but only 23 per cent did so from the Lancasters. Wireless-operators and navigators had a better chance in the Halifax due to their position in the long nose of this aircraft being close to its forward escape hatch. The safest position in either aircraft was that of the bomb-aimer, relatively remote from the effects of German fighter fire and close to a hatch through which the escape drill demanded he should be the first to go. Even so, two out of every three bomb-aimers were killed on the Nuremberg Raid. A surprising number of Lancaster pilots survived when their aircraft blew up – it was rumoured that this aircraft usually broke apart near the pilot's position – but Lancaster tail gunners fared badly, with only four surviving from sixty-four Lancasters shot down.

Regular crews hated taking inexperienced pilots as passengers on operations and many considered it unlucky to do so. Out of forty-one 'second dickeys' on the Nuremberg Raid, nine were killed and two became prisoners – double the average casualty rate for the night. One of the two who were captured, Pilot Officer Park, of 166 Squadron, expressed great disappointment that, after more than two years spent in training and with 472 hours flying to his credit, he would never fly on operations with his own crew (they were all killed later with another pilot). The other seemed quite pleased to be safely out of it.

All nine squadron commanders who flew returned safely but at least nine flight commanders went missing, all killed. 427 (Lion) Squadron lost both A and B Flight commanders – Squadron Leaders Bissett, D.F.M., and Laird, D.F.C., both Manitobans. Bissett's crew had already caused anxiety on the squadron when starting their second tour by their apparent unconcern at the importance of keeping on course and his loss was not unexpected. In fact, Bissett's Halifax had crashed almost exactly on track south of Aachen.

One Bomber Command statistic was faithfully followed, that of the vulnerability of new crews. Exactly half of the missing crews had less than ten completed operations behind them; thirty, almost one third of those lost, were in the dangerous first five operations area and nine unfortunate crews were on their very first flight. Nine second-tour crews were missing – five from the Main Force and four Pathfinders.

Ten German aircraft were claimed as destroyed by Bomber Command crews – nine by heavy bombers and one by a Serrate Mosquito. A further five were claimed as probably destroyed and twenty-three as damaged. The only known German document that records Luftwaffe casualties is I Fighter Corps' War Diary. This shows that the 1st, 2nd and 3rd Fighter Divisions lost five aircraft 'missing', five more 'over 60 per cent destroyed' and three 'damaged'. Slightly damaged aircraft were probably not recorded. Unfortunately the War Diary does not cover the activities of the 4th Fighter Division, from II Corps, which was also involved in the battle.

The ten German aircraft claimed as shot down were identified by the British crews involved as: four Junkers 88s, three Messerschmitt 109s, two Focke-Wulf 190s and one Messerschmitt 110. If their claims are accurate, two comments can be made. The loss of five single-engined fighters shows how unsuitable these Wild Boar aircraft were for a basically Tame Boar situation and the destruction of only one Messerschmitt 110 shows how effectively this night-fighter type had performed on that night.

The War Diary shows that three night-fighter crew members had been killed, eight were missing and one had been wounded. This casualty list of only twelve men, compared with the R.A.F.'s huge loss, requires no further comment.

It is impossible to say exactly how many human beings had become casualties in all the incidents of that one night of war but the following table shows the death roll where that is known:

Allied	Numbers killed
Royal Air Force	545
English civilian (by Halifax crash at Ryhope)	1
Belgian civilians (Ostend)	36
Belgian Resistance (in secret operations Halifax)	2
Workers from occupied countries in Nuremberg (15) and Cologne (5)	20
Total	**604**

German	Numbers killed
Luftwaffe	11
Flak units	8
Nuremberg and surrounding villages	69
Schweinfurt and surrounding villages	2
Oberhausen (Oboe Mosquito's bomb)	23
Cologne (Mosquito spoof raid)	14
Kassel (Mosquito spoof raid)	2
Total	**129**

16

An Analysis

Failure cries out for explanation but success, like charity, covers a multitude of errors.   Erwin Rommel

There are few who would deny that the Nuremberg operation had been a failure for Bomber Command. The German city it had sought to destroy had been only lightly damaged; there had been a tragically heavy loss of bombers and crews. But, in many ways, it had been a simple, straightforward operation and to find the explanation as to why it had turned out to be a failure for the British is not difficult, providing one takes this raid in isolation and away from the overall context of the bombing war.

The first and obvious explanation of the disaster is that the decision to mount the operation at all had been faulty. To send this large force of bombers deep into Germany when the moon was up was a two-way gamble: firstly, that the Germans would fail to intercept the bombers; secondly, if contact was made, there would be cloud in which the bombers could seek cover.

The gamble on the German reaction deserves examination. The Americans were claiming to have destroyed large numbers of German fighters on their recently resumed daylight bomber raids. Since the Germans had introduced the single-engined Wild Boar type of night fighter it was felt that there was a strong link between the fortunes of the German day fighters and of their night fighters – the British were meeting single-engined fighters by night; the Americans were meeting twin-engined types, apparently night fighters, by day. The American victories were, therefore, felt to be affecting the night-fighter units. Unfortunately the American claims later proved to have been exaggerated and the relationship between the German day and night units was not, in fact, a strong one.

By night, Bomber Command's own recent operations had not, with one exception, been subject to heavy casualties. Bomber Command papers clearly show that its seventy-three losses on the Berlin raid six nights before Nuremberg were thought to have been caused not by fighters, but by strong winds blowing a scattered bomber-stream over the Ruhr where radar-predicted Flak had shot them down. In fact, the German night fighters had made their most effective Tame Boar interception to date on that occasion.

Intelligence in a rapidly changing war is always a chancy business and it is likely that these two faulty assessments – that of the supposed effects of American daylight raids on the German night-fighter force and the failure to realize that the German Tame Boar night tactics could sometimes achieve great success – probably lulled Bomber Command into a false sense of security.

The gamble on the frontal cloud was entirely different. The morning forecast by Mr Spence only said that such cloud was a possibility; the reports of the Mosquito weather reconnaissance flight and Mr Spence's subsequent forecasts showed that the possibility was non-existent. There would be no cloud on the outward route. The operation should have been cancelled at that moment. General Walter Grabmann, whose 3rd Fighter Division at Deelen had handled the first phase of the fighter battle, says 'it was a gross tactical error to make a major attack in such weather conditions'.*

Given that this cancellation did not occur, could the operation have been planned and mounted better? The Official History refers to 'uncharacteristically bad and unimaginative operational planning'.† Is this fair comment? These are difficult questions to answer and the discussion revolves mainly about two aspects of the plan – the choice of the route and the diversionary effort.

A route had to do two things: to get the bombers to the target and home again with a minimum of losses and to conceal the identity of that target from the enemy for as long as possible. With the German Tame Boar tactics in the ascendant, the second aim was more easily achieved than the first. Lured by the possibility of high cloud cover and the probability of a strong tail wind, the planners had chosen this relatively direct approach over Belgium and Germany in preference to a longer flight over France. But the choice of the Cologne-gap route had placed the bombers within reach of every night-fighter Gruppe the Germans had in the West.

* Letter to author, 11 July 1972.
† The Official History, Vol. II, p. 209.

The absence of cloud made this route a potential death trap. The swift reaction of the Germans and their choice of beacons Ida and Otto as fighter assembly points turned the potential into reality.

The Long Leg, which came in for so much criticism, was not in itself a fault. The pattern of bomber losses in the map on page 330 shows that the course alteration at the end of the Long Leg made little difference to the effectiveness of the German fighter opposition. In the bright moonlight, the Germans had been able to follow the course change. Had there been more turning-points, as some had wanted, there is little likelihood that these would have thrown off the German fighters already in the stream and the resultant longer flight to Nuremberg would only have extended the duration of the fighter battle.

It should not be forgotten that the front of the bomber-stream did slip past the Germans assembling at the fighter beacons. The Germans fighters had only a small speed advantage over the bombers. If the bombers had been a little earlier or the fighters a little later, there would have been no massive interception; instead a long stern chase with the Germans snapping at the heels of the bomber-stream rather than tearing the heart out of the stream as they did. If the Germans had delayed just twenty minutes in ordering up their fighters, the casualty list for the British would have been only a small one. If this had happened, the choice of the Nuremberg route would have been hailed as bold and imaginative.

The German achievement should not be under-estimated. The shape of Britain does not lend itself easily to a comparison but it is as though a Fighter Command controller had been told of German bombers detected near Antwerp and flying towards East Anglia on a strong tail wind at the same time as another force was flying across the North Sea towards Newcastle. By the time the main body of German bombers were crossing the Belgian coast, the controller had decided to ignore the diversion to the north. He had immediately ordered up night fighters from airfields as far apart as Cornwall, Kent and Scotland and had been able to assemble the majority of the fighters at a radio beacon near Nottingham just before the Germans flew south of that city. The resulting air battle would then have raged all the way to the bomber's target at Glasgow.

The route did achieve its second object. The War Diary of the German I Fighter Corps contains a passage explaining the failure of their Wild Boar fighters. It is quite clear from this that once the bombers had flown past the Ruhr and then Frankfurt, the Germans had no idea at all of what the target would be. The diarist pays this tribute to Bomber Command's choice of route: 'The frequent change of course by the British bombers and the decoy manoeuvres using Mosquitoes prevented an early recognition of the target.'

This passage helps also to evaluate the effectiveness of the diversionary effort. The first attempt to deceive the Germans had been the dispatch of the Halifax mining force over the North Sea towards Hamburg. Unfortunately this was a ploy that had outworn its usefulness; it had been used five times in the previous nine major raids. The Germans, with much practice behind them, had been able to guess correctly which of the two forces was the diversion and had assembled their fighters in the path of the main attack. Commenting on this stage of the night's operations, General Grabmann says that 'the diagnosis of the situation was relatively uncomplicated'. However, it would seem that on the evidence of the German War Diary the Aachen and Cologne spoofs by 8 Group's Mosquitoes did confuse the Germans slightly and possibly the Kassel spoof also momentarily drew their attention to the north of the Long Leg. None of this saved the bombers from the attentions of the Tame Boar fighters which were already in contact with them but the spoofs certainly helped to ensure that the sky over Nuremberg would be free of a considerable Wild Boar effort that might otherwise have been assembled there.

Minor aspects of the operation show a degree of inevitable decline in effectiveness following the long phase of deep-penetration raids during the Battle of Berlin. These had tired the British but given the Germans many opportunities to respond to British tactics and equipment. Because the Germans were able to size up the situation at an early stage the first wave of Intruders were left patrolling empty airfields. The new SN–2 radar had left the Serrate Mosquitoes groping ineffectually for the elusive radar signal without which the Serrate set was useless, while British H2S signals, on the other hand, were being tracked by the Germans from Norwich onwards. Gee was jammed, resulting in all sorts of navigational difficulties, and Oboe would not reach beyond the Ruhr. The combined efforts of twenty-six A.B.C. Lancasters had been insufficient to jam the broadcast of the German running commentary.

The cream of Bomber Command were the Pathfinders, yet Bennett's men had not had a happy night. By 8 Group's admission, many of their Windfinder crews had failed to operate effectively. One certainly and probably two more of their aircraft had marked a target fifty-five miles from Nuremberg, although the second and third Pathfinders may well have rallied the scattered bombing there. At Nuremberg itself, a year and a half after the establishment of the Pathfinder Force, faulty marking had led most of the Main Force to bomb well away from the target.

Let me hasten to say that to place skymarkers accurately, especially beyond Oboe range and in an unexpectedly strong cross wind, was a most difficult problem that was never solved during the war. Let it also be said that these observations are not criticisms of the brave men who flew in Bennett's squadrons nor of Bennett and his staff. Too many good men had been shot down in the Battle of Berlin both in the Pathfinders and in the Main Force squadrons that provided Pathfinder reinforcements. There was no shortage of willing crews but the average level of experience had fallen too low.

Bomber Command was tired and some, at least, of its tactics were played out.

Leaving the tactics of the operation, it can even be asked whether Bomber Command should have been raiding Nuremberg at all. A specific directive had been received at the beginning of March stating that Harris should give priority to the attack of six German targets yet the month had passed without one of these being intentionally bombed. But the poor bombing results at Nuremberg and the accidental bombing of Schweinfurt show that there was some justification for the reluctance of Harris to follow the directive. Five of the priority targets were smaller than Nuremberg. Those crews who had bombed Schweinfurt had demonstrated that the navigational difficulties were such that an aircraft could easily be fifty-five miles astray at the end of an approach flight and those who did reach Nuremberg could hardly hit this large city because of marking difficulties

Harris said that he could not guarantee that his bombers could find and destroy small targets beyond the range of Oboe using existing tactics. The events of the night went a long way to proving him to be right. The sixth target on the list was Leipzig, roughly the same size as Nuremberg. Harris had attacked this target late in February and lost seventy-eight bombers and their crews in doing so.

One part of the Nuremberg plan is difficult to understand. I was more moved by the bombing of Ostend, the 'last resort' target, than by any other incident of the night. Within the overall context of the war, the German cities and civilians might be expected to have to take their chance against the bombers, but the selection of Ostend as a target in the furtherance of the policy that not a single bomb should be wasted seems an unreasonable sacrifice to ask of the friendly citizens of that town considering the known bombing accuracy of bomber crews.

Bomber Command was not run by a committee or board but by one man. Sir Arthur Harris had taken the decision to raid Nuremberg; he had approved the plan and the route; he had decided not to cancel the operation when Saundby showed him the revised weather forecast. Hindsight gives us the ability to judge that Harris was solely to blame for the decision to mount this raid and then persist with it, but hindsight does not give us the right to be over-critical. An admiral might fight one major battle in his lifetime. A general might fight three such battles. Harris committed the whole of his front line force to combat approximately ten times in each month for three and a quarter years. Many raids that were subsequently successful would never have taken place if Harris had waited for perfect conditions. On this occasion, he took one chance too many. Those who knew him say that he would later grieve over the losses as deeply as anyone.

The attack on the battleships at Wilhelmshaven, München-Gladbach (the first bombing of a German city), the first Area Bombing success on Lübeck, the Thousand-Bomber Raid against Cologne, the Oboe-marked destruction of the Ruhr, the Dams Raid, the firestorm in Hamburg, the attempt to destroy Berlin – these had been the turning-points of Bomber Command's war. And now Nuremberg. Like many of the others, it was not a sharply defined landmark and was not recognized at the time to be of much significance. But, for several reasons, Nuremberg deserves a place in this growing list.

Nuremberg's record bomber casualties, which were never surpassed, were certainly one of the highlights, but of greater importance were the causes of the losses and the tactical changes that they forced. The basis of Bomber Command's tactics since the Thousand-Bomber Raid on Cologne had been the attack on one major target carried out by the maximum number of heavy bombers flying in one stream. Attempts had been made to protect this single bomber-stream by the introduction of an increasing number of electronic devices and tactical diversions and by the use of more Serrate and Intruder Mosquitoes. These tactics had succeeded against shallow penetration targets like the Ruhr and Hamburg but the long flights to targets deeper in Germany had proved to be increasingly costly.

The five-month period now known as the Battle of Berlin had cost Bomber Command 1,128 aircraft missing over enemy territory plus an unknown number that had crashed in England. The Official History points out that this far exceeded the entire front-line strength of Bomber Command at that time. Flak and single-engined Wild Boar fighters defending the target itself had caused some of this loss, but it was the Tame Boar tactics of intercepting the bombers while they were flying to and from the target that had been mainly responsible. The longer the routes, the more success-ful were the Tame Boar fighters. In the barely remembered Essen operation four nights before Nuremberg only nine bombers had been lost. But Essen although a heavily defended target was only ten minutes' flying time beyond the German border. Compare the Essen loss with the results of raids on distant targets such as Leipzig in February and Berlin, six nights before Nuremberg, when seventy-eight and seventy-three bombers had not returned. Now Nuremberg had hap-pened with its huge loss. Bomber Command was in a dilemma. Its existence could not be justified by raiding only those targets just across the German border yet it could not continue to fly deeper into Germany and sustain the heavy losses of Leipzig, Berlin and Nuremberg.

There was a lull in operations following Nuremberg and the whole tactical problem was thrashed out. The most important of several changes made was that the single

bomber-stream principle was abandoned. At one meeting of
Bomber Command's Tactical Planning Committee early in
April, it was even suggested that the bomber-stream be given
up entirely and each aircraft should choose its own route to
and from the target as they had done earlier in the war, but
this drastic solution was rejected. It was decided, however,
that in future smaller streams of bombers would attack more
than one target during a night. Nuremberg was the last
occasion that Bomber Command flew out to Germany in one
huge stream.

Another change was the immediate reinforcement of the
infant 100 Group. The Mosquito night fighters defending
England were equipped with the Mark X radar which was
superior to anything the Serrate Mosquitoes were allowed to
carry over Germany. Harris suggested that the embargo on
using the Mark X over Germany should be lifted as the need
to protect his bombers was now greater than that of home
defence. He asked for ten of these under-employed squadrons
to be transferred to 100 Group but he only received three.
A big impetus was, however, given to the supply of equipment and aircraft to the radio counter-measures squadrons
in 100 Group.

There was another aspect of the raids on long-distance
targets, other than their high cost, that was causing dismay.
Not only could Bomber Command not reach the distant
targets without suffering crippling losses, but the bombs
eventually dropped there rarely achieved the desired effect.
The Essen raid, a few nights earlier, had been highly successful in terms of bombing accuracy although the target had
been cloud-covered throughout the raid. The reason why
this could not be repeated on Nuremberg and other targets
deep in Germany was, of course, the limited range of Oboe.

The Air Ministry had been hoping for some time that
Harris could solve this problem so that bombing in general
could be more effective and so that the priority targets in
particular could be eliminated.

617 Squadron had been retained in 5 Group after its historic raid on the German dams and was now regularly
achieving pinpoint bombing accuracy in attacks on small
targets. In the early months of 1944, a 617 Squadron aircraft
had sometimes flown low over lightly defended French
targets to drop markers for the remainder of the squadron.

This low-level marking had been successful and Wing Commander Leonard Cheshire, the gifted leader of 617 Squadron, then flying his fourth operational tour, suggested to his group commander that the technique might be suitable for attacks by bomber forces larger than his own squadron. Cochrane, who was always looking for greater bombing accuracy, was interested but first Cheshire had to learn to fly the Mosquito which was a more suitable aircraft than the Lancaster as the low-level marker. On 30 March, just as preparations were going ahead for the Nuremberg Raid, Cheshire made his first solo flight in a Mosquito from the fighter station at Coleby Grange near Lincoln.

At some stage in the affair, the suggestion that targets be marked from low level had been put to the Pathfinders but Bennett had demurred, partly on account of the risk involved over the average German target and partly because of various technical difficulties that he forecast would occur. Cochrane now suggested that 5 Group should be allowed to experiment, with 617 Squadron doing the marking and the rest of the group providing a miniature Main Force. Cochrane requested Harris's permission for this and also for two Mosquitoes as low-level marker aircraft.

In the period of tactical reappraisal that was then taking place, Cochrane's suggestion found Harris in a receptive mood. Less than a week after Nuremberg, Cheshire flew in a Mosquito and marked an aircraft factory at Toulouse from under 1,000 feet. He continued to orbit the target at low level acting as Master Bomber while Lancasters of 617 Squadron backed up his markers from a medium height and 140 more Lancasters bombed with unprecedented accuracy from their normal altitude.

Cochrane reported this success to his chief next day and asked for two more Mosquitoes. To the 5 Group commander's astonishment, Harris sent not two Mosquitoes but the whole of 627 Squadron from 8 Group. In addition, the two Lancaster squadrons, 83 and 97, that 5 Group had sent to form the Pathfinders in 1942 were returned. Cochrane was told to bomb certain specially selected German targets using the Mosquitoes as low-level primary markers, 83 and 97 Squadrons as backers-up and the two hundred or more Lancasters of 5 Group as the bombing force. Cochrane and Cheshire were delighted to be pioneering a new phase of bomber operations. Bennett was, to put it mildly, disappointed that his old rival Cochrane had been responsible for ending 8 Group's exclusive sovereignty in Pathfinding matters.

Before that month of April was out, the reinforced 5 Group carried out three accurate attacks on distant targets – Brunswick, Munich and Schweinfurt. It is significant that two of these targets were in the priority list that Harris had previously been reluctant to attack. For his courage while acting as Master Bomber at a few hundred feet over these heavily defended targets, Wing Commander Cheshire was awarded the Victoria Cross.

There were limitations to the new technique. It could not be used on a cloud-covered target; it would not, for instance, have been of any use over Nuremberg. When cloud was encountered, the Lancaster Pathfinders in 5 Group had to revert to conventional marking methods. Nor could the 5 Group method be used for large forces whose bombs would obliterate the small number of markers used and who could not be kept orbiting a target while the Master Bomber readjusted the marking as Cheshire and his pilots often did.

It is ironical that Cheshire had earlier almost joined the Pathfinders on the completion of his third tour of operations. Bennett said that he would accept Cheshire if he could prove his flying to be of the required standard. 'Rather ungraciously I suppose,' writes Cheshire, 'I told him that, if that was the case, I would see if I could find somewhere else to go!' It is also of interest that no 5 Group Mosquito was ever lost over a target while flying as a low-level marker except for one piloted by the famous Guy Gibson, v.c.

The fact that Bennett had failed to grasp the opportunity to develop low-level marking should not detract from his splendid achievements in establishing the Pathfinders in 1942 and pioneering the earlier marking techniques. Critics of Harris will say that improved marking should have been introduced earlier. This may be true but his decisive action a week after Nuremberg certainly got things moving again. It can be counted one of Harris's achievements that, by this eventual arrangement, he got the best out of both Bennett and Cochrane, his two brilliant but so different group commanders.

Nuremberg was destined to be the last operation of the Battle of Berlin. The coming of the shorter nights and the proved dominance of the German night fighters were two reasons for this but a third was that a new phase of the bombing war was to open on 1 April. Until then, Bomber Command had always been under the control, albeit a very loose control, of the Air Ministry; for over two years, Harris's theoretical boss had been Sir Charles Portal, Chief of the Air Staff. Now, with the Allied invasion of Europe only a few weeks away, Bomber Command was to come under S.H.A.E.F. (Supreme Headquarters, Allied Expeditionary Force) so that the heavy bomber effort could be fully harnessed to Overlord, the vital landings in France due to take place early in June. For the next five months, Harris would owe nominal allegiance to an American, General Dwight Eisenhower. During this period, Harris could only pursue his general offensive against Germany's industrial centres when his bombers were not needed to bomb Overlord targets.

This divide between the end of the Battle of Berlin and the intensification of the pre-Overlord campaign marks the greatest historical significance of the Nuremberg Raid. The cornerstone of R.A.F. policy before the war had been that a sustained offensive by heavy bombers against an enemy's industrial capacity would cause that enemy to collapse and render 1914-style land campaigns unnecessary .This was the Bomber Dream – that air power and not armies and navies would decide future wars. The early disappointments – the vulnerability of the daylight bomber and the difficulty of accurate bombing by night – had caused many of the bomber enthusiasts to modify their ambitions. The bomber could still play a large part in victory but would not, on its own, be decisive. The decision, late in 1941, not to build up Bomber Command to 4,000 front-line aircraft appeared to seal the fate of the strategic bomber theory.

But some never accepted the demise of the theory; they found their champion in Sir Arthur Harris. The successful Battles of the Ruhr and Hamburg gave promise that a bomber victory could yet be achieved. However, a combination of circumstances – the curvature of the earth which stopped the Oboe beams being used beyond the Ruhr, the fallibility of H2S marking, the German night fighters with their Wild and Tame Boar tactics – all these robbed Harris of that vital third success. He had claimed that Berlin would be wrecked 'from end to end' and that there would be 'a state of devastation in which surrender is inevitable'. No man had tried harder than Harris to beat the Germans without the necessity of a land campaign but he had now to subordinate his bombers to that same land campaign.

Nuremberg was the end of the Battle of Berlin. The Battle of Berlin was the end of the Bomber Dream.

17

Was the Nuremberg Raid Betrayed?

'The Germans must have known we were coming.' So said many an R.A.F. man who had flown on the Nuremberg raid. It was an understandable reaction. It was unusual for German fighters to have intercepted the bomber stream so early in the outward flight, and the ease with which the fighters remained in the stream from there to Nuremberg sowed the seed in the minds of many men that the Germans had known the route and laid an ambush.

It was not the only time that such a theory was discussed by bomber crews after a bad raid and, in England at least, interest in the possibility soon faded. Among R.A.F. prisoners-of-war in Germany, however, talk of possible German foreknowledge persisted. The Germans encouraged this and many of the men shot down on the Nuremberg operation were told by the interrogation officers at Oberursel that both the target and the route had been known to the Luftwaffe on the afternoon *before the raid* and the Germans attributed their night-fighter victory to this advance intelligence. Most of the Nuremberg raid prisoners realized that the Germans could easily have produced both the story and the display of maps showing the route in the interval between their being shot down and their arrival at Oberursel. On the other hand, the Germans do not appear to have used this ploy often and the R.A.F. men had not been warned of it. Some of the Nuremberg prisoners believed the story and, when they reached their permanent prison camps, it became a subject for discussion among hundreds of other bored aircrew prisoners.

The possibility of an intelligence leak was mentioned in several post-war publications. It is a subject of great importance and I devoted a considerable research effort into following up every lead given. Oberst Erich Killinger, the German commanding officer at Oberursel at the time, was found, but he denied any foreknowledge: 'We never knew with any certainty nor did we ever discover what the next target of

the R.A.F. was going to be.'* An R.A.F. prisoner-of-war –
claimed in one book† to have been at Oberursel on the afternoon before the Nuremberg raid and to have been told the
name of the target for that night, but only the name, not the
route to be taken – turned out to have been a character based
on no more than hearsay evidence. I was able to find no R.A.F.
men who were at Oberursel on the relevant day and who
were informed of the target during their interrogations. I
did find four men who were at Oberursel on that day who
never heard the subject mentioned. There has never been any
firm, first-hand evidence to support the Oberursel story.

It is important to what follows in this chapter to state that
everything written in it so far appeared in the first edition of
this book which was published in 1973.

The subject of German foreknowledge was reopened in
dramatic manner by the publication of a new book, *Bodyguard
of Lies*, in 1975.‡ The author, Anthony Cave Brown, an
Englishman and a former journalist who had settled in the
United States, wrote a history of intelligence deception
practised by the Allies during the Second World War. Cave
Brown devoted one chapter§ of his book to a contention that
an Allied intelligence organization had deliberately given
details of the Nuremberg raid to the Germans by means of a
German agent who had been captured in England.¶ The
Germans were intended to believe that their agent was still
operating normally but the Allies were using him to help
build up the important deception that the main landings of the
invasion in the summer of 1944 would take place in the Pas de
Calais area and not in Normandy. To confirm the continuing
credibility of the spy, the Allies had to allow him to send some

* Letter to author, 1971.
† David Irving, *Und Deutschlands Städte Starben Nicht: Ein Dokumentar-
bericht*, Schweizer, Zürich, 1963.
‡ Anthony Cave Brown, *Bodyguard of Lies*, published by Harper and Row,
New York, in 1975 and W. H. Allen, London, in 1976. A German edition was
published by Kurt Desch, Munich, in 1976.
§ The chapter, 'Nuremberg', is on pp. 500–516 of *Bodyguard of Lies*.
¶ The organization carrying out this work was the XX Committee – the
Double-Cross Committee – controlled by B.1.A which, in turn, was part of
M.I.5, Military Intelligence Branch No. 5.
More about the work of the XX Committee can be read in *The Double-Cross
System in the War of 1939–1945* by J. C. Masterman, published by Yale Univer-
sity Press in 1972. Approximately 120 German agents were captured, 'turned'
and worked as double agents by the committee.

true information to his former masters. Cave Brown claimed that the deliberate leaking of the Nuremberg raid and the subsequent heavy losses were necessary sacrifices that had to be accepted to ensure the success of the invasion and the eventual saving of a greater number of lives.

When Cave Brown's book became available in Britain in 1976, the Nuremberg story attracted particular attention. The popular press had a field day and the families of the R.A.F. men killed in the raid suffered new distress. But the suggestion that Bomber Command was used in this way is of serious, historical interest and the distress of relatives should not, at this stage, be allowed to cloud an examination of the subject.

Cave Brown's Nuremberg story started with Major-General Sir Francis de Guingand who, in the spring of 1944, was Chief of Staff in Montgomery's 21st Army Group which was due to land in Normandy in June. One of de Guingand's tasks was to ensure that military planning conformed to the deceptions being practised by the intelligence authorities. In this role, he would have come into contact with the organization handling the German double agent but would not have been directly involved in the details of that operation. De Guingand informed Cave Brown, in 1970, that he had been told that the identity of a target in Germany 'for a major air attack' had been revealed to the Germans in order to ensure the continuing credibility of the agent. According to Cave Brown, de Guingand 'seemed to remember' that the identity of this target was Stuttgart but he did not state whether it was the R.A.F. or the U.S.A.A.F. whose raid was involved.

Let us firstly examine in what form information on a future raid could have been transmitted to the Germans. It has been described earlier how both R.A.F. Bomber Command and the American Eighth Air Force in England conducted operations under the guidance of a series of directives. It would have been an easy matter – and almost a matter of routine – for the intelligence authorities to have been given copies of these directives. If the Germans had to be told the identity of the target, it would have been simple to choose a name from the current list and send this to the Germans in the expectation that the R.A.F. or the U.S.A.A.F. would bomb it during the following weeks. In this way, no one outside the intelligence organization would need to be involved. However, to be told the day or the night of any raid on the target thus given to the enemy, or the routes to and from that target, would have required either the involvement of someone at the head-quarters of Bomber Command or the Eighth Air Force or detailed knowledge from inside those headquarters during the few hours available between the decision taken to mount a raid and the actual execution of it.

As has been stated in an earlier chapter, the current directive to the Allied heavy-bomber commanders concen-trated on the German ball-bearing and fighter-aircraft industries. Stuttgart, with the V.K.F. ball-bearing factory in the suburb of Bad Canstatt, was prominent in the latest variation of the directive* *as a priority target for the U.S.A.A.F.* Bomber Command was ordered to support this ball-bearing and fighter-factory campaign although its first six priorities did not include Stuttgart. Of all the targets in that directive, Stuttgart was the closest to Germany's western frontier. It lay only fifty miles inside Germany and bombers could reach it by means of routes across Northern France which were not, at that time, heavily defended by the Germans. The Americans did bomb Stuttgart, on 25 February 1944; their losses are not recorded but are known to have been light. Bomber Com-mand also raided the city, attacking it three times between 21 February and 16 March. Its losses in these raids were forty-nine bombers from 1,989 sorties dispatched – a loss rate of 2·5 per cent compared with an average loss rate for all raids on Germany in February and March of 4·6 per cent.

If de Guingand was right and if Stuttgart was divulged to the Germans as a target for the Allied bombers, then the four raids on that city in twenty-four days should have amply con-vinced the Germans that their agent in England was still sending reliable information, and this intelligence ploy by the Allies would have been undertaken successfully without undue loss of aircraft and crews.

Cave Brown's reaction to all this was curious. He appar-ently did not consider that the air attack divulged might have been an American one. He did not mention the series of four raids on Stuttgart, only the two R.A.F. ones in the first half of March. His book does not mention any primary research which he carried out into the Stuttgart possibility. When I wrote to Stuttgart, inquiring into this matter, I was told of

* Issued on 28 January 1944, The Official History, Vol. IV, pp. 162–3.

the former head of the city's *Flugwachtkommando*, a Major Engelhorn, speaking before his death of a 'sensation' in being warned by Berlin *before* the last R.A.F. raid in March that Stuttgart was to be bombed that night; and that the city's sirens sounded thirty-six minutes before the first bombs dropped on that night. The extent of this warning time should be remembered.

But the four Stuttgart raids of that period had not, until then, attracted much attention and there were no published works on them. As has been stated, no primary research into the possibility of a Stuttgart disclosure was mentioned in Cave Brown's book. Instead, he dismissed the subject: 'Neither [*sic*] Stuttgart raid showed signs of German fore-knowledge.' But two full-length books about the Nuremberg raid of 30/31 March 1944 appeared in 1973.* Cave Brown leaned heavily on these books and on other published works for the sensational story which he then wrote, asserting that Nuremberg and not Stuttgart was the target disclosed to the Germans. He referred to me as 'an historian of the Nuremberg raid' and quoted from my book on many occasions. The implication of this is that Cave Brown had available to him all the evidence presented in the first sixteen chapters of this book – to which no changes have been made in this revised edition – and the earlier paragraphs of this chapter which deal with the Oberursel story. The remainder of this chapter will examine each major part of Cave Brown's story.

In examining the British planning of the Nuremberg raid and the decision to reveal it through the double agent, Cave Brown presented a theory. 'It was essential to bring on an immense night battle where the best of the German night fighters might be destroyed.' That, claimed Cave Brown, was 'certainly a principal intention of the raid' and is his explanation for the justification for disclosing information of a raid to the Germans; a raid not on a target just over the German border, but one deep in Germany – and to be carried out on a moonlit night which would favour the German night fighters. It was important to take this double risk, said Cave Brown, to destroy the German night-fighter aircrews who, he suggested,

* The second of these books, *The Bombing of Nuremberg* by James Campbell, was published in London by Allison and Busby on the same day as my own book.

were expected to conduct the majority of the German air operations against the coming D-Day landings. But the whole emphasis of Bomber Command training and tactics was to avoid fighters and, for a drastic change such as the one suggested by Cave Brown to be implemented on this one night, dozens of officers must have been involved in the planning. No one concerned has ever mentioned this. Such planning must certainly have involved Sir Arthur Harris, indeed must have been co-ordinated by him. If Cave Brown had approached Harris – and Harris says he did not – he would have received a vigorous denial that he had ever been ordered to bomb Nuremberg on that particular night and that any part of Cave Brown's story was true. 'I don't believe a word of it,' Harris says.* Those who know Harris well will state that he would never have allowed Bomber Command to be used in this way. Also, Sir John Masterman said of the work of the Double-Cross Committee: 'We never gave the enemy information that would have cost Allied lives.'†

Cave Brown went on to claim that the bombers were deliberately routed 'close to the thick concentration of German night-fighter bases around the Ruhr' and 'directly over the fighters' assembly beacons at Aachen (codenamed Ida) and Frankfurt (Otto)'. He also stated that Harris had ordered, earlier in March, that, because of recent heavy losses, 'bomber streams should henceforward be split up to approach their targets from different directions' to deceive the German fighters. The single stream chosen for the Nuremberg raid was exceptional, he claimed, and was a further device to enable the Germans to find the bombers and provoke a battle. In addition, Cave Brown said that the Nuremberg plan 'called for some seventy to eighty long-range Mosquito night fighters to accompany the main force' and engage the German night fighters. '*These were not the usual tactics,*' wrote Cave Brown.

Routine research at the Public Record Office shows that Mosquitoes had been attempting to support the bomber force since early January 1944, that only fifty-five Mosquito night fighters flew on the Nuremberg operation, that only nineteen of these actually flew with the bomber stream and that the tactics used on this night were entirely normal. As

* Letter from Sir Arthur Harris to author, 2 May 1976.
† Masterman interview with Cave Brown.

for the route chosen, maps in my own book, known to have been studied by Cave Brown, show that there was no undue concentration of German fighter bases near the Ruhr and that the Nuremberg route was not 'directly over' but exactly half way *between* the two assembly beacons. The Germans had at least twenty-one such beacons at that time and no route into Germany could avoid passing near some of them. Again, on the use of a single stream to Nuremberg, Harris had thought about changing to split streams in February, not March as stated by Cave Brown, but Bomber Command only tried the new method twice in six weeks and, far from Nuremberg's single stream being an exception, the single stream had been used in the last six raids before Nuremberg! The failure to use split streams on the Nuremberg raid has no significance.

Cave Brown then turned to the reaction of the Germans, dealing firstly with the forecast by their radio–listening service that between seven and eight hundred bombers would attack Germany that night. Cave Brown stated that, because 'Bomber Command was striking everywhere from Murmansk to Milan', this forecast may have been evidence of fore-knowledge of the attack on Nuremberg. But Public Record Office documents show that Bomber Command had not mounted a single major attack outside Germany for more than seven months. Forty-five consecutive raids without a break had fallen on Germany! The truth is that, once the R.A.F. bomber's test radio transmissions had been picked up, the German forecast that Germany was likely to be raided that night was no more than routine.

Cave Brown then stated categorically that, during the afternoon or early evening of 30 March, the Germans brought some of their more distant night–fighter units nearer to beacons Ida and Otto. But the only recorded move I have been able to discover during that day is of a mere four fighters of II/NJG1 which had recently been bombed out of their own airfield and had since been shuffled fom one airfield to another. Their move that afternoon, from St Trond in Belgium to Laon in France, was from an airfield directly on the bombers' route to Nuremberg to another airfield a hundred miles away!

In his description of the flight of the bombers into Germany that night, Cave Brown wrote of the interception of the bomber stream in the so-called ambush. The Germans had, he said, 'calculated the estimated time of arrival of the main force . . . with remarkable precision', completely ignoring the statement by General Grabmann that he had taken the decision to order the night fighters to Ida and Otto almost on the spur of the moment. Cave Brown also ignored these examples of failure by the Germans in the handling of their night fighters that night: the premature commitment of most of the Wild Boar fighters near the Ruhr, the holding back of the 1st Fighter Division's Wild Boars to cover Berlin, the failure of Nuremberg's local Wild Boar fighter units at Neuberg even to take off, and the action of the Messerschmitt 110 Gruppe at Stuttgart which flew half way round Germany chasing the bomber stream when they could so easily have been kept back to intercept it when it flew back almost over their home airfield.

The main public warning siren in Nuremberg, the *Flieger-alarm*, sounded at 12.38, twenty-two minutes before the first Pathfinders appeared over the city and the first bombs fell. Cave Brown quoted this information from my own book but went on to state: 'Again, it seems that the Germans had fore-knowledge . . . for normally the Germans were able to provide their cities with only a few minutes' warning, if any at all.' The truth is that, by March 1944, the Germans had a well-developed warning system which enabled any threatened city to be warned well before bombers arrived. Nuremberg city archives show that, for the seven major attacks on Nuremberg during the period for which records are available between mid-summer 1942 and the end of the war, the average interval between the sounding of the *Fliegeralarm* and the arrival of the first bombers was twenty minutes. May I remind the reader that the Stuttgart raid of 15/16 March, which Cave Brown said showed 'no signs of German foreknowledge', had a thirty-six-minute warning period before the first bombs dropped!

Finally, in concluding his case, Cave Brown presented the old story of the British aircrew prisoners-of-war who were at Oberursel on the afternoon before the raid.

British airmen would state after the war that . . . they were told . . . about five hours before the bomber stream took off . . . that the target for the raid that night was Nuremberg. At least one prisoner claimed that he saw that someone in the Luftwaffe had marked the route to be taken . . . on a wall map.

This was presented as a bald statement of fact, without any qualification. It was also presented without any source reference. Cave Brown used the names of many R.A.F. aircrew in his Nuremberg chapter – these names all coming from other publications – but he did not name this airman, or any other of the prisoners at Oberursel. It can only be assumed that his statement here is based on the old hearsay evidence quoted in other books but never confirmed. Despite intense press publicity when *Bodyguard of Lies* was published in Britain, still no ex-Oberursel R.A.F. prisoner has yet come forward to confirm this old story.

Not one of the statements and theories put forward by Cave Brown to support his claim that it was Nuremberg that was disclosed to the Germans and not Stuttgart, as de Guingand originally said, stands up to examination. What is asked to pass as history should be written from actual evidence. If such evidence is conclusive, then truth is established. If the evidence is not conclusive, then theorizing and supposition, as Cave Brown might claim he is carrying out with Nuremberg, is permissible – *but only as long as all the available evidence is submitted.* In this case it is known that the writer had other material in his hands. In Cave Brown's list of sources, he included the '1st Air Corps (Luftwaffe) War Diary and scattered associated documents'. There is no evidence to show what the 'scattered associated documents' were, but the diary is that of the German I Fighter Corps referred to in my own book. Cave Brown can be assumed to have studied the many references in my own book to this War Diary; it is, after all, the main German source on the Nuremberg operation. But he failed to present any of the following extracts from the War Diary:

The frequent changes of course by the British bombers and the decoy manoeuvres using Mosquitoes prevented an early recognition of the target. The early commitment of some Wild Boar units was a precautionary measure in the event of an attack on Frankfurt . . . The choice of the Ida and Otto beacons was a fortunate coincidence . . . The command of I Fighter Corps recognized relatively late that the British attack was meant for Nuremberg.

Cave Brown omits all of this vital evidence.

From a lead given to him about the disclosure of the identity of Stuttgart as a possible target for Allied bombers,

Cave Brown thus developed his own sensational story that the R.A.F. raid on Nuremberg must have been the subject of the disclosure, with the night and the route chosen both being part of the disclosure. In doing so, he produced no new evidence, he quoted only one new source – and that was de Guingand, who had said 'Stuttgart'; he failed to include or comment upon counter-evidence which he knew existed. Not one serious historian has endorsed Cave Brown's Nuremberg story and his book collected some scathing reviews from top men in the field into which he chose to venture.

Why devote so much effort to exposing such a weak case now? Unfortunately, the general reader too often assûmes that anything in print must contain an element of truth. Cave Brown has never, to my knowledge, attempted to answer publicly the charges on Nuremberg made by his critics, nor expressed any regret for what he has written. I felt it important that a reasoned reply should appear in book form and stand as a permanent record on the library shelf, partly so that families of the Nuremberg dead, so deeply hurt by Cave Brown's story, may be reassured, but primarily so that students in years to come may study both Cave Brown's contention and this reply.

It is my opinion that the old legend, 'the Germans knew we were coming', turned by Cave Brown into his more dramatic, 'the Germans were told we were coming', should be laid to rest.

18

The Years that Followed

For exactly six months following the Nuremberg Raid, Bomber Command faithfully carried out its allotted duties in connection with the invasion of France. A great variety of targets were attacked during this period. The French railway system was bombed in such a way that Normandy was isolated from the remainder of France thus delaying the arrival of German reinforcements until the troops had secured a foothold behind the invasion beaches. Military targets of all kinds were attacked both before and after the invasion; sometimes German troop concentrations only a mile or so beyond friendly ground positions were heavily bombed. When the German flying-bomb launching sites were discovered, these too were dealt with by Bomber Command.

All this was a complete contrast to Bomber Command's operations over the previous years and for the crews who had flown the first part of their tour in the Battle of Berlin it was an exhilarating, if hectic, period. Initially, at least, they were delighted to be on shorter raids, often by day and with fighter cover, and usually over less heavily defended targets than those they had been used to attacking. There was satisfaction too that they were making a more direct contribution to the war effort.

Every now and then we realized that we were hitting civilians when bombing German targets and we tried to shut this out of our minds. We felt much better when we went on to marshalling yards; we felt that we were fighting like the Eighth Army or the Battle of Britain boys. It was good clean fighting. (Flying Officer J. Chatterton, 44 Squadron)

Not all the raids were connected with the invasion. Whenever he had the chance, Harris still sent part of his bomber force to Germany. With the more accurate 5 Group marking he was now prepared to devote more effort to the directive targets and many of these were effectively bombed. Harris also found time to return occasionally to the general area offensive against German industrial centres.

In these hectic six months Bomber Command dispatched 91,368 bombing sorties, half as many again as it had sent out in the whole of 1943. 1,392 aircraft were lost during the period but the loss-rate of 1·5 per cent was easily the lowest since 1939. But the improving casualty figures concealed some bad incidents. The German night-fighter force remained strong and effective, and although there was never a repetition of the Nuremberg massacre, smaller forces of bombers were sometimes caught, to their terrible cost, particularly when operating over Germany. In a raid on 21 June by half of 5 Group on a synthetic petroleum plant at Wesseling, only forty miles beyond the German border, thirty-seven Lancasters, or 28 per cent of the attacking force, were shot down!

The German fighters also started reacting to raids on France and there occurred another disaster on the night of 3 May when 1 and 5 Groups attacked an important Panzer training unit alongside the French village of Mailly-le-Camp. Wing Commander Cheshire, acting as Master Bomber for a 5 Group-type attack, had the difficult task of ensuring that bombs fell on the German camp but not the village. The Lancasters had to wait until Cheshire saw that the markers were in the right place. Then Cheshire's Mosquito suffered a partial radio failure. The long delay gave the German night fighters time to arrive and forty-two out of 346 bombers were lost. 1 Group had suffered the greater loss and after this raid was reluctant to operate with 5 Group again.*

After Mailly-le-Camp there were protests by the bomber crews that these raids still only counted as one third of an operation. This rule was immediately amended and attacks on French targets counted the same as those over Germany.

Many of the men who had flown to Nuremberg and returned safely did not survive that summer and were shot down attacking such targets as Wesseling and Mailly-le-Camp. Most of the remainder completed their operational

* When I visited Mailly-le-Camp in 1967 to find the grave of my friend Flying Officer Archard I was told that Cheshire had done a good job. The raid had caused heavy damage to the military camp but the only civilian casualties had been caused by crashing bombers. The Germans were furious at their losses and would not allow the French to gather in the bodies of the many bomber men scattered over the area until three days later.

tour and the war would not last long enough for more than a few to come back for a second tour.

Among the men who had flown on the Nuremberg Raid and were later shot down were two Pathfinder pilots. Flight Lieutenant Ronald Walker of 83 Squadron came down in Holland following the Wesseling raid. He managed to contact the Dutch section of the escape route, but was in a 'safe' house in Tilburg when it was raided by the Germans. Walker and two other R.A.F. men, all wearing civilian clothes, were coldbloodedly shot by Gestapo men who were themselves later sentenced to death for war crimes.

Squadron Leader Edward Blenkinsopp, a British Columbian with 405 (Vancouver) Squadron, was shot down while flying as Deputy Master Bomber on a raid. Blenkinsopp met up with the Belgian Resistance and apparently made no attempt to return to England. In December 1944 he was with a party that set out to blow up a Gestapo-occupied house but were themselves trapped and captured. The Canadian either did not disclose his identity or else failed to convince the Germans of it, for he was next reported in St Gilles Prison in Brussels. An American airman in a neighbouring cell heard Blenkinsopp tapping out a message in Morse saying that he had been condemned to death. However, the sentence was not carried out for he was next seen in Hamburg working as a forced labourer in a shipyard. Apparently he escaped from here during an air raid but the final report of this gallant and long-suffering Canadian's career placed him in Belsen Concentration Camp where German records show him as dying from 'heart failure'. He has no known grave.

At the end of September 1944 Bomber Command was officially released from its commitment to S.H.A.E.F. and came once more under the nominal command of the Chief of the Air Staff, Sir Charles Portal. Harris continued to receive requests to help the Army and the Navy by attacking tactical targets and his bombers often aided the other services in the following months, but a great debate ensued in the highest circles on exactly how the main effort of the still growing strength of Bomber Command should be used in the remaining months of the war.

One view was strongly pressed by Air Marshal Sir Arthur Tedder, Eisenhower's Deputy Commander at S.H.A.E.F.

Tedder felt that if both British and American heavy-bomber forces were used in a tactical role to isolate the European battlefield from the remainder of Germany, the land battle, and therefore the war, could be more quickly brought to an end. This was loosely known as the Communications Plan.

Sir Charles Portal, one of the original proponents of the theory that the strategic use of the heavy bomber could bring a decisive end, maintained that the bomber could still bring about the collapse of the enemy if used selectively against particular sections of German industry. In particular, Portal favoured an all-out attack on the German petroleum industry. This was the Oil Plan.

To Sir Arthur Harris this was the ball-bearing panacea all over again. To him, the continuing destruction of the major German industrial cities would inevitably cause the collapse of that elusive German morale and will to resist that Harris had earlier sought. He claimed that his bombers could completely destroy German cities at the rate of two-and-a-half per month and that only twelve outstanding cities now stood between him and victory. It is interesting to note that Nuremberg stood seventh on this list. Harris told Portal that 'this vast task' should not be abandoned 'just as it nears completion'.*

So those who had it in their power to direct the fortunes of Bomber Command for the remainder of the war had three paths from which to choose. The decision would rest with Portal and ultimately with Churchill. Would it be Tedder's Communications Plan, Portal's own Oil Plan or Harris's Area Bombing? In the end, it was the view of that single-minded man Sir Arthur Harris that prevailed. The crunch appears to have come when Harris stated that he should either be left free to follow his own policy or be replaced. But Harris stood so high in the esteem of the bomber crews and of the British public that his sacking at this time would have been a terrible blow to the morale of both aircrew and civilians. Furthermore, there was a possibility that the Americans might then attempt to bring Bomber Command into a unified Allied Air Command. If this happened, the new air commander would probably be an American. Bomber Command was practically the last independent force still under British control and the submission to Harris was the price Portal had

* The Official History, vol. III, page 82.

to pay for the retention of that independence. If Harris had been replaced by a British commander, it is interesting to speculate whether Saundby or Cochrane would have been promoted or whether Portal would have brought someone in from outside Bomber Command.

And so the final phase commenced. Directives continued to arrive at High Wycombe ordering Harris to attack specific target systems as they had in the old days and, to be fair to Harris, he did devote a considerable effort to following these but his main attention was to the area offensive.

In the six months since Nuremberg, the aerial balance of power had shifted drastically in favour of the bombers. Allied troops now occupied most of France and Belgium and raids to Germany were often routed over this friendly territory. The Germans had also lost their forward airfields and a large part of their early-warning radar system. Their fighter force had suffered in the battles of the past summer and those that remained were subject to an increasingly drastic shortage of petrol. The radio counter-measures squadrons in 100 Group also achieved their greatest successes during these last months and the Germans found it more and more difficult to distinguish reality from deception. But in one vital and little appreciated respect the situation had changed even more decisively in favour of the bombers. When the land forces had advanced through France and Belgium, they had been followed by mobile Oboe ground stations. Targets in Germany, which for years had been almost immune from really accurate bombing, now came within range of the Oboe beams. Bennett's Pathfinders took full advantage of this.

There is no need to dwell long on these last six months. Bomber Command flew nearly 100,000 sorties, about one third of which were by day. The loss-rate fell to less than 1 per cent. The German cities suffered appallingly as ever-increasing bomb tonnages descended on them with ever-increasing accuracy. Dresden, attacked on 13 February 1945, became a symbol of these terrible months for the Germans. At the end of March 1945, exactly one year after Nuremberg, the end of the war was clearly in sight and a halt was at last called to Area Bombing. The heavy bombers were then put to dropping food into starving Holland and bringing home liberated prisoners-of-war.

On the night of 2 May, 125 of Bennett's Mosquitoes raided Kiel in Bomber Command's last raid. Four days later Germany surrendered.

55,573 bomber men had died in helping to secure that victory.*

By the time the war ended in Europe, Bomber Command had grown to be a mighty force that could deploy 1,600 bombers at any one time. The aircrew who manned these contained very few men of the March 1944 era let alone from earlier years. The loss-rate had fallen so low towards the end that there was a huge surplus of fully trained crews who would never fly on operations. The Empire governments, especially those of Australia and New Zealand, had late in 1944 started to insist that their men should return home after only one tour. A farmer from Victoria describes his feelings as he left England.

I had been lighting fires on Germany for over six months but we had been ourselves burnt out at home in Australia – mile upon mile of fencing, 1,700 sheep lost and no labour left! For me, the war was over. Home James and don't spare the horses. We had run our course, had fought the battle and had seen the Germany of Hitler being slowly crushed to death. But they won that night on Nuremberg. (Warrant Officer G. C. Notman, 550 Squadron)

1 Group in north Lincolnshire found itself the strongest group in Bomber Command at the end of the war. The group policy of carrying maximum bomb loads had ensured that it had delivered a colossal tonnage during its career. 100 Squadron at Grimsby, that had been one of the few to return without loss from Nuremberg, had again been lucky when it flew 800 sorties during a three-month period late in 1944 without losing a single crew.

The smaller 3 Group in East Anglia, which also finished with an all-Lancaster force, had performed a vital function in the last year. Its aircraft had been fitted with a very accurate blind-bombing device called G-H. This had enabled it to lead other groups in precision daylight bombing through cloud by the simple expedient of allowing two or more ordinary bombers to formate on each 3 Group aircraft. When the G-H crew bombed, everyone bombed. The results were

* Fuller details of Bomber Command's casualties are contained in Appendix 5.

excellent and the ability to operate by daylight allowed a strong fighter escort to deal with the Germans.

4 Group, in Yorkshire, never got rid of their Halifaxes and finished with twelve squadrons, two of which were manned by the Free French. After the 1944 changes, 4 Group had been used as much as possible on the less dangerous targets and it never again incurred the terrible casualty rates it had suffered during the Battle of Berlin.

In Lincolnshire, 5 Group retained both the Dambusters as precision bombing experts and its three Pathfinder squadrons – this last being a sore point with 8 Group who even had to train their replacement crews. More and more, Cochrane's bombers had operated independently and they had carried out many highly successful raids on targets too small or difficult for a larger force.

The Canadian squadrons in north Yorkshire continued at full group strength to the very end. They never managed to convert entirely to Lancasters and finished with six squadrons of Halifaxes and eight of Lancasters, many of the Lancasters being Canadian-built.

8 Group, the Pathfinders, finished the war as a dual force. The Lancaster squadrons continued to serve most of Bomber Command under all manner of weather conditions and they were often at full-stretch marking for several different operations at once. The rigorous qualifications and the extended tours for their crews were never relaxed. The second 8 Group component was its eleven Mosquito bomber squadrons. Some of these were Oboe and marker squadrons but the majority were the Light Night Striking Force which operated independently of the heavy bombers. Berlin was a favourite target for these aircraft; the German capital was once raided on 200 consecutive nights. Sometimes, in the long winter nights, one Mosquito would bomb Berlin, return, change crew and go back to Berlin again.

100 (Bomber Support) Group in Norfolk had also grown rapidly. For example, it had been able to dispatch 1,578 sorties in aid of the bombers during March 1945 compared with only 217 such sorties in the same month of 1944. The radio counter-measures effort of the group became very successful and the Serrate squadrons had made some contribution to the shortage of good German pilots although the

difficulties of successful fighter-to-fighter interception at night remained immense.

Of the group commanders, Rice of 1 Group, Carr of 4 Group and Cochrane of 5 Group all stood down early in 1945 so that other promising officers could be given command experience before the war ended.

Bomber Command flew in strength to Nuremberg eleven times during the war and the Americans at least three times. The city which had escaped so lightly in March 1944 finally succumbed when 521 Lancasters visited it in the evening of 2 January 1945. The Pathfinders found good visibility on this occasion and carried out a perfect Newhaven marking. Only six bombers were lost. The Americans followed this up with two heavy daylight attacks in February and Nuremberg joined the long list of ruined German cities. 1 Group and the Pathfinders went there again on the night of 16 March but the German night fighters scored one of their last successes when they intercepted this small force and shot down twenty-four Lancasters, all from 1 Group.

Bomber Command alone dropped 13,807 tons of bombs on Nuremberg and the city's archives disclose that 6,369 Germans had been killed – 6,111 civilians and 258 military personnel. But the archives show that 1,707 foreigners had also perished in the raids – 825 civilian workers, many of whom would be forced labourers, and 882 prisoners-of-war. Over 13,000 people had been wounded and 350,000 had lost their homes. The Altstadt had been hard hit in Bomber Command's January 1945 raid and the important M.A.N. and Siemens-Schuckert factories also finished up in ruins although they had not been seriously hit until almost the very end.

Because of Nuremberg's pre-war association with the Nazi Party, the Allies chose the city as the scene of the famous Nuremberg Trials, when many of the surviving Nazi leaders were tried and sentenced for their war crimes. One man cheated the hangman though; Hermann Goering, the former Luftwaffe leader, took poison and died here.

When the war in Europe ended, Bomber Command immediately started to organize some of its squadrons into the so-called Tiger Force which was to go to the Far East and help finish off Japan but events overtook this plan. In August, an American Superfortress dropped the Atom Bomb on

Hiroshima, an event witnessed from another American bomber by the British representative, Group Captain Leonard Cheshire. A few days later, the Nagasaki bomb was dropped and the Second World War was over.

During the war that had just ended the bomber leaders and the men who had flown over Germany had been everyone's heroes but after the fighting ceased a subtle and disturbing change occurred. 'Bomber' Harris, who had once stood so high in the esteem of the British public, failed to be recognized in the distribution of post-war honours and his request that a special Bomber Command Campaign Medal be awarded to his crews was refused although a similar decoration was given to the Fighter Command men who had fought in the Battle of Britain. No one would wish to deprecate the valiant and decisive part played by the fighter pilots in the summer of 1940 but the bomber crews had fought for five long years in the dangerous night skies over Germany. Over twice as many men flew on the Nuremberg Raid alone as had taken part in the entire Battle of Britain; 545 bomber men died during that one night compared with the total number of 507 deaths among the Battle of Britain men. Why had the shadows fallen on Harris and his men?

Throughout the war, the press and radio had inferred that the heavy bomber raids had been directed only onto industrial and military targets. If historic buildings and works of art had been destroyed or civilians killed, then that had been accidental. But after the war, with thousands of British servicemen now stationed in or near the ruined German cities and the press inclined to be more critical and realistic, the true nature of Area Bombing gradually became known.

There were those in high places who never forgave Harris for his independent stand on target priorities and particularly for his successful fight against Tedder and Portal late in 1944. Churchill, who had so often backed Harris in the past, was no longer in office and the new Labour Government had little time for the man who had been so closely associated with the now embarrassing Area Bombing. Portal, who had prepared the Area Bombing Directive early in 1942 *before* Harris took over Bomber Command, became Viscount Portal of Hungerford. Harris, just like Haig after 1918, retired unhonoured to obscurity. It was not until eight years later, when Churchill was again Prime Minister, that Harris became a Baronet – an honour often awarded to minor politicians for long service. In the ensuing years, the R.A.F. glorified each anniversary of the Battle of Britain but little was made of the sacrifice by the thousands who had died over the Ruhr, Berlin and such cities as Nuremberg.

Much has been written and spoken since the war about Harris, about the effectiveness of the Strategic Bomber Offensive and about its morality. History has seen many great land and naval battles but the Strategic Bomber Offensive may never be repeated and will undoubtedly continue to interest historians for many years. It may be that the further passage of time will resolve some of the aspects of this controversial encounter.

It must be conceded that the original aim of the bomber theorists – to cause the collapse of Germany without land battle – was not realized. The morale of the German people never broke; Germany did not seek a surrender until land armies had physically occupied her territory after the most bitter fighting. But this does not mean that the theory was wrong; only that it had not been proved. What might have happened if Harris had been given the 4,000 heavy bombers that others had decided upon as the minimum requirement for the great aim of bombing Germany into submission? What might have happened if, as has been estimated, 55 per cent of Bomber Command's effort had not been directed elsewhere? What if the Russians had not pressed so forcefully for the land invasion of Europe and the bombers could have gone on for another year with their steadily improving techniques – low-level marking, G-H blind bombing, improving radio counter-measures?

No one can prove that Germany would have collapsed, although Albert Speer, the German armaments minister, says that if the successes against the Ruhr and Hamburg could have been repeated Germany could not have continued. If this had happened and the army casualties in Europe had been saved, then the determination and single-mindedness of Harris would have been seen as the attributes of a truly great man and both he and the bomber crews would have been marked as heroes alongside the Battle of Britain men. British military leaders are often accused by historians of being hidebound by tradition but these historians later gave short shrift to those who had attempted this new, unconventional approach.

Surely it is significant that Japan, just as resilient an enemy as Germany, gave in after two atom bombs – new weapons in one way but explosives delivered from the air none the less. Also, we have now had almost thirty years of world peace during which the defence plans of all major nations have been based upon the nuclear deterrent – the mutual fear that cities can be ruined and populations killed by a fresh generation of aerial explosives. War only thrives now in those places where there is not the threat of this massive destruction. Maybe the memory of Coventry, Dresden and Hiroshima lives on. Harris and the Lancaster and Halifax crews who flew to Nuremberg helped develop the attitude that mankind can no longer afford all-out world wars. History may one day conclude that this was their greatest achievement.

Let it not be forgotten also that Bomber Command made a most valuable contribution to the overall war effort although that had not been its primary aim. The list is a long one – the sowing of mines in German waters, the bombing of German submarine pens, the attacks on the flying-bomb launching sites, the brilliant part played in the interdiction of communications before the invasion, the frequent bombing in support of the land battles. Harris in his book points out that his command destroyed six German capital ships by bombing or mining compared with only four sunk by the entire Royal Navy and the Official History estimates that Bomber Command, with the American bombers, was responsible for the destruction of two hundred and seven German submarines either during building in shipyards or after completion. A mass of statistics is also available showing that the bombers tied down a huge quantity of German manpower and weapons in home defence and the air-raid services.

Could it have been done better? Certainly it could, but the defects in every military campaign or human endeavour can be distinguished afterwards. A fine job was done in 1942 and early 1943 in revitalizing Bomber Command – the introduction of new tactics, aircraft and equipment and above all the renewal of the crews' morale. To Harris must go the credit for much of this and for the subsequent victories of the Battles of the Ruhr and Hamburg. It was the next engagement, the Battle of Berlin, that was the crucial point of the bombing war. Harris put everything he had into it; he did not want to be sidetracked by ball-bearing directives or by subordinates who wanted to experiment with new tactics. He wanted the maximum strength of his command to be applied at what he thought to be the decisive point – the attitude of mind shown by most great military commanders.

In the end, Harris failed to destroy Berlin. It is only with hindsight that it can now be seen that he should have tackled the marking problem earlier and that if he had to go any-where at all on that moonlit night at the end of March 1944 he would have made a more useful contribution to the war if he had chosen Schweinfurt as the target and not Nuremberg. Again, it is now clear that Harris should not have returned so determinedly to Area Bombing after the invasion.

Surely, however, no one can question the high principles of this man who had tried so hard to defeat Germany without repeating the terrible carnage of a prolonged land campaign.

Close on the heels of the discussion as to whether the bomber campaign had been effective came the questioning of the morality of it. Had it been right to attempt to gain victory by adopting a policy that would result in the deaths of civilians and the destruction of historic buildings and treasures?

The German propagandists labelled the bomber crews as *Terrorfliegers* but Bomber Command never, at any time, descended to the level of pure terrorism The city attacked had always been of industrial, military or communications importance. The Germans could have evacuated their cities of all but essential workers and then there would have been no 'innocent' casualties. This would have imposed an in-tolerable strain on Germany, which is what the R.A.F. wanted, but the Germans chose to leave the workers' families in the cities and there they died. The intention of Area Bombing had been to break the morale and will to carry on the war of the German civilian population; this is not the same as attempting the systematic killing off of those civilians. The methods used were not forbidden by the Geneva Convention and were no worse in their effects than the slow starvation by naval blockade in the previous war which probably killed twice as many civilians as did the bombing.

316 The Nuremberg Raid

The bombing of German cities started in 1940, after the German bombing of Warsaw and Rotterdam but before that on London and Coventry. For well over a year the bomber crews were given as their Aiming Points such morally acceptable targets as individual factory buildings. It was only when it was realized that the bombers could not hit such precise targets that the entire industrial city became their objective. By then the Luftwaffe had already 'blitzed' London and Coventry.

I can remember 1940 after the fall of France. Britain did not have an ally in the world other than her own distant Empire. My family prepared to move to the Lake District for we genuinely expected the Germans to land at any time on the East Coast. We would have been refugees. My boyhood nightmare was that I would awake to find a Nazi paratrooper at the window.

As we now know, Fighter Command saved us in 1940 but for the next two years it was only the bombers, flying to Germany several times a week together with a small Commando raid every six months or so, that were capable of any offensive action against the Germans.

It is perhaps significant that in the post-war controversy, the least noise was made by the Germans themselves. Without real provocation, Hitler had gone to war with most of Europe. The Nazis had systematically exterminated the Jewish race, had declared all Slavic peoples to be *Untermenschen* – sub-humans. The Gestapo had tortured and terrified throughout Occupied Europe and countless thousands of innocent men and women had been dragged off to work in German factories almost as slaves. Post-war German historians realized that it was the Nazis who had sown the wind and the now-dead Hitler, whom they once followed so faithfully, received much of the blame for the retaliation.

The wartime actions of Bomber Command or of any other service should not be judged out of the context of the period. When did the outcry against bombing start – in 1940 or after the war when the dream of a Nazi paratrooper was no longer a cause of terror? There was only a tiny questioning of the morality of bombing later in the war and that by religious leaders not by politicians or historians. A country fighting for its very existence cannot afford to have strict boundaries of morality in the means by which it saves itself. It is sheer humbug to suggest that the use of the bombers at this time was wrong when it was touch and go whether Britain survived at all.

It is small wonder that the bomber men felt baffled and hurt when their actions were later declared to be unworthy. They fought with the highest ideals against a ruthless and sometimes barbaric enemy. The memory of those who died should not be tarnished. The survivors should not be made to feel other than proud to have played the part they did play.

What are their thoughts now, those men who flew on that moonlit night at the end of March 1944?

It was a time not without its excitement and heroism and dread. (Pilot Officer J. R. Ison, 199 Squadron)

It was a bastard raid in its conception. Unless there was a really compelling need to go there, the thing was a double failure. But I am not bitter – I could tell you of many more raids that were cleverly executed and the desired result obtained. (Flight Lieutenant B. D. C. Patterson, 426 Squadron)

The only thing the Nuremberg Raid achieved was probably to raise morale in the Third Reich. (Sergeant R. A. Anderson, 420 Squadron)

I didn't hate the Germans at all. I went into that job for the kicks, the flying and the adventure. I know it sounds corny but I felt we were all Knights of the Air going out to have a go at each other. I enjoyed it all although we only did five trips before being shot down. (Sergeant N. Wilmott, 10 Squadron)

Even now, when I see a bright moon, I think of it as a Nuremberg Moon. (Flight Sergeant K. A. Bush, 640 Squadron)

I thought then and I still think that we in Bomber Command saved hundreds of thousands of soldiers' lives. (Flying Officer J. Dougall, 429 Squadron)

Is it any wonder that I avoid memorial services, for I cry very easily, that this day the sound of the Air Force march brings memories flooding back and the tears with them. Men are not supposed to cry but this one does mostly in private, for how many are there who can even begin to understand? (Flight Sergeant R. Rhodes, 35 Squadron)

Anyway, it never really happened. How could you fight a war and be able to walk through the Backs at Cambridge the next day? (Sergeant C. A. Thompson, 7 Squadron)

As to my personal feelings, they were at a higher pitch of terror and fear than on any previous raid. If, after that raid, I could have seen my way clear to stop flying then I would have done so. My personal thoughts about Harris and Churchill were, to put it mildly, extremely unpatriotic. (Flight Sergeant L. Wayte, 166 Squadron)

It was acknowledged that it was a short but not necessarily happy life. However, I have never regretted the experience. (Sergeant N. Binnie, 420 Squadron)

These are the survivors. One hopes that their dead comrades will not be forgotten.

R.A.F. and Luftwaffe Aircraft involved in Air Operations, 30–31 March 1944.*

PART 1 R.A.F. AIRCRAFT

AVRO LANCASTER MARKS I, II AND III

Type: Four-engined heavy bomber.

Crew: Pilot, flight engineer, navigator, bomb-aimer, wireless-operator, mid-upper gunner, tail gunner.

Engines:
Mark I – 1,460 h.p. Rolls-Royce Merlin 22.
Mark II – 1,735 h.p. Bristol Hercules VI or XVI.
Mark III – 1,460 h.p. Packard Merlin 28.

Dimensions: Length – 69·6 feet, height – 20·6 feet, wing span – 102 feet, wing area – 1,297 square feet.

Weight: Empty – 41,000 pounds, fully loaded – 68,000 pounds (Mark II – 63,000 pounds).

Armament: Eight 0·303-inch machine-guns in three turrets (some Mark IIs also had a 0·5-inch machine-gun in mid-under position with a third gunner).

Payload: Maximum bomb load – 14,000 pounds, fuel capacity – 2,154 gallons (with auxiliary tanks – 2,954 gallons), maximum combined bomb and fuel load – 27,000 pounds (Mark II – 22,000 pounds).

Performance:	Marks I and III	Mark II
Rate of climb	480 ft. per min.	450 ft. per min.
Ceiling	24,500 feet	22,000 feet
Maximum speed	287 m.p.h.	265 m.p.h.
Cruising speed	216 m.p.h.	167 m.p.h.
Range		
with maximum bomb load	1,660 miles	1,500 miles
with maximum fuel load	3,150 miles	2,550 miles

* It must be stressed that these statistics are intended to be of *typical* aircraft in use at that time. There were a great many minor variations in every type and only the more important of these variations will be mentioned. It should also be stated that maximum performances could rarely be achieved with heavily laden aircraft under operational conditions.

HANDLEY PAGE HALIFAX MARK III

Type: Four-engined heavy bomber.
Crew: As the Lancaster.
Engines: 1,650 h.p. Bristol Hercules XVI.
Dimensions: Length – 70·1 feet, height – 20·75 feet, wing span – 104 feet, wing area – 1,275 square feet.
Weight: Empty – 42,860 pounds, fully loaded – 65,000 pounds.
Armament: Nine 0·303-inch machine-guns in three turrets.
Payload: Maximum bomb load – 13,000 pounds, fuel capacity – 1,998 gallons (with auxiliary tanks – 2,688 gallons), maximum combined bomb and fuel load – 22,140 pounds.
Performance: Rate of climb – 440 feet per minute, ceiling – 22,000 feet, maximum speed – 281 m.p.h., cruising speed – 225 m.p.h., range with maximum bomb load – 980 miles, range with maximum fuel load – 2,785 miles.

SHORT STIRLING MARK III

Type: Four-engined heavy bomber but, in 1944, no longer flying on Main Force operations.
Crew: As the Lancaster.
Engines: 1,650 h.p. Bristol Hercules XVI.
Dimensions: Length – 87·2 feet, height – 22·75 feet, wing span – 99 feet, wing area – 1,460 square feet.
Weight: Empty – 48,000 pounds, fully loaded – 70,000 pounds.
Armament: Eight 0·303-inch machine-guns in three turrets.
Payload: Maximum bomb load – 14,000 pounds, fuel capacity – 2,254 gallons (with auxiliary fuel tanks – 2,964 gallons), maximum combined bomb and fuel load – 22,000 pounds.
Performance: Rate of climb – 500 feet per minute, ceiling – 17,000 feet, maximum speed – 270 m.p.h., cruising speed – 200 m.p.h., range with maximum bomb load – 590 miles, range with maximum fuel load – 2,440 miles.

DE HAVILLAND MOSQUITO MARK IV (BOMBER)

Type: Twin-engined light bomber and Pathfinder marker aircraft.
Crew: Pilot and navigator.
Engines: 1,460 h.p. Rolls-Royce Merlin 23.
Dimensions: Length – 40·8 feet, height – 15·3 feet, wing span – 54·2 feet, wing area – 454 square feet.
Weight: Empty – 15,318 pounds, fully loaded – 21,462 pounds.
Armament: None.
Payload: Maximum bomb load – 2,000 pounds (some modified to carry a 4,000-pound bomb), fuel capacity – 536 gallons (with auxiliary tanks – 657 gallons), maximum combined bomb and fuel load – 6,144 pounds.

Performance: Rate of climb – 2,500 feet per minute, ceiling – 34,000 feet, maximum speed – 380 m.p.h., cruising speed – 265 m.p.h., range with maximum bomb load – 1,620 miles, range with maximum fuel load – 2,040 miles.

DE HAVILLAND MOSQUITO MARKS II AND VI
(NIGHT FIGHTERS)

Types: Mark II – twin-engined night fighter equipped with A.I. Radar and Serrate. Mark VI – twin-engined Intruder fighter-bomber.

Crew: Pilot and navigator; in Serrate aircraft the navigator also operated the Serrate and Radar sets.

Engines: Mark II (Serrate) – 1,460 h.p. Rolls-Royce Merlin 23, Mark VI (Intruder) – 1,635 h.p. Rolls-Royce Merlin 25.

Dimensions: As Mark IV bomber.

Weight:	Mark II (Serrate)	Mark VI (Intruder)
Empty	13,431 pounds	14,300 pounds
Fully loaded	18,547 pounds	22,300 pounds

Armament: Mark II (Serrate) – four 20-millimetre cannons. Mark VI (Intruder) – four 20-millimetre cannons, four 0·303-inch machine-guns and four 250-pound or 500-pound bombs.

Fuel capacity: 536 gallons (with auxiliary tanks – 616 gallons).

Performance:	Mark II (Serrate)*	Mark VI (Intruder)
Rate of climb	2,100 ft. per min.	2,140 ft. per min.
Ceiling	34,500 feet	33,000 feet
Maximum speed	370 m.p.h.	378 m.p.h.
Cruising speed	255 m.p.h.	260 m.p.h.
Range	1,705 miles	1,705 miles

PART 2 LUFTWAFFE AIRCRAFT

MESSERSCHMITT BF 110G

Type: Twin-engined night fighter.

Crew: Pilot, radar/radio-operator, rear gunner.

Engines: 1,475 h.p. Daimler-Benz DB 605B.

Dimensions: Length – 42·8 feet (which included radar aerials protruding beyond the nose), height – 13·7 feet, wing span – 53·4 feet, wing area – 413 square feet.

Weight: Empty – 11,220 pounds, fully loaded – 21,800 pounds.

Armament: Two 30-millimetre cannons and two 20-millimetre cannons in nose, two 7·9-millimetre machine-guns in rear of

* The Mark II Mosquitoes flown by the Serrate squadrons of 100 Group in March 1944 were mostly old aircraft and it is particularly unlikely that these figures could be achieved. Later in 1944 more advanced Marks of Mosquito became available.

cockpit. Some aircraft had the *schräge Musik* installation of two upward-firing 20-millimetre cannons.

Fuel capacity: 280 gallons (with auxiliary tanks – 676 gallons).

Performance: Rate of climb – 2,170 feet per minute, ceiling – 26,250 feet, maximum speed – 342 m.p.h., cruising speed – around 250 m.p.h., range – 1,305 miles.

JUNKERS 88c*

Type: Twin-engined night fighter.

Crew: As Messerschmitt 110.

Engines: 1,410 h.p. Junkers Jumo 211J.

Dimensions: Length – 49·4 feet (including radar aerials), height – 16·6 feet, wing span – 65·8 feet, wing area – 587 square·feet.

Weight: Empty – 19,973 pounds, fully loaded – 27,225 pounds.

Armament: Three 20-millimetre cannons and three 7·9-millimetre machine-guns in nose, one 13-millimetre machine-gun in rear of cockpit. Some aircraft had the *schräge Musik* installation of two upward-firing 20 millimetre cannons.

Fuel capacity: 369 gallons (with auxiliary tanks – 704 gallons).

Performance: Rate of climb – 1,770 feet per minute, ceiling – 32,480 feet, maximum speed – 307 m.p.h., cruising speed – 263 m.p.h., range – 1,230 miles.

MESSERSCHMITT BF 109G-6

Type: Single-engined day fighter serving as Wild Boar night fighter.

Crew: Pilot.

Engine: 1,475 h.p. Daimler-Benz DB 605A.

Dimensions: Length – 29 feet, height – 8·2 feet, wing span – 32·5 feet, wing area – 174 square feet.

Weight: Empty – 5,893 pounds, fully loaded – 7,491 pounds.

Armament: One 30- or one 20-millimetre cannon and two 13-millimetre machine-guns.

Fuel capacity: 88 gallons (with auxiliary tanks – 154 gallons).

Performance: Rate of climb – 3,110 feet per minute, ceiling – 37,890 feet, maximum speed – 386 m.p.h., cruising speed – 260 m.p.h., range – 620 miles.

FOCKE-WULF 190A-8

Type: Single-engined day fighter serving as Wild Boar night fighter.

Crew: Pilot.

Engine: 1,700 h.p. BMW 801D.

Dimensions: Length – 29·4 feet, height – 12·9 feet, wing span – 34·4 feet, wing area – 197 square feet.

---

* The much improved 88G was just starting to appear with operational units at this time.

Weight: Empty – 7,652 pounds, fully loaded – 10,800 pounds.

Armament: Four 20-millimetre cannons and two 13-millimetre machine-guns.

Fuel capacity: 115 gallons (with auxiliary tanks – 247 gallons).

Performance: Rate of climb – 2,350 feet per minute, ceiling – 37,400 feet, maximum speed – 408 m.p.h., cruising speed – 298 m.p.h., range – 942 miles.

Appendix 2

Order of Battle of R.A.F. Bomber Command, 30 March 1944

1 GROUP
(Air Vice-Marshal E. A. B. Rice)
H.Q. Bawtry Hall

Squadron	Station	Type of Aircraft
12 Squadron	Wickenby	Lancaster
100 Squadron	Grimsby	Lancaster
101 Squadron	Ludford Magna	A.B.C. Lancaster
103 Squadron	Elsham Wolds	Lancaster
166 Squadron	Kirmington	Lancaster
300 (Polish) Squadron	Faldingworth	Wellington/ Lancaster *
460 (R.A.A.F.) Squadron	Binbrook	Lancaster
550 Squadron	North Killingholme	Lancaster
576 Squadron	Elsham Wolds	Lancaster
625 Squadron	Kelstern	Lancaster
626 Squadron	Wickenby	Lancaster

3 GROUP
(Air Vice-Marshal R. Harrison)
H.Q. Exning, Newmarket

Squadron	Station	Type of Aircraft
15 Squadron	Mildenhall	Lancaster
75 (New Zealand) Squadron	Mepal	Stirling/Lancaster
90 Squadron	Tuddenham	Stirling
115 Squadron	Witchford	Lancaster
149 (East India) Squadron	Lakenheath	Stirling
199 Squadron	Lakenheath	Stirling
218 (Gold Coast) Squadron	Woolfox Lodge	Stirling/Lancaster

* This and similar entries mean that the squadron was in the process of converting to Lancasters.

514 Squadron	Waterbeach	Lancaster
622 Squadron	Mildenhall	Lancaster

Secret Operations Squadrons:

138 Squadron	Tempsford	⎰ Halifax, Liberator,
161 Squadron	Tempsford	⎱ Hudson, Lysander

4 GROUP
(Air Vice-Marshal C. R. Carr)
H. Q. Heslington Hall, York

10 Squadron	Melbourne	Halifax
51 Squadron	Snaith	Halifax
76 Squadron	Holme-on-Spalding-Moor	Halifax
77 Squadron	Elvington	Halifax
78 Squadron	Breighton	Halifax
102 (Ceylon) Squadron	Pocklington	Halifax
158 Squadron	Lissett	Halifax
466 (R.A.A.F.) Squadron	Leconfield	Halifax
578 Squadron	Burn	Halifax
640 Squadron	Leconfield	Halifax

5 GROUP
(Air Vice-Marshal The Hon. Ralph Cochrane)
H.Q. Morton Hall, Swinderby

9 Squadron	Bardney	Lancaster
44 (Rhodesia) Squadron	Dunholme Lodge	Lancaster
49 Squadron	Fiskerton	Lancaster
50 Squadron	Skellingthorpe	Lancaster
57 Squadron	East Kirkby	Lancaster
61 Squadron	Coningsby	Lancaster
106 Squadron	Metheringham	Lancaster
207 Squadron	Spilsby	Lancaster
463 (R.A.A.F.) Squadron	Waddington	Lancaster
467 (R.A.A.F.) Squadron)	Waddington	Lancaster
617 Squadron	Woodhall Spa	Lancaster
619 Squadron	Coningsby	Lancaster
630 Squadron	East Kirkby	Lancaster

6 (CANADIAN) GROUP
(Air Vice-Marshal C. M. McEwen)
H.Q. Allerton Park Castle, Knaresborough

408 (Goose) Squadron	Linton-on-Ouse	Lancaster
419 (Moose) Squadron	Middleton St George	Halifax/ Lancaster
420 (Snowy Owl) Squadron	Tholthorpe	Halifax
424 (Tiger) Squadron	Skipton-on-Swale	Halifax
425 (Alouette) Squadron	Tholthorpe	Halifax
426 (Thunderbird) Squadron	Linton-on-Ouse	Lancaster
427 (Lion) Squadron	Leeming	Halifax
428 (Ghost) Squadron	Middleton St George	Halifax
429 (Bison) Squadron	Leeming	Halifax
431 (Iroquois) Squadron	Croft	Halifax
432 (Leaside) Squadron	East Moor	Halifax
433 (Porcupine) Squadron	Skipton-on-Swale	Halifax
434 (Bluenose) Squadron	Croft	Halifax

8 (PATHFINDER) GROUP
(Air Vice-Marshal D. C. T. Bennett)
H.Q. Castle Hill House, Huntingdon

7 Squadron	Oakington	Lancaster
35 (Madras Presidency) Squadron	Graveley	Lancaster
83 Squadron	Wyton	Lancaster
97 (Straits Settlements) Squadron	Bourn	Lancaster
105 Squadron	Bourn	Oboe Mosquito
109 Squadron	Marham	Oboe Mosquito
139 (Jamaica) Squadron	Upwood	Mosquito
156 Squadron	Upwood	Lancaster
405 (Vancouver) Squadron R.C.A.F.	Gransden Lodge	Lancaster
627 Squadron	Oakington	Mosquito
635 Squadron	Downham Market	Lancaster
692 (Fellowship of the Bellows) Squadron	Graveley	Mosquito
1409 (Meteorological) Flight	Wyton	Mosquito

100 (BOMBER SUPPORT) GROUP
(Air Commodore E. B. Addison)
H.Q. Bylaugh Hall, East Dereham

141 Squadron	West Raynham	Mosquito
169 Squadron	Little Snoring	Mosquito
192 Squadron	Foulsham	Halifax, Wellington and Mosquito
214 (Federated Malay States) Squadron	Sculthorpe	B-17 Fortress
239 Squadron	West Raynham	Mosquito
515 Squadron	Little Snoring	Mosquito

Luftwaffe Night Fighter Order of Battle, 30 March 1944

Geschwader, Gruppe and Staffel are not translated because there are no exact R.A.F. equivalents. Only the main aircraft types of each unit are given; many also contained a few obsolete Dornier 217s. The Germans often used a double-name airfield style, e.g. Bonn/Hangelar which signifies that the airfield was Hangelar near Bonn.

I FIGHTER CORPS
(Generalleutnant Josef Schmidt)
H.Q. Zeist, Holland

1ST FIGHTER DIVISION (Oberst Hajo Herrmann)
H.Q. Döberitz, Berlin

	Airfield	Type of Aircraft
Nachtjagdgeschwader 5		
I Gruppe	Stendal	Messerschmitt 110
II Gruppe	Parchim	Messerschmitt 110
III Gruppe	Brandis	Messerschmitt 110
IV Gruppe	Erfurt	Messerschmitt 110
Jagdgeschwader 300 (Wild Boar)		
I Gruppe	Jüterbog	Messerschmitt 109
II Gruppe	Ludwiglust	Messerschmitt 109
III Gruppe	Zerbst	Messerschmitt 109
Nachtjagdgruppe 10 (Research)	Werneuchen with forward base at Bonn/Hangelar	Various types
Behelfs Beleuchter Staffel 1 (Illuminator)	Celle	Junkers 88
Luftbeobachtungsstaffel 1 (Reconnaissance)	Neurrupin	Junkers 88

2ND FIGHTER DIVISION (Generalmajor Max Ibel)
H.Q. Stade, Hamburg

Nachtjagdgeschwader 3
  I Gruppe   Vechta   Messerschmitt 110
  II Gruppe   Vechta   Junkers 88
  III Gruppe   Stade   Messerschmitt 110
  IV Gruppe   Westerland   Junkers 88,
                                               Messerschmitt 110

Jagdgeschwader 301 (Wild Boar)
  III Gruppe   Oldenburg   Messerschmitt 109,
                                               Focke-Wulf 190

Luftbeobachtungsstaffel 2
  (Reconnaissance)   Stade   Junkers 88

3RD FIGHTER DIVISION (Generalmajor Walter Grabmann)
H.Q. Deelen, Holland
Nachtjagdgeschwader 1
  I Gruppe   Venlo   Messerschmitt 110,
                                               Heinkel 219
  IV Gruppe   Saint-Trond   Messerschmitt 110
Nachtjagdgschwader 2
  I Gruppe   Bad Langensalza   Junkers 88
  II Gruppe   Quackenbrück   Junkers 88
  III Gruppe   Langendiebach   Junkers 88
                            and Twenthe

Nachtjagdgeschwader 4
  III Gruppe   Mainz/Finthen   Messerschmitt 110
Jagdgeschwader 300 (Wild Boar)
  I Gruppe   Bonn   Messerschmitt 109
  II Gruppe   Rheine   Focke-Wulf 190
  III Gruppe   Wiesbaden/   Messerschmitt 109
                            Erbenheim
Behelfs Beleuchter Staffel 3 Munster/
  (Illuminator)   Handorf   Junkers 88
Luftbeobachtungsstaffel 3   Deelen   Junkers 88
  (Reconnaissance)

7TH FIGHTER DIVISION (Generalleutnant Joachim Huth)
H.Q. Schleissheim, Munich
Nachtjagdgeschwader 6
  I Gruppe   Mainz/Finthen   Messerschmitt 110
  II Gruppe   Stuttgart/
                            Echterdingen   Messerschmitt 110
Jagdgeschwader 301 (Wild Boar)
  I Gruppe   Neuburg an der
                            Donau   Messerschmitt 109
Luftbeobachtungsstaffel 7   Stuttgart/
  (Reconnaissance)   Echterdingen   Junkers 88

II FIGHTER CORPS
(Generalleutnant Werner Junck)
H.Q. Chantilly, Paris

4TH FIGHTER DIVISION (Oberst Karl Wiek)
H.Q. Metz.

Nachtjagdgeschwader 1		
II Gruppe	Saint-Dizier	Messerschmitt 110
III Gruppe	Laon/Athies	Messerschmitt 110
Nachtjagdgeschwader 4		
I Gruppe	Florennes	Messerschmitt 110
II Gruppe	Coulommiers	Messerschmitt 110

Group and Squadron Performances

This appendix will provide a statistical record of the part played by R.A.F. and Empire groups and squadrons in the air operations of 30–31 March 1944.

The 108 aircraft which were a total loss are identified by their manufacturer's serial number and by the names of their pilots. Each lost aircraft will be given a number (e.g. '48th down') which corresponds with its position on the map 'Missing and Crashed R.A.F. Aircraft' on the following page. The first loss is that of the Lancaster which crashed on take-off at Skellingthorpe and the sub-sequent numbering roughly follows the course of the raid. Where possible, the cause of the aircraft's loss is also given but it should be remembered that, because of the intense air action, such information should be regarded as no more than a best estimate.

With shot-down crews and those where crashes resulted in the loss or break-up of the crew, their operational record is also given, the Nuremberg raid being included. Where a crew contained a replacement for a regular member, the number of operations is that of the majority and, where the crew was thoroughly mixed, it is the best estimate of their average number of operations.

The number of aircraft shown as having 'bombed' are those believed to have bombed Nuremberg or some other specific target in Belgium or Germany; such totals include aircraft shot down later in the raid.

The following abbreviations are used:

Squadron Leader	S/L
Flight Lieutenant	F/L
Flying Officer	F/O
Pilot Officer	P/O
Warrant Officer	W.O.
Flight Sergeant	F/Sgt
Sergeant	Sgt

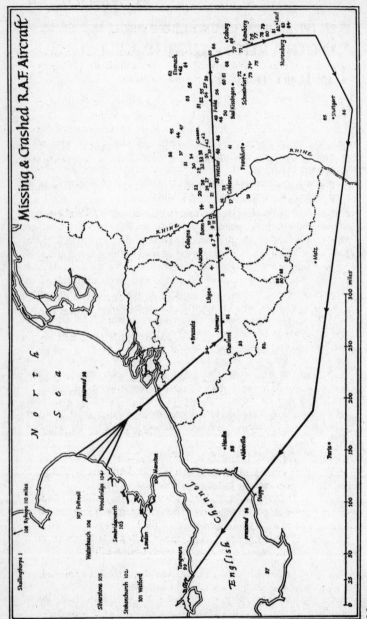

Missing & Crashed R.A.F. Aircraft

Map 12

THE NUREMBERG FORCE

1 GROUP. 180 Lancasters dispatched, 151 bombed, 21 missing, 1 wrecked in crash, 12 damaged. 134 men killed, 21 prisoners, 1 evaded capture, 6 wounded in returned aircraft.

12 Squadron, Wickenby. 14 Lancasters dispatched, 12 bombed, 2 missing, 3 damaged. 15 men killed, 2 returned wounded.

Lancaster ND562 (F/L A. J. Cook, killed), 8th down probably by fighter attack; crashed at Holzheim, 12 kms south west of Euskirchen. Crew on 22nd operation, 8 killed.

Lancaster ND441 (F/L D. M. Carey, D.F.C.), 36th down by fighter attack; crashed at Dotzlar, 30 kms north east of Siegen. Crew on 3rd operation, some of 2nd tour, 7 killed.

100 Squadron, Grimsby. 18 Lancasters dispatched, 17 bombed, 3 damaged. No aircrew casualties.

101 Squadron, Ludford Magna. 26 A.B.C. Lancasters dispatched, 20 bombed, 6 missing, 1 wrecked in crash. 47 men killed, 8 prisoners, 1 evaded capture.

Lancaster DV264 (P/O W. I. Adamson, D.F.C.), 7th down mistakenly hit by fire from a Halifax; crashed at Gemünd, 20 kms south west of Euskirchen. Crew on 29th operation, 5 killed, 1 prisoner, 1 evaded capture.

Lancaster LL832 (F/Sgt G. Tivey, killed), 17th down by Coblenz Flak; crashed at Rubenach, 5 kms west of Coblenz. Crew on 10th operation, 8 killed.

Lancaster LM463 (P/O A. E. Lander, prisoner), 31st down by fighter attack; crashed at Dillenburg. Crew on 2nd operation, 6 killed, 2 prisoners.

Lancaster LL861 (P/O D. J. Irving, killed), 62nd down by fighter attack; crashed at Lauterbach, 10 kms north of Eisenach. Crew on 9th operation, 8 killed.

Lancaster ME618 (F/Sgt C. R. Harnish, killed), 67th down by fighter attack; crashed at Simmershausen, 20 kms east of Fulda. Crew on 6th operation, 4 killed, 4 prisoners.

Lancaster DV276 (P/O J. Batten-Smith, D.F.C., killed), 84th down by fighter attack; crashed on Autobahn junction 6 kms east of Nuremberg. Crew on 22nd operation, 8 killed.

Lancaster DV290 (F/Sgt E. R. Thomas, killed), 101st down in crash at Welford, Berks. Crew on 5th operation, 8 killed.

103 Squadron, Elsham Wolds. 16 Lancasters dispatched, 13 bombed, 2 missing, 1 damaged. 13 men killed, 1 prisoner.

Lancaster JB736 (F/O J. G. Johnston, killed), 28th down by Westerburg Flak; crashed at Bilkheim, 7 kms south of Westerburg. Crew on 3rd operation, 6 killed, 1 prisoner.

Lancaster ND572 (P/O R. R. J. Tate, killed), 54th down by fighter attack; crashed at Morles, 12 kms north east of Fulda. Crew on 1st operation, 7 killed.

166 Squadron, Kirmington. 20 Lancasters dispatched, 15 bombed, 4 missing, 1 damaged. 19 men killed, 3 prisoners, 1 returned wounded.

Lancaster ND798 (P/O W. H. Burnett, killed), 18th down by fighter attack; crashed at Griesenbach, 25 kms east of Bonn. Crew on 16th operation, 3 killed, 5 prisoners.

Lancaster ME638 (F/L F. Taylor, prisoner), 25th down by fighter attack; crashed at Weidenhahn, 7 kms south west of Westerburg. Crew on 18th operation, 2 killed, 6 prisoners.

Lancaster ME624 (F/Sgt R. B. Fennell, killed), 42nd down by fighter attack; crashed on Giessen airfield. Crew on 13th operation, 6 killed, 1 prisoner.

Lancaster ME686 (F/L G. A. Proctor, killed), 52nd down by fighter attack; crashed at Michelsrombach, 10 kms north of Fulda. Crew on 2nd operation, 8 killed.

460 (R.A.A.F.) Squadron, Binbrook. 24 Lancasters dispatched, 21 bombed, 3 missing. 17 men killed, 4 prisoners.

Lancaster ND750 (P/O P. R. Anderson, killed), 16th down by Rhine Flak; crashed at Rodenbach, near Neuwied. Crew on 5th operation, 4 killed, 3 prisoners.

Lancaster ND361 (S/L E. A. G. Utz, D.F.C. and Bar, killed), 56th down by fighter attack; crashed at Obernhausen/Rhon, 17 kms south east of Fulda. Crew on 18th operation of 2nd tour, 6 killed, 1 prisoner.

Lancaster ND738 (F/Sgt C. H. Hargreaves, killed), 81st down by fighter attack; crashed at Gräfenburg, 20 kms north east of Nuremberg. Crew on 4th operation, 7 killed.

550 Squadron, North Killingholme. 17 Lancasters dispatched, 15 bombed, 2 missing, 1 damaged. 11 men killed, 3 prisoners, 2 returned wounded.

Lancaster LM425 (F/Sgt A. Jefferies, killed), 4th down by Liège Flak; crashed at Gileppe, 8 kms east of Verviers. Crew on 19th operation, 4 killed, 3 prisoners.

Lancaster ND423 (F/Sgt C. G. Foster, killed), 73rd down by Schweinfurt Flak; crashed at Unterspiesheim, 10 kms south of Schweinfurt. Crew on 17th operation, 7 killed.

576 Squadron, Elsham Wolds. 16 Lancasters dispatched, 14 bombed, 1 missing. 5 men killed, 2 prisoners.

Lancaster LM470 (F/L P. E. Underwood, prisoner), 57th down by fighter attack; crashed at Oberweid, 25 kms east of Fulda. Crew on 6th operation.

625 Squadron, Kelstern. 13 Lancasters dispatched, 12 bombed, 1 missing, 2 damaged. 7 men killed, 1 returned wounded.

Lancaster W5009 (S/L T. M. Nicholls, killed), 5th down by fighter attack; crashed at Udenbreth, 20 kms north of Prüm. Crew on 21st operation.

626 Squadron, Wickenby. 16 Lancasters dispatched, 12 bombed, 1 damaged. No aircrew casualties.

3 GROUP. 56 Lancasters dispatched, 42 bombed, 8 missing, 2 wrecked in crashes, 5 damaged. 41 men killed, 17 prisoners, 6 injured in crashed aircraft.

15 Squadron, Mildenhall. 11 Lancasters dispatched, 10 bombed, 2 damaged. No aircrew casualties.

115 Squadron, Witchford. 10 Lancasters dispatched, 8 bombed, 2 missing, 1 damaged. 7 men killed, 7 prisoners.

Lancaster LL704 (F/Sgt T. Fogaty, D.F.M., prisoner), 86th down, partly by fighter attack, partly by Flak; crashed at Neckartenzlingen, 15 kms south of Stuttgart. Crew on 14th operation, 7 prisoners.

Lancaster LL622 (F/Sgt R. Thomas, killed), 94th down by fighter attack; crashed at Braine d'Alleud, 35 kms south of Brussels. Crew on 1st operation, 7 killed.

514 Squadron, Waterbeach. 19 Lancasters dispatched, 11 bombed, 4 missing, 2 wrecked in crashes, 1 damaged. 20 men killed, 10 prisoners, 6 injured in crashes.

Lancaster LL738 (P/O G. S. Hughes, D.F.C., killed), 11th down by fighter attack; crashed at Westum, near Sinzig. Crew on 19th operation, 6 killed, 1 prisoner.

Lancaster LL698 (F/Sgt F. Gregory, killed), 14th down by fighter attack; crashed at Oberpleis, 12 kms south east of Bonn. Crew on 8th operation, 6 killed, 1 prisoner.

Lancaster DS836 (P/O D. C. C. Crombie, killed), 61st down by fighter attack; crashed at Eichhausen, 4 kms north east of Bad Neustadt. Crew on 14th operation, 5 killed, 2 prisoners.

Lancaster LL696 (F/O P. J. K. Hood, prisoner), 76th down by fighter attack; crashed at Memmelsdorf, near Bamberg. Crew on 16th operation, 1 killed, 6 prisoners.

Lancaster LL683 (W.O. W. L. McGown), 103rd down in crashlanding near Sawbridgeworth, Herts. 1 man injured.

Lancaster LL645 (P/O E. W. Chitty, injured), 106th down in crash at Waterbeach. 2 men killed, 4 injured.

622 Squadron, Mildenhall. 16 Lancasters dispatched, 13 bombed, 2 missing, 1 damaged. 14 men killed.

Lancaster ED619 (P/O J. Sutton, killed), 23rd down by fighter attack; crashed at Baumbach, 12 kms north east of Coblenz. Crew on 12th operation. 7 killed.

Lancaster ND767 (F/Sgt E. Picken, killed), 89th down after collision with 427 Squadron Halifax, crashed at Rachecourt, 13 kms south west of Arlon, Belgium. Crew on 5th operation, 7 killed.

4 GROUP. 119 Halifaxes dispatched, 81 bombed, 20 missing, 3 wrecked in crashes, 7 damaged. 116 men killed, 41 prisoners, 2 wounded in returned aircraft and 4 injured in crashes.

10 Squadron, Melbourne. 13 Halifaxes dispatched, 8 bombed, 1 missing. 4 men killed, 3 prisoners.

Halifax LV881 (F/Sgt W. T. A. Regan, killed), 46th down by fighter attack; crashed at Steinheim, 20 kms south east of Giessen. Crew on 5th operation.

51 Squadron, Snaith. 17 Halifaxes dispatched, 11 bombed, 5 missing, 1 wrecked in crash, 1 damaged. 35 men killed, 7 prisoners, 1 wounded in returned aircraft.

Halifax LV822 (F/Sgt E. Wilkins, killed), 30th down by fighter attack; crashed at Guntersdorf, near Herborn. Crew on 6th operation, 7 killed.

Halifax LW544 (F/Sgt G. G. Brougham, killed), 47th down by fighter attack; crashed at Wahlen, 10 kms north west of Alsfeld. Crew on 1st operation, 5 killed, 2 prisoners.

Halifax LV857 (Sgt J. P. G. Binder, killed), 55th down by fighter attack; crashed at Schwarzbach, 13 kms north east of Fulda. Crew on 3rd operation, 7 killed.

Halifax LW537 (F/Sgt M. Stembridge, killed), 59th down by fighter attack; crashed at Fladungen, 30 kms east of Fulda. Crew on 6th operation, 2 killed, 5 prisoners.

Halifax LV777 (S/L F. P. Hill, D.F.C., killed), 85th down, probably by Stuttgart Flak; crashed at Bietigheim, 15 kms north of Stuttgart. Crew on 13th operation, possibly of 2nd tour, 7 killed.

Halifax LW579 (P/O J. Brooks, killed), 102nd down in crash at Stokenchurch, Oxfordshire. Crew on 19th operation, 7 killed.

76 Squadron, Holme-on-Spalding-Moor. 14 Halifaxes dispatched, 10 bombed, 3 missing, 1 written off after battle damage. 13 men killed, 9 prisoners.

Halifax LK795 (F/L H. D. Coverley, prisoner), 22nd down by fighter attack; crashed at Hamm, 25 kms south west of Siegen. Crew on 9th operation (pilot of 2nd tour), 1 killed, 6 prisoners.

Halifax LW696 (S/K K. A. Clack, D.F.M., killed), 33rd down by fighter attack; crashed at Daubhausen, 10 kms north west of Wetzlar. Crew on 4th operation of 2nd tour, 7 killed, 1 prisoner.

Halifax LW647 (F/O G. C. G. Greenacre, killed), 49th down by fighter attack; crashed at Niedermoos, 20 kms south west of Fulda. Crew on 21st operation, 5 killed, 2 prisoners.

Halifax LW628 (F/L R. J. Bolt), 99th down, written off after battle damage; no casualties.

78 Squadron, Breighton. 16 Halifaxes dispatched, 10 bombed, 3 missing. 17 men killed, 4 prisoners.

Halifax LK762 (Sgt R. A. Horton, killed), 13th down by fighter attack; crashed at Westum, near Sinzig. Crew on 1st operation, 4 killed, 3 prisoners.

Halifax HX241 (F/L H. M. Hudson, killed), 44th down by fighter attack; crashed at Allendorf, 25 kms east of Marburg. Crew on 27th operation, 6 killed, 1 prisoner.

Halifax LV899 (P/O F. W. Topping, killed), 92nd down, probably by fighter attack; crashed at Girondelle, 23 kms north west of Charleville. Crew on 3rd operation, 7 killed.

158 Squadron, Lissett. 16 Halifaxes dispatched, 10 bombed, 4 missing, 1 damaged. 14 men killed, 12 prisoners, 2 evaded capture.

Halifax HX349 (S/L S. D. Jones, D.F.C., killed), 26th down by Westerburg Flak; crashed at Hachenburg, 16 kms north west of Westerburg. Crew on 12th operation of 2nd tour, 2 killed, 5 prisoners.

Halifax LW724 (W.O. E. R. F. MacLeod, killed), 34th down by fighter attack; crashed at Herbornseelbach, near Herborn. Crew on 1st operation, 6 killed, 1 prisoner.

Halifax LW634 (W.O. S. Hughes, prisoner), 88th down by Metz Flak; crashed at Eischen, near Arlon. Crew on 8th operation, 5 prisoners, 2 evaded capture.

Halifax HX322 (F/Sgt A. Brice, killed), 95th down by fighter attack after earlier Flak damage; crashed at Caumont, 10 kms south of Hesdin. Crew on 4th operation, 6 killed, 1 prisoner.

466 (R.A.A.F.) Squadron, Leconfield. 16 Halifaxes dispatched, 12 bombed, 1 damaged. No aircrew casualties.

578 Squadron, Burn. 11 Halifaxes dispatched, 7 bombed, 1 missing, 2 wrecked in crashes, 1 damaged. 15 men killed, 3 prisoners, 1 wounded in returned aircraft and 4 injured in crashes.

Halifax MZ505 (F/Sgt A. E. Pinks, killed), 79th down by fighter attack; crashed at Kunreuth, 22 kms north of Nuremberg. Crew on 1st operation, 7 killed.

Halifax LW478 (S/L M. McCreanor, killed), 105th down in crash at Silverstone. Crew on 14th operation, 7 killed, 1 injured.

Halifax LK797 (P/O C. J. Barton, v.c., killed), 108th down in crash at Ryhope, Co. Durham. Crew on 18th operation, 1 killed, 3 injured.

640 Squadron, Leconfield. 16 Halifaxes dispatched, 13 bombed, 3 missing, 3 damaged. 18 men killed, 3 prisoners.

Halifax LW555 (F/O C. O'Brien, killed), 27th down by fighter attack; crashed at Halbs, 5 kms north of Westerburg. Crew on 4th operation, 7 killed.

Halifax LW549 (F/O J. D. Laidlaw, killed), 58th down by fighter attack; crashed at Wölferbütt, 25 kms south west of Eisenach. Crew on 21st operation, 4 killed, 3 prisoners.

Halifax LW500 (P/O D. W. Burke, killed), 96th down, presumed by coastal or naval Flak near Dieppe and crashed into sea. Crew on 5th operation, 7 killed.

5 GROUP. 201 Lancasters dispatched, 168 bombed, 21 missing, 3 wrecked in crashes, 14 damaged. 114 men killed, 32 prisoners, 5 evaded capture, 6 wounded in returned aircraft.

9 Squadron, Bardney. 16 Lancasters dispatched, 12 bombed, 1 missing, 2 damaged. 7 men killed (one in a returned aircraft), 1 prisoner, 1 wounded in returned aircraft.

Lancaster W5006 (F/O J. G. R. Ling, killed), 40th down by fighter attack; crashed at Cleeburg, 5 kms south west of Giessen. Crew on 25th operation, 6 killed, 1 prisoner.

44 (Rhodesia) Squadron, Dunholme Lodge. 16 Lancasters dispatched, 14 bombed, 2 missing, 1 damaged, 13 men killed, 1 prisoner.

Lancaster ME629 (P/O C. A. Frost, killed), 53rd down by fighter attack; crashed at Landershausen, 10 kms south east of Bad Hersfeld. Crew on 6th operation, 7 killed.

Lancaster ND795 (P/O T. G. W. Charlesworth, killed), 68th down by fighter attack; crashed at Unteressfeld, 30 kms west of Coburg. Crew on 7th operation, 6 killed, 1 prisoner.

49 Squadron, Fiskerton. 16 Lancasters dispatched, 13 bombed, 2 missing, 2 damaged. 11 men killed, 3 prisoners, 1 wounded in returned aircraft.

Lancaster JB314 (P/O L. G. Kellow, killed), 37th down by fighter attack; crashed at Quotshausen, 20 kms west of Marburg. Crew on 1st operation, 6 killed, 1 prisoner.

Lancaster JB466 (F/O W. A. Colhoun, killed), 65th down by fighter attack; crashed near Schleusingen, 25 kms north west of Coburg. Crew on 7th operation, 5 killed, 2 prisoners.

50 Squadron, Skellingthorpe. 19 Lancasters dispatched, 15 bombed, 3 missing, 1 wrecked in crash, 1 damaged. 15 men killed, 7 prisoners.

Lancaster W4933 (F/Sgt G. C. Bucknell), 1st down, crashed on take-off. No casualties.

Lancaster R5546 (F/Sgt D. G. Gray, prisoner), 15th down by fighter attack; crashed at Waldbreitbach, 12 kms north of Neuwied. Crew on 4th operation, 4 killed, 3 prisoners.

Lancaster LM394 (F/L M. U. Robinson, killed), 32nd down by fighter attack; crashed at Beilstein, 10 kms south west of Herborn. Crew on 19th operation, 8 killed.

Lancaster EE174 (F/Sgt G. A. Waugh, prisoner), 71st down by fighter attack; crashed near Ebern, 20 kms north of Bamberg. Crew on 13th operation, 3 killed, 4 prisoners.

57 Squadron, East Kirkby. 18 Lancasters dispatched, 18 bombed, 1 missing. 4 men killed, 3 prisoners.

Lancaster ND622 (F/L E. W. Tickler, c.g.m., prisoner), 70th down by fighter attack; crashed at Bischwind, 20 kms south west of Coburg. Crew on 13th operation, 4 killed, 3 prisoners.

61 Squadron, Coningsby. 14 Lancasters dispatched, 10 bombed, 2 missing, 3 damaged. 16 men killed (2 after parachuting into the North Sea from a returning aircraft), 4 wounded in returned aircraft.

Lancaster DV311 (S/L E. H. Moss, d.f.c., killed), 51st down by fighter attack; crashed at Rimbach, 20 kms north west of Fulda. Crew on 20th operation, 7 killed.

Lancaster R5734 (P/O J. A. Haste, killed), 91st down by fighter attack; crashed at Monin, 25 kms south east of Namur. Crew on 8th operation, 7 killed.

106 Squadron, Metheringham. 17 Lancasters dispatched, 12 bombed, 3 missing, 1 wrecked in crash. 17 men killed, 4 prisoners.

Lancaster JB566 (F/Sgt T. W. J. Hall, d.f.m., killed), 35th down by fighter attack; crashed at Berghausen, 7 kms north west of Wetzlar. Crew on 2nd operation, 5 killed, 2 prisoners.

Lancaster ND535 (P/O R. Starkey, prisoner), 38th down by fighter attack; crashed at Königsberg, 8 kms north of Wetzlar. Crew on 22nd operation, 5 killed, 2 prisoners.

Lancaster ND585 (P/O W. G. Moxey, killed), 93rd down, probably by fighter attack; crashed at Villers Deux Églises, 20 kms south of Charleroi. Crew on 16th operation, 7 killed.

Lancaster ND332 (F/O E. R. Penman), 100th down in crash landing at Manston. No casualties.

207 Squadron, Spilsby. 18 Lancasters dispatched, 16 bombed, 2 missing, 2 damaged. 14 men killed.

Lancaster LM436 (P/O B. C. Riddle, killed), 50th down by fighter attack; crashed at Freiensteinau, 25 kms south west of Fulda. Crew on 5th operation, 7 killed.

Lancaster ND588 (P/O J. H. Thornton, killed), 72nd down by fighter attack; crashed at Schweinfurt. Crew on 11th operation, 7 killed.

463 (R.A.A.F.) Squadron, Waddington. 18 Lancasters dispatched, 17 bombed. No aircraft or aircrew casualties.

467 (R.A.A.F.) Squadron, Waddington. 17 Lancasters dispatched, 14 bombed, 2 missing, 3 damaged. 4 men killed, 5 prisoners, 5 evaded capture.

Lancaster LM376 (F/L A. B. Simpson, D.F.C., evaded capture), 3rd down by fighter attack; crashed at Creppe, 4 kms south of Spa. Crew on 22nd operation, 2 prisoners, 5 evaded capture.

Lancaster DV240 (P/O R. E. Llewelyn, killed), 12th down by fighter attack; crashed Westum, near Sinzig. Crew on 7th operation, 4 killed, 3 prisoners.

619 Squadron, Coningsby. 16 Lancasters dispatched, 15 bombed, 1 wrecked in crash. No aircrew casualties.

Lancaster LM418 (Sgt J. Parker), 104th down in crash landing at Woodbridge, Suffolk.

630 Squadron, East Kirkby. 16 Lancasters dispatched, 11 bombed, 3 missing. 13 men killed, 8 prisoners.

Lancaster ND337 (P/O R. L. Clark, killed), 19th down by fighter attack; crashed at Bickenbach, 25 kms south of Coblenz. Crew on 1st operation, 6 killed, 1 prisoner.

Lancaster ME664 (F/O J. Langlands, prisoner), 63rd down by fighter attack; crashed at Ruhla, 10 kms south east of Eisenach. Crew on 3rd operation, 3 killed, 4 prisoners.

Lancaster JB288 (P/O A. G. C. Johnson, killed), 78th down by fighter attack; crashed at Altendorf, 15 kms south east of Bamberg. Crew on 16th operation, 4 killed, 3 prisoners.

6 (CANADIAN) GROUP. 93 Halifaxes and 25 Lancasters dispatched, 76 Halifaxes and 22 Lancasters bombed, 11 Halifaxes and 3 Lancasters missing, 5 Halifaxes damaged. 67 men killed, 26 prisoners, 3 evaded capture, 1 injured in crash.

408 Squadron, Linton-on-Ouse. 12 Lancasters dispatched, 11 bombed, 1 missing. 3 men killed, 5 prisoners.

Lancaster LL633 (F/O J. G. White, prisoner), 75th down by fighter attack; crashed at Gerolzhofen, 17 kms south east of Schweinfurt. Crew on 20th operation.

420 Squadron, Tholthorpe. 14 Halifaxes dispatched, 12 bombed, 1 damaged on landing. No aircrew casualties.

424 Squadron, Skipton-on-Swale. 12 Halifaxes dispatched, 8 bombed, 2 missing, 1 damaged. 13 men killed, 1 prisoner.

Halifax LV879 (F/O J. Doig, killed), 43rd down by fighter attack; crashed at Altenbuseck, near Giessen. Crew on 2nd operation, 6 killed, 1 prisoner.

Halifax LW944 (S/L H. W. Metzler, killed), 74th down, probably by Schweinfurt Flak; crashed at Falkenstein, 15 kms south east of Schweinfurt. Crew on 23rd operation, 7 killed.

425 Squadron, Tholthorpe. 12 Halifaxes dispatched, 10 bombed, 1 missing. 7 men killed.

Halifax LW429 (F/L J. R. Taylor, killed), 83rd down by fighter attack; crashed at Tauchersreuth, 10 kms north east of Nuremberg. Crew on 7th operation. This aircraft is believed to have shot down the Me 109 which was attacking it.

426 Squadron, Linton-on-Ouse. 13 Lancasters dispatched, 11 bombed, 2 missing. 9 men killed, 5 prisoners.

Lancaster DS852 (F/Sgt R. G. Douglass, prisoner), 64th down by fighter attack; crashed at Brotterode, 15 kms south east of Eisenach. Crew on 2nd operation, 2 killed, 5 prisoners.

Lancaster DS840 (F/L W. C. Cracknell, killed), 82nd down by fighter attack; crashed at Ermeuth, 20 kms north west of Nuremberg. Crew on 5th operation, 7 killed.

427 Squadron, Leeming. 16 Halifaxes dispatched, 13 bombed, 3 missing, 1 damaged. 22 men killed, 1 evaded capture.

Halifax LV898 (S/L J. M. Bissett, D.F.M., killed), 6th down by fighter attack; crashed at Herhahn, 65 kms south west of Euskirchen. Crew on 4th operation of 2nd tour, 8 killed.

Halifax LW618 (F/O W. N. McPhee, killed), 60th down by fighter attack; crashed at Hohenroth, near Bad Neustadt. Crew on 1st operation, 7 killed.

Halifax LV923 (S/L G. J. Laird, D.F.C., killed), 90th down in collision with 622 Squadron Lancaster; crashed at Rachecourt, 13 kms south west of Arlon. Crew on average of 15th operation, 7 killed, 1 evaded capture.

429 Squadron, Leeming. 13 Halifaxes dispatched, 12 bombed, 2 missing, 1 damaged. 1 man killed, 2 evaded capture, 5 prisoners, 6 rescued (1 injured) from crash in sea.

Halifax LK800 (P/O K. H. Bowly, prisoner), 87th down by fighter attack; crashed at Weiler-la-Tour, 8 kms south east of Luxemburg city. Crew on 17th operation, 2 evaded capture, 5 prisoners.

Halifax LK804 (F/O J. H. Wilson, killed), 97th down, crashed in English Channel after being damaged by fighter and running out of fuel. Remainder of crew rescued and returned to England.

432 Squadron, East Moor. 14 Halifaxes dispatched, 12 bombed, 2 missing. 7 men killed, 7 prisoners.

Halifax LW682 (P/O C. R. Narum, killed), 21st down by fighter attack; crashed at Grossmaischeid, 10 kms north west of Coblenz. Crew on 5th operation, 4 killed, 3 prisoners.

Halifax LK754 (F/O E. K. Reid, killed), 41st down by fighter attack; crashed on railway line south of Friedberg, 7 kms north of Frankfurt. Crew on 10th operation, 3 killed, 4 prisoners.

433 Squadron, Skipton-on-Swale. 12 Halifaxes dispatched, 9 bombed, 1 missing, 1 damaged. 5 men killed, 3 prisoners.

Halifax HX272 (P/O C. Nielson, prisoner), 77th down by fighter attack; crashed at Friessen, 10 kms south east of Bamberg. Crew on 27th operation.

8 (PATHFINDER) GROUP. 107 Lancasters dispatched, 94 bombed, 11 missing, 1 destroyed in crash, 5 damaged. 68 men killed, 11 prisoners.

7 Squadron, Oakington. 20 Lancasters dispatched, 16 bombed, 2 missing, 1 crashed, 1 damaged. 14 men killed.

Lancaster ND443 (S/L C. H. Wilson, D.F.C., killed), 48th down by fighter attack; crashed at Obermoos, 25 kms south west of Fulda. Crew on 4th operation, possibly some on 2nd tour, 7 killed.

Lancaster JB722 (F/L S. Evans, killed), 80th down by fighter attack; crashed at Kunreuth, 20 kms north of Nuremberg. Crew on 26th operation, 7 killed.

Lancaster ND350 (F/L A. H. McGillivray), 107th down, crash-landed and burnt out at Feltwell. No casualties.

35 Squadron, Graveley. 14 Lancasters dispatched, 14 bombed, 1 damaged. No aircrew casualties.

83 Squadron, Wyton. 14 Lancasters dispatched, 14 bombed. No aircraft or aircrew casualties.

97 Squadron, Bourn. 14 Lancasters dispatched, 12 bombed, 2 missing, 1 damaged. 14 men killed.

Lancaster ND640 (F/L L. V. Hyde, D.F.C., killed), 39th down by fighter attack; crashed at Münchholzhausen, 5 kms east of Wetzlar. Crew on 29th operation, 7 killed.

Lancaster ND390 (F/L D. H. Rowlands, D.F.C., killed), 69th down by fighter attack; crashed at Ahorn, near Coburg. Crew on 3rd operation of 2nd tour, 7 killed.

156 Squadron, Upwood. 17 Lancasters dispatched, 13 bombed, 4 missing. 24 men killed, 6 prisoners.

Lancaster ND476 (Captain F. Johnsen, killed), 9th down by fighter attack; crashed at Vischel, 8 kms west of Ahrweiler. Crew on 25th operation, 8 killed.

Lancaster ND406 (W.O. J. A. Murphy, killed), 10th down by fighter attack; crashed at Holtzweiler, near Ahrweiler. Crew on 19th operation of 2nd tour, 6 killed, 1 prisoner.

Lancaster ND492 (P/O L. Lindley, prisoner), 20th down by fighter attack; crashed at Ober Irsen, 30 kms east of Bonn. Crew on 19th operation, 6 killed, 1 prisoner.

Lancaster ND466 (S/L P. R. Goodwin, prisoner), 66th down by

fighter attack; crashed at Eisfeld, 18 kms north of Coburg. Crew on 17th operation of 2nd tour, 4 killed, 4 prisoners.

405 (R.C.A.F.) Squadron, Grandsen Lodge. 14 Lancasters dispatched, 14 bombed, 2 damaged. No aircrew casualties.

635 Squadron, Downham Market. 14 Lancasters dispatched, 11 bombed, 3 missing. 16 men killed, 5 prisoners.

Lancaster ND711 (F/L H. J. L. Webb, killed), 24th down by fighter attack; crashed at Steinen, 10 kms west of Westerburg. Crew on approximately 20th operation, 7 killed.

Lancaster JB706 (F/L J. H. Nicholls, D.F.C., prisoner), 29th down by Westerburg Flak; crashed at Mademühlen, 14 kms north east of Westerburg. Crew on 35th operation, 2 killed, 5 prisoners.

Lancaster JB366 (F/L C. A. Lyon, killed), 45th down by fighter attack; crashed at Erksdorf, 20 kms north east of Marburg. Crew on 16th operation, 7 killed.

100 GROUP OPERATIONS

(For the remainder of this Appendix it can be assumed that squadrons did not suffer casualties unless stated.)

141 Squadron, West Raynham. 5 Serrate Mosquitoes dispatched, 1 damaged.

169 Squadron, Little Snoring. 7 Serrate Mosquitoes dispatched.

192 Squadron, Foulsham. 2 Halifaxes and 2 Mosquitoes dispatched on radio counter-measures operations.

239 Squadron, West Raynham. 7 Serrate Mosquitoes dispatched, 1 damaged.

515 Squadron, Little Snoring. 1 Intruder Mosquito dispatched.

8 GROUP MOSQUITO BOMBER OPERATIONS

105 Squadron, Bourn. 12 Oboe Mosquitoes dispatched, 1 damaged.

109 Squadron, Marham. 15 Oboe Mosquitoes dispatched.

139 Squadron, Upwood. 11 Mosquitoes dispatched.

627 Squadron, Oakington. 10 Mosquitoes dispatched.

692 Squadron, Graveley. 12 Mosquitoes dispatched.

INTRUDER OPERATIONS

21 Squadron, Hunsdon. 3 Mosquitoes dispatched. 1 missing, 2 men killed.

Mosquito HX950 (F/O R. H. Osborn, killed), 98th down from unknown cause; presumed in North Sea.

418 (City of Edmonton) Squadron, Ford. 11 Mosquitoes dispatched.

487 (R.N.Z.A.F.) Squadron, Hunsdon. 4 Mosquitoes dispatched.

605 (County of Warwick) Squadron, Bradwell Bay. 11 Mosquitoes dispatched.

613 (City of Manchester) Squadron, Lasham. 6 Mosquitoes dispatched.

U.S.A.A.F. Detachment, Little Snoring. 2 Lightnings and 2 Mustangs dispatched.

SECRET OPERATIONS

90 Squadron, Tuddenham. 5 Stirlings dispatched.

138 Squadron, Tempsford. 5 Halifaxes dispatched, 1 missing. 3 men killed, 4 prisoners, 1 evaded capture.

Halifax LL287 (F/L B. B. Mills, evaded capture), 2nd down by Flak; crashed into River Scheldt, 2 kms west of Hansweert. 2 Belgian Resistance men also killed; one was Lieutenant Robert Deprez from the town of Deerlijk; the identity of the second is unknown.

149 and 199 Squadrons, Lakenheath. 7 Stirlings dispatched.

196 Squadron, Keevil. 1 Stirling dispatched.

295 and 570 Squadrons, Harwell. 4 Albemarles dispatched.

296 and 297 Squadrons, Brize Norton. 6 Albemarles dispatched.

298 and 644 Squadrons, Tarrant Rushton. 6 Halifaxes dispatched.

620 Squadron, Fairford. 1 Stirling dispatched.

MINING OPERATIONS

75 (New Zealand) Squadron, Mepal. 4 Stirlings dispatched.

77 Squadron, Elvington. 10 Halifaxes dispatched.

102 Squadron, Pocklington. 10 Halifaxes dispatched.

149 and 199 Squadrons, Lakenheath. 2 Stirlings dispatched.

419 (Moose) and 428 (Ghost) Squadrons, Middleton St George. 22 Halifaxes dispatched.

434 (Bluenose) Squadron, Croft. 7 Halifaxes dispatched.

LEAFLET OPERATIONS

92 Group O.T.U. 8 Wellingtons dispatched from Silverstone and Bruntingthorpe, 1 damaged.

422 Bomb Squadron, U.S.A.A.F., Chelveston. 6 Fortresses dispatched.

Appendix 5

Bomber Command Casualties 1939–45

(This Appendix is based entirely on various tables in the Official History, Volume IV, pages 429–44.)

PART 1 – AIRCRAFT

Bomber Command dispatched 364,514 bombing and leaflet sorties from which 8,325 aircraft were missing. This gives a missing rate of 2·28 per cent. These figures cover both day and night raids but not the considerable mining effort or secret operations for which figures are not available. It is probable that a further 330 aircraft were missing, mainly from mining and secret operations. Approximately 1,500 more aircraft were written off following severe battle damage or crashes.

Yearly Totals of Bombing and Leaflet Raids

Year	Sorties	Aircraft missing	Loss-Rate
1939	333	33	9·9 per cent
1940	20,809	494	2·4 per cent
1941	30,608	914	3·0 per cent
1942	35,050	1,400	4·0 per cent
1943	64,528	2,314	3·6 per cent
1944	148,448	2,573	1·7 per cent
1945	64,738	597	0·9 per cent

PART 2 – AIRCREW

55,573 aircrew, 1,363 male ground staff and 91 W.A.A.F.s died while serving with Bomber Command. It is not known exactly where all the aircrew had their homes but the following table shows in which air forces they were serving at the time of their deaths:

Royal Air Force	38,462 (69·2 per cent)
Royal Canadian Air Force	9,919 (17·8 per cent)

Royal Australian Air Force   4,050 (7·3 per cent)
Royal New Zealand Air Force   1,679 (3·0 per cent)
Polish Air Force   929 (1·7 per cent)
Other Allied Air Forces   473 (0·9 per cent)
Other Dominions   34
South African Air Force   27 (0·1 per cent)

Acknowledgements

Before all others I would like to thank the following men, both Allied and German, who flew in the air operations of 30–31 March 1944 and those men and women who were involved in the planning or preparation of the Nuremberg Raid or were otherwise closely associated with it. Without their generous and willing help this book could not have been written.

(Abbreviations not used earlier are: Air Marshal – A.M., Air Vice-Marshal – A.V.M., Air Commodore – Air Cdre, Group Captain – Gp Capt., Wing Commander – W/Cdr. Ranks quoted are those held on 30 March 1944.)

THE BRITISH

AIRCREW FLYING ON 30–31 MARCH 1944

7 Squadron: F/L F. Bell, F/L T. G. Dill, Sgt H. Maxwell, F/O M. H. Michael, F/O G. E. Parkes, F/L G. J. South, W.O. T. H. Strong, Sgt C. A. Thomson, F/L H. C. Williams.

9 Squadron: F/O M. E. Anderton, Sgt H. Hannah, Sgt D. B. Pinchin, W.O. G. F. Ridley.

10 Squadron: F/Sgt L. W. Duncan, F/Sgt A. Hampson, F/Sgt J. S. Manson, F/Sgt J. Street, P/O J. D. Whiteman, Sgt N. Wilmott.

12 Squadron: Sgt W. J. Blackburn, Sgt F. V. Shaw, F/Sgt J. B. Starr.

15 Squadron: P/O V. Brooks, P/O S. Fisher, F/O E. S. Henzel, S/Ldr P. J. Lamason, W/O E. G. Spandier, F/Sgt H. Sutcliffe.

21 Squadron: F/L J. K. B. Purves.

35 Squadron: W.O. J. M. Colledge, W/Cdr S. P. Daniels, P/O A. V. Hardy, F/Sgt M. Ladyman, P/O H. A. Millar, F/Sgt R. Rhodes.

44 Squadron: F/L S. Burrows, F/O J. Chatterton, P/O F. G. Davey, F/Sgt G. M. Gebhard, W/Cdr F. W. Thompson.

49 Squadron: Sgt A. W. Black, Sgt R. H. Eeles, P/O T. Jones, Sgt A. J. McAvoy.

50 Squadron: P/O E. Berry, F/Sgt D. G. Gray, F/Sgt G. W. Hughes, Sgt D. C. Lynch, F/L D. J. Oram, Sgt E. D. Rowlinson, Sgt M. R. Sinton, F/Sgt G. Wallis.

51 Squadron: Sgt P. Bailey, F/Sgt J. H. Gowland, Sgt J. M. MacCoss, F/Sgt R. J. K. Murphy, F/Sgt H. B. Pettifer.

57 Squadron: F/Sgt A. G. Buckley, Sgt R. Hammersley, Sgt

R. I. Hudson, F/O H. B. Mackinnon, F/O J. R. Maunsell, Sgt J. K. Ronald, Technical Sgt W. E. Steeper, F/L F. A. Thomas, F/L E. W. Tickler.

61 Squadron: F/L G. A. Berry, F/Sgt D. R. Chinery, F/Sgt R. A. F. Griffin, F/Sgt R. Jones, Sgt J. T. McQuillan, Sgt D. G. Patfield, F/O A. E. Stone.

76 Squadron: F/L R. J. Bolt, F/L H. D. Coverley, Sgt G. L. Edwards, P/O F. P. G. Hall, P/O A. Monk, Sgt M. Ransome, P/O V. A. Thomson.

78 Squadron: Sgt H. M. Chittenden, Sgt J. H. Connoley, F/Sgt L. Nugent, P/O J. C. Palmer.

83 Squadron: F/L R. A. C. Hellier, W/Cdr A. S. Johnson, W.O. K. A. Lane, F/Sgt W. G. Trotter.

90 Squadron: F/L W. A. Kirk, F/L W. J. Ralph, F/O S. T. Smith, W.O. F. G. Smithies.

97 Squadron: F/O W. H. Benton, F/L C. S. Chatten, F/Sgt M. H. McBride, F/L C. B. Owen, F/L G. H. R. Polson, W.O. J. E. Rimmington.

100 Squadron: P/O R. J. Booth, F/Sgt H. R. Crompton, Sgt G. D. Dixon, F/L D. F. Gillam, F/L J. K. Hamilton, Sgt T. McCartney, F/L G. R. Ross.

101 Squadron: F/Sgt E. R. Barlow, Sgt D. Brinkhurst, F/O K. D. Connell, F/Sgt A. P. Farquharson, Sgt A. H. Grainge, W.O. A. G. Hall, F/Sgt R. J. Hardacre, Sgt T. Haycock, F/Sgt I. R. Hill-Smith, P/O E. J. Holland, Sgt H. A. Jamieson, P/O A. E. Lander, Sgt A. R. Luffman, Sgt H. S. Nunn, F/O W. D. Menger, F/O P. J. W. Raine, F/O C. R. S. Ricketts, F/Sgt H. F. Scott, F/Sgt J. Williams.

103 Squadron: Sgt A. F. Carter, F/Sgt M. C. Coughlan, Sgt F. Fealy, F/Sgt D. T. Mitchell, Sgt N. T. L. Storey, F/O L. Young.

105 Squadron: F/O H. Mills, F/L V. E. Piper.

106 Squadron: F/O R. F. Anderson, Sgt R. D. Dack, F/L C. J. Ginder, F/O E. L. Hogg, Sgt H. W. Hudson, F/O G. S. Milne, F/O D. A. Pagliero, F/O G. B. Remigio, F/O W. G. Seymour, F/L E. Sprawson, F/O R. Starkey.

109 Squadron: F/O H. C. Boyd, F/L I. O. Breckon, F/L A. T. Buckland, S/L R. C. Cobbe, F/O K. L. Pring.

115 Squadron: Sgt J. W. Carter, F/Sgt H. Durham, F/Sgt T. N. H. Fogaty, Sgt D. Guard, Sgt E. Oliver, F/O P. H. Paddon, Sgt J. G. Swan.

138 Squadron: F/Sgt G. W. Kimpton, W.O. J. Weir.

139 Squadron: F/O J. G. Alcock, F/O A. S. C. Brown, F/O E. A. F. Jackman, F/O C. S. Richards, F/L G. W. Salter.

141 Squadron: P/O E. W. Rolfe.

149 Squadron: F/Sgt A. M. Millar, F/O S. R. Pryor.

156 Squadron: S/L P. R. Goodwin, F/O W. C. Isted, W.O. R. W.

Parrisien, P/O A. M. Robb, Sgt L. Wooliscroft.

158 Squadron: Sgt W. Crafer, Sgt R. S. Cripps, Sgt K. Dobbs, F/O W. C. Graham, Sgt A. Herring, F/O L. A. Ingram.

166 Squadron: F/Sgt R. H. Bannister, F/Sgt W. J. C. Keigwin, W.O. W. G. Knowles, Sgt A. G. Manuel, F/O P. N. J. Noble, P/O V. W. R. Park, F/Sgt G. G. H. Rodwell, F/Sgt W. R. Swaffield, F/L F. Taylor, F/Sgt L. Wayte, F/Sgt S. N. Whitlock, Sgt B. Wilkinson, P/O P. J. Wilson.

169 Squadron: F/L J. S. Fifield, F/O A. P. Mellows, F/L R. G. Woodman.

192 Squadron: Sgt E. R. Cookson, F/O H. T. John, W.O. G. H. Moon.

196 Squadron: Sgt D. E. Royston.

199 Squadron: P/O J. R. Ison, F/O W. C. Pacholka.

207 Squadron: F/Sgt R. A. Austin, F/Sgt L. B. Briggs, Sgt S. W. Carter, F/Sgt D. G. J. Griffiths, P/O K. W. McSweeney, F/O D. S. P. Smith.

405 Squadron: F/L J. W. Perry, F/O J. D. Routledge, S/L H. W. A. Trilsbach, F/O A. J. Van Rassel, F/L R. W. Wright.

408 Squadron: F/O W. C. Burns, F/O R. W. Butcher, F/L W. F. Hales, W.O. M. J. Harrison, F/Sgt J. R. Hughes, Sgt G. A. Reid.

418 Squadron: F/L J. M. Connell.

420 Squadron: Sgt R. Anderson, Sgt N. Binnie, W.O. J. Broadley, F/Sgt P. A. Dubois, Sgt R. E. Freeman, Sgt M. E. Meech, W.O. L. O'Shell, Sgt A. Read, Sgt W. Watts.

424 Squadron: Sgt A. Green, F/O F. F. Hamilton, F/O J. R. Mason.

425 Squadron: F/O F. D. Hagen, F/O O. J. Harper, F/O D. Stubbs.

426 Squadron: P/O J. Hollingworth, F/L B. D. C. Patterson, F/L F. R. Shedd, Sgt H. E. Sjöquist.

427 Squadron: F/O M. H. Albers, F/O N. Dubeski, F/Sgt W. Fox, P/O J. Moffat, F/O G. C. Southcott, F/Sgt S. Welch.

429 Squadron: P/O K. H. Bowly, Sgt R. Chamberlain, Sgt J. D. Donaldson, F/O J. Dougal, P/O F. Finlay, Sgt L. M. Shetler, F/O W. C. Shields, F/Sgt J. Robson.

432 Squadron: Sgt J. J. Barr, F/L J. H. Cooper, F/Sgt R. P. Goeson, P/O J. Gouinloch, P/O D. A. McCoy, F/O A. Raetzen.

433 Squadron: F/Sgt R. C. Reinelt.

460 Squadron: F/L M. W. Dale, F/O A. W. Delohery, F/Sgt W. A. Gourlay, Sgt T. Mortimer, F/Sgt D. R. Riddell, W.O. M. Stafford, P/O R. N. T. Wade, W.O. L. E. Welldon, F/Sgt H. J. Whittick, F/O R. L. Woods.

463 Squadron: F/O T. J. Foster, F/Sgt J. H. Frith.

466 Squadron: F/O T. C. Drake-Brockman (later Australian Minister for Air), F/Sgt D. C. Gordon, F/Sgt S. G. Waller.

467 Squadron: Sgt L. W. Bird, W.O. J. Bormann, F/Sgt C. A.

Campbell, Sgt C. P. Curl, P/O D. L. Gibbs, F/O D. L. Harris, P/O G. G. Johnson, F/Sgt O. J. Jones, F/Sgt T. E. Pollard, F/O G. W. H. Venables, Sgt J. Wesley.

514 Squadron: Sgt A. W. Birse, F/O H. G. Darby, Sgt R. Fox, W.O. A. D. Hall, F/Sgt P. Henser, F/O P. J. K. Hood, F/Sgt L. W. C. Lewis, F/Sgt A. McPhee, F/O F. J. Parker, Sgt T. J. Saint, F/O R. J. S. Wilton.

550 Squadron: S/L G. D. Graham, Sgt S. A. Keirle, W.O. G. C. Notman, Sgt R. H. J. Pearce, Sgt W. G. Upton.

576 Squadron: P/O M. A. Frost, F/L S. Slater, W.O. A. H. Young.

578 Squadron: Sgt R. C. Corker, Sgt M. Trousdale.

605 Squadron: F/L W. A. Bird, F/O B. J. Duncan, F/L L. H. Hodder, P/O R. E. Lelong, F/L J. G. Musgrave (died 1972), F/L J. I. Pengelly, F/L G. C. Wright.

619 Squadron: F/Sgt F. H. Baynton, F/Sgt E. Booth, P/O P. A. Buttar, F/O R. A. Marshall, P/O R. W. Olsen.

622 Squadron: Sgt. C. R. Bright, P/O R. Curling, Sgt J. W. Farrow, Sgt R. V. Francis, F/Sgt E. C. Hazelwood, P/O W. L. Wilson.

625 Squadron: Sgt A. W. Brickenden, P/O J. E. Goldsmith, S/L R. W. H. Gray, Sgt R. A. Verry.

626 Squadron: F/Sgt M. H. Hawkins, P/O D. J. Henty, P/O A. H. Rew, F/Sgt F. A. Taylor, Sgt E. Wilkins.

627 Squadron: F/O J. R. Goodman, F/O A. J. L. Hickox, F/Sgt J. Marshallsay.

630 Squadron: F/Sgt D. Cooper, W.O. D. J. Freeman, F/O R. M. Guthrie, Sgt W. Pearson, F/Sgt L. N. Rackley, Sgt G. E. Watts.

635 Squadron: F/O L. Henson, F/L J. H. Nicholls, F/Sgt W. D. Ogilvie, F/L C. R. Snell, W/Cdr J. B. Voyce, F/L L. J. D. Wheble, S/L J. R. Wood.

640 Squadron: F/Sgt K. A. Bush, F/L R. K. Cassels, P/O J. Cotter, S/L L. D. Leicester, F/Sgt J. Varty, F/O C. E. Willis.

692 Squadron: F/L H. H. E. P. Cairns, F/L J. E. L. Gover, F/O D. N. Riley.

1409 (Meteorological) Flight: F/L R. G. Dale, P/O N. Gilroy, F/O T. Oakes.

BOMBER COMMAND HEADQUARTERS

A.M. Sir Robert Saundby, Deputy C. in C. (died 1971), A.V.M. H. S. P. Walmsley, S.A.S.O.; Air Cdre H. A. Constantine, Deputy S.A.S.O.; Gp Capts. S. C. Elworthy, W. I. C. Inness, and M. T. Spence; W/Cdrs G. A. Carey-Foster and F. A. B. Fawssett.

GROUP, STATION AND SQUADRON COMMANDERS
(not on raid)

A.V.M. C. R. Carr, 4 Group (died 1971); A.V.M. The Hon. Ralph Cochrane, 5 Group; A.V.M. D. C. T. Bennett, 8 Group; Air Cdre E. B. Addison, 100 Group; Gp Capt. H. Mahaddie, R.A.F. Warboys; Gp Capt. R. H. Waterhouse, R.A.F. Leconfield; W/Cdr R. C. Ayling, 51 Squadron; W/Cdr E. D. M. Nelson, 103 Squadron; W/Cdr G. H. Womersley, 139 Squadron; W/Cdr E. P. M. Fernbank, 192 Squadron; W/Cdr G. L. Cheshire, 617 Squadron.

GROUP AND STATION STAFFS

1 Group: Air Cdre H. I. Cozens, W/Cdr R. F. Budden (died 1972), S/L A. R. Glading; 3 Group: W/Cdr W. J. Burnett; 4 Group: S/L R. C. Smylie; 5 Group: S/L R. G. Churcher; 8 Group: Air Cdre C. D. C. Boyce; 100 Group: Gp Capt. R. A. E. Chisholm; R.A.F. Leconfield: F/L W. L. Harrison.

AIR MINISTRY

Air Cdre S. O. Bufton, Director of Bomber Operations.

MINISTRY OF ECONOMIC WARFARE

C. E. R. Sherrington, Esq.

THE W.A.A.F.S

Leading Aircraftwoman Anne Butler, R.A.F. Spilsby; Section Officer Lorraine Plunkett, R.A.F. Waddington; Assistant Section Officer Patricia Bourne, 101 Squadron; Sgt Jessie Waldron, R.A.F. Waddington.

PRISONERS OF WAR AT DULAG LUFT, OBERURSEL

Gp Capt. N. W. D. Marwood-Elton, ex-Station Commander R.A.F. Burn; Sgt R. A. Hide, ex-7 Squadron; W.O. W. Housley, ex-97 Squadron; F/Sgt G. Tipping, ex-78 Squadron.

THE GERMANS

GERMAN AIRCREW FLYING ON THE NIGHT OF THE RAID

Oberleutnant Martin Becker, Major Martin Drewes, Unteroffizier Heinrich Frankenbach, Unteroffizier Erich Handke, Major

Wilhelm Herget, Major Hans-Joachim Jabs, Oberleutnant Fritz Lau, Major Rolf Leuchs, Hauptmann Berthold Ney, Leutnant Fritz Rumpelhardt, Major Rudolf Schoenert, Oberleutnant Helmut Schulte, Leutnant Wilhelm Seuss, Hauptmann Gustav Tham.

GERMAN COMMANDERS AND STAFFS

Generalleutnant Werner Junck, Commander II Fighter Corps; Generalmajor Max Ibel, Commander 2nd Fighter Division; Generalmajor Walter Grabmann, Commander 3rd Fighter Division; Oberst Erich Killinger, Commandant Dulag Luft; Hauptmann Heinz Rökker, I/NJG 2; Oberleutnant Dieter Birk, Radio Monitoring Officer, 2nd Fighter Division.

WITNESSES FROM BOMBING AREAS

Nuremberg: Karl Eh, Hilde Gregori, Fritz Leidhäusel, Dr E. Neupert, Johann Völkel, Else Weber. Schweinfurt: Rudi Heym, Alfred Popp, Hermann Schumann, Gerhard Spitzner.

WITNESSES FROM AREAS WHERE BOMBERS CRASHED

Werner Gross, Philip Retzmann and W. Scheidweiler of Westerburg; Helmut Schnatz and Walter Zimmerman of Coblenz; Helmut Ecker and Walter Vogt of Neuwied; Rosemarie Bongart and Heinz Schmalz of Sinzig; Horst Barthelmes, Obernhausen; Fritz Heusler, Dillenburg; Anni Hickmann, Mühlpfad; Erna Spies, Falkenstein; Richard Metz, Eichenhausen and Heinz Schonsges, Andernach.

Personal Acknowledgements

I would like to record my thanks to many people and organizations for their most generous help in connection with the preparation of this book.

Two people in particular gave willingly of their free time: Anthony Sharp of Boston Grammar School diligently translated a large German correspondence and many research documents and John Chatterton of Horncastle, who piloted a Lancaster on the Nuremberg Raid, carefully examined all the draft chapters and not only saved me from committing technical errors but also offered many valuable suggestions.

The following also helped in a great variety of ways: the order in which their names appear does not imply any order of merit: John Sharpe, Bill Pengelly and George Whitehead, all of Boston; Roger Boast and others in the Meteorological Office at R.A.F. Coningsby; F/L Alfred Price, F/L Jack Simpson and my brothers F/L Peter and W/Cdr Gregory Middlebrook, all of today's R.A.F.; Ron Carabine of Maidenhead, Bob Church of South Norwood, Capt. Roy Benwell of Woking, Dr Noble Frankland (ex-50 Squadron), Patrick Mahoney of Chadwell Heath, F. M. Underhill of Upton, Berks and Alan Woolard of Wallingford.

I would also like to thank three ladies – Janet Mountain, Jean Smith and Molly Stevens – who between them coped so well with the typing of a huge correspondence, the research notes and, finally, the manuscript. My appreciation also to my wife Mary and daughters Jane, Anne and Catherine for their help in many ways.

I am most grateful to Mrs P. J. Voysey of New Malden for valuable help in connection with the story of her brother, Pilot Officer Cyril Barton, V.C.

I was surprised at the depth and thoroughness of the help given by various departments of the Ministry of Defence in view of the fact that those involved had no idea as to whether the book would ultimately be favourable to the R.A.F. or not. I am very pleased to be able to acknowledge the help of these departments (names in brackets are of those people with whom I came most frequently into contact): at Adastral House – AR8b (Mr T. P. Tracey), AR9 (Mrs E. C. M. Ford and Miss F. E. Vaughan) and the Air Library (Mr F. White); the Air Historical Branch at Dean Farrer Street (Mr E. B.

Haslam and many others); the Personnel Management Centre at Gloucester. I thank Gp Capt. C. B. Owen and the Intelligence Staff for detaching at short notice an officer from the R.A.F. Language School to act as interpreter for a research trip to Germany.

Other organizations who have been of great assistance are: the Imperial War Museum, the Commonwealth War Graves Commission (Miss I. Doig and Miss M. Bosticco), the Meteorological Office, the German Embassy (Mrs Holland and Major R. Müller), the R.A.F. Association, the R.A.F. Escaping Society, the Pathfinder Association and the Lincolnshire Aviation Society.

The Air Forces of overseas countries whose men once flew with Bomber Command were all willing to help trace men who took part in the Nuremberg Raid and with other requests. In Canada I thank the Directorate of History, the Department of Veterans Affairs and the Canadian Forces Record Centre, all at Ottawa; in Australia, the War Memorial and the Department of Air's Records Section, both at Canberra, and in New Zealand, F/L J. S Barclay, the historian of 75 Squadron, Royal New Zealand Air Force. In the United States I thank the National Personnel Records Center, St Louis, the Office of Air Force History, Washington, and the Albert F. Simpson Historical Research Center, Maxwell Air Force Base, Alabama. Individuals who helped from overseas are John Barton and Terry Cook both of Auckland, New Zealand, Mr P. R. Sara of Punchbowl, New South Wales, and Charles Whitmore of Hantsport, Nova Scotia.

I was most fortunate in being able to obtain much valuable material from Germany. To Dr Erich Mulzer, Rudolf Hofmann, Rudolf Tyrassek and the staff of the Nürnberg Stadtarchiv I give my warm thanks for help in connection with two pleasant and useful visits to Nuremberg and, in Schweinfurt, Johannes-Curt Rust, Helmut and Willy Bach, Herr K. H. Leuschner and Siegfried Reissman were also of great assistance. I wish also to thank Dr Ludwig Hässlein of Lauf, Horst Diener of Dortmund, Else Hille of Oberursel and Norbert Krüger of Essen.

I will not name in this English publication the municipal authorities of the many cities, towns and villages who answered my letters of inquiry about the events of the night of 30–31 March 1944 but I am most grateful to them all. I would also acknowledge the Bundesarchiv offices at Koblenz and Freiburg, the Bundesminister der Verteidigung at Bonn, the Gemeinschaft der Jagdflieger and the Waffenring der Flakartilleristen und Flugabwehr.

OTHER ACKNOWLEDGEMENTS

Acknowledgements for permission to include quotations from the following published works and public documents are gratefully given: *The First and the Last* to Methuen and Co., *The Bombing of Germany* to Frederich Muller Ltd. Quotations from Crown copyright records in the Public Record Office and from the Official History of the Second World War appear by permission of the Controller of H.M. Stationery Office.

THE PRESS

To find the men who participated in the Nuremberg Raid I mounted an appeal campaign through newspapers and magazines in many parts of the world. The following publications printed my appeals, always without charge, and I am pleased to be able to acknowledge this valuable help.

UNITED KINGDOM

Belfast Telegraph, Birmingham Mail, Bradford Telegraph and Argus, Daily Telegraph, Eastern Daily Press, Glasgow Daily Times, Grimsby Evening Telegraph, Lincolnshire Chronicle, Lincolnshire Echo, Lincolnshire Standard, Liverpool Daily Post, London Evening News, Manchester Evening News, Middlesbrough Evening Gazette, Newcastle Evening Chronicle, Nottingham Guardian Journal, Sheffield Telegraph, Surrey Comet, Western Morning News, York Evening Press. Air Mail, Air Pictorial, B.E.A. House Journal, B.O.A.C. News, Control Column, Guild of Air Traffic Control Officers' Bulletin, R.A.F. News, R.U.S.I. Journal, Royal British Legion Journal.

CANADA

Barrie Examiner, Brandon Sun, Calgary Albertan, Calgary Herald, Edmonton Journal, Galt Evening Reporter, Halifax Chronicle-Herald, Hamilton Spectator, London Free Press, Medicine Hat News, Montreal Gazette, Ottawa Journal, Owen Sound Sun Times, Peterborough Examiner, Red Deer Advocate, Regina Leader Post, Sarnia Observer, Saskatoon Star Phoenix, St Catherine's Standard, St John Telegraph-Journal, Sudbury Star, Toronto Daily Star, Toronto Globe and Mail, Toronto Telegram, Vancouver Sun, Victoria Colonist, Windsor Star, Winnipeg Free Press. Canadian Flight, Canadian Forces Sentinel, Canadian Military Journal, The Legion, Wings at Home.

AUSTRALIA

Adelaide Sunday Mail, Australasian Post, The Australian, Bendigo Advertiser, Border Morning Mail, Burnie Advocate, Canberra Times, Daily Telegraph, Dandenong Journal, Hobart Mercury, Launceston Examiner, Melbourne Herald, Melbourne Sun, Northern Star, Perth Sunday Times, Queensland Courier Mail, Queensland Telegraph, The Sun, Truth. Australian Journal of Politics and History, 'Gen',

Journal of the Royal Australian Historical Society, Legion Magazine, Reveille, Wings.

NEW ZEALAND
Auckland Star, The Dominion, Evening Star, Nelson Evening Mail, New Plymouth Daily News, New Zealand Herald, Otago Daily Times, The Press. National Air Corporation Staff Magazine, National Airways Staff Magazine, New Zealand Listener.

GERMANY
Giessener Allgemeine, Nürnberger Nachrichten, Nürnberger Zeitung, Rhein Zeitung, Schweinfurter Volkszeitung, Schweinfurter Tagblatt, Süddeutsche Zeitung, Westerwälder Zeitung, Der Adler, Jägerblatt, Luftwaffen-Revue.

U.S.A.
American Legion Magazine, Stars and Stripes, Veterans of Foreign Wars Magazine.

Bibliography

OFFICIAL HISTORIES

Webster, Sir Charles, and Frankland, Noble, *The Strategic Air Offensive Against Germany, 1939–1945*, 4 vols, H.M.S.O., 1961.
Herrington, John, *Australia in the War of 1939–1945*, Australian War Memorial, 1954.

Anderson, William, *Pathfinders*, Jarrolds, 1970.
Andrews, Allen, *The Air Marshals*, Macdonald, 1968.
Bekker, Cajus, *The Luftwaffe War Diaries*, Macdonald, 1968.
Bennett, D. C. T., *Pathfinder*, Frederick Muller, 1958.
Chisholm, Roderick, *Cover of Darkness*, Chatto and Windus, 1953.
Divine, David, *The Broken Wing*, Hutchinson, 1966.
Frankland, Noble, *Bomber Offensive*, Macdonald, 1970.
Frankland, Noble, *The Bombing Offensive Against Germany*, Faber, 1965.
Galland, Adolf, *The First and the Last: German Fighter Force in World War II*, Methuen, 1970.
Garbett, Mike, and Goulding, Brian, *The Lancaster at War*, Ian Allan, 1971.
Green, William, *Warplanes of the Third Reich*, Macdonald, 1970.
Harris, Sir Arthur, *Bomber Offensive*, Collins, 1947.
Irving, David, *Und Deutschlands Städte Starben Nicht*, Schweitzer, Zürich, 1963.
Johnen, Wilhelm, *Duel under the Stars*, William Kimber, 1969.
Lawrence, W. J., *No. 5 Bomber Group R.A.F.*, Faber, 1953.
Moyes, P. J., *Bomber Squadrons of the R.A.F. and Their Aircraft*, Macdonald, 1964.
Price, Alfred, *Instruments of Darkness*, William Kimber, 1967.
Robertson, Bruce, *Lancaster: Story of a Famous Bomber*, Harleyford, 1964.
Rumpf, Hans, *The Bombing of Germany*, Frederick Muller, 1963.
Saundby, Sir Robert, *Air Bombardment*, Chatto and Windus, 1961.
Saward, Dudley, *The Bomber's Eye*, Cassell, 1959.
Sharp, C. M., and Bowyer, M. J. F., *Mosquito*, Faber, 1967.
Speer, Albert, *Inside the Third Reich*, Weidenfeld and Nicolson, 1970.
Verrier, Anthony, *The Bomber Offensive*, Batsford, 1968.
Wiener, Ludwig, *Schweinfurt Sollte Sterben*, Verlags Neues Form, Schweinfurt.

Index

Passing references to individual aircraft of frequently mentioned types and to technical devices and tactical terms have not been indexed in the chapters covering the actual Nuremberg operation.